European Monetary Union

Transition, International Impact and Policy Options

Springer-Verlag Berlin Heidelberg GmbH

Paul J. J. Welfens (Ed.)

European Monetary Union

Transition, International Impact and Policy Options

With 50 Figures
and 31 Tables

Springer

Professor Dr. Paul J. J. Welfens
University of Potsdam
European Institute for International
Economic Relations
August-Bebel-Str. 89
14482 Potsdam
Germany

ISBN 978-3-642-63827-5

Cataloging-in-Publication Data applied for
Die Deutsche Bibliothek - CIP-Einheitsaufnahme

European monetary union: transition, international impact and policy options; with 31 tables / Paul J.J. Welfens (ed.). - Berlin; Heidelberg; New York; Barcelona; Budapest; Hong Kong; London; Milan; Paris; Santa Clara; Singapore; Tokyo: Springer, 1997

ISBN 978-3-642-63827-5 ISBN 978-3-642-59039-9 (eBook)
DOI 10.1007/978-3-642-59039-9

Originally published by Springer-Verlag Berlin Heidelberg New York in 1997
Softcover reprint of the hardcover 1st edition 1997

Hardcover-Design: Erich Kirchner, Heidelberg

SPIN 10635904 42/2202-5 4 3 2 1 0 – Printed on acid-free paper

TABLE OF CONTENTS

III. Fiscal Aspects of the Maastricht Treaty and Political Economy of Transition

Introduction

Paul J.J. Welfens

European monetary union has been discussed for more than three decades and is likely to be realized in 1999. One may anticipate generous interpretations of the fiscal convergence criteria. Such generosity consistent with the Maastricht Treaty might impair the credibility of the ECB and the stability of the Euro, respectively, despite the fact that inflation is a monetary phenomenon and has little to do with government deficits, unless they were financed via the printing press, which is excluded in the Maastricht Treaty. The European Commission's forecast of spring 1997 suggests that Italy will have problems in joining the EMU starter group as the Italian deficit/GDP ratio is expected to be 3.2% in 1997 and even 3.9% in 1998. A fully developed EMU group (with all 15 countries included) would represent 38% of the OECD GDP, slightly higher than the U.S. with 33% (Japan 21%). The exports/GDP ratio of EU countries is 30%, the ratio with respect to exports outside the EU would be 10% (Japan, U.S. 8%). The share of the U.S. dollar in international currency reserves fell from 67% to 40% in 1995, while the share of European currencies increased from 13% to 37%.

Prior to the EMU, market participants have to anticipate whether a transition to 1999 will bring windfall losses or gains in various bond markets. Germany as a country, where the public is rather sensitive and skeptical to the project of monetary union, is of particular interest. Jeromin Zettelmeyer's contribution is "EMU and Long Interest Rates in Germany" and tests the hypothesis that the EMU project has pushed up interest rates in Germany. By examining the co-movements of German and other European yields, as well as the exchange rate of the private ECU - in reaction to events affecting the probability that EMU will be realized. Days with good, bad or neutral press news about EMU are taken into account. If other EU countries expect lower yields from EMU, their yields should fall in response to events making EMU more likely, while interest rates in Germany should rise. Surprisingly, the relationship between German and other European yield reactions to EMU related events is significantly positive rather than negative. Similarly, events leading to an appreciation of the private ECU are associated with a decline in German yields. In this perspective, markets seem to expect rather low inflation rates or real interest rates in the EMU area in comparison to the regime of the Deutsche Bundesbank. German markets might still be skeptical about EMU, but they seem to prefer the successful completion of this process to the risks associated with its disruption.

Jens Weidmann's comments shed further light on the "EMU interest hypothesis" and his detailed analysis also suggests that the likelihood of EMU does not affect long yields in Germany. He proposes an alternative methodology which relies on conditional probabilities with respect to EMU using the deviations of the actual ECU forward interest rates from their theoretical values.

Low Euro rates could also in principle be related to an expected Euro devaluation in comparison to the average mid-1990 dollar exchange rate of the EMU starter group. If this depreciation was strong enough representing an overshooting effect, it could cause expectations about a long-term Euro appreciation; so the interest rate for the EMU starter group could be rather low. Risk-averse investors in EU countries are likely to favor a more short-term portfolio investment in the US dollar, the Swiss franc and the British pound in the uncertain transition period rather than in the long term. When rising EMU capital imports (reversal of "excessive" capital exports) occur some time after 1999, one should see an Euro appreciation and falling interest rates. One may notice that EU countries, disregarding Greece, achieved very low inflation rates in the run-up to 1999 so that the initial inflationary record of the ECB could be rather favorable. Moreover, given the ECB's natural aim to build up reputation, it is likely to adopt a rather strict monetary policy stance in the early years of EMU. By contrast, the starting position with respect to the employment record will be rather poor as the unemployment rate could be around 10 percent, and a rather strict monetary policy could further aggravate this problem. At the same time there is no reason to believe that poorly functioning labor markets cannot be reformed in the EMU regime as easily or difficultly as in the EMS-I-area.

The EU's low capital productivity - relative to the US - is indirectly part of the European unemployment problems and should increase under the pressure of more integrated financial markets and an intensified merger and acquisition process in Europe. For EU countries there could indeed be major disadvantages of staying outside EMU which are not related to higher interest rates but to slower growth prospects as well. This compounds existing budget deficit problems and hence prospects for meeting the convergence criteria. It will be important how the new

European Monetary System works and which countries its members will be and which ones are not included. The design for EMS II linking the EMU area and the outsiders is a copy of the institutional arrangements in the final stage of EMS I. It will rely rather on wide exchange rate margins than on narrow ones.

Paul Bergin and Mathias Moersch analyzed the relationship between "EMU and Outsiders: Fixed versus Flexible Exchange Rates". Strict enforcement of the Maastricht criteria will lead to the creation of a two-speed Europe, consisting of a monetary union of the core, and the outsiders, who are initially not part of the union. This will exert pressure on the outsiders to return to floating exchange rates versus the core, since for a number of reasons the return to pegged rates is no longer possible. With markets ruling out strictly fixed, i.e. pegged exchange rates and the rules of the game precluding currency union, the next logical question is how to assess the effects of flexible exchange rates. Using a simple simulation model, the authors argue that a flexible regime will not be seriously disruptive to the common goods market or worsen foreign welfare. It also is argued that the de-valuations of 1992 and 1993 are not a warning against adopting a flexible exchange rate regime, but rather are a reaction to exchange rate misalignment that developed earlier. While flexible exchange rates did not support convergence, they are no more damaging to it than pegged rates.

Max Corden gives important and detailed comments about whether a flexible exchange rate regime is favorable or unfavorable for preserving free trade. Monetary integration in the presence of new trade barriers would hardly generate economic benefits.

While fixed rates (in the lose sense of EMS II) might facilitate the process of disinflation and interest rate convergence, fully flexible rates have the advantage of coping with shocks and major reforms in the political system This includes the switch to a higher share of social security outlays financed by higher value-added taxes (as a means not impairing exports in the case that the VAT rate of the importing country is applied). The switch to this type of partial pension financing, dominant in Denmark and discussed in Germany in early 1997, will cause an appreciation of the currency. This is the result of the decrease in imports in the high-VAT country and thus import prices will have to fall. If the whole EU would apply a higher VAT rate while reducing income taxes - a reasonable reform in favor of higher growth - the world market prices of tradables would indeed fall since the EU is large enough to cause a terms of trade improvement through increases in tariffs or value-added tax rates.

Financial markets and monetary policy are affected by EMU and the Euro, respectively. A crucial question concerns the relative importance of the $ and the Euro which is not backed by a banking system as powerful, innovative and internationalized as the US system. Hence, there could be some currency substitution after 1999 in favor of the US $. The Euro is unlikely to quickly exceed the DM share (e.g. 15% in 1996) in international currency reserves or international bond issues. An important aspect of the coming $-Euro rivalry concerns the question of the role the new European currency could play in foreign exchange trading. Philipp Hartmann deals with "Foreign Exchange Vehicles Before and After EMU: From Dollar/Mark to Dollar/Euro?" In the theoretical part, the structure of currency exchanges is explained by trading costs, as measured by the dealer bid-ask spreads. A necessary condition for the emergence of vehicle currencies is that the increased trading volume reduces its bid-ask spreads. The econometric part of the paper tests this relationship by extracting the predictable part from foreign exchange trading volumes and estimating its impact on forex dealer spreads. Evidence for a negative volume coefficient is found. Predictable exchange rate volatility increases spreads. Finally, scenarios of future Euro foreign spot exchange volumes are simulated from BIS turnover data. The analysis suggests that the Euro will gain some role as a forex vehicle currency, but cannot challenge the Dollar´s position in the medium-term.

This paper is commented on by Emil Claassen who uses the analogy of a barter trade model to highlight the importance of a vehicle currency which allows to reduce transaction costs dramatically. However, as he points out, one has to explain why two (or more) vehicle currencies can co-exist. The fact that after 1973 two currency blocks co-existed - a dollar block and a DM block - can apparently explain this phenomenon.

An important issue in the formation of EMU is the optimum currency literature where discussion has recently been focused on the problem of symmetric and asymmetric shocks. Marie Demertzis, Andrew J. Hughes Hallet and Ole Rummel extend this literature in various ways in their paper "Does a Core-Periphery Regime Make Europe into an Optimal Currency Area?"

Previous investigations into the possibility that the European Union (EU) could form an optimal currency area (OCA) have focused on the traditional arguments for an OCA. Namely the size and correlation of shocks hitting the individual economies. In addition, such analyses are usually carried out with respect to an anchor-area. Such studies have found that only Germany and her immediate neighbors may form an OCA within the EU. This paper tries to extend this analysis by looking at the size and correlation of price and output shocks on two European country aggregates. The member countries of the EU are thus divided into a core, comprising Austria, Belgium, Denmark, France, Germany, Luxembourg and the Netherlands. The periphery consists of Finland, Greece, Ireland, Italy, Portugal, Spain, Sweden and the UK. Shocks hitting these economies are then analyzed with respect to the core and periphery averages. The authors find that the evidence for an OCA is severely weakened, and only exists on the supply side. And even if shocks hitting EU economies were of similar size and highly positively correlated, the authors find marked differences in the transmission mechanisms of European economies. Therefore, symmetric shocks can still have asymmetric effects, thereby weakening the arguments for an OCA further. In the absence of supporting policies to balance those asymmetries, the arguments for the EU as an OCA are tenuous at best.

The comments by Hans G. Monissen point to some other important issues, including the trade-off between employment and the real exchange rate. It also gives an interesting perspective on the "true price index" and emphasizes the problems of strategic interdependencies for the central banks involved. In this perspective EMU can be welfare enhancing not in the least because it reduces the strategic interaction costs on noncooperative central banks.

Lukas Menkhoff analyzes the crucial questions of monetary policy, namely "Competitive Neutrality of Monetary Policy Instruments for EMU". Given the divergence of traditional monetary policy instruments across EU countries the choice of future Euro monetary policy instruments is important, both in the effectiveness and efficiency of policy as well as for its impact on the banking systems and competition between large and small banks in various EMU countries.

The area of monetary policy instruments for European Monetary Union is still open for debate. The dispute is related to the instruments of lending facilities and reserve requirements. Here, the complement of the policy goal "efficiency" by the "competitive neutrality" leads to the proposal of introducing the disputed instruments into the European Central Bank's toolbox. There exist banks in many countries which do not automatically benefit from an international monetary union and internationalized money markets. These banks should be treated fair. For example, giving them an effective chance of a direct refinancing with the central bank via a certain facility that takes into account their institutional characteristics. Alternative proposals are discussed in detail in this paper.

Heinz Herrmann from Deutsche Bundesbank emphasizes in his comments that the set of monetary instruments available is not simply an issue of technical merit but has to be seen in the context of monetary policy control as well as the rapid growth and deepening of the financial and foreign exchange markets.

Greg Steinmetz (Wall Street Journal) chaired a lively panel discussion on "Necessary Amendments for a Functional EMU". Stefan Collignon, AUME, Paris, Robert Raymond, European Monetary Institute, Frankfurt, Michèle Schmiegelow, Catholic University of Louvain and Matti Vanhala from the Bank of Finland also participated. As the views published here indicate there was no common perspective on this critical issue - possibly because in 1996 the final blueprint for the stability pact was not yet clear.

The fiscal aspects of the Maastricht Treaty and the political economy of the transition process are quite important. Daniel Gros took a fresh look at "Self-Fulfilling Public Debt Crises" which is particularly relevant for highly indebted EMU candidates. The paper argues that there are two equilibria in the model where credibility is important: Under one equilibrium the authorities have initially a strong anti-inflationary credibility so that interest rates and the debt service burden remain rather low. Under the other equilibrium, credibility is initially weak so that the government, if it keeps inflation low, has to pay a very high ex post real interest rate. With the risk of interest rates rising further the government could finally press for loosening monetary policy. The experience of Belgium and Italy suggest that the existence of two equilibria is a real possibility.

Helmut Wagner offers his comments on the innovative aspects of the model, the empirical part of the paper and the institutional implications of the model results. One might add that Italy's government under Ciampi and Prodi were at least credible enough to strongly reduce the inflation rate which points to the virtue of having a former central bank governor and an economist from academia as the head of government in times of low initial credibility.

Reading the many debates about fiscal debt and deficit criteria one wonders why governments of EMU countries are not obliged to regularly publish standardized figures on public investment and the value of public capital stock (including the value of natural resources). A gross debt GDP limit is clearly very doubtful from a theoretical point of view, but in any case it would be desirable to have more transparency in the field of gross and net debt of general government and the social security system.

Richard Jackman gave a paper on "EU Labor Markets Inside and Outside the Monetary Union". Labor market developments are different across EU countries, but generally the unemployment figures and especially long-term unemployment rates are high. Jackman's starting point is that the adoption of a single currency largely eliminates the exchange rate as an instrument of adjustment. Thus the nominal wage flexibility becomes quite important. His paper argues, largely on the evidence of the 1992 devaluations that nominal wage rigidities now appear empirically important. It is argued that the evidence suggesting that nominal rigidities were negligible in European economies derives largely in part during historical instances when inflation was rapid and volatile, and does not carry over to current conditions of subdued and stable inflation rates. The paper also questions the claim that a fixed exchange rate system protects an economy from financial shocks, on the grounds that the same degree of protection can be achieved under flexible rates provided by monetary policy. It is based on an interest rate rather than a money supply target. Finally, the author makes some conjectures about the effects of increased cross-country wage comparability although it has to be recognized that monetary union does not necessarily increase the need for the convergence of wage rates across countries.

Michael Burda's comments highlight some additional points and he basically agrees to some of the skeptical views developed by Jackman. Burda emphasizes the role of nominal and real rigidities, but also raises the issue to what extent monetary union will affect labor markets directly and indirectly. He argues that capital mobility, with capital moving away from high wage and high regulatory-regime countries, plays a crucial role for trade unions and that supply side reforms are long overdue on the continent.

Paul Welfens and André Jungmittag focus on the "Political Economy of EMU and Stabilization Policy". They focus both on the question of exchange rate and monetary policy variability which are empirically found to have a negative impact on investment. This supports a quasi-monetarist argument in favor of EMU which could become an area of reduced destabilizing monetary policy impulses. The extent to that the aggregate money demand in the EMU area is less volatile than under the EMS-I-regime facilitates monetary policy control and that money supply of the European central bank. There will be a focus on the average business cycle of the EMU country group which implies less volatile monetary policy reactions than the average monetary policy of EMU candidates in the mid-1990s. One may expect more stable monetary policies. With less policy volatility one can anticipate higher investment growth and higher investment output ratios in an EMU area. This mechanism could explain why firms across EU countries favor monetary union. Since higher investment is the key to more employment and growth - and lower deficit ratios - forming a successful EMU starter group is important. A wide starter group would reduce the risk of competitive devaluations within the EU; a risk which would still persist as long as Italy, Spain and the UK are among the outsiders. Therefore part of industry in the EU is favoring a larger starter group. An argument in favor of a small starter group is the advantage in terms of credibility and therefore the favorable impact on interest rates which, of course, is also crucial to the business community. Depending on the real impact of the creation of EMU and the arguments of various groups in favor of or against EMU one may expect increasing social conflicts in the EMU area.

Willem T.M. Molle offers some critical comments where his major points of disagreement are obvious. He emphasizes the political economic aspects and has a more optimistic view about the impact of regional policy.

The final panel "European Monetary Union from a German Perspective", chaired by Karen Horn from the Frankfurter Allgemeine Zeitung, was quite controversial. Michael Heise, DG Bank, Heinrich Matthes, European Commission, Jürgen Pfister, Commerzbank and Christa Randzio-Plath, European Parliament gave a rather different point of view on the topics raised.

This conference volume is another cornerstone in the series of books which are based on conferences at the European Institute for International Economic Relations (EIIW by its German acronym). European monetary union poses important and difficult issues which the economics profession has to address. Given a few relevant historical precedents on monetary union one may argue that theoretical analysis is of particular importance in the case of EMU. One should not forget that EMU extends beyond Europe since the French Franc Zone in Africa will have to decide about its future monetary regime. The EMU project also extends beyond Western Europe because prospective east European EU member countries will try to shadow the convergence criteria and ultimately become a members of both the EU and EMU.

The Maastricht Treaty suffers from one serious problem, namely the latecomers, who qualified for EMU but chose to opt out initially. They can enter after three years or even earlier. Latecomers should be allowed to enter only after a decade (or paying an entry fee), since this type of sanction is the only way to avoid the free-rider strategies of EU latecomer countries. Without such a clause, the UK and Denmark effectively take a free-rider position with respect to the institutional monetary innovation of the Euro. It can observe the costs of the early starter group and join at a reduced marginal entry cost fairly early if it wants to do so. If the EMU would face massive problems, monetary union could be the starting point for EU disintegration. However, a successful monetary integration could reinforce the single market and create positive welfare effects. The EMU could become, at least after the joining of the UK, a major net exporter of financial services as well as a net exporter of capital, so that sustained EU trade balance deficits could occur.

A successful Euro will cause the City to put maximum pressure on the UK government to finally join the EMU club. Even if the Euro should be weak the new British government is likely to face pressure to join in the medium-term because UK could face a problem similar to that of Germany with its appreciating DM in the first half of the 1990s: A weak Euro will imply a strong dollar and a strong pound, and the latter can hardly be welcome by the British government which under the Thatcher and Major governments attracted many multinational companies by pointing to British (labor) cost advantages. Whether the Swiss Franc will benefit from EMU is doubtful. A massive appreciation - in periods of speculations against the Euro - will further erode the competitiveness of Swiss exports. Thus, a depreciation might be more welcome. Hence, it is clear that the EMU project could create many political and economic pressures for adjustments.

An ideal case of monetary union would be that German monetary dominance - as visible by the Bundesbank's policy - would be replaced by a Bundesbank-like ECB (with an adequate set of policy instruments) and achieve low inflation rates, while not undermining economic expansion. After the D-Mark the European currency would help to save transaction costs and to dramatically increase market transparency. From the case of a reunified Germany, one can also learn that trade unions and employers' federations not necessarily adopt reasonable wage strategies.

Generous conference support is gratefully acknowledged from the European Commission, Brussels, the Fritz Thyssen Stiftung, Cologne, the Landeszentralbank Berlin and Brandenburg, the Landesbank Berlin and the Mittelbrandenburgische Sparkasse, Potsdam. I am most grateful for editorial assistance to Harold Welsand and Alison Sinclair as well as to Tilo Gerstberger and Andreas Schwarz. The index was compiled by Antje Wenk.

EMU will have effects outside Europe. A positive external effect of EMU could be the easier crisis management in the triade, since fewer actors have to be coordinated. A negative internal effect might be that remedying high unemployment in the EU countries could become more difficult since the political conflicts of the stability and growth pact absorb "political consensus capital" to a large extent, leaving national political systems unable of adopting important labor market and capital market reforms. High and sustained unemployment rates undermine the political support for EU integration and cause a dangerous revival of economic nationalism in Western Europe. The row between the German government and the Bundesbank over the revaluation of gold reserves, which the government wanted to use via special profits from revaluation to reduce the budget deficit in 1997 (the crucial year of the convergence test), was an example of poor political management. Confidence of the public in the transition to the Euro was thereby impaired. The independence of the Bundesbank was visibly undermined (and by implication that of the ECB) and the credibility of Germany's government was shattered. The German government which always had criticized creative accounting in France, Italy and other countries weakened the legitimacy of its own criticism by resorting to creative accounting itself. The economics profession will have to closely watch developments in the field of integration.

Potsdam, May 1997 Paul J.J. Welfens

I. Transition and Long Interest Rates in Germany

A. EMU and Long Interest Rates in Germany

Jeromin Zettelmeyer[1]

1. Introduction

Has the expectation that monetary policy might in the foreseeable future be in the hands of a European monetary institution maintained long interest rates in Germany at higher levels then they would otherwise be? Since the future European Central Bank (ECB) might be expected to adopt some weighted average of the traditional monetary policy stances of its members--tougher than most, perhaps, but not as tough as the Bundesbank, implying higher expected inflation and perhaps credibility premia--this idea has a fair amount of intuitive appeal. Moreover, it is consistent with three sets of facts, which have each received considerable attention in recent months:

First, opinion polls indicate that a large majority of Germans (almost two-thirds, according to a September 1995 report in The Economist) oppose a common currency, presumably because the D-Mark has a track record of stability while the future European currency does not[2]. If this view is shared by financial markets, it could contribute to relatively high long yields.

Second, there is anecdotal evidence of a German "capital flight" particularly among small investors and savers into Swiss Franc denominated assets[3].

Third, the shape of the German yield curve relative to the U.S. yield curve has been somewhat puzzling for most of 1995 and early 1996 (figure A.1). From May 1995 to March 1996, German long yields were higher than U.S. long yields even though at the short end German interest rates are below U.S. rates, with the intersection occurring at medium maturities (5-8 years). This pattern--i.e. a positive U.S.-German yield differential at the short end but a negative one at the long end--has not been observed since the mid-seventies (figure A.2). Since the positive differential at the short end can probably be accounted for by differences in the stances of monetary policy and/or business cycle positions, the question becomes what explains the relatively high German rates at the long end. A lack of faith in the anti-inflationary credentials of the future European Central Bank could certainly be among the candidates.

The objective of this paper is to examine whether this potential explanation is valid, i.e. whether skepticism about EMU has in fact exerted upward pressure on long yields in Germany, or at least prevented them from coming down as much as they could have[4]. More precisely, I define the "EMU hypothesis" as the following proposition: if financial markets believe that EMU will come about with positive probability within the next T years, then German bond yields for maturity T will be higher than if financial markets attach zero probability to the event. The objective is to test this hypothesis.

To develop an appropriate test, the paper exploits the following idea. If it is really true that expectations of EMU are keeping German bond yields at higher levels then they would otherwise be, then news which make EMU seem more likely in the foreseeable future should lead to a jump up in German long yields, and vice versa. This suggests that we should examine the reaction of German long yields to events affecting the probability that EMU will realize over the time horizon of the bond.

Figure A.1: U.S. and German Yield Curves, 2/12/96

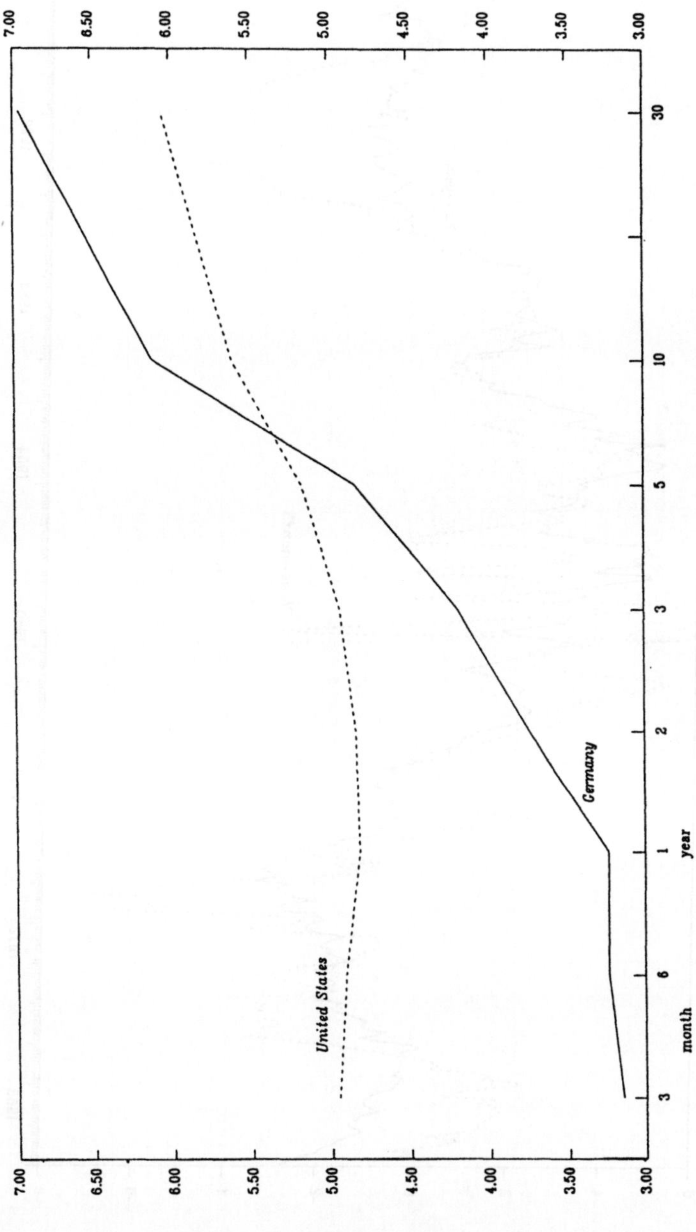

Source: Bloomberg Financial News

Figure A.2: U.S. - German Interest Rate Differentials at the Three-Month and Ten-Year Maturities, January 1967 - January 1996

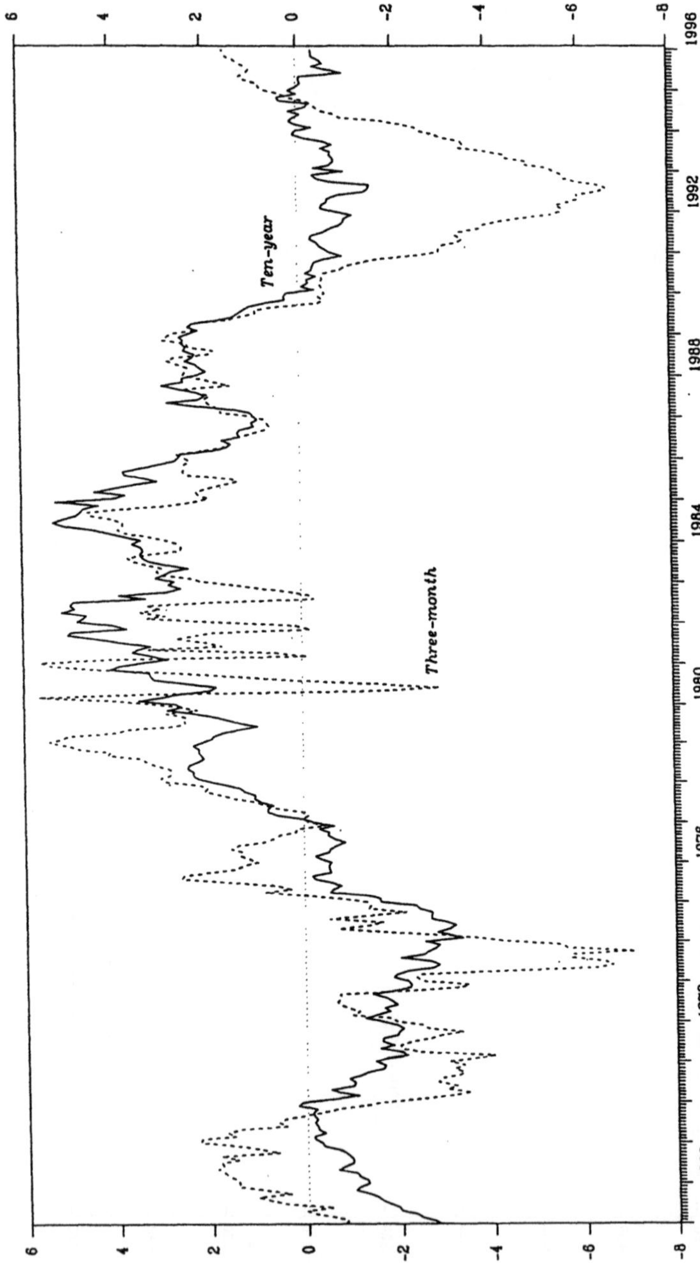

Source: IMF

However, we have a problem in that the magnitude and even the direction in which an event affects the expected timing of EMU are not directly observable. Thus, if German bond yields fail to jump up in response to an event which we classify as making EMU more likely, this might either indicate that the EMU hypothesis is untrue, or it might be due to a misclassification of the news content of the event. Consider, however, bond yields in some other European country i for which the EMU process constitutes a commitment to a tougher anti-inflationary stance than has traditionally been associated with that country. For this country, yields should jump down in response to unanticipated events making EMU more likely, and up in response to bad news about EMU. Thus, if the EMU hypothesis is right we should see a reaction of bond yields in Germany and country i in *opposite* directions in response to an EMU-related event. Under the EMU hypothesis, this prediction will hold irrespective of whether the event had the effect of making EMU more or less likely and whether or not the event was anticipated.

Forty-four political events were selected--beginning with the Maastricht agreement itself, and ending with the recent debate about the EMU timetable in view of large deficits in several European countries--which should have had some effect on the perceived probability of EMU realizing (unless they were entirely anticipated), were not endogenous to same-day economic information, and would not have had significant effects on bond markets except through their implications for EMU. Using an instrumental variables procedure to address the possible simultaneous presence of other economic information to which bond markets might also have reacted, changes in German bond yields *on the days of these events* were then regressed on changes in (i) French, (ii) Belgian, (iii) Italian, (iv) Spanish bonds on the same days. In addition, changes in German bonds on the same event-days were regressed on changes in ECU bonds and the exchange rate of the private ECU relative to the ECU basket; the latter was used as an alternative measure of the news content of the event. The EMU hypothesis predicts negative coefficients in each of these regressions.

The main finding is that, contrary to this prediction, the estimated coefficient is *positive* in all cases, and significant at the five percent level for all regressions except that on changes in the ECU exchange rate ($p=0.11$ in this case). In other words: events that--based on the response of French, Belgian, Italian, Spanish and ECU yields and to a lesser extent the ECU exchange rate--seem to *increase* the chances of EMU coming about, tend to move German yields *down*, not up. On the basis of this result, the EMU hypothesis is rejected.

In the following, the testing methodology summarized above is developed and justified in more detail and in a more formal setup. Next, the criteria for selecting events and the final selection are discussed. We then present the test results, discuss potential sources of bias, and conduct some tests for structural breaks. A final section interprets the results, and concludes.

2. Methodology

For the purposes of developing testable implications, it is useful to state the EMU hypothesis formally. Let $i_g(0,T)$ denote the (annualized) German T-year long interest rate in year zero (i.e. today). For example, $i_g(0,10)$ is today's German ten year rate. Next, let $i_{gD}(t,T)$ denote the annualized German T-year long rate expected today for time t (t being an integer greater zero) assuming that domestic monetary institutions are in place between dates t and t+T. Similarly, let $i_{gE}(t,T)$ denote the annualized German T-year long rate expected today for time t assuming that European monetary institutions will be in place between dates t and t+T. Thus, both $i_{gD}(t,T)$ and $i_{gE}(t,T)$ are today's conditional expectations about long rates of maturity T at time t, conditioning on different institutional settings in each case.

Suppose initially that financial markets are certain that the third stage of EMU will begin at time t, $0 \le t < T$. From the expectations theory of the term structure, we can then write (to a first approximation):

$$i_g(0,T) = \frac{t}{T} i_{gD}(0,t) + \frac{T-t}{T} i_{gE}(t,T-t) \tag{1}$$

Now assume that whether or not EMU will realize at time t is uncertain, but for simplicity retain the assumption that if EMU realizes at all over the maturity period of the bond, it will realize at time t[5]. Define p_g as the probability (from the perspective of financial markets) that a core EMU which includes Germany will realize at time t, and let $i_{gD}(0,T)$ denote the German T-year long rate that would prevail today if it was certain that German institutions would continue in place over the entire maturity period of the bond, i.e. if EMU does not realize at time t. Then, today's German T-year bond yield can be written as

$$i_g(0,T) = p_g\left(\frac{t}{T} i_{gD}(0,t) + \frac{T-t}{T} i_{gE}(t,T-t)\right) + (1-p_g) i_{gD}(0,T) \tag{2}$$

The "EMU hypothesis" is then defined as the following proposition:

$$H_{EMU}: i_g(0,T) > i_{gD}(0,T) \tag{3}$$

or, using (2)

$$H_{EMU}: \frac{t}{T} i_{gD}(0,t) + \frac{T-t}{T} i_{gE}(t,T-t) > i_{gD}(0,T) \tag{4}$$

or equivalently (to a first approximation)

$$i_{gE}(t,T-t) > i_{gD}(t,T-t) \tag{5}$$

In other words, $i_g(0,T) > i_{gD}(0,T)$ will be the case if and only if future interest rates under the European monetary regime are expected to be higher than under the Bundesbank.

Consider now the reaction of $i_g(0,T)$ to a change in the probability that EMU will realize within the maturity period of the bond. Assuming that interest rates conditional on continuing domestic monetary institutions in Germany (i.e. $i_{gD}(0,t)$) are unaffected by changes in p_g[6], we have:

$$\frac{di_g(0,T)}{dp_g} = \frac{t}{T} i_{gD}(0,t) + \frac{T-t}{T} i_{gE}(t,T-t) - i_{gD}(0,T) \tag{6}$$

which under the EMU hypothesis is always greater than zero (equation (4)). Consequently, a test of H_0: $di_g(0,T)/dp_g > 0$ constitutes a test of the EMU hypothesis, since a rejection of the former implies a rejection of the latter.

As mentioned in the introduction, the complication in putting this approach to practical use is that dp_g is not directly observable. Suppose we simply check the reaction of German bond yields to major events influencing the timing and likelihood of EMU--for example, a referendum outcome during the Maastricht ratification process. We could then be vulnerable to two problems. First, a change in p_g and thus a reaction of bond yields will only occur to the extent that the outcome is unanticipated. Thus, for a perfectly anticipated outcome we would not observe any change in yields, even if the EMU hypothesis were true, which could lead us to falsely reject (or at least underestimate the evidence in favor of the hypothesis). Second, and perhaps more importantly, the interpretation of certain events in their effect on EMU may be ambiguous. Consider, for instance, the French referendum, which was won by the pro-Maastricht groups by an extremely narrow margin. What was more newsworthy about this event: the fact of victory for Maastricht, or its narrowness, indicating further resistance to EMU in the future?

The approach suggested here in attempting to resolve these problems is to examine the consequences of EMU related events for the *co-movement* of German bond yields and other forward-looking market variables, rather than for the movement of German bond yields directly. In a sense, the change in these other market variables is used as a measure of the change in p_g resulting from a given event. I make use of two families of variables, which are discussed in turn.

2.1 Tests Based on Domestic Bond Yield Co-Movements

Consider an EMU candidate other than Germany ("country i"). In general, the desire to maintain its exchange rate close to a certain parity to the D-Mark will play a role in the way this country conducts its monetary policy. Consequently, interest rates in this country will be affected by conditions in foreign exchange markets, which in turn may depend on the perceived probability that EMU realizes within a given time period. Based on (2), this leads to the following more general version of equation (6):

$$\frac{di_i(0,T)}{dp_i} = \frac{t}{T}i_{iD}(0,t) + \frac{T-t}{T}i_{iE}(t,T-t) + p_i\frac{t}{T}\frac{\delta i_{iD}(0,t)}{\delta p_i} - i_{iD}(0,T) \qquad (7)$$

The difference between this and (6) is the second to last term, in which we allow for an effect of changes in p_i on interest rates conditional on continuing domestic monetary institutions (i.e. *pre*-EMU interest rates).

Equation (7) implies that $i_i(0,T)$ will *fall* in response to an increase in p_i if the following conditions are satisfied:

(i) future interest rates in country i are expected to be *lower* under EMU than under continuing domestic institutions (i.e. the reverse of what the EMU hypothesis states for Germany):

$$\frac{t}{T} i_{iD}(0,t) + \frac{T-t}{T} i_{iE}(t,T-t) < i_{iD}(0,T) \tag{8}$$

(ii) an increase in the probability of joining EMU within a given period will lower pre-EMU interest rates--for example, because it tends to strengthen the currency against the D-Mark, allowing domestic authorities to relax interest rates[7]:

$$\frac{\delta i_{iD}(0,T)}{\delta p_i} < 0, \quad 0 \leq t < T \tag{9}$$

Suppose, then, we have a country i for which (i) and (ii) are both satisfied. If the EMU hypothesis is true, equations (6) and (7) imply that long bond yields in country i and Germany should move in the *opposite* direction in reaction to an event which affects both Germany's and country i's chances of entry into EMU in the same direction (i.e. for which p_i and p_g move together in response to the event). This implies that the we could test the EMU hypothesis by collecting a set of events which affected the EMU timetable in both countries in the same direction--but had negligible effects on long yields through other channels--and regressing the change in German bond yields on the change in the bond yields of country i *on these event days*. The EMU hypothesis would predict a negative coefficient in this regression. This prediction is independent of the magnitude and direction of the jumps dp_g and dp_i (as long as they have the same sign). As a result, the suggested procedure is valid irrespective of the direction in which a certain event might have affected the probability of EMU, or the extent to which the outcome of the event was anticipated.

I would argue that most signatories of the Maastricht agreement that are either members of the ERM or are shadowing the Bundesbank in order to re-enter into the ERM (such as Italy) are likely to satisfy conditions (i) and (ii)--the possible exceptions being Austria, the Netherlands and, of course, Germany itself. In all other cases, there appears to be a consensus that the EMU process enhances the credibility of tight monetary policy in the country, in the sense that it constitutes a commitment to a more consistently anti-inflationary policy stance than was traditionally associated with the country in the past. Indeed, there is plenty of anecdotal evidence, which we will attempt to confirm more systematically below before conducting our test, that countries in this group have witnessed upward jumps in long yields in response to events that made their EMU participation less likely, and vice versa. This is obvious for high yield countries such as Spain and Italy, but it is also the case for countries such as France or Belgium, which have had, and continue to have, positive interest differentials with Germany at the long end, in spite of the fact that their inflation rates have been somewhat lower than the German inflation rate in recent years.

Moreover, using the reactions of French or Belgian bond yields to EMU-related events as right hand side variables in the regressions proposed has one major advantage over using Spanish or Italian yield reactions, which is that the implication of the events for the German EMU timetable is likely to resemble the implications for France or Belgium much more closely than those for Italy or Spain. In this sense, jumps in French or Belgian yields in response to EMU-related events are likely to be a better proxy for changes in p_g than jumps in Italian or Spanish yields in response to the same events[8]. We thus consider bond yield reactions in all four countries as a potential right hand side variable in the regressions proposed.

2.2 Tests Based on ECU-Denominated Variables

The above discussion suggests another candidate for use as a right hand side variable in the proposed test: ECU denominated bonds. Since converting the D-Mark to a European currency would almost certainly occur if and only if the ECU is converted to this currency, $dp_{ecu}=dp_g=dp$ is automatically satisfied for events affecting the likelihood of EMU. In addition, we would expect the average yield of a basket of bonds in the underlying ECU currencies (the so-called "theoretical yield" of ECU bonds) to react to EMU related events in the same direction as French, Belgian, Italian or Spanish yields: in view of the institutional design of the ECB, inflation and nominal interest rates associated with the future European currency can on average be expected to be lower than the weighted average of inflation and nominal interest rates of the basket currencies (the low interest rate currencies D-mark and Guilder combined have a weight of about 40 percent in the basket). Indeed, this effect--that the ECB would be more credible than the sum of its parts--is one of the principal arguments in favor of EMU relative to the EMS of the 1980s.

However, the relationship between the yield of the ECU bond and its "theoretical" yield is not entirely straightforward. Since November 1988, when ECU clearing banks stopped exchanging ECUs into currency baskets at par, "no active official or private market mechanism guarantees a one-to-one exchange of private ECUs into units of the ECU basket"[9]. As a result, the (private) ECU--the unit of denomination of ECU bonds--fluctuates in value against the currency basket. Consequently, the relationship between the yield on ECU bonds and the yield of the underlying basket is governed by an uncovered interest parity condition. Assuming for simplicity that a (one for one) conversion of the private ECU into the basket and subsequently into the European currency will either happen at time t or never[10], this condition can be written as

$$1 = p\frac{1+i_{ecu}(0,t)}{1+i_b(0,t)}\frac{E \in (t)}{\in (0)} \tag{10}$$

where $\in(0)$ and $E\in(t)$ denote the exchange rate of today's ECU basket to the ECU at time 0 and the exchange rate expected for time t, respectively. Thus, an increase in $\in$ indicates an appreciation of the ECU. The remainder of the notation is unchanged[11].

Consider now, as before, the effects of an increase in p on the various terms in equation (10). While we lack an equilibrium model which would tell exactly us how the terms adjust in response to such a change, the discussion presented in *Folkerts-Landau and Garber (1995)* suggests the following. In general, one would expect an increase in p_g to prompt *both* a change in yield spreads in favor of the ECU (first term under sum declines) *and* a decline in the expected appreciation of the ECU vis-à-vis the basket (second term under sum declines), with the latter taking the form of a jump in the spot rate $\in(0)$. This is because an increase in the probability that the ECU will be converted at par into a European currency which is expected to be more stable than the current basket makes the ECU more attractive relative to the basket. Thus, demand for ECU denominated assets will rise relative to basket assets both on bond and foreign exchange markets, resulting both in a drop in ECU yields relative to basket yields and in an appreciation of the private ECU in terms of the basket.

On the basis of this argument, we include two additional variables among the right hand side variables which we use to test the EMU hypothesis, namely ECU denominated long bonds and the spot value of the private ECU. As before, the test is whether or not these variables move in the opposite direction as German bond yields in reaction to events affecting the probability that EMU will come about within the maturity period of the bond.

Before moving on, it is worth noting that the two families of variables discussed above seem to exhaust the set of market variables for which events affecting the EMU timetable, on an *ex ante* basis, would seem to have unambiguous implications. In particular, and contrary to this author's initial intuition, the response of "safe haven" bond yields--say, Swiss long bond yields--to events affecting the probability of EMU is ambiguous. True, the EMU hypothesis suggests that as EMU becomes more likely, German long bond holders will substitute away from German paper, whose "fundamentals" are affected adversely by EMU, and into "safe haven" paper such as Swiss bonds. However, the same events will make bonds denominated in traditionally less stable European currencies *more* attractive, leading investors to substitute out of "safe haven" paper and into these bonds. The net effect of such an event on the yields of "safe haven" paper is thus ambiguous, as would be the effect of an event that lowers the chances of EMU. Consequently, the EMU hypothesis implies nothing about the co-movement between German yields and "safe haven" yields in response to EMU-related events that could be exploited in order to test the hypothesis.

2.3 Econometric Issues

Before the test suggested in the previous sections can be implemented--regressing the change in German yields on the change of appropriate market variables on the day at which EMU-related events were announced--we need to address the possibility that other shocks affecting bond markets on the same day might confound the underlying structural relationship we are trying to uncover. Some of these shocks might be measurable, and can be controlled for. In particular, as in *Skinner and Zettelmeyer (1995)*, one can control for shocks related to German monetary policy announcements by including the jump in the German three month rate on days of such announcements as a measure of the unanticipated content of the announcement[12]. In other cases, however, shocks might not be easily measured or altogether unobservable.

The presence of these shocks will then constitute a measurement error problem which could seriously bias the OLS coefficient in the suggested regression to test the EMU hypothesis. In particular, the estimated coefficient in a regression of German yield changes on French yield changes on the day of EMU related events might be positive even if the true structural relationship is negative, leading us to falsely reject the EMU hypothesis, and undermining the validity of our test.

This can easily be seen as follows. Assume we select events such that the EMU-shock embodied in the event is unrelated to other economic information on the same day. Then--abstracting from German monetary policy news or other news for which we can control-- the true model can be written as

$$\Delta i_{gt} = \alpha \Delta p_t + \epsilon_{gt}; \quad E\left[\epsilon_{gt} \left| \Delta p_t \right.\right] = 0$$

$$\Delta x_t = \alpha p_t + \epsilon_{xt}; \quad E\left[\epsilon_{xt} \left| \Delta p_t \right.\right] = 0 \qquad (11)$$

where x stands for the market variable which we want to use as a measure of the news content of an EMU-related event (i.e. French, Belgian, Italian Spanish or ECU yields or the ECU exchange rate), and the EMU-shock Δp is measured in the units of the reaction of x.

The EMU hypothesis implies that $\alpha<0$. In order to test this implication, and in view of the fact that the change in the probability p of EMU realizing is not directly observable, the suggestion is to run:

$$\Delta i_{gt} = \beta \Delta x_t + u_t \qquad (12)$$

Substituting (11) into (12), it is clear that $\beta=\alpha$; thus, a consistent estimate of β is a consistent estimate of the parameter we are interested in. The problem is that running OLS on (12) will *not* consistently estimate β, since

$$u_t = \in_{gt} - \beta \in_{xt} \tag{13}$$

Thus, x_t and u_t in equation (12) will be correlated, which implies that the OLS estimator of β is inconsistent. Substituting (11) into the definition of the OLS estimator and taking probability limits, it is easy to show that (under standard assumptions about the existence of probability limits):

$$plim\, \hat{\beta}_{ols} = \frac{1}{1+(\sigma^2_{\in_{xt}} / \sigma^2_{\Delta p})}\alpha + \frac{E\left[\in_{gt} \in_{xt}\right]}{\sigma^2_{\in_{xt}} + \sigma^2_{\Delta p}} \tag{14}$$

The first term on the right hand side of (14) is well known from the textbook measurement error problem. It will be smaller than α in absolute value whenever the noise-to-signal ratio in the numerator is greater than one, biasing the OLS estimator towards zero. This type of bias would of course not produce a change in the *sign* of the coefficient (i.e. the OLS estimator of β being of different sign than α), however, this could well result from the second term on the right hand side of (14). In particular, suppose the EMU hypothesis holds, i.e. $\alpha<0$. If the noise terms in (11) are positively correlated--as would seem likely with integrated capital markets--and this correlation is large enough, then this could still lead to a positive estimate of β.

There are two ways in which one might address this problem. The standard approach is to estimate (12) using an instrumental variables procedure, which will give a consistent estimate of β even if the noise terms in (11) are highly correlated. This raises the question of what would be valid instruments in this context. One obvious choice is to use the *ex ante* categorization of the EMU shocks we are considering--in other words, a classification of each shock as "good news for EMU" ($\Delta p>0$), "bad news for EMU" ($\Delta p<0$), or "ambiguous". If we pick a valid market measure x (i.e. a measure which satisfies assumptions (i) and (ii) of section 2.1) then our ex ante categorization of EMU related events should be negatively correlated with x. Moreover, if the categorization used is truly ex ante in the sense that we classify a particular event as "good for EMU", "bad for EMU" or "ambiguous" purely on the basis of political and economic background information about the event we are considering, i.e. *without* knowledge of the market reaction on the same day, then the instrument will by construction be uncorrelated with the noise terms in (11). Thus, a dummy variable which, for example, assigns a value of 1 to events which are "good for EMU", -1 to events which are "bad for EMU" and 0 to "ambiguous" events would constitute a valid instrument, and (12) can be estimated consistently using two-stage least squares in the usual fashion. The instrument can also be used to perform a *Hausman (1978)* specification test which compares the IV and the OLS estimates of (12). If the null of no misspecification is not rejected, so that OLS be assumed consistent, then OLS can be used as the more efficient of the two estimators.

An alternative would be to pick a subset of events in a way that (a) excludes events which coincided with other published news that might have influenced bond markets and (b) restricts the sample to instances in which the EMU-related event was actually mentioned in bond market reports. One might then hope that this set only includes events with high signal to noise ratios, so that the remaining measurement error problem is negligible and OLS can be assumed to be consistent. This approach was explored in an earlier version of this paper, and led to qualitatively similar results as those presented in section 4[13]. However, it suffers from a series of disadvantages relative to the IV approach. First, it misses unobservable shocks which might still have affected bond prices on the days selected. Second, it is vulnerable to reporting inaccuracies or omissions in bond market reports. For both reasons, it might not be successful in reducing the measurement error problem to an extent at which it can be ignored. Finally, it excludes events which, although they happened to coincide with other major news, contain valuable information about the reaction of bond markets to EMU related shocks. In that sense, it uses information inefficiently. This approach is thus not pursued in what follows, even though it would not have changed the conclusions of the paper.

3. Events

In practice, the events on which our dataset is based were selected according to the following procedure. With the help of past issues of *The Economist* and the *Financial Times* (FT), we compiled an initial set of about 50 candidate events with implications for the likelihood and timing of EMU. In order to generate an event-set that would satisfy the assumptions embodied in system (11) and thus give us a chance at estimating α consistently, we subsequently eliminated events which

i. were endogenous in the sense that they constituted within-day reactions to economic news, and

ii. had direct implications for bond yields in addition to their implications for yields via their effects on the probability of EMU.

An example for ii. is a government defeat over EMU ratification that increases the chances of early elections (as was the case during Britain's EMU ratification process). In addition to hurting the prospects for EMU, an event of this kind affects the chance of a change in government policy in general, which might have consequences for bond yields unrelated to EMU. An example for both i. and ii. is a class of "events" which may have had the largest effect of all on perceptions about EMU, namely ERM currency crises. It is clear that the movement of long bond yields during these crises might be driven as much by perceptions of what these crises implied about the conduct of monetary policies and interest rates in the *pre*-EMU future, as by their implications for EMU itself. In addition, there is no reason to believe that the exchange rate movements defining the EMU crises were exogenous to economic information on the days on which we would be studying jumps in bond yields.

The application of these criteria left us with a set of 44 events for use as the basic sample on which to conduct IV regressions as described in the previous section. For all events included in this set, we used the FT to collect the yields of ten year benchmark government bonds before and after the event from the same FT issues which we used to check the event. The ten year maturity was chosen because it constituted the longest maturity for which yield data was readily available for all countries.

To report on how criteria i. and ii. were applied--and, in particular, why certain events were *not* excluded although they might have been candidates for exclusion under criterion ii.--we now briefly review both the initial set of candidate events and the final event set, which is summarized in table A.1. They can divided into two groups: early events, mostly during 1992 and 1993 and related to the Maastricht ratification process; and more recent events, mostly during 1995 and related to the EMU timetable and to whether or not certain countries--in particular France--would be able to meet the Maastricht convergence criteria in accordance with this timetable.

Table A.1: Broad Event Set

Date	Event	Classi-fication	Changes in ten-year bond yields and the ECU spot rate							
			GER10y	FRA10y	BEL10y	ITA10y	SPA10y	ECU10y	ECUEX	USA10y
12/10/91	Maastricht agreement	G	0.01	-0.11	-0.01	-0.07	-0.14	-0.11	0.00	0.00
06/02/92	First Danish Referendum rejects agreement	B	0.00	0.13	0.08	0.22	0.32	0.23	0.13	0.02
06/18/92	Irish Referendum: M passes by wide margin	G	0.01	0.06	-0.02	-0.08	-0.11	0.01	-0.09	0.04
09/20/92	French Referendum: M accepted very narrowly	A	0.07	0.05	0.01	0.02	0.11	-0.04	-1.66	0.01
11/04/92	First Commons vote won	G	0.02	-0.06	-0.09	-0.01	-0.23	-0.08	0.03	-0.02
12/12/92	EC Edinburgh Summit: success for EMU	G	0.02	0.03	0.02	-0.02	-0.07	-0.02	-0.06	0.05
03/08/93	Commons vote lost after Tory right wing revolt	B	0.02	0.10	0.03	0.09	0.08	0.07	0.02	0.06
05/05/93	UK gov. forced to accept amendment to M bill	B	0.07	0.08	0.05	0.02	0.05	0.08	0.00	-0.01
05/18/93	Second Danish Referendum won	G	0.04	0.04	-0.01	-0.06	-0.13	0.02	-0.01	0.00
07/30/93	UK High Court rejects challenge to M	G	0.02	-0.03	0.06	-0.13	-0.24	0.01	1.60	0.01
10/12/93	German constit. court rejects challenge to M	G	-0.03	-0.02	0.00	-0.05	0.01	-0.06	-0.17	0.01
10/29/93	EU Brussels summit confirms M: timetable	G	0.02	0.06	0.00	0.17	0.09	0.04	0.00	0.12
06/12/94	European Elections: victory for anti-M forces	B	0.10	0.29	0.19	0.37	0.20	0.20	-0.04	0.04
04/09/95	EU CB governors' and Finance Ministers' meet	A	0.01	0.03	0.04	0.01	-0.01	0.08	-0.19	0.01
05/31/95	Eur. Comm. releases "Green Paper" on EMU	G	0.02	-0.01	-0.02	0.02	0.10	-0.01	-0.02	0.00
06/19/95	EU finance ministers write off 1997, affirm 1999	A	-0.02	-0.01	-0.01	-0.19	0.01	-0.01	-0.01	0.03
06/22/95	First Juppé mini-budget	G	-0.06	-0.12	-0.05	-0.08	-0.11	-0.05	-0.01	-0.09
06/26/95	EU Cannes summit reiterates 1999 deadline	G	-0.03	0.00	0.01	0.01	-0.01	0.03	0.10	0.03

(continued)

Table A.1 (continued)

Date	Event	Classi-fication	Changes in ten-year bond yields and the ECU spot rate							
			GER10y	FRA10y	BEL10y	ITA10y	SPA10y	ECU10y	ECUEX	USA10y
08/25/95	Madelin resigns over proposed spending cuts	B	-0.02	0.04	0.01	0.16	0.07	0.02	0.03	0.00
09/20/95	Juppé presents 96 budget; Waigel on ITA ,BEL	A	-0.06	0.04	-0.03	0.10	0.01	0.00	0.02	-0.02
09/21/95	Gaddum: EMU criteria must be strictly satisfied	B	0.03	0.00	0.03	0.10	0.11	0.00	0.05	0.09
09/25/95	OECD report: France unlikely to meet criteria	B	0.01	-0.02	0.02	0.04	0.01	0.08	0.39	0.00
09/28/95	Juppé announces French revenue shortfall	B	-0.05	-0.22	-0.04	0.02	-0.07	-0.03	0.12	-0.08
10/01/95	EU Valencia summit seals 1999 as EU target date	G	-0.04	-0.03	-0.05	0.11	-0.04	-0.07	-0.05	-0.05
10/10/95	First French public sector strike (24 hours)	A	0.00	-0.03	0.00	-0.05	0.00	-0.06	-0.20	0.00
10/26/95	Chirac committs to deficit-cutting as no. 1 priority	G	0.01	-0.10	0.01	-0.07	0.01	-0.04	-0.35	-0.02
11/07/95	French cabinet resigns	G	0.01	-0.08	-0.02	-0.07	-0.04	-0.09	-0.06	0.03
11/07/95	Composition of new cabinet announced: fiscally conserv.	G	-0.04	-0.11	-0.05	-0.10	-0.10	-0.10	-0.07	-0.06
11/14/95	EMI presents EMU blueprint	G	-0.01	0.00	-0.02	-0.07	-0.04	-0.02	-0.10	-0.01
11/15/95	Juppé unveils welfare reform package	G	-0.02	-0.10	-0.04	-0.03	-0.09	-0.03	-0.15	0.04
11/23/95	French railway strike begins	B	-0.02	-0.05	-0.03	-0.02	-0.08	-0.08	-0.31	-0.03
11/27/95	EU fin. min. favorable on Waigels "stability pact"	G	0.03	0.05	0.02	0.04	0.00	0.02	-0.27	0.00
11/29/95	Bundestag hearing on EMU: Germans tough on criteria	B	0.00	0.07	0.03	0.04	0.10	0.08	0.22	-0.05
12/03/95	French Unions vow to intensify strike	B	-0.02	0.06	0.02	0.04	0.04	0.05	0.10	-0.07
12/05/95	Juppé: will not back down on welfare reform	G	-0.04	-0.12	0.04	0.06	-0.02	-0.11	0.14	0.03
12/07/95	Kohl: confidence in early French EMU membership	G	-0.04	-0.05	-0.02	0.02	-0.08	-0.03	-0.05	0.00
12/10/95	Juppé compromises on parts of package	A	0.03	0.03	0.03	-0.04	-0.02	0.02	0.23	0.03
12/13/95	French govt. abandons public pension reform	A	-0.02	0.03	0.02	0.01	-0.05	0.04	0.21	0.02
12/15/95	EMU Madrid summit, end of strike	G	-0.02	-0.08	-0.02	-0.12	-0.09	-0.06	-0.22	-0.02
01/09/96	Waigel: Germany missed M deficit target in 95	B	-0.01	-0.02	-0.03	0.02	0.02	-0.03	-0.11	0.12
01/15/96	Lamfalussy: EMU remains attainable by 1999	G	-0.03	-0.03	-0.05	-0.03	-0.08	-0.03	0.19	-0.09
01/24/96	Giscard: criteria should be relaxed	A	-0.04	-0.02	-0.05	-0.09	-0.05	-0.04	0.10	-0.06
01/25/96	Giscard views sharply ciriticized by FRA, GER	B	0.06	0.06	0.03	0.06	0.11	0.04	0.32	0.11
01/29/96	GER unlikely to meet M criteria in 97; Kohl reassures	A	0.05	0.04	0.04	0.01	0.09	0.06	0.09	0.02

Sources: Financial Times, Kredietbank N.V. "G" stands for "Good News for EMU"; "A" stands for "Ambiguous News", "B" for "Bad News".

3.1 Events Related to the Maastricht Ratification Process

Depending on the stipulations of each national constitution, the Maastricht agreement needed to be ratified either by parliament or through a referendum in each country. Most of the referenda involved substantial ex ante nervousness about the outcome, in particular after the unexpected defeat of Maastricht in the first Danish referendum. Their outcomes typically constituted major news both in the political sections of the FT and in the bond market reports, were not influenced by any within-day economic news, and had no implications on bond markets except through their implications for EMU. They thus constitute ideal "events" for our purposes. Parliamentary ratification, on the other hand, was never in doubt in view of ruling party majorities in parliaments, except for the U.K., where there was cross-party opposition to the ratification process. U.K. parliamentary votes on Maastricht were thus included in the event set with the exception of the final U.K. Maastricht votes on July 22 and 23, 1993, which constituted news primarily because they almost led to a collapse of the Conservative government. Since the implications of these votes for the Maastricht timetable was clearly secondary to their general political implications, these events were excluded under criterion ii.

In addition, we included the EC's Edinburgh summit in December 1992, which was crucial for EMU in that it put the Maastricht process back on track by reaching a compromise with Denmark, and two major court decisions--in Germany and the U.K.--which could have derailed the treaty.

3.2 EMU Related Events Following Maastricht Ratification

Following the EU Brussels summit at the end of October 1993, which confirmed the beginning of the second stage of EMU with the creation of EMI in January 1994, Maastricht was largely out of the headlines until the European election of June 1994, which in most countries constituted the first opportunity for the general public to cast a vote on Maastricht. In the event, anti-Maastricht groups made substantial gains, and the election was primarily interpreted as a setback for EMU. However, in some countries--notably Spain, where the Socialists' poor showing prompted fears of political instability and early elections--the domestic implications of the election may have outweighed its implications for EMU. We thus ran our regressions both including and excluding this datapoint (see section 4).

After the election until early 1996, there was a large number of political events with implications for EMU, which can be roughly divided as follows: (1) various EU summits, declarations and blueprints designed to salvage the 1999 deadline for the beginning of the third stage and put some flesh on the EMU process both until 1999 and thereafter; (2) French efforts to reduce the budget deficit in order to meet the Maastricht convergence criteria, including a wave of strikes triggered by the government's fiscal reform plans; (3) German officials' remarks emphasizing the need to adhere strictly to the Maastricht convergence criteria and suggesting that certain countries might not make it into the first group of EMU members.

While events in the first category rarely constituted large surprises and were often ignored in bond market reports, they are unproblematic in terms of criteria i. and ii. above, and were thus generally included in our event set. Interpreting the remaining events primarily in terms of their implications for the likelihood that EMU will be achieved within a certain time--changes in p, in the notation of the previous sections--is more problematic, and needs to be justified.

In the case of the French consolidation and welfare reform efforts and the public protests which they gave rise to, the problem is that these events carry obvious direct implications for the French economy in addition to the prospects for joining EMU, and that these in themselves can be expected to affect long rates (for example, through the effect of fiscal consolidation on real interest rates). We would argue, however, that both the urgency of the government in pushing these reforms and the reaction of bond markets to the proposals were primarily driven by the implications of the proposed reforms for France's chances to join EMU in 1999. Both general press reports on the events in France and bond market reports support this view[14]. Thus, bond market reactions would primarily reflect the effect of the events on the probability of joining EMU. Moreover, to the extent that there was a direct effect on long real rates, it would tend to push French bond yields in the same direction (i.e. down for events increasing the chances of a lower deficit in the future). Thus, the basic prediction regarding the expected co-movement between French and German yields is unaffected, unless the French fiscal reform also implies lower long real rates in *Germany* through integrated capital markets. In view of the magnitude of adjustment involved (reducing the French deficit from about 5.5 to about 3 percent) and the size of French public borrowing relative to the integrated capital market among industrial nations, this effect would seem sufficiently small to be neglected, in the sense that it would not generate a correlation between Δp and the error terms in system (11)[15]. The dataset underlying the initial set of results presented in the next section thus includes events based on French fiscal reform efforts; however, in section 4.2 we return to this issue and test whether our conclusions would be affected if we had excluded this class of events.

In the case of German officials remarks about the need to scrupulously observe the Maastricht criteria, the issue is that these remarks can be somewhat ambiguous in their implications for EMU itself. While they were interpreted by the press and--according to the FT--by bondmarkets as making EMU more difficult for the majority of European countries, including France, and thus the 1999 deadline less realistic, their main intention was presumably to reassure the German public on the prospects for low inflation under the third stage of EMU. In general, we would thus expect these remarks to have two effects: first, to reduce the probability that EMU will come about within a given time period ($p_i(T)$ falls); second, to lower inflationary expectations and thus nominal interest rates conditional on European monetary institutions ($i_{iE}(t,T)$ falls). Under the EMU hypothesis, these would work in the same direction for Germany (namely, pushing yields down) but in opposite directions for the other countries, i.e. France, Belgium, Spain and Italy. In these cases, the effect of the remarks on the EMU timetable would tend to push yields up, while their effect through inflationary expectations conditional on EMU materializing would push them down. On the other hand, in the cases of Belgium, Italy and Spain we would also expect the effects of these remarks on the respective EMU timetables to be more severe than for Germany, since the remarks specifically address criteria that might be harder for these countries to satisfy than for France and Germany. This would tend to offset the potential decline in yields through $i_{iE}(t,T)$. On the whole, thus, our priors are that a country such as Belgium, Spain or Italy and probably also France would evaluate remarks of this kind primarily in terms of its chances to participating in EMU. Indeed, in only one case out of twelve (Belgium, 9/20/95--see table A.1) do we observe a fall of French, Belgian, Italian or Spanish yields on the day of on which one of the German statements became public, and in only in one instance do we register no reaction at all (France, 9/21/95). Our approach was thus to retain the statements of German officials and to run our regressions both with and without the corresponding datapoints to ensure that our results are not sensitive to their inclusion.

In principle, the same ambiguity applies for ECU bond yields and the value of the private ECU. Statements emphasizing the need to apply tough convergence criteria can affect the value of the ECU and ECU yield differentials vis-à-vis the basket in at least two ways: first, through expectations that the beginning of the third stage will be delayed--the effect we want to capture; second, through expectations that the ECU might be converted into a smaller basket which only includes traditionally stable European currencies. Since these currencies would, in general, tend to be strong within their ERM bands, this expectation could, by itself, strengthen the private ECU and lower ECU bond yields. Again, we have two potentially offsetting effects, and again the observed reaction suggests that the former is stronger at least in its effect on the private ECU, which depreciates (jumps up) in all cases. The ECU yield, on the other hand, jumps up in one case but shows no reaction in the two others. As in the case of regressions involving yield changes on the right hand side, we thus decided to run the regressions based on changes in the value of the ECU and ECU yields both including and excluding the datapoints in question.

Table A.1 presents all events included in the final event set with their classification in terms of their presumed unanticipated effects on EMU which is to be used as an instrument as described in section 2.3 ("good news", "bad news" and "ambiguous"). Note that in one case two EMU-related events coincided, so that bond yields are interpreted to reflect their net implications for EMU (09/20/95), whereas in another case--the November French cabinet reshuffle--news of the reshuffle were spread over two days, because bond markets learned about the resignation of the old cabinet during the trading session, while the composition of the new cabinet became known after markets had closed (11/07/95).

4. Results

4.1 Basic Regressions

Table A.2 presents the results from the regression-based tests proposed in section 2.3. The upper panel presents the coefficient and standard errors from first stage of the IV regression; the dependent variables are the six market variables listed in the heading of each group of columns. In the main panel ("Second Stage Regression"), the dependent variable is the change of the German ten year government bond yield on the days selected, and the six market variables listed in the headings of the columns are now the main right hand side variables of interest; their coefficients are reported in the line "Measure". For each of these six right hand side variables, we run three regressions: an IV regression using the ex-ante interpretation of the events as an instrument, denoted "INTERPR" (see table A.1 and section 2.3); an OLS regression on the same right hand side variables as the IV regression, and a second OLS regression which in addition includes the change in the US ten year bond yield--as a proxy for changes in the world interest rate--on the right hand side. This second OLS regression model must be interpreted with care. If the Hausman test based on the comparison of the first two regressions has rejected the null of no misspecification then one cannot, in general, expect this regression to be correctly specified. Even if the Hausman test has not indicated misspecification of OLS(1), the presence of the US ten year bond yield in OLS(2) may introduce an endogeneity problem of its own through reverse causality. If, however, reverse causality is not deemed to be a problem (for example, it might be argued that the German bond market is small relative to the U.S. bond market) and the Hausman test can*not* reject no misspecification of the OLS(1) regression model, then the OLS(2) model offers the opportunity of a more efficient use of information, since a proxy for changes in the world interest rate is directly included as a regressor whereas in IV and OLS(1) it is not[16].

Table A.2: Results from IV and OLS Regressions

	Right-Hand Side Measure of EMU Shock																	
	FRA 10y			BEL10y			ITA10y			SPA10y			ECU10y			ECUEX		
	IV	OLS (1)	OLS (2)	IV	OLS (1)	OLS (2)	IV	OLS (1)	OLS (2)	IV	OLS (1)	OLS (2)	IV	OLS (1)	OLS (2)	IV	OLS (1)	OLS (2)
First Stage Regression:																		
INTERP	-0.04	...	...	-0.03	...	...	-0.06	...	...	-0.07	...	...	-0.05	...	...	-0.07	...	...
S.E.	0.014	...	...	0.007	...	...	0.015	...	...	0.015	...	...	0.010	...	...	0.027	...	...
CONST	0.01	...	...	0.01	...	...	0.03	...	...	0.01	...	...	0.02	...	...	0.02	...	...
S.E.	0.013	...	...	0.006	...	...	0.014	...	...	0.014	...	...	0.009	...	...	0.025	...	...
Second Stage Regression:																		
Measure	0.29	0.26	0.21	0.50	0.47	0.36	0.22	0.11	0.06	0.16	0.12	0.07	0.26	0.22	0.16	0.18	0.00	0.00
S.E.	0.118	0.051	0.051	0.191	0.098	0.100	0.106	0.052	0.048	0.081	0.048	0.046	0.114	0.069	0.064	0.109	0.034	0.029
GER3m	0.63	0.65	0.75	0.34	0.36	0.53	0.65	0.70	0.85	0.69	0.70	0.84	0.49	0.53	0.70	0.50	0.75	0.88
S.E.	0.358	0.354	0.331	0.397	0.372	0.354	0.456	0.431	0.387	0.426	0.421	0.382	0.423	0.411	0.371	0.585	0.442	0.380
USA10y	...	...	0.23	...	...	0.23	...	...	0.33	...	...	0.31	...	...	0.30	...	...	0.35
S.E.	...	...	0.085	...	...	0.089	...	...	0.096	...	...	0.097	...	...	0.090	...	...	0.090
R^2	...	0.42	0.51	...	0.39	0.48	...	0.15	0.34	...	0.19	0.42	...	0.25	0.41	...	0.07	0.33
N	44	44	44	44	44	44	44	44	44	44	44	44	44	44	44	42	42	42
Hausm. p		0.76			0.84			0.19			0.52			0.67			0.03	

Notes: Hausman p denotes the significance level at which the Hausman test would reject no misspecification of the OLS(1) model.

In all regressions, we control for influences of German monetary policy on the German ten year bond yield by including the change in the German three month interbank rate in our regression whenever German monetary policy actions or related news (e.g. about German monetary aggregates) were mentioned in bond market reports; this occurred on sixteen occasions. In other words, the variable "GER3m" contains a zero entry except for these sixteen occasions, when it contains the change of the German three month rate on that day. To satisfy ourselves that the inclusion of events which coincided with German monetary policy announcements did not bias the results in spite of our attempt to control for the announcements, we also ran the OLS regressions without GER3m after dropping the events in question. Not surprisingly, we obtained larger standard errors, but the regression coefficients on the market variables of interest were very similar to those reported in the OLS columns of table A.2.

Finally, note that the sample for the regressions using ECUEX, the spot exchange rate of the private ECU relative to the ECU basket, is slightly smaller than that for the remaining regressions. According to *Folkerts-Landau and Garber (1995*, p. 135*)*, the market for private ECUs "did not operate for a week after September 16, 1992" (the date of the first ERM crisis). While exchange rates are still quoted for this week, typical day-to-day changes are about ten times larger than usual, indicating that the market was very thin and not functioning normally. September 20, 1994 was thus excluded from the regressions involving ECUEX, and July 30, 1995, which coincided with the second ERM crisis, was excluded on similar grounds.

Consider first the upper panel in table A.2, which reports the results from the regression of the market variables listed in the column group headings on the instrument "INTERPR". As can be seen, the coefficient on "INTERPR" is highly significant in all cases. This is interesting not only because it suggests that "INTERPR" is a reasonable instrument (well correlated with the variable we are instrumenting for), but as a way of confirming the basic property assumed in section

2 for the right hand market variables used as a measure for EMU shocks, namely that "good news for EMU" reduces the yields of these variables (leads to an appreciation), and conversely for "bad news". The significant negative coefficients on INTERPR imply that, assuming that the classification embodied in INTERPR tends to correctly capture the direction of the true underlying EMU-related shocks, the market variables we picked for our test really react to these shocks in the direction in which they were assumed to react.

A further point to note from the upper panel of table A.2 are the relatively large standard errors of INTERPR in the ECUEX regressions, suggesting that ECUEX, the daily change of the spot rate of the private ECU relative to the ECU basket, may be a noisier measure of EMU-related shocks than changes in the long yields of the bonds chosen. Finally, note that the constant in the first stage regression is positive throughout, although typically not significant. This implies that events whose news content was classified as "ambiguous" on average lead to slight increases in yields, or depreciations--thus, the "bad" news content of these ambiguous cases seems to have dominated slightly.

Now turn to the lower panel of the table. To begin with, note that the Hausman test rejects the null of no misspecification strongly in only one case (p=0.025), namely in the model with ECUEX as right hand side market measure. This is not surprising given the "noisiness" of ECUEX as apparent from table A.1, the large standard errors in the first stage regression, and the catastrophic R^2 of the OLS (1) specification; all these suggest that the ϵ_{xt} noise term in system (11), which drives misspecification, has high variance for this particular variable. In addition to ECUEX, in the case of ITA10y the p-value of the Hausman statistic is much lower than for the other yield variables. If we are worried about misspecification--as we should, given the priors established in sections 2.3 and 3--this, too should be interpreted as a rejection; in other words, we should work with an alpha level of at least 0.2.

It follows that for ITA10y and ECUEX, we should trust only the results from the IV regressions. In all other cases, the use of the OLS(1) regression would seem safe. What about OLS(2)? Comparing the standard errors of OLS(1) and OLS(2), it is clear that OLS(2) does not buy us much in terms of estimating "measure", our main variable of interest, more precisely. On the other hand, OLS(2) has not been subjected to a specification test. Thus, this author prefers to stick to OLS(1). On the other hand, it is true that OLS(2) gives a better fit and that USA10y is significant in the OLS(2) regressions. If the reader feels comfortable with the idea of treating USA10y as exogenous, he or she can work with OLS(2) instead. Either way, the qualitative implications are largely the same.

This leads to the main result of table A.2: in all IV regressions, and in all OLS(1) regressions which were not rejected as misspecified, the coefficient on the right hand side yield variables is *positive* rather than negative, as implied by the EMU hypothesis, and significant at the five percent level for all specifications except ECUEX (in which case p=0.11). This implies that the null hypothesis of a true negative coefficient on "measure" should be rejected at the 2.5 percent significance level on the basis of all regressions except for ECUEX, where the likelihood that the regression result is consistent with a true negative coefficient on ECUEX is about 6.5 percent[17].

Less importantly for our purposes, note that the coefficient on GER3m, the proxy variable for German monetary policy or expectations of German monetary policy, comes out positive, as expected, although it is fairly imprecise. Finally, the presence of USA10y in the OLS(2) regressions leads to slightly lower estimates for the "measure" variables relative to the OLS(1) specification, but that with one exception (SPA10y) the OLS(2) estimates for "measure" are still highly significant whenever the OLS(1) specification was not found to be misspecified.

4.2 Robustness and Stability

The results presented above constitute strong evidence against the null that German bond yields and the remaining market variables studied respond to EMU related events in opposite direction. Before we conclude that the EMU hypothesis should be rejected, however, we should address the possibility of bias resulting from the inappropriate inclusion of certain events. Section 3 reported on three types of events--the European election, German officials' statements about the need to apply the Maastricht criteria "strictly", and events related to French fiscal consolidation efforts-- whose inclusion was debatable on the grounds of criterion ii., i.e. because they may have contained information which could have exercised a major effect on bond yields in other ways than through changes in the perceived probability of EMU. In terms of system (11), the risk of inappropriately including these events is to generate a correlation between Δp and the errors ϵ_{gt} and ϵ_{xt}. In this event, (11) cannot be estimated consistently through any of our methods, including IV, since IV will only protect us from the measurement error problem (i.e. the presence of ϵ_{xt} and its likely correlation with ϵ_{gt}) *assuming* that the assumptions of system (11) are satisfied, i.e. that ϵ_{gt} and ϵ_{xt} are orthogonal to the EMU shock.

The most straightforward way of checking whether the inclusion of these event-groups is driving our result is to re-estimate table A.2 excluding each of the questionable event groups. However, this is a bit cumbersome since we would have to go through various combinations of excluded groups, and provides no information beyond making the basic point. An easier and more informative alternative is to use the graphic structural stability analysis capabilities of PCGIVE 8.0, the econometric package used for the earlier regressions, to check how the inclusion of any of these events groups modifies the regression results and at the same time take the opportunity to check parameter stability in general.

In order to apply the graphical analysis functions of PCGIVE to our problem, we take advantage of the fact that our sample has no dynamic structure and re-order the sample such that the event-groups whose properties we want to test are ordered last, as follows: the first 27 observations of the sample are all "unproblematic" events, in chronological order, i.e. all events related to the Maastricht ratification process and all EMU related summits and statements excepting the three statements by German officials discussed in section 3. These three are next (observations 28, 29 and 30), followed by twelve events related to the French fiscal consolidation efforts of 1995 (observations 31 to 43). The European election of June 1994, which stands out because of the exceptionally large reactions in European bond markets, comes last (observation 44).

We then estimate the coefficient on each of the six measures of EMU-related shocks by applying OLS (for FRA10y, BEL10y, SPA10y and ECU10y) or two-stage least squares (for ITA10y and ECUEX) recursively, i.e. beginning with the first few observations and extending the regression over the whole sample observation by observation, and plot (a) the resulting coefficients with standard errors, (b) the t-statistics and (c) the Chow breakpoint N↓ and N↑ statistics. These constitute two variants of the Chow test for predictive stability. The former tests for a structural break between the first t observations in our sample and the last N≡44-t observations (the "forecast period"). For each t between a fixed observation M, which is defined initially, and 44, PCGIVE plots the value of the Chow statistic which tests whether t is a breakpoint; the test is referred to as N↓ because the "forecast period" gets smaller as t approaches 44. The N↑ test, on the other hand compares a fixed "estimation period" comprising observations 0 to M-1 with a "forecast period" comprising observations M to t≥M. It is called N↑ because the forecast period increases as t approaches 44[18]. In our case, we first set M-1 equal to 11, which is the number of events from the initial Maastricht ratification process in our sample. We subsequently repeated the Chow tests after setting M-1 equal to 27 so that the null of the N↑ test referred to the structural equality of a growing forecast period which included increasing numbers of events belonging to the three "problematic" groups, and the set of "unproblematic" events.

Figure A.3: Tests for FRA10Y

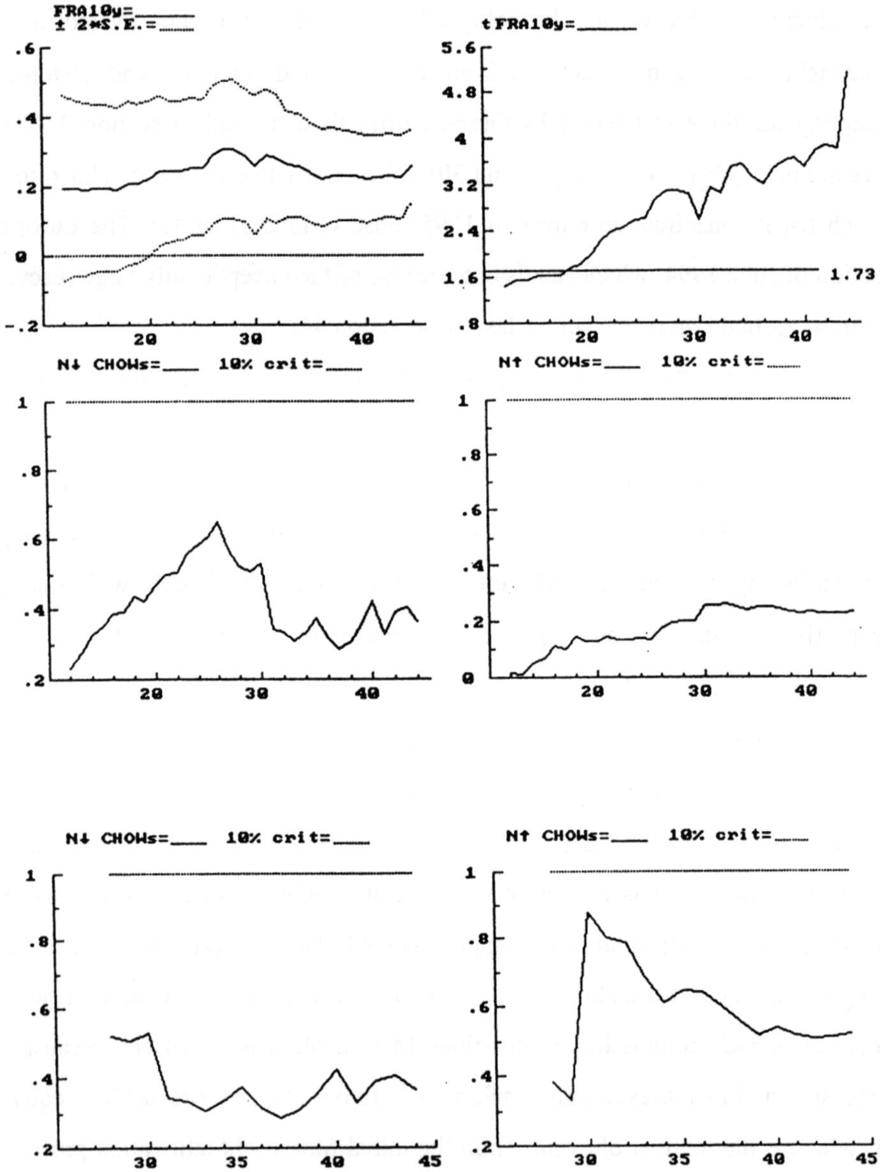

Figure A.4: Tests for BEL10Y

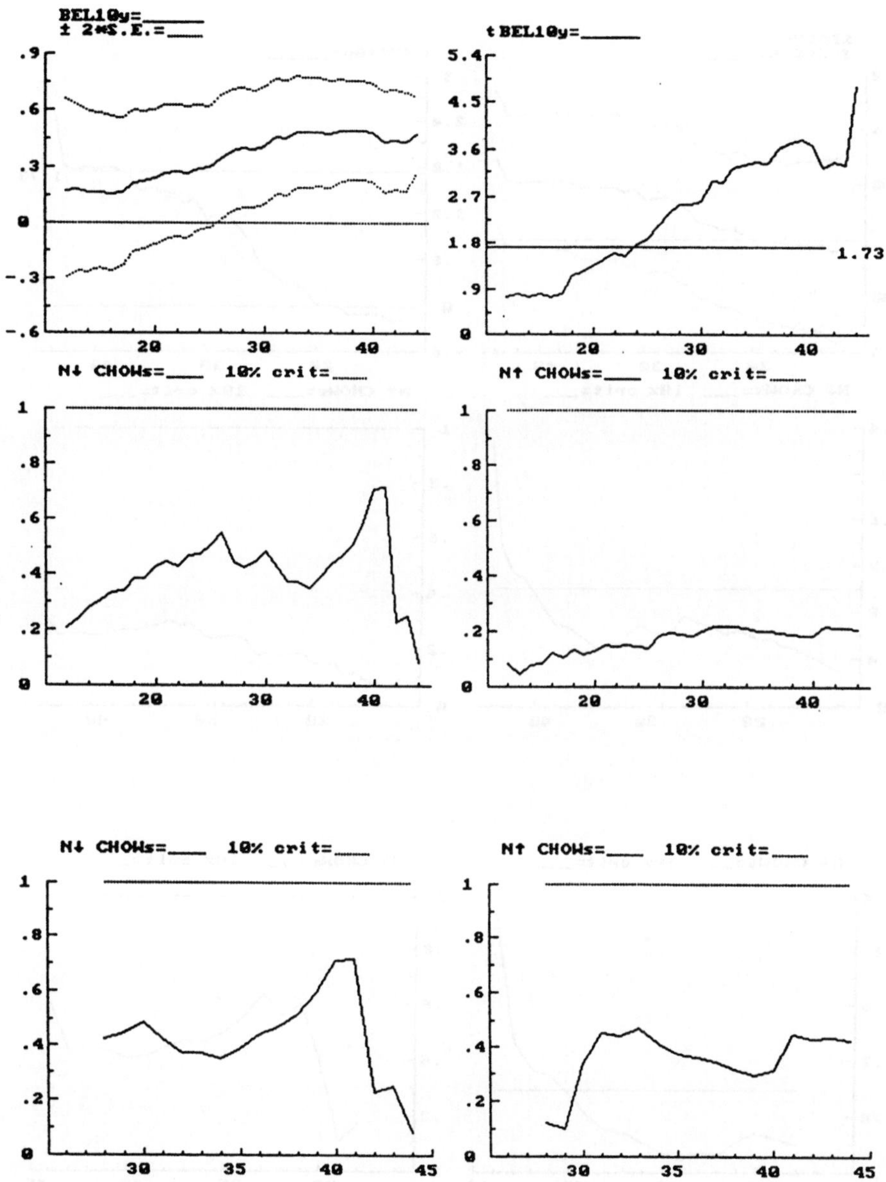

Figure A.5: Tests for SPA10Y

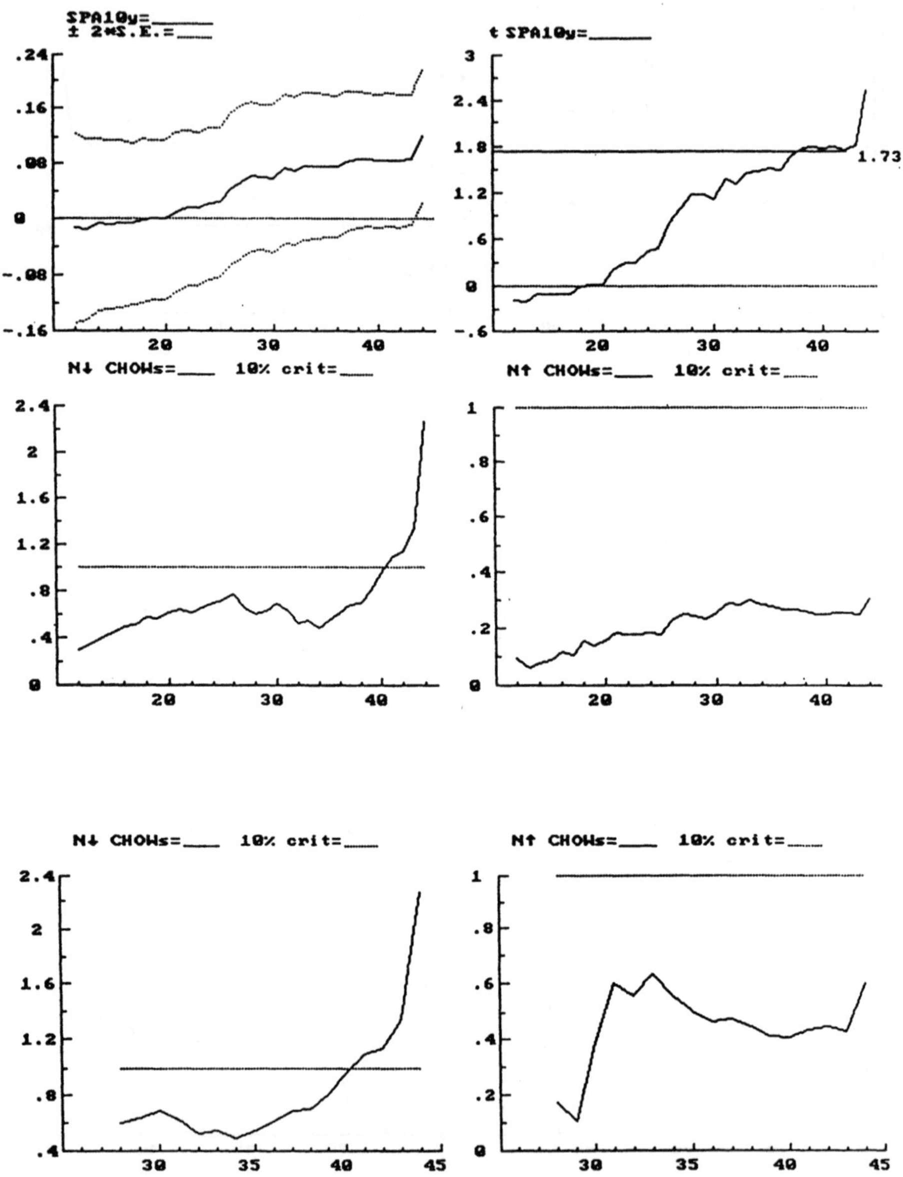

Figure A.6: Tests for ECU10Y

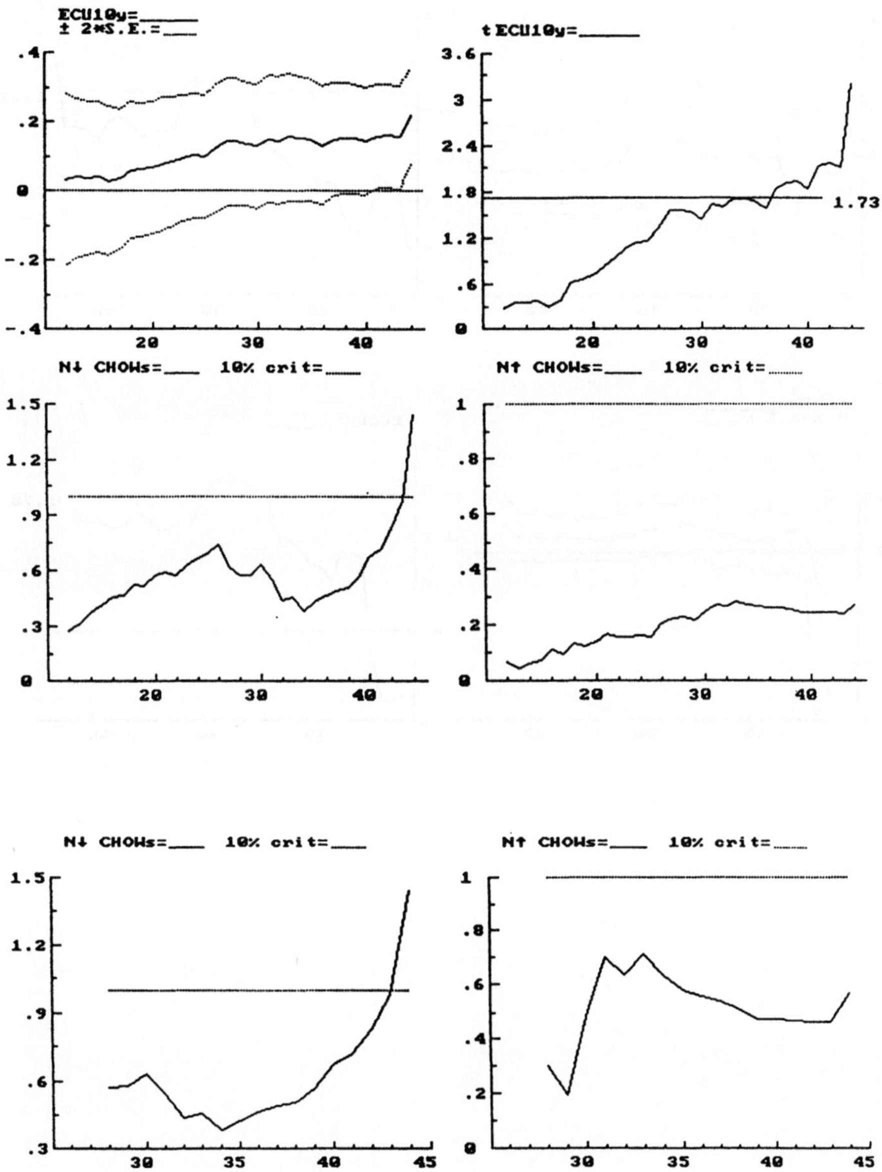

Figure A.7: Coefficients on ITA10Y and ECUEX

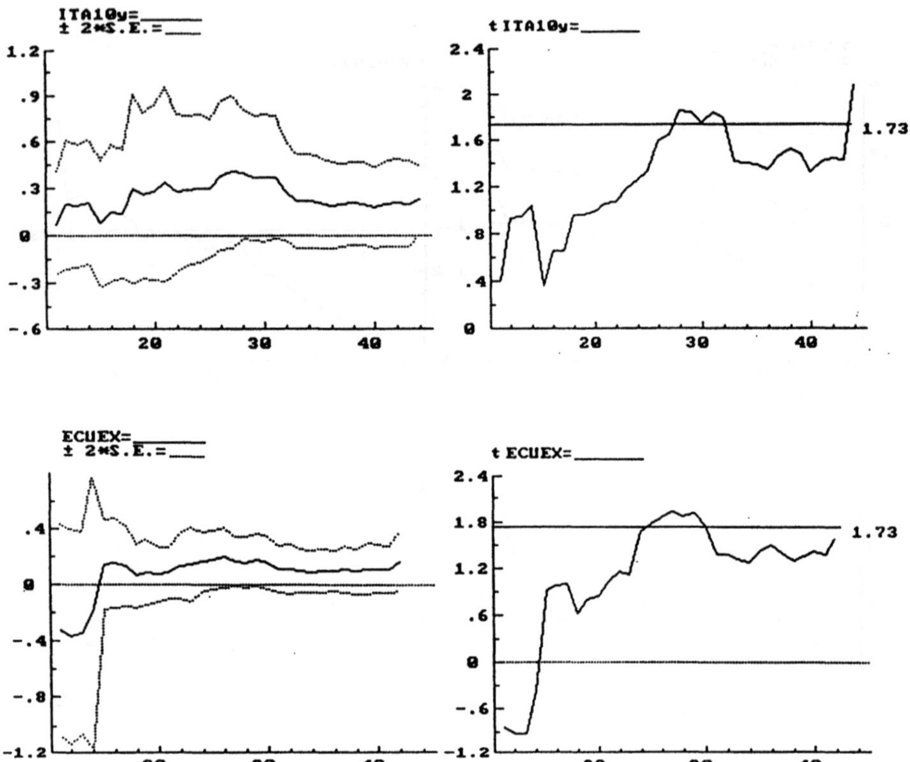

Figures A.3 to A.6 show these plots for the variables for which we can use OLS. In each figure, the upper two plots show the recursive regression coefficients with standard errors and the t-statistics as t approaches 44, the next two the N↓ and N↑ Chow tests setting M-1=11, and the bottom two the two Chow tests with M=27. Figure A.7 contains only the first two plots for the right hand side variables ITA10y and ECUEX, which required IV and for which Chow tests could not be performed. The main results are as follows:

1. The last observation in our reordered sample, i.e. the reactions to the European election, has a disproportionate affect on our t-values--witness the sharp surge at the end of all t-value graphs--and generates a structural break (at the ten percent level) in two cases (see N↓ graph for SPA10y and ECU10y). It seems to be a clear outlier and should probably be excluded on those grounds. Note, however, that its exclusion will not affect the rejection of the EMU hypothesis, whose critical value at the 5 percent alpha level (t = 1.73) is shown in the graphs, except for the case of ITA10y. In all other cases, the test still rejects whenever it rejected over the whole sample. Even in the case of ITA10y, we are not far off. In that sense, the conclusions of the previous section are robust to the exclusion of this datapoint.

2. No other structural break is detected at the ten percent level. However, in some instances the Chow statistics gets close to its critical values; in particular, the N↓ test does reject at t=26 at the 20 and 25 percent levels, respectively, for SPA10y and ECU10y and at t=40 at the 15 percent level for BEL10y (all for M-1=11). After setting M-1=27, the N↑ tests rejects at t=30 at the 15 percent level for FRA10y and at the 25 percent level for ECU10y. Whether or not this is enough to conclude that the event groups related to German official's remarks and French fiscal reform should be excluded is debatable. However, note that even if they are entirely excluded (along with the European elections datapoint), so that the sample is reduced to observations 1 to 27, the EMU hypothesis would still be rejected at the

five percent level by the tests involving FRA10y, BEL10y, ITA10y and ECUEX (see the t-value plots in all these cases), and at the 10 percent level for ECU10y. Thus, the basic result is robust to the exclusion of *all* "problematic" events from the sample.

3. In no case could the EMU hypothesis have been rejected on the basis of the events associated with the Maastricht ratification process alone. This may not just be a small sample problem, since the estimated coefficients actually appear lower for the first dozen or so observations in the sample (see top right charts showing coefficients and standard errors). This is particularly striking for SPA10y, ECU10y and ECUEX, which have coefficients close to zero in the first part of the sample, but is also suggested by the graphs of BEL10y and ITA10y. Only in the case of FRA10y does the graph suggest reasonable parameter constancy across the event groups according to which the samples were ordered. While imprecise estimations preclude the detection of a structural break which would distinguish the 1992-93 events from later events, the evidence in favor of a true positive relationship between GER10y and the other market variables for the early part of the sample is much weaker than over the whole sample.

5. Conclusions

The main result in this paper is that German bond yields appear to react to events affecting the probability that EMU will in fact happen over the medium term in the *same*, rather than the opposite direction as French, Belgian, Spanish, Italian and ECU bond yields. In most cases, the hypothesis of a true negative relationship can be rejected at the five percent level. In addition, EMU related events that lead to an appreciation of the private ECU relative to the ECU basket tend to be associated with declines in German bond yields, and vice versa. On this basis, we conclude that the "EMU hypothesis" as defined in the introduction should be rejected: events making EMU more likely have, on average, led to lower, not higher long interest rates in Germany.

We also find that the apparent positive association between German and other European bond yields in response to events affecting the probability of EMU is mainly driven by the way German bonds react to EMU related events after 1993--i.e. after the Maastricht process was ratified--in the sense that the hypothesis could not have been rejected based on German yield reactions to Maastricht ratification events alone. For this early event subset, the reactions of German yields are essentially uncorrelated with the reactions of other European yields. This suggests a change in the way German yields reacted to EMU related events. Initially, German bond markets seem fairly indifferent to events with large implications for EMU, showing very little reaction to events such as the Maastricht agreement itself, the first Danish referendum or the Irish referendum--in sharp contrast to the behavior of bond yields elsewhere in Europe. Eventually, however, German bond markets begin reacting to EMU related events in line with the reaction of other European bond markets. For example, German and French bond reactions to news about EMU are correlated from about September 1992 onwards (the French referendum, see table A.1), while German and ECU bond reactions to EMU news appear correlated from about the summer of 1993 onwards.

Two alternative interpretations are consistent with these findings. One is simply that the EMU process has put no pressure on German yields, and that German bond markets, if anything --perhaps after a short period of indifference following the Maastricht agreement--are happy with the idea of European monetary union. Maybe German markets expect the European Central Bank to be as tough on inflation as the Bundesbank, or perhaps they expect lower real interests under EMU (for example, as a result of the application of the Maastricht criteria) which would offset slightly higher inflation rates under the ECB. Under this interpretation, one would need to look elsewhere for explanations why German yields were higher than

U.S. yields at the long end during most of 1995 and early 1996--for instance, at expectations regarding U.S. fiscal consolidation.

On the other hand, the results presented still allow for one interpretation in which the EMU process as a whole might have raised the level of German yields, even if the EMU hypothesis as defined in the introduction and section 2 is rejected. Markets may not like the idea of EMU per se, but conditional on the EMU process having been initiated, prefer the successful completion of this process to the disruptions which would ensue if the process were called off. In this interpretation, German yields might well be lower now if the Maastricht agreement had never been signed, or had not included a commitment to a single currency. Yet, after this fact--or at least after German markets became aware of the disruptive implications of a failure of the EMU process--one would observe German yields rising in reaction to events which threaten the process, and falling at events that enhance it.

This idea has some appeal not only as a logical possibility but also in view of the indifference of German yields to EMU related events which we found early on in the sample. As described above, the behavior of German bond markets in reaction to EMU related shocks seems to undergo a change either in the late 1992 or mid 1993, depending on the right hand side variable we use to measure these shocks. This happens to coincide with the timing of the two ERM crises. There is thus some support for the idea that German bond markets, after an initial period of indifference or even skepticism, became supporters of the EMU process only after they realized that it could no longer be called off without major disruptions in Europe's monetary system. Specifically, these crises may have led to the perception that a plain and simple return to the old EMS was no longer feasible.

While one cannot tell which of these two interpretations is right, distinguishing between the two may be interesting primarily from the perspective of economic history. As to the present, the results of this paper are unambiguous: German bond markets seem to prefer the successful completion of the EMU process as envisaged by Maastricht and subsequent EU summits to the perceived alternatives if the third stage is not attained.

Endnotes

1. The views expressed in this paper are the author's and do not necessarily represent those of the International Monetary Fund. I am indebted to Mohan Kumar for pointing out the U.S.-German long yield differential as a topic for research. I also wish to thank, without implication, Guy Debelle, Burckhardt Drees, Mark Griffiths, Robert Hauswald, Russell Kincaid, Mohan Kumar, Paul Masson, Don Mathieson, John Montgomery, Jorge Roldós, Jens Weidmann, seminar participants at the IMF and conference participants at EIIW, Potsdam for helpful comments and suggestions, and Jeff Gable for outstanding research assistance.

2. The Economist, 9/16/95, pp. 58-59; The Economist, 11/11/95, p. 47.

3. In particular, The Ecnomist, 9/16/95, pp.58-59. The Swiss National Bank also hints at capital flows into Switzerland in response to fears about EMU, although it does not say where these capital flows come from. See *Swiss National Bank Monthly Reports*, October 1995, p. III and November 1995, p. III.

4. Whenever "EMU" is referred to in this paper, I mean in particular the third stage of EMU with the irrevocable fixing of exchange rates and the move to a common European Central Bank.

5. The more general case in which the timing of EMU is altogether uncertain is examined in a longer version of this paper (IMF Working Paper 96/133, December 1996); it does not affect the conclusions of this section.

6. This is justified if we assume that the Bundesbank mostly pays attention to domestic economic conditions in setting interest rates. For example, the Bundesbank's interest rate policy for the next two years is unlikely to be affected by events affecting the probability that EMU will materialize three years from now.

7. To clarify this mechanism, consider the following two period example. In period zero, domestic monetary authorities in country i set interest rates $i_i(0,1)$ in order to maintain their currency at a given parity to the DM. In period one, EMU succeeds with probability p_i and permanently fails with probability $1\text{-}p_i$. A third possibility--that EMU is postponed--can be introduced if we extend the model to more than two periods; it would not affect the economic mechanism illustrated in the two-period example.

   If EMU succeeds at the beginning of period one, then the period zero exchange rate to the DM is frozen irrevocably and interest rate $i_E(1,1)$ will apply in country i. If EMU fails, then the exchange rate to the DM depreciates by k relative to period zero, the currency returns to floating vis-à-vis the DM and a given interest rate $i_i(1,1)>i_E(1,1)$ applies. Thus, country i's term structure at time 0--today's long and short rates--is determined as follows:

$$i_i(0,2) = \frac{1}{2} i_i(0,1) + \frac{1}{2}\left[p_i i_E(1,1) + (1-p_i) i_i(1,1)\right]$$

$$i_i(0,1) = i_g(0,1) + E[\Delta e(0)] = i_g(0,1) + (1-p_i)k$$

   Consequently, an increase in p_i will lead to a decline in country i's long rate through two effects: (a) expected future interest rates decline because the probability of having low "European" rates in period two is higher; (b) pre-EMU short rates decline because the chance that country *i*'s currency will depreciate at the end of period 1 is lower:

$$di_i(0,2) = \frac{1}{2}\{[i_i(1,1) - i_E(1,1)] - k\}dp$$

8. This is most obvious in the case of France, for which $dp_g = dp_i$ was probably literally satisfied given a general view--emphasized on many occasions by German policy-makers--that a common European currency would be "unimaginable" without the participation of France. See, for example, remarks by German Finance Minister Theo Waigel on September 20, 1995 (FT 9/21/95, p.2).

9. *Folkerts-Landau and Garber (1995),* p. 135. For a detailed description on the institutions and practices governing the use of the private ECU and the ECU bond market, see *Mehnerts-Meland (1994).*

10. It is straightforward to generalize this to the case where the timing of EMU is uncertain; see the longer version of this paper (IMF WP 96/133) and Folkerts-Landau and Garber.

11. The condition is derived at follows. Suppose we knew with certainty that EMU would realize at time *t*. At this time, the ECU will be exchanged into an ECU basket with fixed weights which is subsequently converted into the European currency. The weights in that basket are uncertain at time zero, in particular, they might differ from the current weights in the basket. As a result, even though we know with certainty that at time *t* the ECU will be exchanged into the new basket at par, its exchange rate at *t* vis-à-vis the old basket might differ from par, and is uncertain at time zero. Consequently, the following standard UIP condition applies:

$$1 + i_b(0,t) = (1 + i_{ecu}(0,t))\frac{E \in (t)}{\in (0)}$$

Equation (10) follows if there is a (1-*p*) probability that EMU will not will realize at time *t* and if in this case the private ECU will never be converted into the underlying basket.

12. The idea is that the three-month interest rate is (1) sufficiently short to react to unexpected monetary policy actions (or news which lead to the expectation of such an action in the future) and (2) sufficiently long such that it will only react to monetary policy actions (or news relevant to policy) to the extent that these were *unanticipated.* Thus, changes in the three month rate following monetary policy actions or policy-relevant news can be used as a proxy for the unexpected monetary policy content of such news (see *Skinner and Zettelmeyer (1995)*).

13. "EMU and Long Interest Rates in Germany", presented at the Conference "European Monetary Union: Transition, International Impacts, and Policy Options", at the European Institute for International Economic Relations, Potsdam, April 1996.

14. See, for example, reports on President Chirac's October 26, 1995 commitment to reduce the deficit (*FT, 10/27/95*, p. 2; *The Economist*, 11/04/95, p.55), on market's reaction to that announcement (*FT, 10/28/95*, pp. 2 and 13), on the Nov. 7 cabinet reshuffle (*FT 11/08/95*, p.3, *The Economist*, 11/11/95, p.47), and on the Nov. 15 welfare reform package (*FT 11/16/95*, p. 26, *The Economist*, 11/18/95, p.57). The most drastic reference to the connection between the French fiscal reform struggle and EMU is made in *The Economist*, 12/09/95, where the cover

shows log-burning demonstrators on the Champs Elysées along with the headline "France prepares for EMU".

15. As long as this is not the case, the presence of an independent fiscal shock as part of the error terms of (11) is not problematic, since the IV procedure suggested in Section 2.3 is designed to deal with this.

16. Ideally, one would want to test the specification of OLS(2) directly. Unfortunately, this was not possible since we could not come up with a good instrument for the change in the US ten year bond yield.

17. Since we are testing a one-sided hypothesis, the p-values associated with the usual significance test must be divided in half.

18. See *Doornik and Hendry (1995)*, p. 328-329 for a definition of the test statistics and details.

References

DOORNIK, J. A.; HENDRY, D. F. (1995), PcGive 8.0. An Interactive Econometric Modelling System, London: International Thomson Publishing.

FOLKERTS-LANDAU, D.; GARBER, P. M. (1995), Determining the Value of the a Financial Unit of Account Based on Composite Currencies: The Case of the Private ECU, IMF Staff Papers Vol. 42 No.1, March 1995, 134-157.

HAUSMAN, J. A. (1978), Specification Tests in Econometrics, in: Econometrica, Vol. 46, No 6, November 1978, 1251-1271.

IMF (1996), Germany - Recent Economic Developments and Selected Issues, IMF Staff Country Report, Appendix III, forthcoming.

MEHNERTS-MELAND, R. J. (1994), Ecu in Business. How to Prepare for the Single Currency in the European Union, London: Graham & Trotman.

SKINNER, T. J.; ZETTELMEYER, J. (1995), Long Rates and Monetary Policy: Is Europe Different?, in: J. Zettelmeyer, Essays on Monetary Policy, Ph.D. dissertation, MIT, February 1995, 12-107.

Comments on: EMU and Long Interest Rates in Germany

Jens Weidmann[1]

Does the looming European Monetary Unification (EMU) cause German agents to revise their inflation expectations upwards, thereby inducing "high" long-term interest rates in Germany? This scarcely explored issue, investigated in Zettelmeyer's interesting and stimulating paper, has the utmost political and economic relevance for two reasons: First, the answer to the aforementioned question could teach us about the credibility of the European Central Bank (ECB) in financial markets. Second, the prospect of EMU could have real effects on long-term interest rates and thus the investment/saving decision.

Jeromin Zettelmeyer starts with observing that German long-term interest rates were „relatively high" in recent times, and suggests that we can blame the prospect of EMU for this fact. The situation is as follows: If market participants believe the future inflationary stance of the ECB to be less impressive than that of the German Bundesbank, then the more likely EMU becomes, and the higher the expected inflation rate is in Germany. Following the author, the converse holds true for the other potential member countries of EMU.

This "EMU hypothesis", is then tested using event-study techniques. Zettelmeyer isolates those days on which news about EMU was reported in the press, classifies them as bad, good, or ambiguous, and then investigates whether markets react in a systematic manner to theses announcements. The author's main findings can be readily summarized: In all countries, shown in his table A.2, interest rates do react significantly to the news dummies. Unfortunately, the results for Germany, the country in which Zettelmeyer is mainly interested in, have been omitted. Since I believe that these estimated results can provide us with some insights, they are reported in table A*.1 below. Surprisingly, they suggest that the dummy variable has no significant influence on German long-term yields.

Table A*.1: Dummy Regression for German 10-Year Interest Rates

Variable	Coefficient	Std. Error	$\overline{R}^2$
Constant	0.0029	0.0055	0.03
Dummy	-0.0099	0.0062	

Furthermore, in contrast to his "EMU hypothesis", Zettelmeyer finds that interest rate changes in Germany and other EMS countries are positively correlated. According to the author these results unambiguously signify that "German bond markets seem to prefer the successful completion of the EMU process [...]." Given that there is not overwhelmingly compelling empirical evidence, this conclusion might be a bit speculative.

Let me note what I consider the most important points of the paper and suggest some caveats. I will start my comments with some remarks on the paper's null hypothesis, then I will make some observations on the key variable of this paper, the probability of EMU. Finally, I have some comments on the empirical method and I will suggest an alternative. I believe in a more straight-forward method to investigate the question raised by Zettelmeyer. A simple and tentative estimation exercise confirms my suspicion that the likelihood of EMU does not affect long-term yields in Germany.

1. The "EMU Hypothesis"

The "EMU hypothesis" means that Germany holds an inflation leadership position, implying that interest rates (and inflation expectations) in Germany and the other potential EMU candidates are affected in opposite directions by news about EMU.

It is only under the assumption that the German inflation rate lies below that of all other potential EMU participants, that we can expect interest rates to react differently to a change in the likelihood of EMU. This may have been true some years before German unification. At least since then, however, Germany has lost its inflation leadership position to Belgium, France, and the Netherlands who have reached an inflationary stance comparable or even superior to that of Germany. Figure A*.1 depicts the 10 year interest rates for the most important EMS countries for the sample period of the paper. Clearly, two groups of countries are discernible. The interest rate spreads among the "ins" are negligible, e.g., the spread between the French and German long yield reaches its high at roughly 0.8%. Consequently, I would not expect that interest rates in these countries react differently to news about EMU.

There is another point that may cast some doubt on the existence of an unequivocal relation between the likelihood of EMU and long-term yields: The expected inflation record of the ECB is presumably inversely correlated with the probability of EMU. I shall explain. If the potential candidates make some progress in achieving fiscal and monetary stability, they are more likely to fulfill the Maastricht criteria which in turn raises the probability of EMU. On the other hand, the more the candidates have proven their commitment to monetary and fiscal stability in the advent of EMU, the lower the expected inflation rate is under EMU. Evidently, this mechanism induces a negative relationship between the likelihood of EMU and long-term yields in Germany and all other countries. This counteracts the effects described by Zettelmeyer.

Figure A*.1: 10-Year Interest Rates

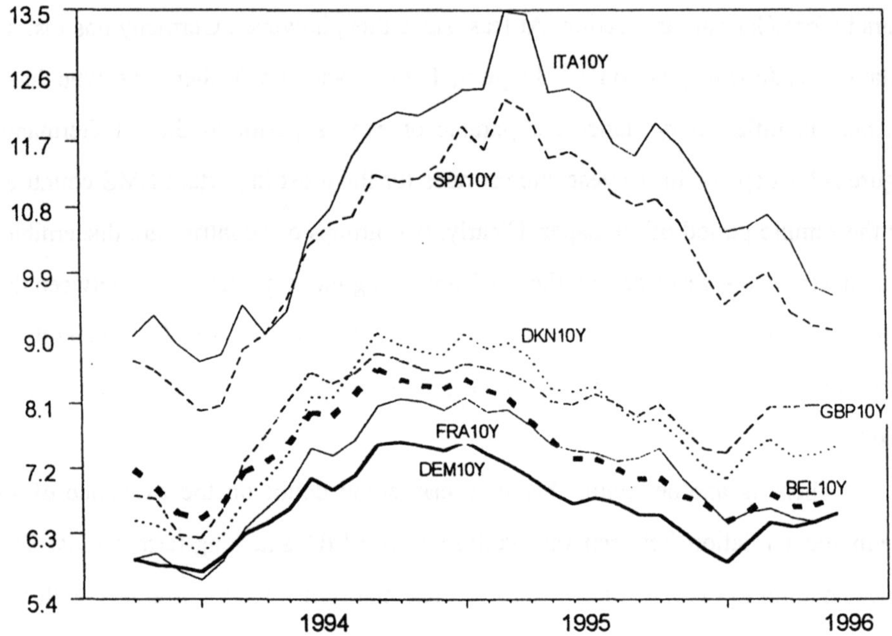

Note: As in Zettelmeyer's paper DEM10y denotes the German, FRA10y the French, BEL10y the Belgian, SPA10y the Spanish, ITA10y the Italian, DKN10y the Danish, and GBP10y the British 10 year interest rate.

2. Some Remarks on Probabilities

I will now examine the central variable, the probability of EMU. I think it is helpful to understand that the probability that Country l is part of EMU, P_l is the probability that Country l belongs to the core given that EMU realizes times the probability that EMU comes about.

$$P_l = P(l \in core | EMU) P(EMU)$$

Examining it in this manner, illustrates the important difference between core and periphery, presenting the problem of the domestic component of EMU related news.[2] The relevant variable for interest rate (or inflationary expectations) reactions in Country l is P_l and not P(EMU). As EMU without Germany, France, and the Netherlands is not conceivable $P(l \in core | EMU)$ is close to one and $P_l \approx P(EMU)$. Today, however, Spain and Italy are far from meeting the Maastricht criteria and cannot considered to be likely candidates (i.e. $P(l \in core | EMU)$ is very small). Recent opinion polls (see *Bank for International Settlements, 1996*) revealed that less than 10 percent of market participants expect these countries to participate in the single currency project at the outset. With the probability of belonging to the core being negligible their interest rate reactions to changes in P(EMU) will be minimal, as well. I am thus a bit surprised by the result that the dummy variable significantly influences the interest rate in countries that are almost surely not part of EMU, whereas German rates are not affected. This points to another problem of the event-study methodology.

3. Event-Study Methodology: A Caveat

The main problem with the event-studies is the correct selection of the events. For the empirical inference to be valid, the news dummy must exclusively capture news related to the likelihood of EMU. Any event included with direct implications for bond yields violate the assumption underlying system (11) and renders the results meaningless. Let me clarify this point by means of an example: On June 22, 1995 the French Prime-Minister Alain Juppé announced a first mini-budget and French long-term yields declined. The question now is why do bond markets react to this news? Is it: (a) because the fiscal discipline entailed in Juppé's proposal indirectly makes EMU more likely or (b) because the proposal has direct implications for domestic capital markets? If the answer is (b) or if we cannot tell, subsequent regressions of the dummy variable on interest rates hardly teach us anything about EMU. Now, if theoretically the two effects influence interest rates in the same direction the dummy regression produces significant results even if the likelihood of EMU plays no role in the determination of interest rates. But even in the case where the event has no direct, domestic implications it may still only affect $P(l \in core|EMU)$ but not P(EMU). Under these circumstances, only the long-term yield in Country l should react.

I am afraid that some events captured in the paper's table A.1 are presumably dominated by their domestic component. Much of the 1995 news related to the strike movement and budgetary problems in France. Others are compounded by the interest rate cuts in France and Spain. The direct domestic implications for France and Spain would be in-line with the empirical findings of a strong reaction to the news dummy in France and Spain, and the absence of a significant reaction in Germany.

But what about the second stage regression? On any arbitrary day, the interest rates of EMS countries are likely to move because of uncovered interest rate parity (UIP) in the same direction. Taking any events that influence interest rates in France and then running an IV regression between French and German interest rate changes would have yielded the same result. A positive correlation between the two interest rate changes exists. To illustrate this point, table A*.2 shows the regressions of the change in the German 10 year rate on a constant and the change in the corresponding rate in France, Belgium, Italy, and Spain. As predicted by UIP, the coefficients are all significantly positive. Moreover, these results prove to be robust for the inclusion of changes in German short term rates to control for influences of German monetary policy. Consequently, I am inclined to think that the author is not on safe ground when it comes to the interpretation of his second stage regression.

Table A*.2: Results from OLS Regression

	Explanatory Variable			
	ΔFRA 10y	ΔBEL 10y	ΔITA 10y	ΔSPA 10y
Constant	0.000 (0.001)	0.001 (0.002)	-0.001 (0.002)	-0.001 (0.002)
Coefficient	0.448 (0.031)	0.645 (0.026)	0.275 (0.017)	0.333 (0.024)
$\bar{R}^2$	0.26	0.52	0.32	0.25

Notes: The following regression was run with daily data covering Zettelmeyer's observation period: $\Delta DEM10y = \alpha + \beta \Delta l10y,\ l = FRA, BEL, ITA, SPA$

4. An Alternative Method

To test the "EMU hypothesis", one could follow Zettelmeyer and resort to event-study methods (i.e. study the reaction of long yields on days where news suggest that the probability of EMU has changed). However, as outlined above I have some reservations regarding this approach. Thus, I will finish my comments by sketching an alternative method to investigate the issues raised in the paper.

The basic idea is to calculate the probability of EMU and then the conditional probabilities using deviations of the actual ECU forward interest rates from their theoretical values (see *de Grauwe, 1996* and *Weidmann 1996*). Following this approach the likelihood of EMU can be computed as follows:

$$P_t(EMU) = 1 - \frac{s_t^{ECU,f,m}}{E(s_{t+f}^{ECU,m} | \overline{EMU})}.$$

In this formula $s_t^{ECU,f,m}$ stands for the observed spread between ECU and DEM forward interest rates with a settlement time t+f (t+f > January, 1st 1999), where $s_t^{ECU,m}$ denotes the spread between ECU and DM interest rates of maturity m at time t. $E(\cdot | \overline{EMU})$ is the expectation operator conditioned on the non-realization of EMU. Since this variable is unobservable it has to be proxied. Assuming the basket definition of the ECU remains unchanged from now on, $E(s_{t+f}^{ECU,m} | \overline{EMU})$ equals the weighted mean of the DEM spread over all basket currencies, with the weight simply corresponding to the actual weight of the respective currency in the ECU basket. Though computed according to the same principle, the formulas for the conditional probabilities are more cumbersome and thus are omitted for space considerations.

These computed probabilities can be shown to be broadly consistent with political events and opinion polls. Figure A*.2 shows P(EMU) while figure A*.3 depicts the conditional probabilities $P(l \in core | EMU)$. Let me begin with some observations on figure A*.3. In accordance with recent opinion polls among market participants (*Bank for International Settlements, 1996*) it is assumed that $P(DEM \in core | EMU) = 100\%$. Conversely, the probability that Italy and Spain will belong to the "insiders" is negligible and thus not shown.[3] Again, given these figures it escapes me why Italian and Spanish long-term yields should react to news about EMU if not because they coincide with some domestically relevant news.

Figure A*.2: Probability of EMU

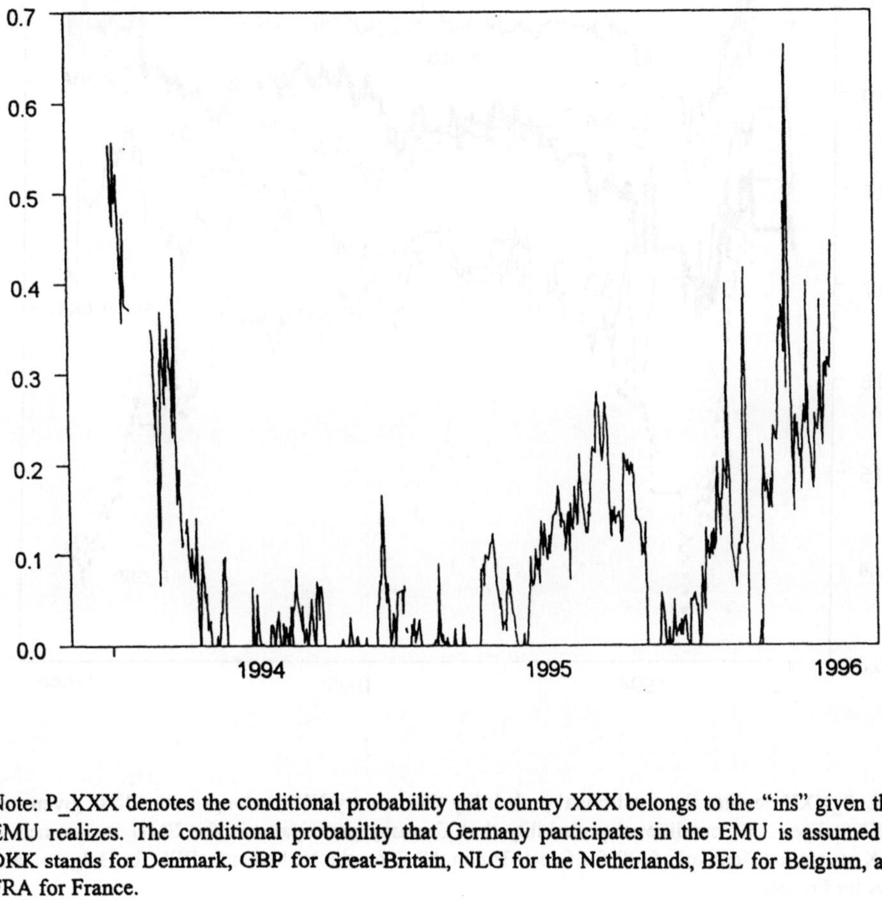

Note: P_XXX denotes the conditional probability that country XXX belongs to the "ins" given that EMU realizes. The conditional probability that Germany participates in the EMU is assumed 1. DKK stands for Denmark, GBP for Great-Britain, NLG for the Netherlands, BEL for Belgium, and FRA for France.

Figure A*.3: Conditional Probability of Country I in EMU

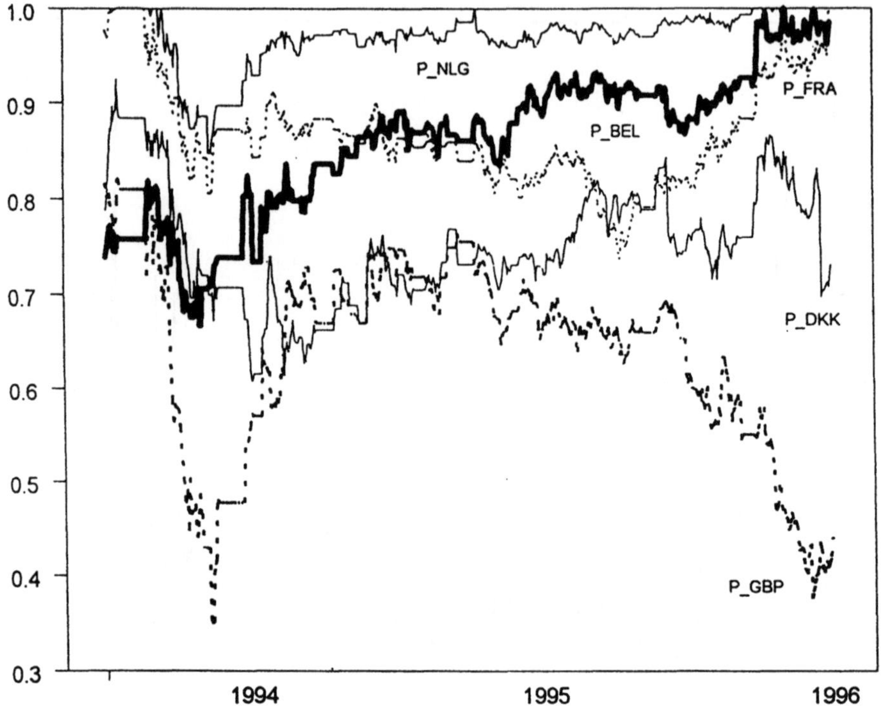

Note: P_XXX denotes the conditional probability that country XXX belongs to the "ins" given that EMU realizes. The conditional probability that Germany participates in the EMU is assumed 1. DKK stands for Denmark, GBP for Great-Britain, NLG for the Netherlands, BEL for Belgium, and FRA for France.

A first visual inspection of figures A*.2 and A*.3 casts some doubt on the hypothesis that P(EMU) exerts a significant influence on long-term yields in any of these countries. Evidence from regression analysis, omitted for space considerations, corroborates this suspicion. There is neither a significant effect of the changes in P(EMU) on the changes in the interest rates or the spread nor a co-integration relation between the variables. Of course, these results could signify that the approximation of P(EMU) is bad and further research is certainly needed. But perhaps the result that P(EMU) has no influence on German long-term rates, in accordance with the evidence from the dummy regression shown in table A*.1, is not that implausible. The institutional framework for the European Central Bank comes very close to that of the German Bundesbank, and the monetary authorities of the most likely candidates for EMU have proven their commitment to price stability during the last years. Evidently, the future behavior of the ECB is not known, but there are some reasons to believe that during her first years the ECB will rather be strenuous on inflation to build-up a reputation as inflation fighters.

Therefore, I think that the empirical evidence presented so far does not support the notion that financial market participants expect the inflationary stance of the monetary authorities to change with EMU. This conclusion is also in line with a recent empirical study by *Heinemann (1995)* who does not find any significant influence of several proxies for EMU on German long-term yields and the French-German interest rate differential.

To conclude, event studies such as the one presented by Jeromin Zettelmeyer, are always a massive undertaking and I cannot but admire the author's efforts. However, I feel somewhat uncomfortable with Zettelmeyer's interpretation of the empirical results. Nevertheless, the author should be commended for a serious effort at investigating this new and highly relevant issue.

Endnotes

1. I wish to thank Gottfried Hörich of J.P. Morgan, Frankfurt, for providing me with the forward interest rate data.

2. Evidently, a sufficient number of countries in the core is necessary to get EMU started, so that the two probabilities on the r.h.s. show some interdependencies. For expositional convenience, let us abstract from this possibility.

3. Only 7 percent of the interviewees believed that Spain will be part of the single currency project in 1999. The picture is still worse for Italy. 98 out of 100 respondents expect Italy not to participate in the EMU (see *Bank for International Settlements, 1996*). The conditional probabilities computed in *Weidmann (1996)* are still smaller.

References

BANK FOR INTERNATIONAL SETTLEMENTS (1996), International Banking and Financial Market Developments, Basle, August 1996.

DE GRAUWE, P. (1996), Forward Interest Rates as Predictors of EMU, CEPR Discussion Paper No. 1395.

HEINEMANN, F. (1995), Währungsunion und deutsche Kapitalmarktzinsen, ZEW Discussion Paper 96-05.

WEIDMANN, J. (1996), The Likelihood of European Monetary Union, University of Bonn, Sonderforschungsbereich 303 Discussion Paper No. B-382.

B. EMU and Outsiders: Fixed versus Flexible Exchange Rates

Paul Bergin and Mathias Moersch[1]

1. Introduction

If European Monetary Union (EMU) commences as planned under the timetable and convergence criteria of the Maastricht treaty, a two-speed arrangement likely will follow. Under this arrangement a core of countries will form a monetary union, leaving a periphery that does not initially participate. The existence of such a periphery raises the issue of the appropriate exchange rate relationship vis-à-vis the core. This paper analyses some key aspects of this choice.

In doing this, the paper takes a number of factors as given. First, the debate about costs and benefits of a monetary union is not reopened; it is simply assumed that some, but not all European countries will go ahead with monetary union. Second, it is assumed that the European Central Bank (ECB) will conduct monetary policy in keeping with the mission of delivering stable prices. Third, the Maastricht criteria, without discussing their merits, are taken as given. Finally, existing opt-out clauses also allow for countries that are voluntarily excluded from monetary union.

Given that a currency union with the core is ruled out, there are two options left to the periphery: a peg to the core currency or a freely floating exchange rate. Following *Obstfeld and Rogoff (1995a)*, we refer to pegged exchange rates as being subject to the domestic monetary authority's announcement of buying and selling rates for its currency at which it is willing to trade unlimited amounts. Historically, pegged exchange rate systems allowed narrow bands within which the currency was allowed to fluctuate. Under the Bretton Woods system, exchange rates were allowed to fluctuate by one percent in either direction vis-à-vis the dollar. Before August 1993 the allowed fluctuations in the European Monetary System (EMS) were 2.25 percent.

Under a flexible exchange rate system, no commitments by central banks to defend their currencies exist. Of course, as exchange rate bands are widened, the pegged exchange rate mechanism more and more resembles a regime of floating exchange rates. Use of the term pegged exchange rate therefore also implies that the constraint on the exchange rate is binding at least some of the time[2].

The second section of this paper draws on models of speculative attacks to argue that a conventional peg is even less credible for a periphery than it has been under the EMS, and therefore is not advisable. This leaves some form of flexible exchange rate regime as the remaining option.

The third section of this paper argues from a theoretical viewpoint that this option, though often dismissed, is worth reconsidering. While it is typically feared that flexible exchange rates would invite competitive depreciations and beggar-thy-neighbor spillovers, there are good arguments to discount these fears. A simulation model based on agent optimization, calibrated to Italy and Germany, is used to consider the likely current account and welfare effects of a periphery depreciation. While the events of 1992-93 are often spotlighted as a warning against competitive depreciations, section four of the paper reconsiders and reinterprets the empirical evidence.

The fifth section analyzes the issue of convergence and eventual admission of the outsiders to the core. It argues that flexible rates do not represent an additional hindrance to convergence. Section six concludes.

2. Pegging to the Core

The standard argument for a fixed exchange rate is that at the price of abandoning independent monetary policy, a country gains not only a reduction in exchange rate fluctuations, but also the monetary policy of the country to which it pegs. Especially pegging to a low-inflation country will help to reign in domestic inflationary pressures. The commitment to a credible peg makes this policy of fighting inflation easier. A second argument is that exchange rate volatility and misalignments have potentially negative effects on trade and real output.

Both arguments for a peg have received considerable attention in the recent debate over future exchange rate arrangements in Europe (see *Barber, 1996*; *de Grauwe, 1995a*). The misalignment argument, discussed in detail below, states that devaluations can greatly benefit, at the expense of their neighbors, the devaluing countries. Especially since the suspension of the narrow exchange rate bands in 1993, some European countries have been accused of obtaining an unfair advantage over their competitors by devaluing. The credibility argument states that pegging to the core allows the borrowing of the core's monetary policy and the resumption of convergence. If the peg to the core is fully credible, the periphery can enjoy the monetary policy of the core, even without being a member of the currency union. Once convergence has been achieved, entry into the monetary union can take place at that exchange rate[3].

In the following we argue that there are a number of rather sizeable obstacles to the strategy of pegging the exchange rate to the core. Essentially, a system of pegged exchange rates not only suffers all the problems of the old EMS, but, due to the asymmetry in the relationship between the core and the periphery, is subject to additional strains.

First, the establishment of the currency union, which is expected to be beneficial for a number of reasons, can lead to a sizeable revaluation of the core currency (the Euro). A peg to the Euro will be subjected to considerable pressure, similar to that experienced in the early nineties, when Germany's currency experienced a real appreciation. Second, even if exchange rate appreciation is not an issue, the credibility of the peg can be questioned. Given the disadvantages that the outsiders face concerning the cost of their debt service, pegging to the core may be too costly politically and economically. Third, even in the absence of any fundamentals justifying exchange rate movements, self-fulfilling speculative attacks are a danger to pegged exchange rates.

2.1 Monetary Union as a Real and Monetary Shock

One reason for the exchange market crises in the EMS was the shock to fundamentals caused by German unification. A positive demand shock, the large German fiscal deficit, as well as a negative supply shock, the large increase in east German wages, contributed to a rise of the relative price of German output, i.e. a real appreciation of the DM (see *Cobham, 1994*).

It is quite likely that a similar real shock results from a currency union. With the exchange rate of the Euro defined as units of home currency per foreign currency we get

$$e^N = e^R (P / P^*) \tag{1}$$

e^N is the nominal exchange rate, e^R the real exchange rate, P is the domestic price level and P^* the foreign price level.

The positive impulse for efficiency and growth, based on the elimination of transaction costs and exchange rate uncertainty has always been named as an important benefit of a currency union (see *Commission of the European Communities, 1990; Gros and Thygesen, 1994*). Of course, these efficiency gains will only be available to the core countries and not the periphery. Hence, efficiency gains will induce an asymmetric real shock which will, in the absence of relative price movements, require an adjustment in the nominal exchange rate. The direction of the shock is not however clear a priori. This is because the gains from monetary union can be modeled as both a positive supply and a positive demand shock. While a positive demand shock leads to a real appreciation of the currency, a real supply shock leads to a real depreciation. In addition to this theoretical ambiguity, there is also a question about the empirical relevance, since estimates about the magnitude of the gains from integration vary considerably (see *Eichengreen, 1993; Isaac, 1994*).

A second disturbance which may be expected to change the value of the core currency relative to the periphery in the years following monetary union is the changing status of the Euro in the world economy, possibly challenging the dominant role of the US dollar. Increased use as reserve- or vehicle-currency, as predicted, for example, in *Kenen (1995a)*, will tend to put upward pressure on the Euro. This can be seen by extending equation (1) to include money market equilibrium (see *Frenkel and Mussa, 1988*) as follows

$$e^{N}=e^{R}\frac{\frac{M^{S}}{M^{S*}}}{\frac{M^{D}}{M^{D*}}}$$

M^D and M^S are the demand for real balances and the nominal money supply respectively. A * denotes a foreign variable. An increase in the relative demand for the Euro, the home currency, will lead to a decrease in e^N, a nominal appreciation.

Overall, there are a number of channels, both real and monetary, through which a peg to the core can come under pressure, especially in the years after the formation of the currency union. The empirical magnitude of these effects over time remains hard to assess, which makes finding a stable parity at which to peg the nominal exchange rate extremely difficult.

2.2 The Peg as an Anchor for Credibility

Pegging to the core signals that the periphery is interested in importing the monetary policy of the core. If credible, adherence to this policy can facilitate convergence with respect to the Maastricht criteria, because lower inflation, inflationary expectations and interest rates can be imported from the core.

There is however considerable tension between obtaining a credible peg and the fact that by excluding the countries from the core, they have already been given a vote of no confidence. Doubts about the commitment to defend the exchange rate, however, make convergence much harder to achieve, since they can lead to higher real interest rates in the periphery (see *de Grauwe, 1995b*). Higher interest rates are the consequence of risk premia, asked by financial markets to compensate for the risk of devaluation. These risk premia will be asked as long as there is doubt about the credibility of defending the exchange rate, whether an actual devaluation materializes or not. The higher real interest rates will also increase the debt burden and therefore make fiscal consolidation, and thus meeting the fiscal criteria much harder.

The peg thus can only be helpful in obtaining convergence if it is fully credible. Unfortunately, the credibility of the outsiders is likely to be low, certainly lower than that of the participants of the EMS in 1992. This casts doubts on the usefulness of the peg in supporting convergence.

2.3 Global Capital Markets

During most of its history, the EMS operated under various forms of capital controls. These capital controls made divergent monetary policies, even under a system of pegged exchange rates, possible, at least for limited periods of time. The Single European Act forced the elimination of capital controls by July 1, 1990[4, 5]. This led to the co-existence of the fundamentally incompatible conditions of independent monetary policy, a pegged exchange rate, and free movement of capital. Once the stability of this system came into question, speculative attacks forced the devaluation of a number of currencies.

This account leads to the general proposition that financial market deregulation and the globalization of financial markets has made fixed exchange rates impossible; a proposition forcefully argued by *Eichengreen (1994)*. The point is not so much that it is technically impossible to defend a pegged exchange rate, but that the defense comes at a high price concerning other policy objectives. *Obstfeld and Rogoff (1995a)* show that all that is needed for a successful defense of the currency is the ability to buy back the monetary base, that is currency in circulation and deposits with the central bank. They also show that most countries which came under pressure in the 1990s had this technical ability. However, the drawback of this defense of the currency will be sharp increases in short-term interest rates with potentially strong adverse affects for other important policy variables like output, unemployment and the public debt. In light of those adverse effects, a commitment to defend the exchange rate at all cost, even if technically feasible, will lack credibility.

Models of speculative exchange rate attacks come in two versions. In the first kind, exemplified by *Krugman (1979)* and *Flood and Garber (1984)*, attacks on the exchange rate are triggered by problems in economic fundamentals. In the second class of models, speculation can occur and succeed even in the absence of economic fundamentals justifying the attack. Recent examples are *Obstfeld (1994, 1995)*. In these newer models the focus is on the government's willingness to defend its currency, continuously weighing costs and benefits of the peg. The self-fulfilling speculative attack succeeds because it changes conditions sufficiently to make defending the exchange rate after the attack no longer desirable.

The possibility discussed in section 2.1 -- a currency union leading to sizeable efficiency gains for the core, which suggest an eventual realignment -- is an example for fundamentals prompting a speculative attack. The scenario in section 2.2, namely the peg as an anchor to obtain convergence belongs in the second category. Consider that the periphery country pegs to the Euro in hopes of achieving lower interest rates and therefore lower debt-servicing costs. If speculators decide to attack the currency, the required defense will drive up current and expected future interest rates, increasing the current and expected debt burden and moving the country further away from the convergence criteria that would allow joining the monetary union. Now the policy maker needs to reassess the strategy of pursuing the convergence criteria. Faced with the temporarily higher costs of debt servicing, she may choose to abandon the original plan.

2.4 Supporting Pegged Exchange Rates

Maintaining pegged exchange rates may still be possible if restrictions are put either on the free movement of capital or on independent monetary policy. All speculative attacks can technically be repelled if the core and the periphery join forces in defending the exchange rate. All that is needed is an agreement between the core and the periphery to coordinate monetary policy with the goal of stabilizing the exchange rate. Again, however, this defense may be costly. In the case of the ECB in particular, it may come in conflict with the main goal of price stability. Also, it appears that the most natural candidate for monetary coordination, namely a currency union, is currently rejected. It thus appears doubtful whether monetary policy coordination can be relied on in a crisis situation. The experience during the EMS crisis in 1992 and 1993 serves as a reminder of the limits of policy coordination during periods of distress[6].

Capital controls are no longer an option to contain exchange rates because they are ruled out by the Maastricht treaty. Absent this possibility, flows of speculative capital may still be slowed by making them costly. *Eichengreen, Tobin and Wyplosz (1995)* propose a number of taxes to contain the movement of speculative capital. These measures are aimed at discouraging short-term speculation, but not long-term investment. Unlike capital controls, these taxes will not insulate the policy makers permanently from market forces, but they will allow more time to organize policy coordination or a realignment.

Both *Garber and Taylor (1995)* and *Kenen (1995b)* criticize the transactions tax. They doubt that the tax could be implemented successfully. Rather, they argue that a tax would create unwanted distortions in other sectors of the economy and lead to efforts by speculators to evade it. *Eichengreen et al. (1995)* realize these shortcomings, but argue that faced with independent monetary policy and capital mobility, a transactions tax may be the only tool available to make a system of pegged exchange rates workable.

Currency boards have recently been proposed as a means to obtain a credible peg, even in the face of capital mobility (*Gros, 1996*). A currency board has two distinguishing features. First, the monetary base is completely backed by foreign reserves. Second, the monetary authority is reduced to one function, namely the issuance of domestic money backed by foreign reserves.

As noted above, the mere fact that a country possesses ample reserves has in the past not prevented speculative attacks, mainly because the defense of the currency remains costly in terms of other domestic objectives. This is the reason why in addition independent monetary policy must be formally abandoned to make a currency board credible. The proposal is different from the call for policy coordination, as it puts no responsibility on the core countries, but asks the periphery country to unilaterally peg to the Euro.

While the currency board is a credible arrangement as far as the defense of a pegged exchange rate is concerned, it also suffers from a number of shortcomings. First, abandoning all monetary policy sovereignty means that there exists no lender of last resort. This function of a central bank is important whenever a crisis develops in the domestic banking system. While the ECB may be asked to assist, there certainly cannot be a formal obligation to do so.

Second, the money supply is entirely determined by the ability to obtain foreign reserves. The money supply can thus only be increased when corresponding capital- or current-account transactions occur. This constraint on the ability to create money can lead to deflationary pressures in the economy.

Both points show that a currency board is still different from a monetary union, simply because there is no central bank that is responsible for the country operating under a currency board arrangement. It merely forces a country to subordinate all domestic considerations to pegging the exchange rate[7]. It thus appears that a currency board, while being an appropriate tool to stop hyper-inflation, may be too costly as a measure to obtain a credible peg. This is all the more so as a credible peg alone does not necessarily guarantee subsequent admission to the monetary union.

The above discussion clearly illustrates the problems associated with pegging exchange rates when capital is freely mobile and monetary policies are independent. Moreover, a return to a system of pegged exchange rates is not merely a return to the EMS as it existed before the exchange rate crises in 1992 and 1993, but leaves the periphery in a much weaker position. Given the many reasons to question the reliability of this credibility anchor, it is doubtful whether abandoning monetary policy sovereignty is a price worth paying.

Ruling out a peg leaves freely floating exchange rates as the most natural alternative arrangement. In the next section we therefore consider benefits and costs of this option.

3. Flexible Exchange Rate Arrangements

This section argues that a system of flexible exchange rates may not be as hazardous as many policy discussions suggest. In particular, fears are probably exaggerated that competitive exchange rate depreciations in the periphery will generate beggar-thy-neighbor current account surpluses and thus threaten the single goods market.

3.1 Costs of Flexible Exchange Rates

Current fears about flexible exchange rates in Europe have tended to focus on competitive depreciations and the resulting misalignments, rather than on exchange rate volatility and its adverse effects on trade and investment flows. Perhaps this is because these volatility effects appear to be small. First regarding trade flows, most empirical studies conclude the effect of exchange rate volatility is not strong (see *Frankel, 1992; Baily, Tavlas and Ulan, 1986*; *Hooper and Kohlhagen, 1978*; see *Cushman, 1983 and 1988a,* for an opposing view.) *Frankel (1992)*, for example, finds in a cross-sectional study that doubling the standard deviation of the real exchange rate reduces the volume of trade by only 0.7 percent. Second, foreign direct investment might be expected to respond more sensitively than goods trade to exchange rate uncertainty, since the service life of plant and equipment may well exceed the term to maturity of available forward contracts. Yet evidence is still very mixed (see *Morsink and Molle, 1991,* for evidence identifying a significant effect; see *Kenen, 1979,* and *Cushman, 1988b*, for evidence against.)

Regarding competitive depreciations, it is widely feared that flexible rates might undermine the common goods market in Europe, because this open single market has increased the vulnerability of European countries to the distribution effects of currency swings. By devaluing, a member may be able to increase the price competitiveness of its goods and flood its neighbors with exports. These neighbors might well be expected to object to this beggar-thy-neighbor policy and impose countervailing duties on the devaluer or erect other protectionist measures.

There are reasons to doubt the relevance of this competitive depreciation story for the current debate. Most significantly, engineering a depreciation in the context of a flexible exchange regime would entail a loosening of monetary policy, which might strongly shape the implications of a depreciation.

Bryant, Henderson, Holtham, Hooper and Symansky (1988) compare simulations of monetary expansions and resulting depreciations for eleven prominent macroeconometric forecasting models. Eight of the eleven predict that the policy would actually generate a current account deficit in the depreciating country. The list of models suggesting this surprising conclusion include the Multicountry Model of the U.S. Federal Reserve, the Interlink model for the Economics and Statistics Department at the OECD, as well as the forecasting models of DRI and the Wharton group. Further, *Hughes-Hallett and Wren-Lewis (1995)* have argued using a two-country model that Britain's devaluation in 1992 may have entailed significant monetary loosening and resulted in positive spillovers for its neighbors[8].

Part of the explanation for the surprising current-account effects above is the fact that the monetary expansion associated with a depreciation can have positive effects on domestic demand by lowering interest rates. But interest rates are not the whole story. In several of the macroeconometric forecasting models above, interest rate effects cannot be sufficient alone to overcome the expenditure switching effect and generate a net current account deficit[9]. Another part of the explanation may be that monetary policy stimulates domestic demand by improving expectations of future profitability. In the section below, a dynamic general equilibrium model is constructed to analyze both expectations effects and interest rate effects[10].

3.2 Depreciation in a Model with Microfoundations

Appendix A develops a model that attempts to update the Mundell-Fleming framework with utility theoretic micro-foundations[11]. Simulations with this model, presented below, suggest the potential importance of several effects that might be expected to lessen the beggar-thy-neighbor spillovers of competitive depreciations.

The model consists of two countries, each of which contains a representative household, a representative firm, and a government. The households derive utility from consumption of the home and foreign goods and from leisure. Profit-maximizing firms produce output using as inputs the labor they hire and the capital they rent from households. Wage stickiness is modeled as a set of overlapping contracts which predetermine the nominal wage. The government in each country sets its respective money supply, conducting monetary policy through open market operations on the nominally-denominated, interest-bearing debt it issues.

Calibration and simulation are conducted on a version of the model linearized around steady state. The model is calibrated to represent Italy and Germany. Values are chosen for the elasticities and other parameters from various econometric studies and to fit the steady state of the model to features of 1994 data for the two countries (see Appendix B).

Simulations involve an easing of monetary conditions in Italy which leads to a depreciation of the Italian currency. We are interested in the effects of the monetary easing on the current account and three scenarios are considered. The basic case strongly predicts a current account deficit, because of a surge in investment demand. Dampening investment demand by introducing adjustment costs in scenario two moderates the current account decrease but still does not reverse it. Scenario three is able to get a current account surplus by additionally decreasing the response of consumption demand. This is achieved by lowering the elasticity of substitution between consumption and leisure.

Figure B.1: Depreciation, Basic Case

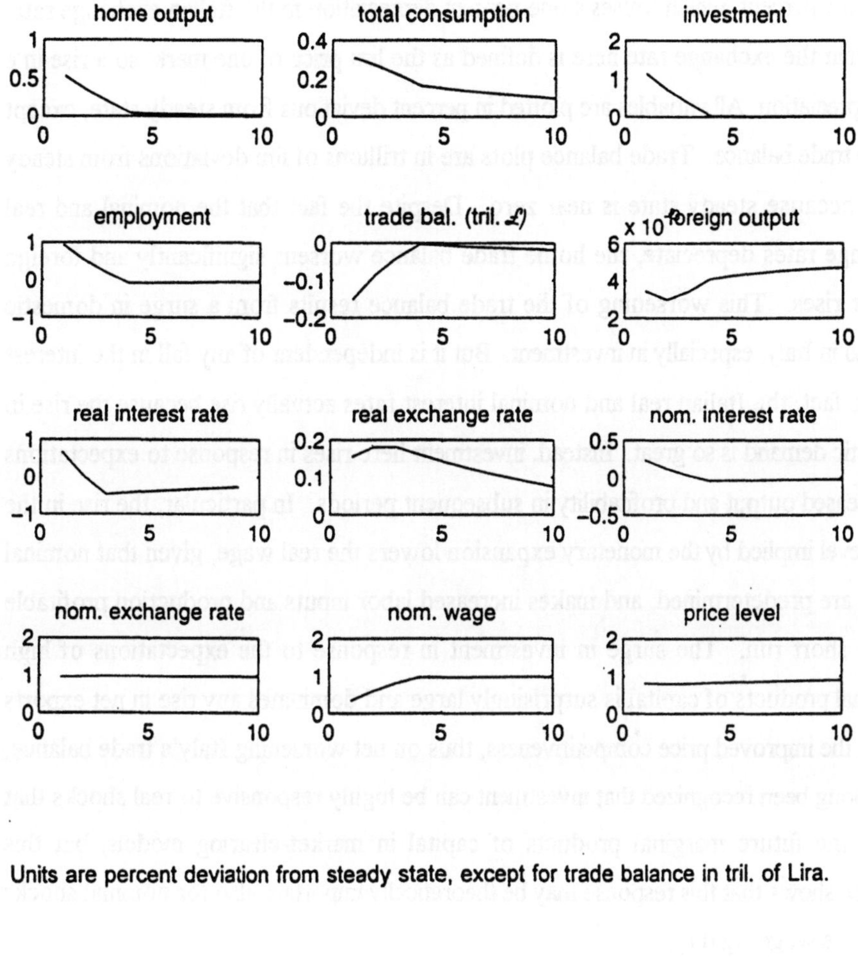

Units are percent deviation from steady state, except for trade balance in tril. of Lira.

Source: Authors' calculations

Figure B.1 shows impulse responses for an experiment in which money supply in Italy is raised 1 percent, which causes a one-percent depreciation in the Italian exchange rate. Note that the exchange rate here is defined as the lira price of one mark, so a rise in e is a depreciation. All variables are plotted in percent deviations from steady state, except for the trade balance. Trade balance plots are in trillions of lira deviations from steady state, because steady state is near zero. Despite the fact that the nominal and real exchange rates depreciate, the home trade balance worsens significantly and foreign output rises. This worsening of the trade balance results from a surge in domestic demand in Italy, especially in investment. But it is independent of any fall in the interest rate; in fact, the Italian real and nominal interest rates actually rise because the rise in domestic demand is so great. Instead, investment here rises in response to expectations of increased output and profitability in subsequent periods. In particular, the rise in the price level implied by the monetary expansion lowers the real wage, given that nominal wages are predetermined, and makes increased labor inputs and production profitable in the short run. The surge in investment in response to the expectations of high marginal products of capital is surprisingly large and dominates any rise in net exports due to the improved price competitiveness, thus on net worsening Italy's trade balance. It has long been recognized that investment can be highly responsive to real shocks that affect the future marginal products of capital in market-clearing models, but this exercise shows that this response may be theoretically important also for nominal shocks if there is wage rigidity.

The response of investment may be overstated since there are costs to adjusting the capital stock on short notice, so we add quadratic adjustment costs to the model, as shown in equation A2 in Appendix A. Investment can be dampened sufficiently for the monetary expansion to lower the nominal interest rate in the model if the adjustment parameter, ψ, is chosen to be 7.7 or greater. This value implies that for a one percent increase in the capital stock, adjustment costs must be forfeited equal to 7.7 percent of the capital accumulation. It is difficult to say exactly what would be a reasonable value for this parameter, but econometric work by *Galeotti (1990)* suggests it might be as high as 60, while previous simulations have usually used lower values, such as 2.5 (see *Schmidt-Hebbel and Serven, 1994*). Even though a high value of adjustment costs can dampen investment enough to allow nominal and real interest rates to fall in Italy, the Italian trade balance still does not improve. Even for a very large value of ψ, such as 100,000, the trade balance still worsens.

Figure B.2: Depreciation, Dampened Investment

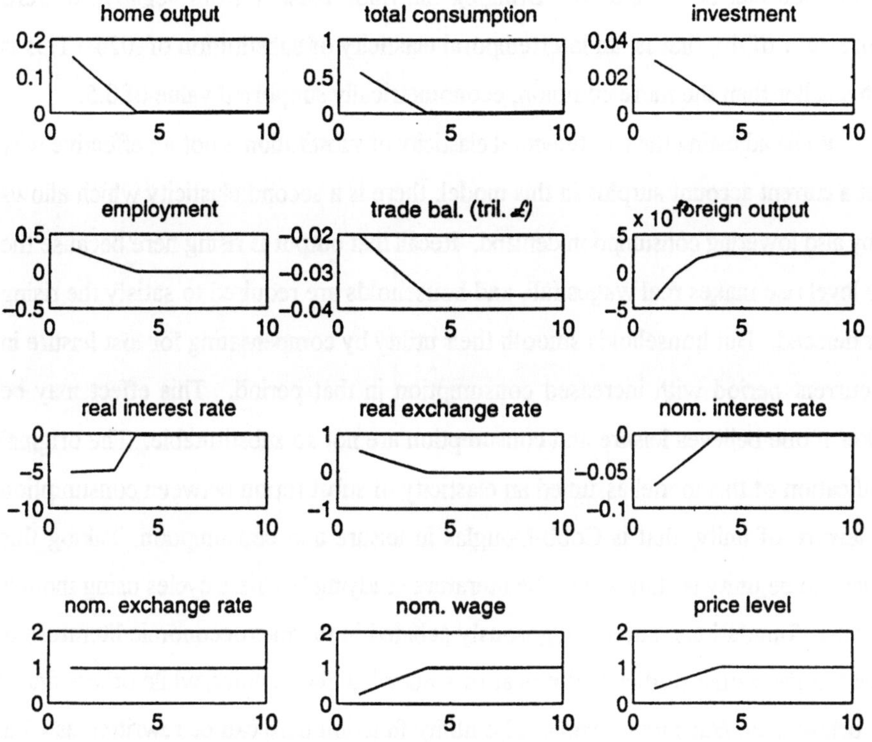

Units are percent deviation from steady state, except for trade balance in tril. of Lira.

Source: Authors' calculations

An illustrative case is shown in figure B.2, where adjustment costs are incorporated by setting $\psi = 100$. The explanation for the worsening current account is a surge in consumption. This is due, in part, to the fall in the real interest rate, which makes current consumption more attractive relative to future consumption. This effect would be smaller, depending on the household's intertemporal elasticity of substitution. Indeed, if this elasticity is made smaller (choosing the parameter σ larger) the surge in consumption can be dampened. Bringing the trade balance from negative to zero requires a σ of 40, that is, an intertemporal elasticity of substitution of .025. This is much smaller than the more common, econometrically supported value of 0.5.

While adjusting the intertemporal elasticity of substitution is not an effective way to get a current account surplus in this model, there is a second elasticity which allows this by also lowering consumption demand. Recall that output is rising here because the price level rise makes real wages fall, and households are required to satisfy the rising labor demand. But households smooth their utility by compensating for lost leisure in the current period with increased consumption in that period. This effect may be weaker if one believes leisure and consumption are not so substitutable. The original specification of this model assumed an elasticity of substitution between consumption and leisure of unity, that is Cobb-Douglas in leisure and consumption. Taking this elasticity to be unity is standard in the literature studying business cycles using models with microfoundations, but it is vigorously debated in the microeconomic literature in public finance. Some studies find it near or somewhat above unity, while others find it well below (see *Hausman, 1985*). The utility function here can be rewritten as CES to allow for different values, depending on the value ν. If now this elasticity is lowered a bit from unity to .92, consumption is just sufficiently dampened to push the trade balance into improvement. If the very low value of 0.1 is chosen, the balance improves noticeably (see figure B.3). But this increase is still not big, about 0.024 percent of steady state output and is not the dominant component of the increase in Italian output. It contributes only about 30 percent to Italian output, while domestic demand contributes the remaining 70 percent. In this case German output does fall.

Figure B.3: Depreciation, Dampened Investment and Consumption

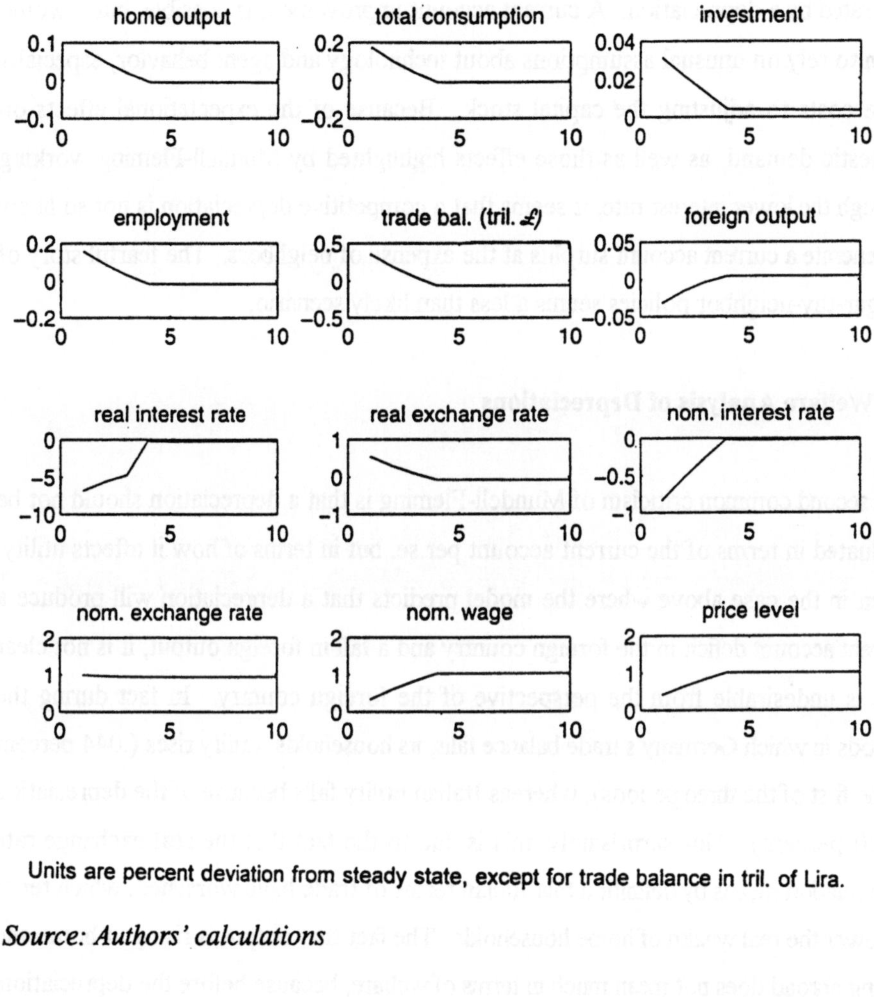

Units are percent deviation from steady state, except for trade balance in tril. of Lira.

Source: Authors' calculations

The lesson is that if the effects of expectations on domestic demand are taken at full value, they tend to restrict any improvement in the current account that might be generated by a depreciation. A current account improvement is possible, but it would seem to rely on unusual assumptions about technology and agent behavior, especially large costs to adjusting the capital stock. Because of the expectational effects on domestic demand, as well as those effects highlighted by Mundell-Fleming working through the lower interest rate, it seems that a competitive depreciation is not so likely to generate a current account surplus at the expense of neighbors. The fearful story of beggar-thy-neighbor policies seems a less than likely scenario.

3.3 Welfare Analysis of Depreciations

The second common criticism of Mundell-Fleming is that a depreciation should not be evaluated in terms of the current account per se, but in terms of how it affects utility. Even in the case above where the model predicts that a depreciation will produce a current account deficit in the foreign country and a fall in foreign output, it is not clear this is undesirable from the perspective of the foreign country. In fact during the periods in which Germany's trade balance falls, its households' utility rises (.044 percent in the first of the three periods), whereas Italian utility falls because of the depreciation (.020 percent). Not surprisingly, this is due to the fact that the real exchange rate depreciation means by definition that Italian terms of trade have worsened, which tends to lower the real wealth of home households. The fact that output is rising at home and falling abroad does not mean much in terms of welfare, because before the depreciation, the marginal utility and marginal cost of producing were equated, maximizing utility. When output is stimulated by the depreciation, the home country is producing more, but this is at an almost offsetting cost in terms of decreased leisure. Thus a depreciation does not seem to benefit the home country at the expense of neighbors.

This point has been made most strongly in a recent paper by *Obstfeld and Rogoff (1995b)*. Their modeling framework differs somewhat from that proposed in this paper mainly in that producers are modeled as monopolistic competitors. The prices of the monopolists' goods are held above the marginal cost and output is held below the economically efficient level. A monetary expansion and exchange rate depreciation may generate expenditure switching from foreign to home goods, but there will also be a general increase in demand. The demand stimulation effect, shared by home and foreign consumers, has welfare implications an order of magnitude larger than the expenditure switching effects, which were beggar-thy-neighbor. The welfare effects for producers are second order, since by construction marginal costs and marginal revenue were equal at the starting equilibrium. However, because output started out at a suboptimally low level from the perspective of consumers, with marginal benefits exceeding marginal costs, an increase toward the economically efficient level means that there are first-order benefits to consumers.

All this suggests that the danger of competitive depreciations has been exaggerated. It is not clear they would generate current account surpluses, and even if they did, this likely would not harm the welfare of their neighbors.

4. The European Experience in the 1990s

In this section we turn to an empirical assessment of the devaluations in the EMS which began in 1992. This episode is viewed widely as an example of what might happen in the future if exchange rates are not locked in. For example, the EU commissioner for the internal market, Mario Monti has warned of "growing concern among industrialists that the lira's devaluation is giving Italian companies an advantage over their European competitors..." and that "It was impossible to have a guaranteed single market in a situation where currency fluctuations remained unchecked"[12] .

Rather than providing a full econometric analysis, we present a number of statistics and correlations describing the recent experience[13, 14]. Table 1 presents percent changes in the nominal exchange rate, output, real exports and prices from 92:II until 95:III. Also reported is the level of interest rates in 92:II and 95:III for 12 European countries.

The first observation is that nominal exchange rate devaluations translated into real devaluations and thus into gains in competitiveness in all cases. Cumulative changes in inflation vary from 6% for Sweden to 16.9% for Portugal. Nominal exchange rate changes have been much larger and range from an appreciation of 2.4% versus the SDR in the Netherlands and Belgium to a depreciation of 46.9% in Italy.

Export performance varied widely. Germany and Austria essentially were unable to improve real exports over the period, while Sweden's exports increased by 63%. There is also a very close link between depreciations and export performance, captured in figure B.4. The larger the devaluations, the better the export performance appears to be.

Table B.1: Key Economic Data for 12 European Countries (92:II-95:III)

	Change in the Exchange Rate (vs. SDR)	Change in Output (IP)	Change in Real Exports	Change in Prices	Interest Rate 92:II	Interest Rate 95:III
Austria	0.023	0.071	0.009	0.106	9.52	4.40
Belgium	0.024	-0.014	---	0.075	9.57	4.42
France	-0.007	0.019	0.066	0.058	9.91	6.16
Germany	0.023	-0.049	0.010	0.097	9.60	4.40
Ireland	-0.137	0.471	0.360	0.071	10.21	6.09
Italy	-0.469	0.073	0.343	0.155	13.53	10.62
N'lands	0.024	0.025	0.112	0.078	9.37	3.99
Norway	-0.099	0.198	0.156	0.064	10.38	5.44
Portugal	-0.230	-0.034	0.253	0.169	13.22	10.75
Spain	-0.348	0.067	0.480	0.159	11.87	9.86
Sweden	-0.318	0.234	0.628	0.060	11.91	8.94
U.K.	-0.267	0.115	0.319	0.079	9.60	6.60

Notes:
- The change in real exports is measured from 92:II until 95:I. All other changes are measured from 92:II until 95:III, with the following exceptions: Changes in real exports for Austria are through 94:IV, changes in IP for Belgium through 95:II. Interest rates for the late period refer to 95:II in Portugal, and Austria.
- All changes are in percent. For the exchange rate, a negative sign implies a depreciation.
- SDR = Special Drawing Rights, IP = Index of Industrial Production.

Sources: IFS, IMF

Figure B.4: Changes in Exchange Rates and Real Exports (92:II-95:I)

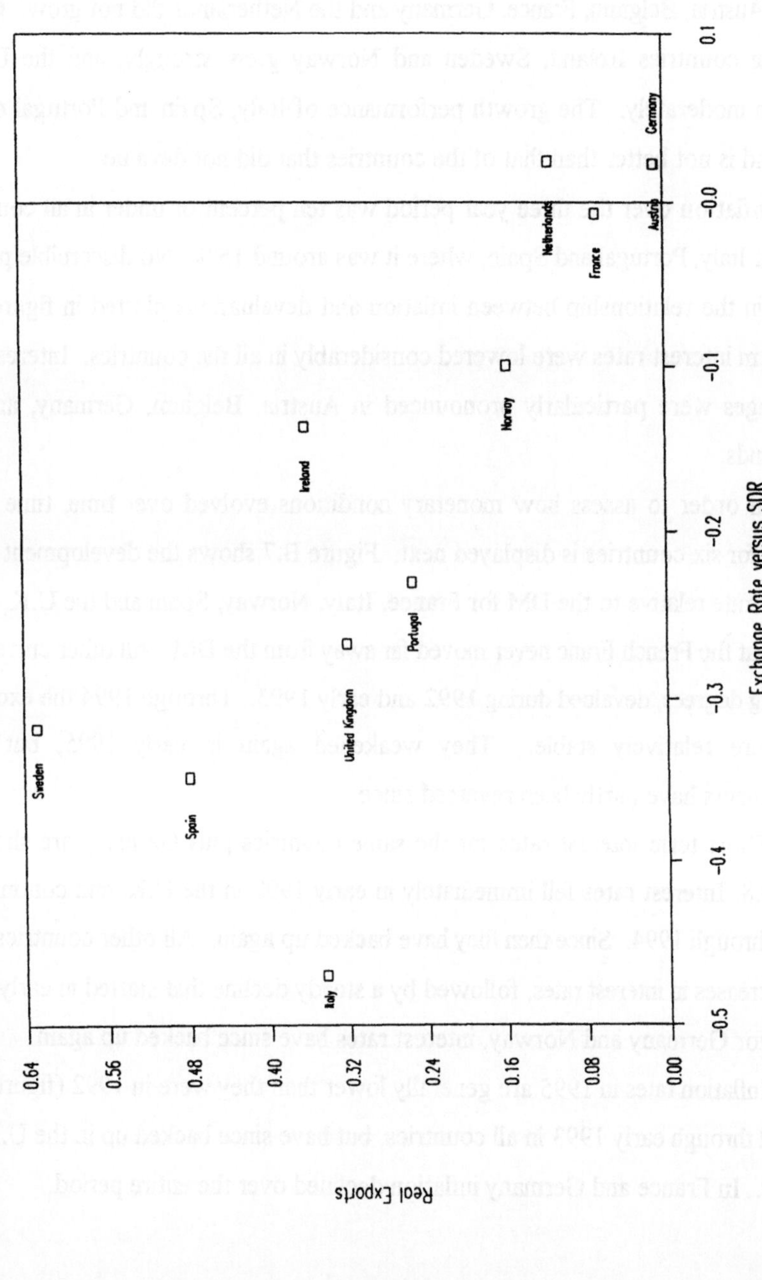

Source: Table B.1

Real output, measured by the index of industrial production also shows considerable variation. However, as can be seen in figure B.5, the link to exchange rate depreciations is not as strong. What is clear however, is that the countries that did not devalue, Austria, Belgium, France, Germany and the Netherlands did not grow. Of the devaluing countries Ireland, Sweden and Norway grew strongly, and the United Kingdom moderately. The growth performance of Italy, Spain and Portugal on the other hand is not better than that of the countries that did not devalue.

Inflation over the three year period was ten percent or under in all countries except for Italy, Portugal and Spain, where it was around 15%. No discernible pattern appears in the relationship between inflation and devaluations plotted in figure B.6. Short term interest rates were lowered considerably in all the countries. Interestingly the changes were particularly pronounced in Austria, Belgium, Germany, and the Netherlands.

In order to assess how monetary conditions evolved over time, time series evidence for six countries is displayed next. Figure B.7 shows the development of the exchange rate relative to the DM for France, Italy, Norway, Spain and the U.K. First, we see that the French Franc never moved far away from the DM. All other currencies, to varying degrees, devalued during 1992 and early 1993. Through 1994 the exchange rates were relatively stable. They weakened again in early 1995, but these developments have partly been reversed since.

Short term interest rates for the same countries plus Germany are shown in figure B.8. Interest rates fell immediately in early 1992 in the U.K. and continued to decline through 1994. Since then they have backed up again. All other countries show initial increases in interest rates, followed by a steady decline that started in early 1993. Except for Germany and Norway, interest rates have since backed up again.

Inflation rates in 1995 are generally lower than they were in 1992 (figure B.9). They fell through early 1993 in all countries, but have since backed up in the U.K. and Norway. In France and Germany inflation declined over the entire period.

Figure B.5: Changes in Exchange Rates and Industrial Production (92:II until 95:III)

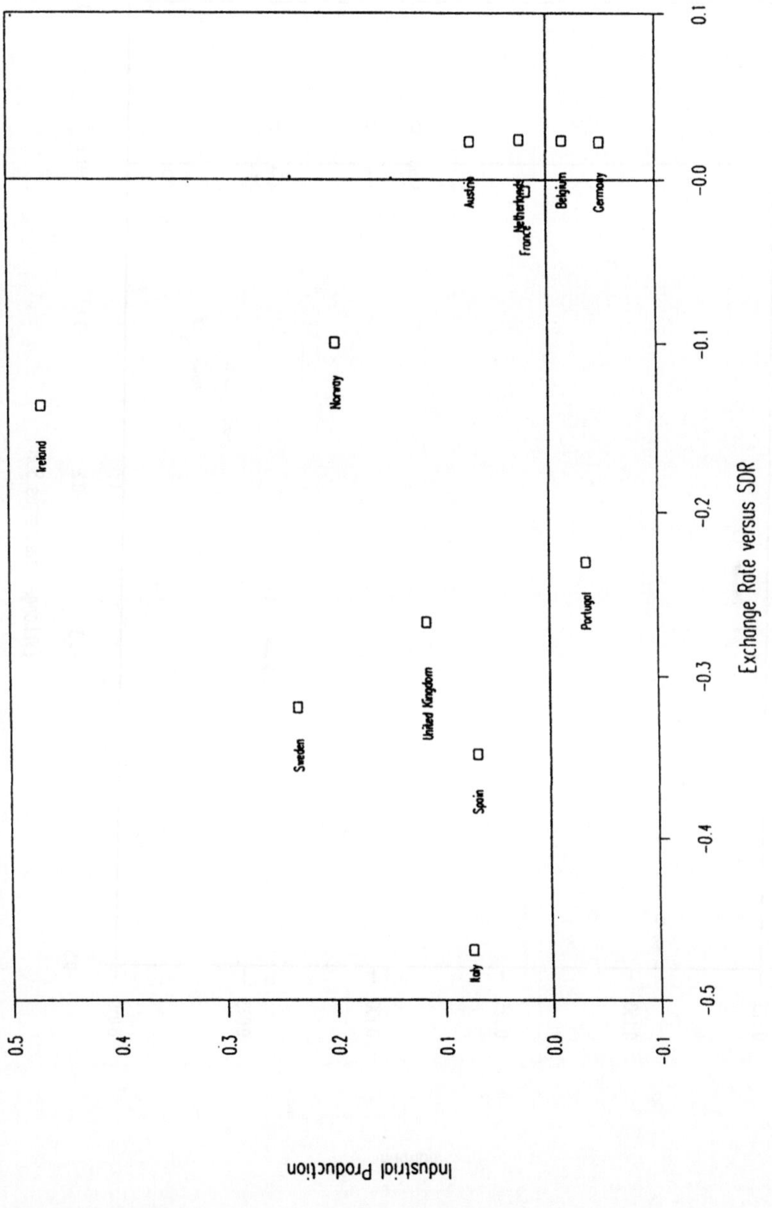

Source: Table B.1

Figure B.6: Changes in Exchange Rates and Inflation (92:II until 95:III)

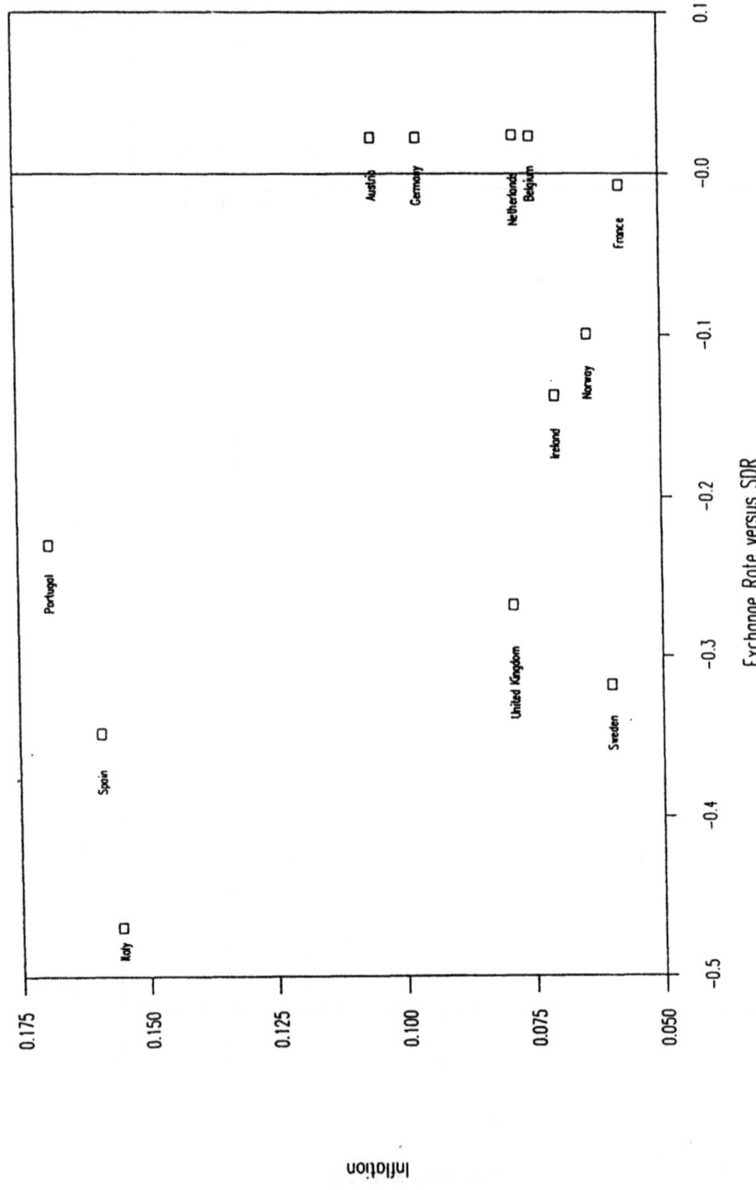

Source:Table B.1

Figure B.7: Exchange Rates vs. Germany (92:II=1.0)

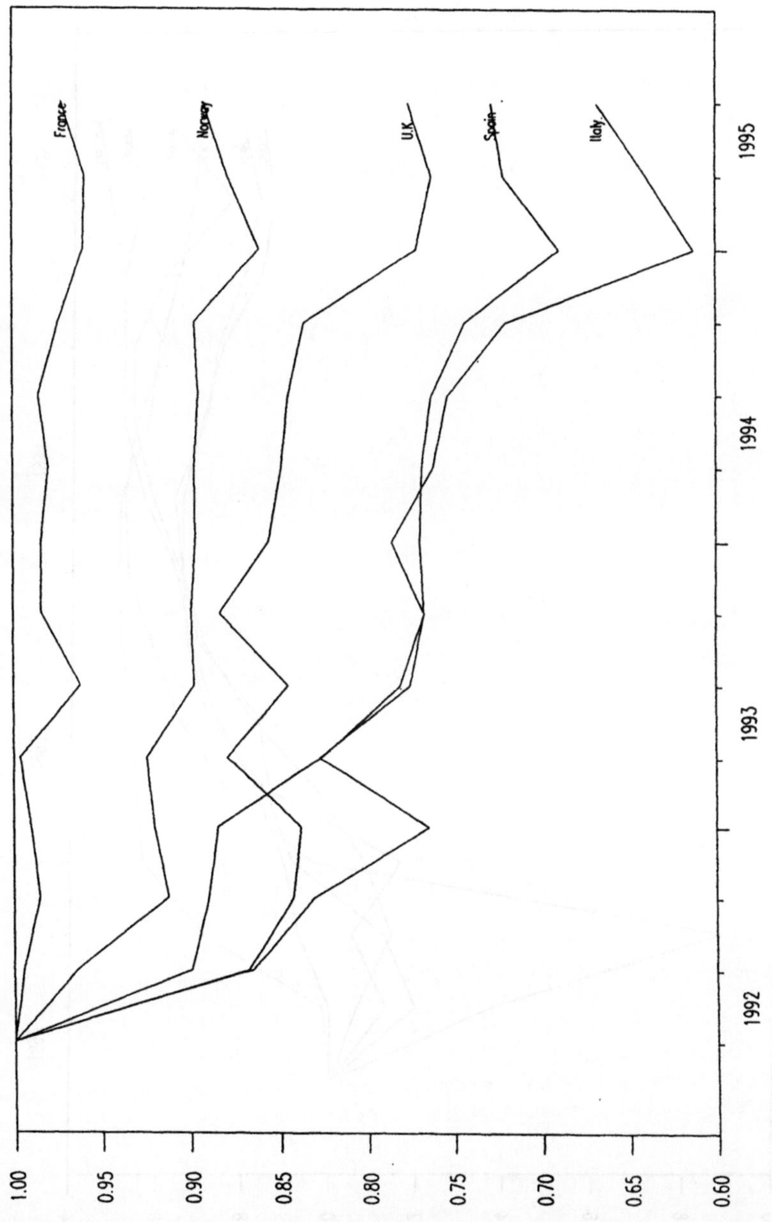

Sources: IFS, IMF

Figure B.8: Short-Term Interest Rates (92:II=1.0)

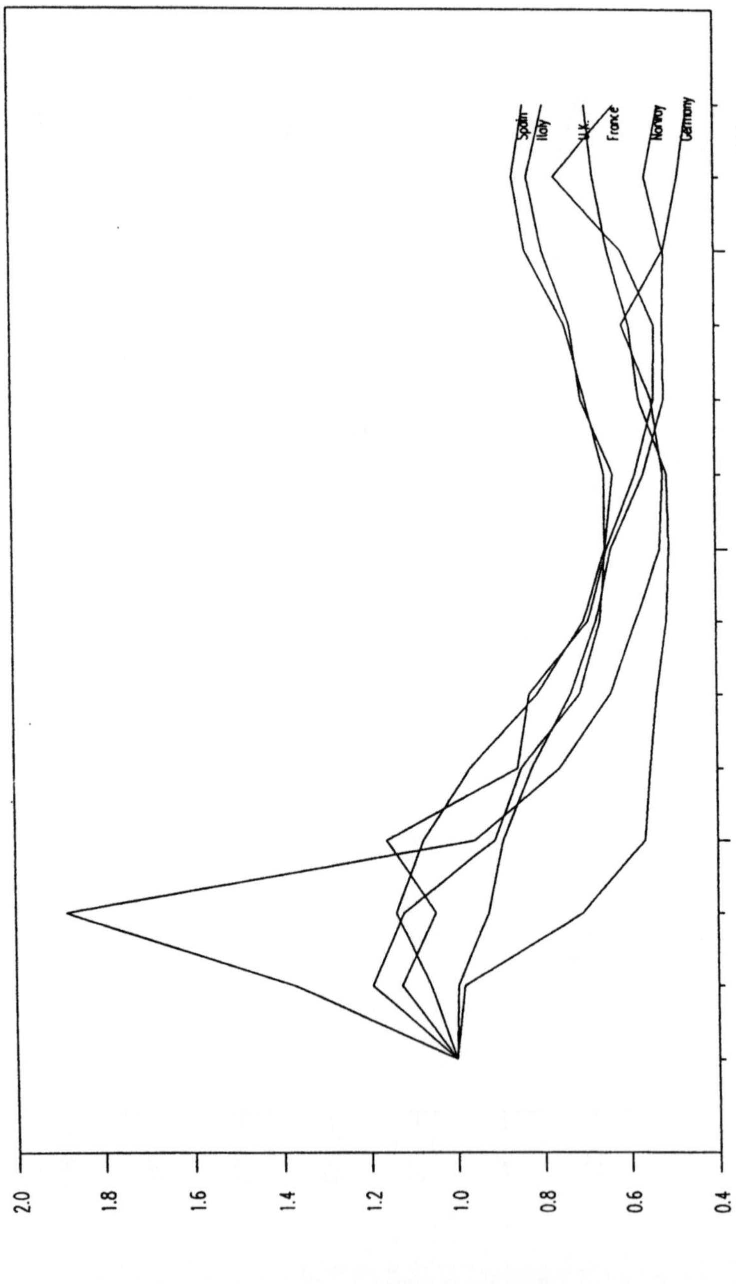

Sources: IFS, IMF

Figure B.9: Inflation Rates

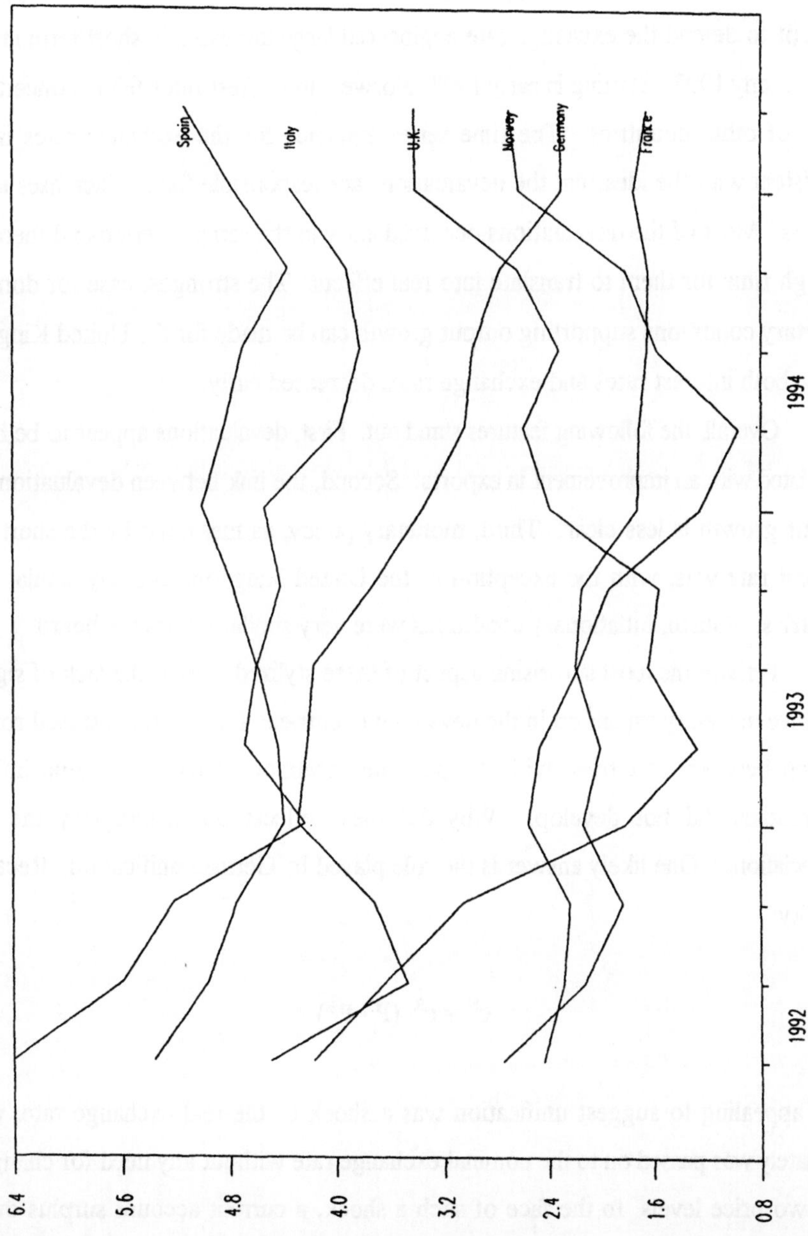

Sources: IFS, IMF

Figures B.7 and B.8 allow a better assessment of the timing of the easing of external and domestic monetary conditions. With the possible exception of the United Kingdom, where short term interest rates fell much earlier than in the rest of Europe, it is hard to explain the differentials in growth by domestic monetary conditions. Interest rates behaved broadly similar through early 1994 in the other countries. Norway, in an attempt to defend the exchange rate engineered large increases in short term interest rates in early 1992. Starting in early 1993, Norwegian interest rates fell in concert with those of other countries. The time series evidence for the exchange rates is also consistent with the idea that the devaluations are responsible for the increases in real exports. Most of the devaluations occurred early in the sample period and there was enough time for them to translate into real effects. The strongest case for domestic monetary conditions supporting output growth can be made for the United Kingdom, where both interest rates and exchange rates decreased early.

Overall, the following features stand out. First, devaluations appear to be highly correlated with an improvement in exports. Second, the link between devaluations and output growth is less clear. Third, monetary policy, as measured by the short term interest rate was, with the exception of the United Kingdom, broadly similar in all countries. Fourth, inflationary conditions were very similar across the board.

Perhaps the most surprising aspect of these stylized facts is the lack of signs of a relative monetary expansion in the devaluing countries. Interest rates stayed roughly in step between countries, with the possible exception of the U.K. And inflation differentials did not develop. Why did these effects not accompany the 1992 depreciations? One likely answer is the role played by German unification. Recall the identity:

$$e^N = e^R \ (P / P^*).$$

It is appealing to suggest unification was a shock to the real exchange rate, which ultimately was passed on to the nominal exchange rate without any need for changes in the two price levels. In the face of such a shock, a current account surplus outside Germany would be a natural counterpart to the deficits in Germany implied by the temporary excess of public consumption over production. The nominal depreciation of the exchange rate and the current account surplus would be parallel results of a common cause, rather than the former being the direct cause of the latter.

A complementary explanation for the episode of 1992 is that inflation rates had failed to converge in some countries such as Italy. This means the monetary expansion responsible for some misalignment preceded the actual devaluation by some time, and hence its implications for inflation and perhaps interest rates were not observed when devaluation finally came.

Of course, speculative attacks also played a role in explaining both the timing and magnitude of some of the devaluations (see *Eichengreen and Wyplosz, 1993*). We focus on the real shock and past inflation differentials to show that they offer a better explanation for the exchange rate movements than contemporaneous relative monetary expansions.

This observation is important, since a monetary expansion is the source of the effects that would be expected to offset current account surpluses, as discussed in the previous section. First, recall that when the price level rises while nominal wages are sticky, the fall in real wages raises production and the marginal product of capital, and thus may strongly stimulate the investment component of domestic demand. Second, recall that in a setting of monopolistically competitive firms, the rise in the price level can strongly stimulate production and generate first-order welfare benefits for home and foreign consumers, even if the current account of neighbors worsens.

The fact that the price level did not rise suggests that these effects were not active in modifying the size and cost of beggar-thy-neighbor effects. The implication is that the episode of 1992 should not be viewed as indicative of what depreciations might be like if a generally flexible exchange rate regime were adopted between a European core and periphery.

5. Problems for Convergence

As spelled out in *Commission of the European Communities (1995)*, the exchange rate relationship between the periphery and the core need not only ensure the efficient and orderly functioning of the single market through exchange rate stability, but should also contribute to the convergence process of non-participating member states. Two different issues must be addressed in this regard. The first concerns the relationship between the choice of an exchange rate regime and the convergence criteria not related to the exchange rate. The second deals with the fact that one convergence criterion deals directly with the exchange rate.

One argument for fixed exchange rates, already discussed in section 2 holds that convergence with respect to the inflation, interest rate and fiscal criteria can be facilitated by using the nominal exchange rate as an anchor for credibility of monetary policy. As has also been shown in section 2, however, it is unlikely that the nominal exchange rate can be used in that function in the future. It is therefore not clear whether a fixed exchange rate provides any advantage over flexible rates as far as the convergence criteria are concerned. In fact it can even be argued that a fixed exchange rate is harmful in this regard. Not only does it rule out needed adjustments in reaction to exogenous shocks discussed in section 2.1, it also provides targets for one way bets for speculators. If the events of 1992 are any indication, a failed attempt to peg, followed by an exchange rate crisis would be a bigger blow to confidence than a conscious assent to market forces moving flexible rates.

A flexible regime would not rule out an attempt at coordinating macroeconomic policies, so as to support convergence of inflation rates. This could promote exchange rate stability to some degree, while still allowing for reasonable adjustments to exogenous shocks and market pressures, in particular in the years following the formation of the core.

Additionally, the problems for the periphery may stem not so much from the choice of the exchange rate regime as from the existence of a core per se. As has been shown by *Alesina and Grilli (1994)*, the mere formation of the core will make it harder for the periphery to join later. If the initial core has a higher preference for price stability than the periphery, it might be rational to make later admissions more difficult, because any such admissions might lower the credibility of a low-inflation policy and lower the welfare of the existing core.

This then leaves the argument that the exchange rates themselves are part of the convergence criteria, which require that the exchange rate be within normal bands of fluctuation within the two years prior to joining EMU. Consequently, a country with flexible exchange rates could never join the core. Even without requiring a change in the Maastricht treaty, however, two lines of defense seem possible.

The first opening for a generous interpretation of the "normal fluctuations" comes from the fact that the treaty bases the allowed fluctuations on the existence of the EMS, which with the beginning of stage three will cease to exist. This oversight clearly calls for some modification of the Maastricht treaty and introduces the space needed to introduce a loose exchange rate arrangement. *Spaventa (1996)* suggests individual and conditional agreements with each outsider, defining the permitted fluctuation margins. It may even be possible to define these individual agreements without any explicit margins, as long as exchange rates are monitored and evaluated by the ECB.

If explicit margins must be set to satisfy the Maastricht treaty, there still is room to opt for wide bands, thus attempting to make pegged exchange rates look like flexible rates. A precedent for such an interpretation appears to have been set by the fact that the new 15% bands in the EMS are still acceptable with regard to the exchange rate criterion.

In sum, there are no economic reasons to think that flexible exchange rates hinder convergence more than fixed rates do. While there is currently a legal obstacle to convergence if flexible rates are adopted, there appears to be the opportunity to deal with this problem within the parameters set in the treaty. A final way around the strait jacket of pegged exchange rates and towards flexible rates lies in a liberal interpretation of the normal bands of fluctuations.

6. Conclusions

This paper strongly suggests the use of a flexible exchange rate arrangement between the outsiders and the core. This suggestion is based mainly on three observations. First, a flexible exchange rate regime need not be seriously disruptive to the common goods market. Second, the events of 1992 and 1993 are not a warning against adopting a flexible rate regime, but rather are the reaction to exchange rate misalignments. Third, fixed exchange rates are not useful as a nominal credibility anchor, supporting convergence in monetary policy. Rather, an ultimately unsuccessful defense of a fixed exchange rate may well put a large burden on the outsiders and further undermine monetary unification.

Appendix A: A Two-Country Model

A1. Model Notation:

c_1	- home consumption of home good
c_2	- home consumption of foreign good
c_1^*	- foreign consumption of home good
c_2^*	- foreign consumption of foreign good
y	- home output
y^*	- foreign output
g	- home government expenditure
g^*	- foreign government expenditure
I	- home investment
I^*	- foreign investment
B_1	- home h'hold holdings of bonds in home currency
B_2	- home h'hold holdings of bonds in foreign currency
B_1^*	- foreign h'hold holdings of bonds in home currency
B_2^*	- foreign h'hold holdings of bonds in foreign curr.
D_1	- home government debt denominated in home currency
D_2	- home gov't debt denom. in foreign currency (neg. exch. reserves)
D_1^*	- foreign gov't debt denom. in home currency (neg. exch. reserves)
D_2^*	- foreign gov't debt denom. in foreign currency
M_1	- home holding of home money
M_2	- home holding of foreign money
M_1^*	- foreign holding of home money
M_2^*	- foreign holding of foreign money
N_1	- money issued by home government
N_2^*	- money issued by foreign government
v_1	- home velocity of home money

v_2 - home velocity of foreign money
v_1^* - foreign velocity of home money
v_2^* - foreign velocity of foreign money
k - home capital stock
k* - foreign capital stock
P_1 - price of home good (in home currency)
P_2^* - price of foreign good (in foreign currency)
e - nominal exchange rate (home currency / foreign)
d - home dividends
d* - foreign dividends
R - home nominal interest rate
R* - foreign nominal interest rate
r - home rental rate on capital
r* - foreign rental rate on capital
T - home income tax rate
T* - foreign income tax rate
q - home lump-sum tax
q* - foreign lump-sum tax
W - home nominal wage
W* - foreign nominal wage
L - home labor
L* - foreign labor

A2. Households and Firms

The households in both countries are endowed each period with one unit of time, which they divide between leisure and work. They derive utility from consumption of the home and foreign goods (c_1 and c_2, respectively) and from leisure (1-L), discounting utility at the rate of time preference β. Households can hold four types of nominal assets: non-interest bearing home or foreign money (M_1 and M_2), or interest bearing government one-period debt denominated in home or foreign currency (B_1 and B_2).

Money holding is motivated via a transactions cost specification, which depends on velocity (v_1). For home households, holding home money lowers the transaction cost of purchasing both domestic and imported goods. An additional transaction cost applies to imports, reflecting the extra cost of dealing with foreign exchange. This extra cost, depending on a second velocity (v_2), motivates home households to hold a certain, but not necessarily a proportionate, amount of foreign currency.

Households make the capital accumulation decision, determining investment (I) subject to convex adjustment costs. (This arrangement is convenient in that it concentrates all intertemporal decisions in the hands of households.) Household income is derived from selling labor (L) to firms, rental of capital (k), dividends from firms (d), and from the interest received on government bonds, less taxes paid on labor income (at rate T) and in lump sum (q).

International linkages in the model work through household trade in the goods market and the market in government debt. There is no trade in firm equities, because the logical result would be a perfect-pooling equilibrium, which would imply that supply shocks are insured between countries in a manner that is empirically counter factual and rather uninteresting. There is also no international mobility in labor.

The home household problem is summarized below. (Here P_1 and P_2^* are home and foreign prices, and e is the exchange rate, defined as the domestic currency price of one unit of foreign exchange. Also W is the wage level, and R and R* are the respective nominal interest rates.)

$$\max E_0 \sum_{t=1}^{\infty} \beta^t U(c_{1t}, c_{2t}, L_t) \qquad \text{(A1)}$$

s.t.

$$\begin{aligned}
&\left(1+\gamma_{1t}v_{1t}\right)\left(c_{1t}+e_t\frac{P^*_{2t}}{P_{1t}}c_{2t}\right)+\gamma_2 v_{2t}\left(e_t\frac{P^*_{2t}}{P_{1t}}c_{2t}\right)\\
&\quad+\left(\frac{B_{1t}-B_{1t-1}}{P_{1t}}+e_t\frac{B_{2t}-B_{2t-1}}{P_{1t}}\right)\\
&\quad+\left(\frac{M_{1t}-M_{1t-1}}{P_{1t}}+e_t\frac{M_{2t}-M_{2t-1}}{P_{1t}}\right)+I_t+\frac{\psi\left(k_t-k_{t-1}\right)^2}{k_{t-1}}\\
&=\left(\frac{R_{t-1}B_{1t-1}}{P_{1t}}+e_t\frac{R^*_{t-1}B_{2t-1}}{P_{1t}}\right)+\left(1-T_t\right)\frac{W_tL_t}{P_{1t}}-q_t+d_t+r_{t-1}k_{t-1}\\
&\qquad \gamma_2\geq 0,\ \psi\geq 0 \qquad (A2)
\end{aligned}$$

where $U(c_{1t}, c_{2t}, L_t)=$

$$\begin{cases}
\dfrac{1}{1-\sigma}\left(\left(a\left(c_{1t}^{\theta}c_{2t}^{1-\theta}\right)^{-\nu}+(1-a)\left(1-L_t\right)^{-\nu}\right)^{-\frac{1}{\nu}}\right)^{1-\sigma} & \sigma\neq 1,\nu\neq 0\\
\dfrac{1}{1-\sigma}\left(\left(c_{1t}^{\theta}c_{2t}^{1-\theta}\right)^{a}\left(1-L_t\right)^{1-a}\right)^{1-\sigma} & \sigma\neq 1,\nu=0\\
\log\left(\left(a\left(c_{1t}^{\theta}c_{2t}^{1-\theta}\right)^{-\nu}+(1-a)\left(1-L_t\right)^{-\nu}\right)^{-\frac{1}{\nu}}\right) & \sigma=1,\nu\neq 0\\
\log\left(\left(c_{1t}^{\theta}c_{2t}^{1-\theta}\right)^{a}\left(1-L_t\right)^{1-a}\right) & \sigma=1,\nu=0
\end{cases}$$

$$\sigma > 0,\ \nu > -1,\ 0 < a < 1,\ 0 < \theta < 1 \qquad (A3)$$

$$\textit{and } v_{1t} = \frac{P_{1t}}{M_{1t}}\left(c_{1t}+e_t\frac{P^*_{2t}}{P_{1t}}c_{2t}\right) \qquad \text{(A4)}$$

$$\text{and } v_{2t} = \frac{P^*_{2t} c_{2t}}{M_{2t}} \tag{A5}$$

$$\text{and } k_t = I_t + (1-\delta) k_{t-1} \quad 0 \le \delta \le 1 \tag{A6}$$

$$B_{1t} > 0,\ B_{2t} > 0,\ M_{1t} > 0,\ M_{2t} > 0 \tag{A7}$$

The problem faced by the foreign household is analogous.

By solving the household budget constraint forward and imposing the transversality condition, which requires that household wealth not explode, an intertemporal budget constraint is obtained:

$$z_t = \sum_{s=t}^{\infty} \left(\prod_{j=t}^{s} (1+R_{j-1})^{-1} \frac{P_{1j}}{P_{1j-1}} \right) \left[(1+\gamma_1 v_{1s}) \left(c_{1s} + e_s \frac{P^*_{2s}}{P_{1s}} c_{2s} \right) + \gamma_2 v_{2s} \left(e_s \frac{P^*_{2s}}{P_{1s}} c_{2s} \right) + q_s - (1-T_s) \frac{W_s L_s}{P_{1s}} - d_s + \frac{\psi (k_s - k_{s-1})^2}{k_{s-1}} + zz_s \right] \tag{A8}$$

$$\text{where } z_t \equiv \frac{B_{1t-1}}{P_{1t-1}} + \left(\frac{1+R^*_{t-1}}{1+R_{t-1}} e_t \right) \frac{B_{2t-1}}{P_{1t-1}} + \left(\frac{1}{1+R_{t-1}} \right) \frac{M_{1t-1}}{P_{1t-1}} + \left(\frac{e_t}{1+R_{t-1}} \right) \frac{M_{2t-1}}{P_{1t-1}} + \left(\frac{1}{1+R_{t-1}} \frac{P_{1t}}{P_{1t-1}} (1 + r_{t-1} - \delta) \right) k_{t-1} \tag{A9}$$

$$and\ zz_s \equiv \left(e_s - \frac{1+R_s^*}{1+R_s} e_{s+1} \right) \frac{B_{2s}}{P_{1s}} + \left(1 - \frac{1}{1+R_s} \right) \frac{M_{1s}}{P_{1s}} \quad (A10)$$
$$+ \left(e_s - \frac{e_{s+1}}{1+R_s} \right) \frac{M_{2s}}{P_{1s}} + \left(1 - \frac{1}{1+R_s} \frac{P_{1s+1}}{P_{1s}} \left(1 + r_s - \delta \right) \right) k_s$$

Firms produce output (y) using a Cobb-Douglas production function, using as input the labor they hire (L) and the capital they rent from households (k). Firms must pay households wage payments and rental payments (at rates W and r). The firms maximize single period net profits, which are paid to households as dividends (d). The home firm's problem is

$$d_t = max \left(y_t - \frac{W_t L_t}{P_{1t}} - r_{t-1} k_{t-1} \right) \quad (A11)$$

$$s.t.\ y_t = A_t L_t^{\alpha} k_{t-1}^{1-\alpha} \quad 0 < \alpha < 1 \quad (A12)$$

The problem faced by the foreign firm is analogous.

The equation system used for simulations uses the Euler equations derived from the problems specified above. First, the choice of home households between the two consumption goods is determined by equating marginal utilities scaled by the relative price:

$$U_{2t} = U_{1t} \left(e_t \frac{P_{2t}^*}{P_{1t}} \right) \left(\frac{1 + 2\gamma_1 v_{1t} + 2\gamma_2 v_{2t}}{1 + 2\gamma_1 v_{1t}} \right) \quad (A13)$$

Second, the intertemporal choice of consumption now or in the future is captured in the Euler equation with respect to home bonds:

$$x_t = \beta(1 + R_t)E_t[x_{t+1}] \tag{A14}$$

$$\text{where } x_t = \frac{U_{1t}}{P_{1t}(1 + 2\gamma_1 v_{1t})} \tag{A15}$$

Here present marginal utility is equated to discounted expected future marginal utility. Third, the above Euler equation substituted into that for home money produces a simple liquidity preference relation:

$$(1 + R_t) = \frac{1}{1 - \gamma_1 v_{1t}^2} \tag{A16}$$

This relation reflects the trade-off money presents between lower transaction costs and foregone interest income from not holding interest-bearing assets. There is an analogous relation for home holdings of foreign money:

$$(1 + R_t^*) = \frac{1}{1 - \gamma_2 v_{2t}^2} \tag{A17}$$

The uncovered interest parity condition emerges when the Euler equation for home bonds above is combined with its counterpart for foreign bonds:

$$e_t = \left(\frac{1 + R_t^*}{1 + R_t} \right) \left(\frac{E_t\left[e_{t+1} x_{t+1}\right]}{E_t\left[x_{t+1}\right]} \right) \qquad \text{(A18)}$$

Note that this parity condition involves marginal utilities, since it is not only the expected depreciation that matters, but the value of expected depreciation in terms of utility.

Investment demand equates the marginal cost of investing (including adjustment costs) to the discounted expected marginal product of capital plus expected saving on future adjustment costs due to a larger capital stock. It is derived by combining the Euler equations of both firms and households with respect to capital:

$$P_{1t} x_{1t} \left(1 + \frac{2\psi\left(k_t - k_{t-1}\right)}{k_{t-1}} \right) = \beta E_t \Big[P_{1t+1} x_{t+1} \Big((1 - a) A_{t+1} L_{t+1}^{\alpha} k_t^{-\alpha} + (1 - \delta) + \left(\frac{2\psi(1 - \delta) k_t \left(k_{t+1} - k_t\right) + \psi\left(k_{t+1} - k_t\right)^2}{k_t^2} \right) \Big) \Big]$$

(A19)

Labor demand equates the real wage to the marginal product of labor:

$$\frac{W_t}{P_{1t}} = \alpha A L_t^{\alpha - 1} k_{t-1}^{1-\alpha} \qquad \text{(A20)}$$

In the flexible-wage version of the model, labor supply equates the after-tax wage to the relative marginal disutility of work:

$$(1 - T_t) W_t = \frac{-U_{Lt}}{x_t} \qquad \text{(A21)}$$

This equation will be suspended in the version of the model where wages are sticky.

The equations discussed above have their counterparts for the foreign agents. The interest parity condition again emerges when the bond equations for the foreign household are combined. This redundancy reflects the fact that, since national bonds are assumed riskless and perfect substitutes, the demand side leaves an indeterminacy in the allocation of bonds between the portfolios of home and foreign households. Governments do nothing on the supply side of the bond market to affect this indeterminacy. To resolve this indeterminacy for the purpose of simulation, an allocation rule is imposed, specifying that foreign agents split their portfolios in a certain proportion, that proportion becoming a calibratable parameter.

$$\frac{B_{1t}^*}{B_{1t} + B_{1t}^*} = \rho_b \frac{B_{2t}^*}{B_{2t} + B_{2t}^*} \qquad \text{(A22)}$$

A3. Wage Rigidity

The nominal wage is predetermined and the equilibrium quantity in the labor market is assumed demand determined. Households take the quantity of labor as given and do not see themselves as having any labor supply decision. So the labor supply Euler equation is suspended. The predetermined wage is set as the rational expectation of the wage that would satisfy this missing Euler equation:

$$W_t = E_{t-1}\left[\frac{-U_{Lt}}{x_t\left(1-T_t\right)}\right] \tag{A23}$$

Hence the optimizing labor supply equation reappears in an altered, expectational form; so the model retains a notion of the incentives of labor-supply to equate the marginal benefits and marginal disutility of additional work. Note that the wage-setting decision involves the rational expectation of how the economy is evolving over time, including the evolution of the capital stock in response to shocks observed in periods prior to the setting of the contract.

In the model, contracts are specified for four periods, in which the wage may be set at different levels for each period. Further, to capture the notion of gradual adjustment to shocks, the model specifies staggered contracts, in which each year one of four contracting groups sets its four-year contract. This implies a group's contract level is affected by what other groups are expected to do in future periods when their contracts come due, and the effects these future decision will have on the evolution of the economy. Finally, the overall wage level prevailing in the economy is approximated by the average over the contract levels of the four groups. In summary, the wage level, W_t is determined by the following expressions:

$$W_t = \sum_{i=1}^{4}\frac{1}{4}W_{it} \tag{A24}$$

where

$$W_{it} = E_{t-i+1}\left[\frac{-U_{Lt}}{x_t\left(1-T_t\right)}\right] \quad for\ i = 1\ to\ 4 \qquad \text{(A25)}$$

A4. Government

The government in each country uses consumption goods (in amount g) for a purpose that yields no utility to consumers. It derives revenue from distortionary taxes on labor income (at rate T), from lump sum taxes on households (q), from issuing money (N_1), and from issuing debt in home and foreign currency (D_1 and D_2). When D_2 is negative, it is the central bank's foreign-currency reserves. The government also expends revenue by paying interest on outstanding debt. The home government budget constraint is as follows:

$$g_t + \frac{R_{t-1}D_{1t-1}}{P_{1t}} + e_t\frac{R^*_{t-1}D_{2t-1}}{P_{1t}} = T_t\left(\frac{W_tL_t}{P_{1t}}\right) + q_t + \left(\frac{N_{1t}-N_{1t-1}}{P_{1t}}\right) + \left(\frac{D_{1t}-D_{1t-1}}{P_{1t}}\right) + e_t\left(\frac{D_{2t}-D_{2t-1}}{P_{1t}}\right)$$

$$D_{1t} \geq 0 \qquad (A26)$$

Monetary policy is described by a rule pegging the money supply:

$$N_{1t} = \overline{N}_1 \qquad \text{(A27)}$$

The monetary shock considered here will be a permanent rise in the level of money $\overline{N}_1$, carried out via open-market operations with government bonds. Assuming a flexible exchange rate regime, foreign exchange reserves are held fixed:

$$D_{2t} = \overline{D_2} \tag{A28}$$

Fiscal policy is described by three policy reaction functions governing expenditure, income taxes, and lump-sum taxes, as follows:

$$g_t = \overline{g} \tag{A29}$$

$$T_t \frac{(W_t L_t)}{P_t} = a_1 + a_2 \left(\frac{D_{1t-1} + e_{t-1} D_{2t-1}}{P_{1t-1}} \right) \tag{A30}$$

$$q_t - q_{t-1} = a_3 \left(\frac{R_{t-1} D_{1t-1} + e_t R^*_{t-1} D_{2t-1}}{P_{1t}} - \frac{R_{t-2} D_{1t-2} + e_{t-1} R^*_{t-2} D_{2t-2}}{P_{1t-1}} \right) \tag{A31}$$

To satisfy dynamic stability, either the income tax rate T_t or the lump-sum tax q_t must respond to changes in the debt burden to keep debt from becoming explosive in the face of shocks. In the simulations that follow, taxes are lump sum, with an "incremental interest payment rule" with $a_3 > 1$. Since the government is guaranteeing dynamic stability of debt, it is sure also to be satisfying its solvency condition, which is necessary if the optimizing households are to be willing to hold government debt:

$$\frac{D_{1t-1}}{P_{1t-1}} + \left(e_t \frac{1 + R^*_{t-1}}{1 + R_{t-1}} \right) \frac{D_{2t-1}}{P_{1t-1}} + \left(\frac{1}{1+R_{t-1}} \right) \frac{N_{1t-1}}{P_{1t-1}}$$

$$= \sum_{s=t}^{\infty} \left(\prod_{j=t}^{s-1} \left(1 + R_j\right)^{-1} \frac{P_{1j}}{P_{1j-1}} \right) \qquad (A32)$$

$$\left[\frac{T_s W_s L_s}{P_{1s}} + q_s - g_s + \left(e_s - e_{s+1} \frac{1 + R^*_s}{1 + R_s} \right) \frac{D_{2s}}{P_{1s}} + \left(1 - \frac{1}{1 + R_s} \right) \frac{N_{1s}}{P_{1s}} \right]$$

The foreign government of course has an analogous budget constraint and policy rules. Finally, the market-clearing conditions must be considered. The money market-clearing conditions are:

$$N_{1t} = M_{1t} + M^*_{1t} \qquad (A33)$$

$$N_{2t} = M_{2t} + M^*_{2t} \qquad (A34)$$

Those for the bond markets are:

$$B_{1t} + B^*_{1t} = D_{1t} + D^*_{1t} \qquad (A35)$$

$$B_{2t} + B^*_{2t} = D_{2t} + D^*_{2t} \qquad (A36)$$

Only one of the goods market clearing conditions is necessary, because of Walras' Law. When it is combined with the budget constraints of the home country, it produces the balance of payments constraint:

$$[net\ \ exports] + [net\ \ interest\ \ income] + [capital\ \ account] =$$

$$\begin{aligned} &\left[P_{1t}c^{*}_{1t} - e_t P_{2t} c_{2t}\right] + \left[e_t R^{*}_{t-1} B_{2t-1} - R_{t-1} B^{*}_{1t-1} - e_t R^{*}_{t-1} D_{2t-1} + R_{t-1} D^{*}_{1t-1}\right] \\ &+ \left[\left(B^{*}_{1t} - B^{*}_{1t-1}\right) - e_t\left(B_{2t} - B_{2t-1}\right) + \left(M^{*}_{1t} - M^{*}_{1t-1}\right) - e_t\left(M_{2t} - M_{2t-1}\right)\right. \\ &\left. - \left(D^{*}_{1t} - D^{*}_{1t-1}\right) + e_t\left(D_{2t} - D_{2t-1}\right)\right] = 0 \end{aligned}$$

$(A37)$

This balance of payments constraint may be regarded as the condition determining the equilibrium exchange rate. If there is an excess demand for foreign currency at a given exchange rate, the home currency will depreciate to clear the market.

Appendix B: Model Calibration

The model is calibrated to represent Italy and Germany. Values are chosen for the elasticities and other parameters from various econometric studies and to fit the steady state of the model to features of 1994 data for the two countries. The share of labor in the production function, α, is taken to be 0.5000 and 0.593 for Italy and Germany respectively, taken from the average labor share for 1960-1985 from the OECD International Sectoral Database. The intertemporal elasticity of substitution, $1/\sigma$, is taken to be 0.5 for both, which is consistent with econometric estimates and preceding simulation studies (see *Stockman and Tesar, 1996; Baxter and Crucini, 1993*). The share of domestically produced goods in the consumption bundle, θ, is 0.75, approximately the average of the values of the two countries. Depreciation, δ, is 0.1 and the rate of time preference, β, is 0.96, which are values common to preceding simulation studies. The technology parameter, A, is chosen to fit steady state output to 1994 output, and is equal to 1.46 and 3.23 respectively. The weighting of leisure in the utility function, a, is set to equate the steady state labor allocation to 0.20 in both countries. The transaction cost parameter, γ, is 0.005 in both countries to set steady state money holding approximately to the levels in 1994. Other steady state values set to 1994 values are tax rates, government debts, foreign reserves, and the net foreign debt of Italy.

The simplest version of the model, simulated in figure B.1, does not include costs of adjustment to the capital stock. Also utility is Cobb-Douglas over consumption and leisure (implying an elasticity of substitution between consumption and leisure equal to unity). In the simulation depicted in figure B.2, the adjustment cost parameter, ψ, is 100. This is also the case in the simulation of figure B.3, where additionally the elasticity of substitution between consumption and leisure, $1/(1+\upsilon)$, is 0.1.

Endnotes

1. This paper was initiated while both authors were participants at a workshop on The Political Economy of European Integration, funded by the German-American Academic Council. We would like to thank conveners Barry Eichengreen and Michael Zürn, and seminar participants for helpful discussions. We are also endebted to our discussant, W. Max Corden, as well as Stanley W. Black, Barry Bosworth, and Silke Fabian Reeves for valuable comments. The affiliations of the authors are: University of California at Davis (Paul Bergin), and American Institute for Contemporary German Studies at The Johns Hopkins University (Mathias Moersch).

2. Variations on the theme of pegged exchange rates, such as managed floats and crawling pegs are not discussed here, but they are subject to essentially the same problems.

3. The call for giving associate membership status in the European currency union to some outsiders (*Gros, 1996)* must be seen in this context. The idea is that associate membership, essentially a unilateral peg to the Euro, facilitates the process of convergence.

4. Spain, Ireland, Portugal and Greece were granted longer transition periods.

5. See *Eichengreen and Wyplosz (1993)* for a history of the EMS from 1987 to 1992.

6. Both the refusal of France to give in to the Bundesbank's request for a devaluation in 1990 and the subsequent refusal of the Bundesbank to support currencies that came under attack in 1992 and 1993 can be cited to illustrate this point. For a discussion of the policy behavior of the two central banks see *Melitz (1994)* and *Sherman and Kaen (1994).*

7. Recent cases of successful currency boards do not fit the situation of the European periphery. Argentina, in addition to a currency board, also has capital ccontrols in place. In Estonia the possibility to devalue the currency is explicitly allowed for (see *Hanke, Jonung and Schuler, 1993).*

8. Historical evidence for beneficial effects of devaluations can be found in *Eichengreen and Sachs (1985).*

9. If the current account were to worsen, this by definition would imply a net capital inflow. But since international capital flows are taken in a simple Mundell-Fleming framework as a function just of the interest rate differential, this would require a rise in the interest rate instead of a fall. Such a rise in interest rate cannot be justified in this simple framework by a large rise in domestic demand; with investment here taken as a function of just the interest rate and current output, investment cannot expand beyond the point where interest rates no longer fall. In graphical terms, the rise in investment will only be a movement along the IS curve; as a result it cannot shift the IS curve so as to raise interest rates and generate a capital inflow. So the simple text-book version of Mundell-Fleming suggests we should expect a depreciation to improve the home current account at the expense of that of foreign neighbors (see *Frankel, 1988; Helliwell and Padmore, 1985*). One rationalization commonly offered for the worsening current account observed empirically in many reduced form models is that expectations of a future policy reversion and exchange rate appreciation might draw capital inflows while the interest rate is still low. An even stronger way to link a depreciation to a worsening current account is to introduce expectations, not just in the capital market, but also in the goods market in the determination of domestic demand. It has been shown in *Risager (1988)* and *Nielsen (1991)* that a devaluation can strongly stimulate investment through expectations of future profitability and hence worsen the current account.

10. The model that follows builds on the intertemporal approach to the current account, in which the much consideration of income effects. It is also distinct from the absorption approach, in which the Harberger-Laursen-Metzler effect focuses on the terms of trade implications for savings behavior, without much consideration for the effects of the monetary policy accompanying the devaluation.

11. Several research efforts have been underway to recast the Mundell-Fleming Framework (*Mundell, 1963; Fleming, 1962*). A significant recent example is *Obstfeld and Rogoff (1995b)*, which combines monopolistic competition and price predetermination in a two-country general equilibrium model. Similar work has been done by *Svensson and van Wijnbergen (1989)* and *Stockman and Ohanian (1993)*. Another approach has been *McKibbin and Sachs (1991)*, which combines sticky wage adjustment with liquidity constrained households.

12. Financial Times, 28 Feb, 1995.

13. A more sophisticated econometric analysis is complicated by at least two factors. First, there is still only a limited amount of post-devaluation time series data available. Second, identification of monetary policy is complicated by the fact that the switch from fixed to flexible exchange rates constitutes a structural break.

14. A more formal treatment of the British experience can be found in *Hughes Hallett and Wren-Lewis (1995)*. Their findings are consistent with our model of the previous section and the empirical analysis that follows. In particular the expenditure switching effect of the real exchange rate depreciation are small, while the stimulation to consumption from lower real interest rates is large.

References

ALESINA, A.; GRILLI, V. (1994), On the Feasibility of a One-speed or Multi-speed European Monetary Union, in: EICHENGREEN, B.; FRIEDEN, J., eds., The Political Economy of European Monetary Union, Westview, 107-127.

BAILY, M.; TAVLAS, G.; ULAN, M. (1986), Exchange Rate Variability and Trade Performance: Evidence for the Big Seven Industrial Countries, Weltwirtschaftliches Archiv, 466-76.

BARBER, L. (1996), EU Looks at Multi-speed Exchange Rate System, Financial Times, January 21.

BAXTER, M.; CRUCINI, M. (1993), Explaining Saving-Investment Correlations, American Economic Review, 417-35.

BRYANT, R.; HENDERSON, D.; HOLTHAM, G.; HOOPER, P.; SYMANSKY, S., eds. (1988), Empirical Macroeconomics for Interdependent Economies, Washington: The Brookings Institution.

COBHAM, D. (1994), European Monetary Upheavals, Manchester: Manchester University Press.

COMMISSION OF THE EUROPEAN COMMUNITIES (1990), One Market, One Money, European Economy, No. 44, October.

COMMISSION OF THE EUROPEAN COMMUNITIES (1995), Exchange Rate Relations Between Participating and Non-Participating Countries in Stage Three of EMU: Interim Report to the European Council.

CUSHMAN, D. (1983), The Effects of Real Exchange Rate Risk on International Trade, Journal of International Economics, 45-63.

CUSHMAN, D. (1988a), U.S. Bilateral Trade Flows and Exchange Risk During the Floating Period, Journal of International Economics, 317-30.

CUSHMAN, D. (1988b), Exchange-Rate Uncertainty and Foreign Direct Investment in the United States, Weltwirtschaftliches Archiv, 322-36.

DE GRAUWE, P. (1995a), An Easier Road to EMU, Financial Times, October 17.

DE GRAUWE, P. (1995b), The Economics of Convergence Towards Monetary Union in Europe, CEPR Discussion Paper, No. 1213.

EICHENGREEN, B. (1993), European Monetary Unification, Journal of Economic Literature, 1321-1357.

EICHENGREEN, B. (1994), International Monetary Arrangements for the 21st Century, Washington: The Brookings Institution.

EICHENGREEN, B.; SACHS, J. (1985), Exchange Rates and Economic Recovery in the 1930s, Journal of Economic History, 925-946.

EICHENGREEN, B.; WYPLOSZ, C. (1993), The Unstable EMS, Brookings Papers on Economic Activity, 51-124.

EICHENGREEN, B.; TOBIN, J.; WYPLOSZ, C. (1995), Two Cases for Sand in the Wheels of International Finance, Economic Journal, 162-172.

FLEMING, M. (1962), Domestic Financial Policies Under Fixed and Under Floating Exchange Rates, IMF Staff Papers 9, 369-79.

FLOOD, R.; GARBER, P. (1984), Collapsing Exchange Rate Regimes: Some Linear Examples, Journal of International Economics, 1-13.

FRANKEL, J. (1988), Ambiguous Policy Multipliers in Theory and Empirical Models, in: BRYANT, R.; HENDERSON, D.; HOLTHAM, G.; HOOPER, P.; SYMANSKY, S, eds., Empirical Macroeconomics for Interdependent Economies, Washington: The Brookings Institution, 17-26.

FRANKEL, J. (1992), Monetary Regime Choices for a Semi-Open Economy, Unpublished manuscript, Berkeley: University Of California.

FRENKEL, J.; MUSSA, M. (1988), Asset Markets, Exchange Rates and the Balance of Payments, in: JONES, R.; KENEN, P., eds., Handbook of International Economics, New York: North Holland, 679-747.

GALEOTTI, M. (1990), Specification of the Technology for Neoclassical Investment Theory: Testing the Adjustment Costs Approach, Review of Economics and Statistics, 471-80.

GARBER, P.; TAYLOR, M. (1995), Sand in the Wheels of Foreign Exchange Markets: A Skeptical Note, Journal of Economics, 173-180.

GROS, D. (1996), Towards Economic and Monetary Union: Problems and Prospects, CEPS Paper, No. 65.

GROS, D.; THYGESEN, N. (1994), Towards Monetary Union in the European Community: Why and How, in: WELFENS, P., ed., European Monetary Integration, 2nd ed., Heidelberg: Springer Verlag, 95-123.

HANKE, S.; JONUNG, L.; SCHULER, K. (1993), Russian Currency and Finance - A Currency Board Approach to Reform, London: Routledge.

HAUSMAN, J. (1985), Taxes and Labor Supply, in: AUERBACH, A.; FELDSTEIN, M., eds., Handbook of Public Economics, New York: North-Holland, 237-283.

HELLIWELL, J.; PADMORE, T. (1985), Empirical Studies of Macroeconomic Interdependence, in: JONES, R.; KENEN, P., eds., Handbook of International Economics, New York: North Holland, 1007-51.

HOOPER, P.; KOHLHAGENS, (1978), The Effect of Exchange Rate Uncertainty on the Prices and Volume of International Trade, Journal of International Economics, 483-511.

HUGHES-HALLETT, A. J.; WREN-LEWIS, S. (1995), Y-a-t'il une Vie Hors du SME? L'Experience du Royaume-Uni, Economie Internationale, 31-54.

ISAAC, A. (1994), Comment on: Towards Monetary Union in the European Community: Why and How, in: WELFENS, P., ed., European Monetary Integration, 2nd ed., Heidelberg: Springer Verlag, 124-131.

KENEN, P. (1979), Exchange Rate Variability: Measurement and Implications, Unpublished Manuscript, Princeton: Princeton University.

KENEN, P. (1995a), Economic and Monetary Union in Europe, Cambridge: Cambridge University Press.

KENEN, P. (1995b), Capital Controls, the EMS and EMU, Economic Journal, 181-192.

KRUGMAN, P. (1979), A Model of Balance-of-payments Crises, Journal of Money, Credit and Banking, 311-325.

MCKIBBIN, W.; SACHS, J. (1991), Global Linkages: Macroeconomic Interdependence in the World Economy, Washington: The Brookings Institution.

MELITZ, J. (1994), French Monetary Policy and Recent Speculative Attacks on the Franc, in: COBHAM, D., ed., European Monetary Upheavals, Manchester: Manchester University Press, 61-77.

MORSINK, R.; MOLLE, W. (1991), Direct Investment and Monetary Integration, European Economy special edition, 36-55.

MUNDELL, R. (1963), Capital Mobility and Stabilization Policy under Fixed and Flexible Exchange Rates, Canadian Journal of Economics and Political Science, 475-85.

NIELSEN, S. (1991), Current-account Effects of a Devaluation in an Optimizing Model with Capital Accumulation, Journal of Economic Dynamics and Control, 569-588.

OBSTFELD, M. (1994), The Logic of Currency Crises, Cahiers Economiques et Monetaires, 189-213.

OBSTFELD, M. (1995), Models of Currency Crises with Self-fulfilling Features, NBER Working Paper, No. 5285.

OBSTFELD, M.; ROGOFF, K. (1995a), The Mirage of Fixed Exchange Rates, Journal of Economic Perspectives, Fall, 73-96.

OBSTFELD, M.; ROGOFF, K. (1995b), Exchange Rate Dynamics Redux, Journal of Political Economy, 624-659.

RISAGER, O. (1988), Devaluations, Profitability and Investment, Scandinavian Journal of Economics, 125-140.

SCHMIDT-HEBBEL, K.; SERVEN, L. (1994), Fiscal Policy in Classical and Keynesian Open Economies, World Bank Policy Research Working Paper, No. 1299.

SHERMAN, H.; KAEN, F. (1994), The Behavior and Thinking of the Bundesbank, in: COBHAM, D., ed., European Monetary Upheavals, Manchester: Manchester University Press, 82-111.

SPAVENTA, L. (1996), Out in the Cold? Outsiders and Insiders in 1999: Feasible and Unfeasible Options, CEPR Discussion Paper, No. 1379.

STOCKMAN, A.; OHANIAN, L. (1993), Short-run Independence of Monetary Policy Under Pegged Exchange Rates and the Effects of Money on Exchange Rates and Interest Rates, NBER Working Paper, No. 4517.

STOCKMAN, A.; TESAR, L. (1990), Tastes and Technology in a Two-country Model of the Business Cycle: Explaining International Comovements, NBER Working Paper, No. 3566, forthcoming in American Economic Review.

SVENSSON, L.; VAN WIJNBERGEN, S. (1989), Excess Capacity, Monopolistic Competition and International Transmission of Monetary Disturbances, The Economic Journal, 785-805.

Comments on: EMU and Outsiders: Fixed versus Flexible Exchange Rates

W. Max Corden

I am in general agreement with the contents of this wide-ranging paper. In these comments (expanded from those presented at the conference) I will highlight and clarify some of the arguments, also directing attention at the end to one issue that is not discussed by the authors.

1. Competitive Depreciation: A Threat to the Single Market?

To start with, the authors address the question: what should be the exchange rate regime of the outsiders - that is, those members of the European Community that are not yet eligible to take part in EMU but hope to do so eventually. Their answer is that (contrary to what has recently been decided) the outsiders would be wise to choose - or be forced to choose - floating exchange rate regimes. Fixed but adjustable regimes, or regimes with narrow bands, have been discredited by the 1992 and 1993 EMS crises. I agree with this. The point is made strongly in *Eichengreen (1994)* and *Corden (1994)* and is coming to be widely accepted, especially since the Mexican crisis. If a country does not choose to join a monetary union nor establish a currency board, a highly flexible exchange rate regime (which does not rule out some intervention or short-term fixing, or even very wide bands) is inevitable.

They then come to the issue that troubled the French after the devaluations of sterling, the lira and the peseta in 1992: if the outsiders have flexible exchange rate regimes of some kind, will they not be able to obtain unfair advantages through "competitive depreciations" ?

The argument common at present in EMU debates is that floating or flexible exchange rates are incompatible with the maintenance of free trade. The countries that lose competitiveness as a result of exchange rate changes - that is, the countries whose exchange rates appreciate relative to their trading partners - will be tempted to reimpose trade restrictions. Hence the survival of the Single Market is threatened. In commenting on this view, the authors also make a correct point. The devaluations of 1992 simply offset earlier real appreciations of sterling, the lira and the peseta resulting from higher inflation rates in the United Kingdom, Italy and Spain relatively to France and Germany - even though the devaluations may have overshot to some extent. These three countries had been gradually losing competitiveness, and in 1992 competitiveness had been restored. If a country such as France felt tempted to impose trade restrictions as a result of the 1992 devaluations (which would, of course, be in breach of the Treaty) one might ask why the three countries that had earlier been losing competitiveness could not also have imposed trade restrictions, using the same argument.

The psychology of the French argument is easy to understand. The argument was also used in some earlier years in Germany in connection with dollar devaluations. When French (or German) competitiveness gradually improves owing to relatively lower French inflation rates this is seen as a reward for virtue - a reward for an admirable monetary policy that has achieved low inflation. It may also be seen as a sign of the high productivity level and general competence of French exporters. When Italian competitiveness is subsequently restored by depreciation of the lira, this is seen as an unfair use of the exchange rate instrument. Given this psychology, the lesson is to avoid jerky exchange rate changes - in other words, to avoid fixed but adjustable regimes which inevitably lead at intervals to large devaluations or depreciations forced by the market.

A distinction must be made between a depreciation that is brought about in the market as a result of changes in market expectations, and one that is deliberately brought about by monetary policy, perhaps combined with some direct official intervention in the market. In both cases "competitiveness" improves, but only in the second case can one say that the depreciation was a deliberate act of policy.

It is the first case that seems to me relevant for the European situation. In a floating rate regime market forces move the exchange rate around, sometimes appreciating it and sometimes depreciating it, and so bring about erratic changes and fluctuations in competitiveness that do not necessarily reflect fundamentals. Uncertainty is created. Whenever a country's exchange rate appreciates relative to trading partners, the result is perceived as "unfair", and pressures for reimposing protection could result. Elsewhere (in *Corden, 1994*) I have labeled the second case "exchange rate protection". A country devalues (or fails to appreciate) and engages in fiscal contraction (or fails to expand sufficiently) in order to generate current account surpluses that favor its tradable sectors relative to its nontradables. Japan and Taiwan have often been accused in the United States of such policies, the claim being that the reasons for these countries' surpluses were not their high private savings ratios but rather a deliberate policy designed to favor their tradable-producing industries.

2. How Would Monetary Expansion Affect the Current Account?

The authors observe that monetary expansion is the way in which competitive depreciation can be deliberately brought about in a floating rate regime with high capital mobility. They are thinking of the second case here. Monetary expansion will depreciate the exchange rate, and presumably that will strengthen a country's "competitiveness" and so have an adverse effect on the export industries of its trading partners. The authors then add the correct point that a monetary expansion could also lead, quite separately, to a demand expansion that will have an offsetting effect - namely worsen the current account of the home country and so increase the exports of trading partners. In other words, the competitiveness or "switching" effect will improve the home country's current account while a demand expansion effect will worsen it. On balance the current account might deteriorate and it is not difficult to find cases where this has been so. Thus trading partners' current accounts might actually improve. If it is indeed so, then trading partners (or, at least, their export industries) should not be concerned about the home country's "competitive depreciation" brought about by monetary expansion. They should welcome the monetary expansion of the home country even though such expansion improves the latter's "competitiveness". To give an example, French exporters may well, on balance, have benefited from the economic recovery in Britain (or avoidance of recession) that resulted from the decision to leave the ERM.

Now the question is: in what circumstances will a monetary expansion lead to a domestic demand expansion? In the simple Mundell-Fleming small country model a demand expansion will *not* result from monetary expansion. The domestic rate of interest stays equal to the given foreign rate of interest and investment just depends on the rate of interest. The exchange rate will depreciate and (assuming the Keynesian case of under-employed resources initially) the current account must improve. Expenditure will stay constant while output and income rises. But the answer changes immediately when this model is modified to allow for imperfect substitutability of foreign and domestic financial assets, so that the domestic interest can diverge from the given foreign interest rate.

We then get the portfolio balance model generally associated with Branson (see, for example, *Branson, 1979*). A monetary expansion leads to some decline in the domestic interest rate. This decline will raise investment and thus lead to a demand expansion. The net result could then be an improvement or a worsening of the current account. One would get the same result when there is imperfect capital mobility owing to some controls. It is surely realistic to suppose that, even with high international capital mobility and no effect on the world interest rate, a monetary expansion will lead to some decline in the domestic interest rate and then demand expansion. (At this point I ignore effects on inflationary expectations). It seems likely that in the short run (when elasticities in international trade are low) the demand effect would outweigh the switching effect, but in time the balance could go the other way. Hence the current account might at first worsen and then improve.

The authors do not refer to the portfolio balance model, but rather introduce another mechanism through which a monetary expansion might lead to a demand expansion. They argue that investment might rise not because the interest rate falls (as in the Branson model) but because of improved profit expectations generated by the prospects of improved competitiveness. That is indeed possible. But there is an alternative possibility which is also plausible. Monetary expansion is likely to increase inflationary expectations which, for various reasons, may have an adverse effect on real profit expectations and thus may actually reduce investment.

Here I should add an additional thought. If a country really wanted to improve its current account through depreciation but also wished to avoid any offsetting effect through demand expansion it should associate monetary expansion with some fiscal contraction.

3. The Central Issue: Is a Flexible Exchange Rate Regime Favorable or Unfavorable for Preserving Free Trade?

I come now to an issue which seems to me very relevant here, and which is both important and of intellectual interest but which the authors do not refer to. (This issue *is* discussed in *Corden,1994* and *Eichengreen, 1996*). How can the following two arguments be reconciled?

On the one hand, there is the argument discussed here. It is said that the preservation of free trade - that is, of the Single Market in the European context - requires or is helped by a fixed exchange rate regime or monetary union. Floating or flexible exchange rates lead to pressures for protection in the countries whose currencies appreciate. In the European Community they might lead to the reimposition of direct or (more likely) indirect trade interventions. This line of thought has now become one of the principal arguments commonly used in favor of European monetary union. Furthermore, the view that floating rates generate protectionism was certainly held in the United States from 1983 to 1985 when the dollar appreciated sharply and pressures for protection intensified. A concern over the revival of protectionism in the United States motivated the Plaza Agreement of 1985 that was designed to depreciate the dollar by means of coordinated intervention.

On the other hand, there is a venerable argument going back to the Bretton Woods era and still widely applied to developing countries which leads to exactly the opposite conclusion: fixed exchange rate regimes lead to protectionism while flexible exchange rate regimes make possible trade liberalization. The empirical evidence for this view is very strong. When a country suffers an adverse external shock and wishes to avoid excessive domestic deflation, it must accompany a reduction in absorption with a "switching" policy. One such policy is devaluation; if it is unable to, or does not wish to, devalue, it will impose or tighten import restrictions instead. Before 1973 a standard argument in favor of exchange rate flexibility was that it would allow countries to avoid the use of import restrictions for balance of payments purposes.

In the current European context, this argument would say that, when a member of the monetary union suffers an adverse shock not shared with other members - that is, an asymmetrical shock - it will be compelled to accept an adjustment through deflation, and in order to moderate the effects of deflation it will be tempted to impose trade restrictions, possibly in various indirect ways. This reaction would be avoided if it were free to devalue.

How can these two views about the effects of the exchange rate regime on pressures for protection be reconciled? I shall not pursue this in depth here, since there is not time and a rigorous analysis has to be fairly elaborate. The answer seems to hinge on two considerations - first, the likelihood of asymmetric shocks combined with downward nominal wage rigidity, and secondly on whether a change in an exchange rate in a flexible rate regime is perceived as a movement in an equilibrating direction, and hence is accepted as equitable in the appreciating country, or whether it is seen as a disequilibrium change, or as unfair, and thus generates a protectionist reaction.

My own inclination is to suggest that the decision whether to form or join a EMU should *not* be governed or greatly influenced by concern with preservation of the Single Market. Areas of free trade can certainly coincide with areas of monetary integration. Indeed, this is the case in most or all countries now. But an area of free trade is also compatible with floating or flexible exchange rates. The best example of the latter is the relationship between Canada and the United States. These two countries have been very open to each other in trade for many years, even before the North American Free Trade Agreement. Of course, there was not complete free trade. At the same time the Canadian dollar has floated relative to the US dollar well before generalized floating in 1973. What one can say is that a regime of fixed but adjustable exchange rates, where exchange rates change sharply and significantly at intervals, is likely to put maximum pressure on a free trade system.

References

BRANSON, W.H. (1979), Exchange Rate Dynamics and Monetary Policy, in: Lindbeck, A., ed. (1979), Inflation and Employment in Open Economies, Amsterdam: North-Holland.

CORDEN, W. M. (1994), Economic Policy, Exchange Rates, and the International System, Oxford: Oxford University Press.

EICHENGREEN, B. (1994), International Monetary Arrangements for the 21st Century, Washington DC: The Brookings Institution.

EICHENGREEN, B. (1996), A More Perfect Union? On the Logic of Economic Integration (The Graham Lecture). Princeton: International Finance Section, Princeton University.

II. Financial Markets and Monetary Policy

C. Foreign Exchange Vehicles Before and After EMU: From Dollar/Mark to Dollar/Euro?

Philipp Hartmann[1]

1. Introduction

The present paper analyzes the phenomenon of media of exchange in the foreign exchange (forex) market in general and then looks at the potential of the euro, as the future single currency of the European Union, to become such a *foreign exchange vehicle* in particular. The forex vehicle function is one dimension of an international medium of exchange. As first described clearly by *Swoboda (1969)*, in a world with N national moneys only a small number of the N(N-1)/2 potential bilateral currency markets is actually open and most of the "cross-currency" transactions is performed through a medium of exchange, the forex vehicle. For example, at the present time the exchange of Canadian dollar (CAD) against Swiss franc (CHF) is most often broken down into two transactions - each one involving the US dollar (USD) - CAD/USD and USD/CHF.[2] However, a forex vehicle does *not* have to be unique (*Hartmann, 1994*). In today's forex markets a Danish kroner (DKK)/French franc (FRF) transaction usually goes through the Deutsche mark (DEM) - DKR/DEM and DEM/FRF - and *not* through the USD (*Danmarks Nationalbank, 1992*). It is important to notice that the roles of the dollar and the mark in these examples are a question of the internal organisation (exchange structure) of the forex market, which differs from the original payments structure in international trade and investment (*Krugman, 1980*).

Of course, the forex vehicle function is not the only medium of exchange function of an international currency. As illustrated in table C.1, international currencies can perform exchange media roles in at least four different ways. By official institutions, most frequently central banks, they can be used as intervention currencies in the forex market. In the use of private agents they can substitute the domestic currency as the local medium of exchange in foreign countries (direct currency substitution; *Giovannini and Turtelboom, 1994*), or play the role of goods exchange medium in international trade (foreign trade vehicles) or currency exchange medium (forex vehicles).

These functions are not unrelated. For example, a decrease of dollar invoicing in international trade reduces dollar forex trading volume, which may also affect its importance as a forex vehicle. Or, when the Australian Reserve Bank wants to prevent the Australian dollar (AUD) from depreciating, then it is most likely to intervene in the AUD/USD market, since the American currency is the forex vehicle for its domestic currency and arbitrage activity by forex dealers will therefore ensure that a change of the AUD/USD rate translates into similar changes of all the other AUD rates. These interdependencies nonwithstanding the present paper will mainly focus on the forex vehicle function alone. Although the mere size of global forex markets (*BIS, 1993, 1995*) and their impacts on national economies prove its importance, this function has not yet attracted as much attention as the other international medium of exchange functions.

Table C.1: Medium of Exchange Functions of International Currencies

	Private use			Official use
Int. medium of exch. function	Substitution currency	Foreign trade vehicle	Forex vehicle	Intervention currency

I proceed as follows. In the next section I illustrate different exchange structures in the global forex market and discuss recent changes in this structure, in particular through the emergence of the Deutsche mark as a competing vehicle currency. In section 3 I sketch a theory, which can explain different exchange structures through micro-structure theory and transaction costs. Section 4 addresses the issue of network externalities in the use of forex vehicles - the fact that the more a medium of exchange is already used the more attractive it becomes to be used even further - from an empirical point of view. The network externality hypothesis is tested by estimating the impact of expected trading volume on transaction costs. Then, the findings in the preceding sections together with forex turnover data, as aggregated by the Bank for

International Settlements (*BIS, 1993*), are employed to estimate the effect of full European Monetary Union (EMU) on the forex exchange structure. These estimations illustrate the potential of the euro to become a vehicle currency upon its introduction with EMU.[3]

2. The Exchange Structure in the Foreign Exchange Market Before EMU

The exchange structure of the forex market can be understood as a network between currencies. One representation is in terms of graphs, as in figure C.1. The currencies are the nodes (USD, DEM etc.), *liquid* bilateral markets are the arcs connecting the nodes with each other. Some bilateral markets may be illiquid (no arc), such as that for Japanese yen (JPY) against CAD in figure C.1.[4] Exchanging these two currencies implies two transactions through two liquid markets, JPY/USD and USD/CAD. The theory sketched in the next section will explain such exchange patterns through the transaction costs of going through a direct bilateral market as compared to the the sum of the transaction costs of using several bilateral markets (indirect exchange).

Figure C.1: "Polar" Forex Market

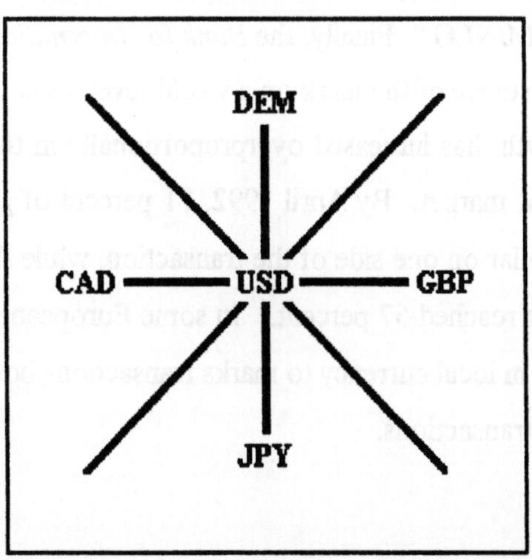

The exchange pattern outlined in figure C.1 describes the basic structure of the foreign exchange market in the 1960s (*Aliber, 1969; Swoboda, 1969*), the 1970s (*Kenen, 1983*) and, at least, the early 1980s (*Black, 1991*). The dollar is the single vehicle currency. Most other "cross-currency" transactions are exercised indirectly involving two USD transactions. Non-USD transactions are a small residual. For example, *Kenen (1983)* estimated that between 90 and 99 percent of all interbank foreign exchange turnover in 1980 had the dollar on one side of the transaction. However, *Black (1991)* observed that the USD share was decreasing in the course of the 1980s.

By the early 1990s the general pattern showed a change. The *Banque de France (1993)* writes in its monthly bulletin: "La progression de la part relative des transactions en DEM/FRF ... confirme les progrès réalisés en matière d'intégration économique et financière européenne. Par ailleurs, elle consacre *le rôle du mark comme monnaie véhiculaire pour les opérations faisant jouer les devises du SME*. Le fait que *la devise allemande ait largement supplanté le dollar dans cette fonction* est reflété par la fraction très substantielle des opérations réalisées au comptant (85 % du total)."[5] Similarly, one reads in Danmarks Nationalbank's Monetary Review (*Danmarks Nationalbank, 1992*): "The great significance of the D-mark reflects that by far the majority of transactions in Danish kroner against other European currencies are made via the D-mark. DKK/NLG trading is thus most often broken down as DKK/DEM and DEM/NLG." Finally, the *Bank for International Settlements (1993)* reports that the importance of the mark on a world level, as compared to US dollar or global volume growth, has increased overproportionally in the last couple of years, especially in the spot market. By April 1992, 71 percent of global *inter-dealer spot* turnover had the dollar on one side of the transaction, while the share of mark inter-dealer spot turnover reached 57 percent.[6] In some European small-to-medium-sized markets the business in local currency to marks transactions now exceeds that of local currencies to dollar transactions.

Figure C.2: Current Structure of Exchange in the Forex Market

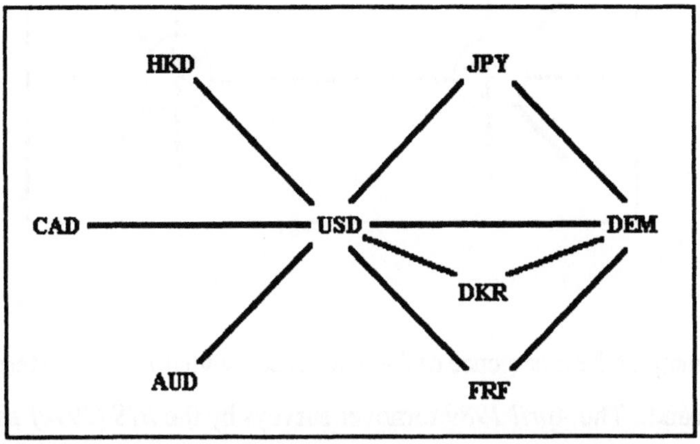

This evidence indicates that by 1992 the DEM has taken over as a vehicle currency in *intra-European* spot forex trading. The current structure of exchange is illustrated in figure C.2. There are two vehicle currencies, the dollar and the mark. However, their respective position is different. While the dollar has relatively liquid markets with practically all other currencies - serving as a global vehicle currency -, the mark's role as a vehicle is largely limited to European currencies. For example DKK/FRF is mainly exchanged through the DEM, while DKK/CAD is mainly exchanged through the dollar. At the current stage there does not seem to be evidence on any currency being connected to all the other currencies through the mark alone (*BIS, 1993*).[7] A "strictly bipolar" system, as illustrated in figure C.3, has *not* (yet) emerged.[8] I also note in passing that there is no evidence either that the yen has gained the role of a vehicle currency in Asian forex trading. In that region the dollar is still predominating and the mark plays a much less important role (*BIS, 1993; Bank of Japan, 1993, 1996*). Therefore, a move to a "tripolar" currency system (*Alogoskoufis and Portes, 1993*) is not visible in the *forex market* at present, but cannot be excluded for the future.

Figure C.3: "Strictly Bipolar" Forex Market

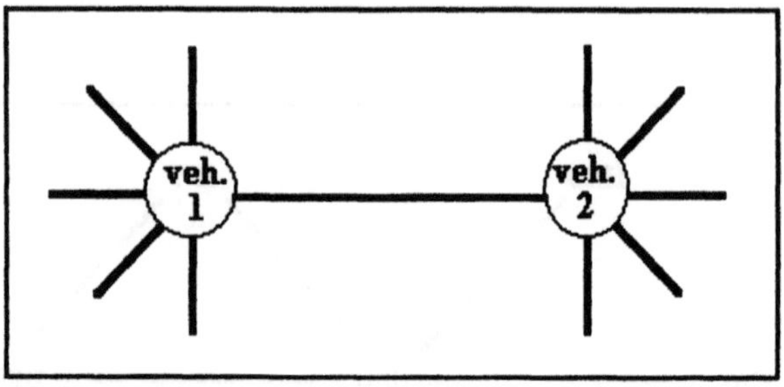

The exact timing of the emergence of the mark is somewhat hard to determine from the evidence at hand. The *April 1989* turnover surveys by the *BIS (1990)* and 19 national central banks do not indicate vehicle use of the mark, but it has to be emphasized that the Bundesbank did not participate in this survey implying some underestimation of DEM trading volume at that time. As will be discussed in more detail below, two major determinants of the potential of a currency to become a forex vehicle are high trading volume and low exchange rate volatility. Another factor, which is not addressed in this paper though, are large and sophisticated domestic financial markets. All three factors seem to have contributed to the emergence of the mark. The creation of the European Monetary System (EMS) in 1978 meant low exchange rate variability of the mark - the currency of the most important trading nation in the European Community - with respect to many other European currencies during the 1980s (*Giavazzi and Giovannini, 1989*). The liberalisation of capital markets in the second half of the 1980s (*Tavlas, 1991*) meant an evolution to greater depth and width of German financial markets. An important development, which may have lifted the mark to todays' status, is related to the phenomenon of convergence trading in Europe at the end of the 1980s and at the beginning of the 1990s (*Group of Ten, 1993*, pp. 10-12, 46f.). In this period many international investors took short positions in DEM in order to benefit from interest rate differentials with other European currencies, believing that there was low realignment risk. This increased the trading activity in the mark culminating in the reversal of these positions and the EMS crises of the early 1990s. Although there is no hard evidence to test that hypothesis, convergence trading and its consequences may have produced the *lock-out* which permitted the forex exchange structure to shift to an equilibrium with the mark as a second, but regional, vehicle currency.

3. Theory of Foreign Exchange Vehicle Currencies

In this section I am presenting a drastically simplified version of the forex vehicle theory developed by *Black (1991)* and *Hartmann (1994, 1996b).* I proceed in two steps. First, transaction costs for each bilateral market are derived from a simple dealer spread model of the Black type and, second, possible exchange structures resulting from these transaction costs are illustrated. In the following section I am going to argue that in spite of the drastic simplifications in the dealer model its two essential predictions are empirically valid.

3.1 Dealer Spreads and Trading Volumes

Consider a bilateral market between currency i and currency j. Let x_{ij} denote the total expected transaction volume in this market and σ_{ij} the expected volatility of the short-run exchange rate in the current trading period, which implies inventory holding costs for a forex dealer making this market. Following *Black (1991)* I assume σ_{ij} to be independent of x_{ij}.[9] The expected long-run exchange rate remains unchanged during this period, but may vary according to a random walk (or another stochastic process) from one period to the other (*Meese and Rogoff, 1983*). The expected profit of the dealer for this period is

$$\pi_{ij}=s_{ij}x_{ij}-\alpha_{ij}\sigma_{ij}\,, \tag{1}$$

where s_{ij} is the (appropriately normalized) dealer spread, the difference between ask rate and bid rate - his choice variable -, which is set symmetrically around the expected long-run exchange rate. α_{ij} is a parameter.

Consider a profit maximizing risk neutral representative dealer in a competitive environment. This dealer will have to set s_{ij} on a level such that his profits vanish ($\pi^*_{ij}[s^*_{ij}]=0$). As a consequence his optimal spread s^*_{ij} varies inversely with the expected trading volume in this market.

$$s^*_{ij}=\frac{\alpha_{ij}\sigma_{ij}}{x_{ij}} \tag{2}$$

Moreover expected exchange rate volatility increases the spread.

Of course, forex spreads may not only reflect inventory holding costs but also order processing and asymmetric information costs (*Flood, 1991; Shastri, 1992*). Order processing costs could be incorporated in the present framework without changing anything substantial for the reasoning below (*Hartmann, 1996b*). As shown in *Bessembinder (1994)* and the next section information costs for dealers are of transitory nature and should therefore have only minor impacts on the emergence of vehicle currencies.

3.2 Structures of Currency Exchange

In order to analyze the phenomenon of vehicle currencies we have to allow for N>2 currencies. Then the exchange structure in the market depends on the spreads in all bilateral markets. In particular for some currency k, the market ij is exchanged directly or indirectly (through k) depending on the spreads in the ij, ik, and kj markets.

$$s^*_{ij} \lesseqgtr s^*_{ik}+s^*_{kj} \tag{3}$$

If the left hand side is larger than the right hand side, then k becomes a vehicle currency. Any transaction, which was originally intended to be i against j is now done in two steps, i against k and then k against j. In other words, all the ij-volume x_{ij} switches to the ik and kj markets, such that the *final* trading volumes (z) become

$z_{ij}=0<x_{ij}$ and $z_{ik}=x_{ik}+x_{ij}$ and $z_{kj}=x_{kj}+x_{ij}$. Following *Krugman's (1980)* terminology, the matrix of originally desired transaction volumes $X=(x_{ij})$ may be named the *structure of payments*, resulting from international trade and investment, and the matrix $Z=(z_{ij})$ may be named the *structure of exchange* in the forex market.

I define a forex market equilibrium, as a (symmetric) matrix of spreads S^*, such that no dealer has an incentive to deviate from the optimal spread s^*_{ij} he has chosen, given the pricing of all the other dealers s^*_{-ij}. Moreover, all the incumbent dealers face the threat of entry by outside dealers in formerly closed markets ($z_{ij}=0$). Formerly outside dealers will reactivate such a market, if they can attract enough volume to make a strictly positive profit. However, reopening a formerly closed market involves some set-up costs γ_{ij} for the entering dealer. For the incumbent dealers these set-up costs are sunk and they only incur the inventory cost of running their market σ_{ij}. Positive set-up costs introduce some inertia in the structure of exchange.

Figure C.4: Equilibrium with a Single Vehicle Currency in a Symmetric Forex Market

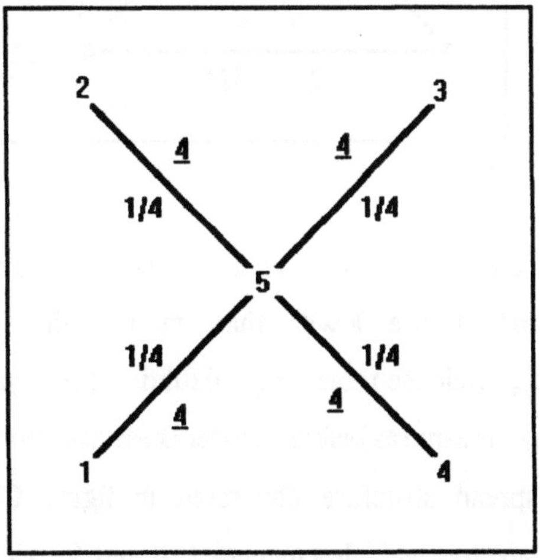

Consider the following "naive" forex market with N=5 currencies: $x_{ij}=1=\alpha_{ij}\sigma_{ij}=\gamma_{ij}$. The number 5 is chosen, because I ultimately aim at equilibria with two vehicle currencies. It is readily verified that the exchange structure illustrated in figure C.4, with currency

5 being the unique vehicle currency, is a forex market equilibrium, as defined above. All transactions are exchanged with or through currency 5. The 5-markets are the only ones actually open and "cross-currency" markets cannot be profitably opened by dealers undercutting the spreads for transactions through the 5-markets. In this particular example the strict symmetry makes the choice of the vehicle currency arbitrary. Any other currency could take the place of 5.

Figure C.5: Equilibrium in an Asymmetric Forex Market with two Vehicle Currencies

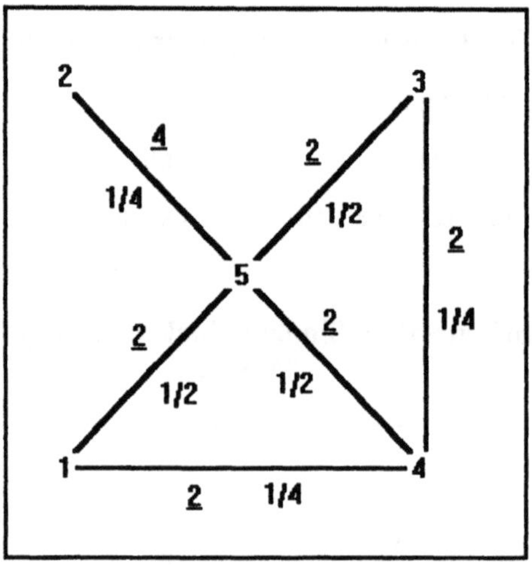

Now let us introduce some asymmetry in exchange rate volatilities. Volatilities among currencies 1, 3, and 4 are lower than in the first example above, say $\alpha_{13}\sigma_{13}=\frac{1}{2}=\alpha_{14}\sigma_{14}=\alpha_{34}\sigma_{34}$, while the remaining volatilities, the payments structure as well as the set-up costs stay the same as before. Under these assumptions I hypothesize that the exchange and spread structure illustrated in figure C.5 is a forex market equilibrium. There are two vehicle currencies, 4 and 5. Currency 2 is exchanged through 5 alone, while currencies 1 and 3 are exchanged against each other through 4. In order to check the sustainability of this structure as an equilibrium two tests need to be undertaken. First, given all the spreads can any bilateral currency exchange be made with lower transaction costs than with the exchange chains hypothesized in figure C.5?

The answer is no. For example exchanging 1 against 3 through 5 would cost ½+½=1 unit, while exchanging 1 against 3 through 4 costs only ¼+¼=½ of a unit. Hence all 1,3 transactions pass through 4.

The second test is a little bit more tricky. Here the question is: Can any one dealer, by setting a different spread or entering a formerly closed market - and taking the other dealers' spreads as given - change the exchange structure such that he realizes a positive profit. It is somewhat cumbersome but straightforward to check that the answer is, again, no. For example, it is impossible to open the 1,2 or the 2,3 market. Similarly, the representative 1,5 and 4,5 dealers cannot sustainably reduce their spread to steer 1,4 volume through 5. The structural similarity between figures C.2 and C.5 is apparent. Therefore we have just shown that exchange structures with two vehicle currencies of quite different status can be sustained as equilibria in the model.

However, as can be easily checked, some asymmetry is necessary for that result. Of course, this asymmetry need not be in volatilities. It can be of a different nature, for example through an asymmetric structure of payments X or asymmetric set-up costs Γ. Although it would also be possible to derive similar or different exchange patterns than those in figures C.4 and C.5 with different assumptions on the exogenous variables of the model, I do not pursue this any further, because the present examples sufficiently illustrate the forex exchange structures discussed in section 2.

Instead I turn to the *choice* of vehicle currencies. The model also illustrates several important factors, which will foster the potential of a currency to become a forex vehicle. This is, first of all, the wide use of this currency in international trade invoicing and international asset denomination, which makes for the structure of payments (X). Second of all, high exchange rate volatility is a factor detrimental for vehicle use. Finally, the cost of changing the structure of exchange (opening of new markets, inertia) together with the increased trading in vehicles and the resulting reduction in transaction costs (network externalities) imply self-fulfiling forces, which give currencies already established as vehicles a competitive advantage over newcoming currencies.

4. Testing for Network Externalities in the Use of Exchange Media

An important element in the theory sketched in the previous section is of course the negative relation between expected trading volumes and forex bid-ask spreads. In this section I provide a test, which shows that both predictions made by the spread model above are empirically valid, the volume-spread as well as the volatility-spread relation. The empirical significance of the negative volume effect reinforces the case for network externalities in the use of forex vehicles. The more a currency is used as a vehicle, the higher its trading volume, the lower the exchange cost through it.

The data used are 5 years of business daily spreads, volatilities, and volumes from the USD/JPY spot market (January 1990 through January 1995, 1246 observations in all). Daily spreads (s_t) are measured as the "tick-by-tick" average of quotes on the Reuters FXFX page between opening and closing of the Tokyo market.[10] Daily volatility (σ_t) is measured as the half-hourly average of absolute middle price changes between opening and closing. Trading volume is that reported by all Tokyo forex brokers to the Bank of Japan for the same interval.

In order to derive an empirically well specified equation I have to extend the spread model (1) in two respects. First, I have to account for some weekly seasonality observed in forex data (*Bessembinder, 1994; Guillaume et al., 1994*). This I do by introducing weekend (w_t) and holiday (h_t) dummies in the equation to be tested. Second, I have to control for information asymmetry effects on bid-ask spreads (*Bagehot, 1971; Glosten and Milgrom, 1985*). The risk to trade with a better informed agent will make dealers increase spreads, when they think that information has been released that they still do not know. According to the mixture of distributions hypothesis daily trading intensity and daily price change are jointly driven by the rate of information arrival during the day (*Clark, 1973*). However, using plain volume as a measure of information arrival risks mixing the positive spread impact of information related volume with the negative spread impact of expected volume derived above (equation (2)). Therefore I fit an ARIMA(9,1,1) on volumes and extract the predictable component (x_t^p) from it to measure expected volume. To measure predictable ("expected") volatility (σ_t^p) I employ a standard GARCH(1,1) specification

(*Bollerslev et al., 1992*).

Then it is claimed that new information cannot be reflected in *predictable* volumes and volatilities, but only in the unpredictable parts. Since the mixture of distributions hypothesis implies that unpredictable volumes and volatilities are highly correlated, I choose only *unpredictable volatility* (σ_t^u) as the measure of asymmetric information costs and exclude unpredictable volume. This is different from *Bessembinder (1994)*, *Jorion (1994)* and *Hartmann (1996a)*, who use unpredictable *volume* and exclude unpredictable volatility. Equation (4) gives the final specification. The equation is estimated with *Hansen's (1982)* heteroscedasticity- and

$$s_t = \beta_0 + \beta_1 x_t^p + \beta_2 \sigma_t^p + \beta_3 \sigma_t^u + \beta_4 w_t + \beta_5 h_t + \varepsilon_t , \quad \varepsilon \sim (0, \Sigma) \tag{4}$$

autocorrelation-consistent Generalized Method of Moments (GMM) estimator with first, second, and third moments as instruments. This gives six degrees of freedom to undertake Hansen's test of the overidentifying restrictions against general misspecification. Autocorrelation correction is done for 20 lags. All variables are in logs to allow for the non-linearities suggested by (1).

Table C.2 summarizes the results found. The predictions of the spread theory seem to be confirmed. In particular, the estimated parameter of predictable volume is negative and significant at the level of 1 percent. This result provides strong evidence in favor of network externalities in the use of vehicle currencies. Inventory and information cost effects through predictable and unpredictable exchange rate volatility are highly significant as well. Weekend effects on spreads are statistically strong, while holiday effects are statistically weak. The test of the overidentifying restriction cannot reject the specification at 10 percent significance. A negative intercept parameter, which has no interpretation, is not reported in the table. Similar estimations were also undertaken with yearly intercept dummies and for the five yearly subperiods separately. In none of these cases slope parameters were significantly changed.

Table C.2: GMM Estimation of Equation (4)

Parameter	β_1	β_2	β_3	β_4	β_5
Estimation	-5.0	25.8	9.8	0.1	0.2
Asy. t-stat.	-2.5	7.8	12.0	3.0	1.5
Test of the overidentifying restrictions: $\chi^2(6)$=9.0 [0.17] adjusted R^2: 0.11					

Notice that, thanks to the volume and volatility decompositions, the volume parameter β_1 has the opposite sign from that found by *Glassman (1987)*, who regressed spreads on *plain* forex futures volumes. However, interpreting the results as evidence in favor of the existence of network externalities also requires a word of caution. In my sample there is a positive correlation between predictable volume and predictable volatility, the coefficient of correlation between these two variables is ρ=0.32. Hence, in the case of certain currencies the primary negative effect of predictable volume on spreads might be compensated by a secondary volume-volatility-spread effect, which cannot be identified from the specification chosen above.

5. The Exchange Structure of the Foreign Exchange Market After EMU: Which Role for the Euro?

The results of the previous two sections together can now be used to interpret scenarios on the structure of exchange in the forex market after the introduction of a single European currency, planned to begin on 1 January 1999 (*European Council, 1992, 1995*). Scenarios on trading volumes can be derived from the *BIS (1993)* turnover survey. I ignore transitional issues here, for example about how quickly all national currencies will effectively be replaced by the euro. Instead I make different assumptions about which countries will join the single currency and assume that there will not be a forex market for the exchange of EMU member currencies against each other any more. Hence, the numbers reported are scenarios for the time when full monetary union is completed 2002 or later.

In order to analyze the possible impact of EMU on the spot forex market it is useful to decompose trading volume in three components. The first one is purely intra-European trading, which I define here to be the turnover between the national currencies of the countries actually participating in EMU (intra-EMU trading). The second one is forex turnover between EMU currencies and currencies of the rest of the world (ROW). And finally, there is intra-ROW trading. Total pre-EMU world forex trade is the sum of intra-EMU, EMU-ROW and intra-ROW turnover; total post-EMU trading volume is the sum of the second and the third component alone. I assume that the switch to the euro is done at current exchange rates with the euro at par with its predecessor, the ecu (*European Council, 1992, 1995*). The first component is simply erased by EMU. The second one switches from EMU-ROW currencies to euro-ROW currencies. The last bit remains unchanged.

At the present time there is some uncertainty about which countries will be members of EMU.[11] However, different assumptions about the "ins" and the "outs" will result in different intra-EMU and EMU-ROW trading volumes. Therefore, I shall, in what follows, compute post-EMU forex turnovers for 6 different scenarios about the "ins" and the "outs", which are listed in column 1 of table C.3. "No EMU" stands for the status quo in April 1992 (no "ins"). "Core EMU" assumes that only countries, which perform reasonably well, as measured by their success to meet the Maastricht criteria (except maybe the budget criterion), are "in". "EMS 1995" means that all countries, which were members of the EMS in 1995 are "in", while "EMS 1992" means that all EMS members *before* the 1992 exchange crisis qualify for EMU. The remaining two scenarios assume that all European Union (EU) countries are "in", in one case excluding the UK and in the other case including the UK.

In the rest of table C.3 the trading volumes from the *BIS (1993)* turnover survey from April 1992 are used to compute hypothetical spot turnovers (inter-dealer *and* dealer-customer), if the switch to the single European currency would have happened around that date. Only the second row contains the actual turnovers in 1992 (without EMU). More recent data from the latest turnover survey are not yet available with the necesary detail to undertake this estimation for a later date (*BIS, 1995*). The survey covers the turnovers in 26 important forex trading centres, with the United Kingdom being the largest and Greece being the smallest.

Table C.3: Changes in the Level and Currency Composition of Spot Forex Trading Through European Monetary Union

EMU scenarios	USD volume		DEM volume		Elim. EU volume		Euro volume		JPY volume		Global volume	
("ins"/"outs")	bio USD	%	bio USD	%	bio USD	%[5]	bio USD	%	bio USD	%	bio USD	%[6]
No EMU (4/92)	283.8	72.1	209.3	53.2	0.0	0.0	(11.7)[1]	(3.0)[1]	79.2	20.1	393.7	200.0
Core EMU[2]	283.8	76.0	0.0	0.0	20.3	5.2	200.2	53.6	79.2	21.2	373.5	200.0
EMS 1995[3]	283.8	76.8	0.0	0.0	24.1	6.1	198.0	53.6	79.2	21.4	369.6	200.0
EMS 1992[4]	283.8	82.1	0.0	0.0	48.1	12.2	212.8	61.6	79.2	22.9	345.6	200.0
Full EU (no UK)	283.8	78.3	0.0	0.0	31.4	8.0	197.7	54.6	79.2	21.8	362.3	200.0
Full EU (w. UK)	283.8	83.1	0.0	0.0	52.1	13.2	211.9	62.0	79.2	23.2	341.7	200.0

Notes: Own calculations from BIS (1993) and national surveys provided by central banks. Numbers based on daily averages over April 1992.
1) Ecu volumes.
2) Austria, Belgium, France, Germany, Luxemburg, Netherlands.
3) Austria, Belgium, Denmark, France, Germany, Greece, Ireland, Italy, Luxemburg, Netherlands, Portugal, Spain.
4) Belgium, Denmark, France, Germany, Ireland, Luxemburg, Netherlands, Portugal, Spain, United Kingdom.
5) Percent of pre-EMU volume (393.7 bio USD)
6) Global volume adds up to 200 percent, because any forex transaction involves two currencies.

The table contains levels of spot trading volumes in USD, DEM, JPY as well as their shares in total spot volume. In columns 4 and 5 I estimate the level of intra-EMU trading volume eliminated through the currency unification and the hypothetical spot trading volume in euro after the switch. Trivially, the first impact of EMU is an overall reduction of world spot forex trading. This reduction is most important (52 bio USD, 13 percent pre-EMU turnover) when the whole EU participates in EMU. It is the lowest (20 bio USD, 5 percent), when only core countries qualify. Although the *levels* of USD and JPY volumes remain unaffected, the reductions in global volumes imply increases in their share of total spot volume from 72 percent to 76-83 percent for the USD and from 20 percent to 21-23 percent for the JPY.

Before EMU 53 percent of overall spot trading had the DEM on one side of the transaction and the ecu accounted for only 3 percent of trading. After EMU euro trading covers a larger *percentage share* of the whole market than DEM trading before. With all EU countries in EMU euro trading would be highest with 62 percent, while with a core EMU euro trading (54 percent) would have only a slightly larger share than the DEM before EMU. Based on these estimations, the *absolute levels* of euro trading would not be very different from those of the DEM before EMU. Under full EU and EMS 1992 it would be slightly higher, in the other cases it would be lower. In other words, the elimination of intra-EMU trading ("lost" for the euro) offsets most of the EMU-external volume "gained" for the euro through the currency unification.

The fact that intra-EMU trading lost is able to offset the increase in EMU-external trading switching to the euro has largely to do with the importance of the DEM as a vehicle for intra-European trading (section 2). In contrast most of USD vehicle transactions are not removed since, to a large extent, they happen outside of the EU. USD turnovers in table C.3 contain much vehicle volume, while euro turnovers contain very little vehicle volume as "inherited" from the DEM.

Of course the scenarios in table C.3 all make use of the drastic simplification that the international structure of payments remains unchanged through EMU. Moreover, it is assumed that there are no qualitative changes in the structure of exchange outside of the EMU area, except the unification of several bilateral markets. That is to say, although the volumes in EMU-ROW currency pairs switch all to the euro, no prediction is made whether this will lead to any secondary switches in the exchange structure, such as the establishment of, say, a liquid CAD/euro market or euro vehicle use replacing bilateral ROW markets (figure C.2).[12]

Concrete predictions about these secondary switches are very difficult. However, in cases of currencies where currently a liquid USD as well as a liquid DEM market exist, the higher bilateral turnover through the switch to the euro is apparent. For example, total CHF/DEM spot trading was 11519.8 bio USD in 1992, total CHF/euro trading would have been 13756.6 bio USD with full EMU. Norwegian kroner (NOK)/DEM trading was 326.2 bio USD and NOK/euro would have been 410.2 bio USD. In the light of Sections III and IV these examples may illustrate the *potential* of the euro to become a forex vehicle for ROW currencies, and therefore challenge to some extent the USD's role. This potential is of course highest for trading between European non-EMU currencies. Central and Eastern European as well as African currencies may also be exchanged through the euro, given that they develop more or less free private markets for foreign exchange. Knowing the current strength of the dollar in the Americas and Asia the chances of the euro as a forex vehicle in these two regions look rather slim though. However, at least some direct markets between the euro and several of these currencies may emerge.[13]

An issue not yet addressed is the attractiveness of the euro in terms of volatility. This will depend on the exchange rate regime with respect to other currencies. Under floating one could expect a higher volatility of the euro exchange rates as compared to ecu exchange rates. But whether its volatility (with respect to non-USD currencies) would become "worse" than that of the dollar in this regime is, again, difficult to predict in advance. The DEM experience suggests that a credible fixed-rate system and European Central Bank (ECB) monetary policy could counter deteriorating volatility effects to the attractiveness of the euro as a vehicle currency.

6. Conclusions

In this paper I have discussed different exchange structures in the foreign exchange market. These exchange structures could be explained with a simple theory of forex vehicle currencies based on transaction costs, as measured by bid-ask spreads of foreign exchange dealers. The basic predictions of the theory, in particular that spreads decrease with *expected* trading volume and increase with expected volatility, were tested with five years of USD/JPY data and could not be falsified.

Different scenarios of potential euro spot trading volumes were computed from BIS turnover data. Very roughly, these data suggest that *total* euro turnover after EMU would be about the same as total DEM turnover before EMU, although the euro would be more important than the DEM as a percentage share of total turnover. However, *bilateral* euro turnovers would be higher than bilateral DEM turnovers. Assuming that exchange rate volatility of the euro with respect to non-dollar currencies will not become excessive after EMU, this suggests the potential of the euro to become a foreign exchange vehicle currency for some currencies outside the EMU area. Nevertheless it seems unlikely that the euro can overtake the dollar shortly after monetary union, although it will be clearly more important than the yen.

One factor also fostering the potential for the internationalization of currencies is the sophistication and depth of their domestic financial markets in general (*Kindleberger, 1993; Swoboda, 1969*). This aspect cannot be addressed within the framework developed in this paper. Although important, it has to be left to future research on forex vehicle currencies.

Endnotes

1. Mailing address: LSE Financial Markets Group, Houghton Street, London WC2A 2AE, Great Britain, Phone: ++44-(0)171-955 7477, Fax: ++44-(0)171-242 1006, Email: hartmann@lse.ac.uk. I would like to thank Richard Portes for his support during the last three years, Thorsten Hens for many valuable discussions and Olsen & Associates (Zurich) for data assistance. Financial support by the UK Economic and Social Research Council (ESRC) and the EU Human Capital and Mobility Programme (contracts ERB-4001-GT92-1175 and CHRX-CT94-0648) is gratefully acknowledged.

2. In order to ensure some uniformity in the notation of currency abbreviations I make use of the United Nations ISO codes in this paper (*UNDP, 1994*).

3. Since *detailed* data from the turnover survey in April 1995 were not yet published by April 1996 (*BIS, 1995*), this study has to resort to the older April 1992 data.

4. The national surveys underlying the BIS reports show some residual turnovers for markets that are considered to be illiquid. However, these turnovers are very small and can be neglected for our purposes (see endnote 6).

5. Italics my own. The number mentioned by the Banque de France applies to the Paris market.

6. The sum of both is larger than 100 percent, because USD/DEM transactions are counted twice in that sum, once in the USD percentage and once in the DEM percentage. Correcting for this source of double counting shows that only 3 percent of global inter-dealer spot forex trading has neither the USD nor the DEM on at least one side of the transaction.

7. Strictly speaking this statement can only be maintained for the 26 currencies of countries with important forex markets participating in the BIS surveys (*BIS, 1993, 1995*).

8. Notice that in the "*strictly* bipolar" system some transactions would have to be made in *three* steps. One currency against vehicle 1, vehicle 1 against vehicle 2, and vehicle 2 against another currency.

9. This assumption is not necessary for our purposes (*Hartmann, 1996b*), but it considerably simplifies the present exposition.

10. One "tick" equals one quote on the screen.

11. For discussions of the insider-outsider problematic see e.g. *Arrowsmith (forthcoming)*, *Goodhart (1996)* and *Gros (1996)*.

12. Spot inter-dealer volume CAD against DEM amounted to a very tiny 8.7 bio USD in April 1992. As a comparison, DEM/CHF spot inter-dealer trading was 9110.2 bio USD during the same period, more than 1000 times higher.

13. Trading volumes in South and Middle American, Eastern and Central European as well as African foreign exchange markets (except South Africa) are currently not covered by the *BIS (1993, 1995)* surveys.

References

ALIBER, Z., ed. (1969), The international market for foreign exchange, New York.

_____ (1977), The future of the dollar as an international currency, New York.

ALOGOSKOUFIS, G.; PORTES, R. (1993), European monetary union and international currencies in a tripolar world, in: Canzoneri, M., Grilli, V., Masson, P. eds. (1993): Establishing a Central Bank - Issues in Europe and Lessons From the US, Cambridge, 273-301.

ARROWSMITH, J. (forthcoming), Pitfalls on the path to a single European currency, EUI Working Paper, European University Institute, Florence.

BAGEHOT, W., pseud. (1971): The only game in town, *Financial Analysts Journal*, vol. 27/2, 12-14, 22.

BANK FOR INTERNATIONAL SETTLEMENTS (1990), Survey of foreign exchange market activity, Basle, February.

_____ (1993), Central bank survey of foreign exchange market activity in April 1992, Basle, March.

_____ (1995), Central bank survey of foreign exchange market activity in April 1995: Preliminary global findings, Press Communiqué, Basle, October.

BANK OF JAPAN (1993), Summary of results of the Tokyo foreign exchange market turnover survey conducted in April 1992, Bank of Japan Quarterly Bulletin, vol. 1/1, 37-45.

_____ (1996), Summary of results of the Tokyo foreign exchange market turnover survey conducted in April 1995, Bank of Japan Quarterly Bulletin, vol. 4/1, 81-91.

BANQUE DE FRANCE (1989), Enquète sur le marché des changes de Paris, Dossier de presse, no. 89-23, November 6, Paris.

_____ (1993), Activité du marché des changes de Paris. Principales tendances., Bulletin Mensuel de la Banque de France, Septembre, 109-116.

BESSEMBINDER, H. (1994), Bid-ask spreads in the interbank foreign exchange markets, Journal of Financial Economics, vol. 35/3, 317-348.

BLACK, S. (1991), Transactions costs and vehicle currencies, Journal of International Money and Finance, vol. 10/4, 512-527.

BOLLERSLEV, T., CHOU, R., KRONER, K. (1992), ARCH modeling in finance - A review of the theory and empirical evidence, Journal of Econometrics, vol. 52, 5-59.

BUERKLE, T. (1996), EU agrees to form new currency grid and cements EMU, International Herald Tribune, April 15, 13, 15.

CHRYSTAL, A. (1984), On the theory of international money, in: Black, J.; Dorrance, G.; eds. (1984), Problems of International Finance, New York, 77-92.

CLARK, P. (1973), A subordinated stochastic process model with finite variance for speculative prices, Econometrica, vol. 41/1, 135-155.

COHEN, B. (1971), The future of sterling as an international currency, London.

DANMARKS NATIONALBANK (1989), Turnover in the foreign-exchange market, Danmarks Nationalbank Monetary Review, November, 8-11.

_____ (1992), Survey of the Danish foreign-exchange market, April 1992, Danmarks Nationalbank Monetary Review, November.

EUROPEAN COUNCIL (1992), Treaty on European Union ("Maastricht Treaty").

_____ (1995), Conclusions of the Spanish presidency, Brussels, December.

FLOOD, M. (1991), Microstructure theory and the foreign exchange market, Federal Reserve Bank of St. Louis Economic Review, November/December, 52-70.

FRANKEL, J. (1993), Is Japan creating a yen block in East Asia and the Pacific?, in: Frankel, J.; Kahler, M. (eds.), Regionalism and Rivalry, Japan and the United States in Pacific Asia, Chicago, 53-85.

GIAVAZZI, F.; GIOVANNINI, A. (1989), Limiting exchange rate flexibility - The European Monetary System, Cambridge (MA).

GIOVANNINI, A.; TURTELBOOM, B. (1994), Currency substitution, in: van der Ploeg, F., ed. (1994.), The Handbook of International Macroeconomics, Oxford, 390-436.

GLASSMAN, D. (1987), Exchange rate risk and transaction costs: Evidence from bid-ask spreads, Journal of International Money and Finance, vol. 6/4, 481-490.

GLOSTEN, L.; MILGROM, P. (1985), Bid, ask and transaction prices in a specialist market with heterogeneously informed traders, Journal of Financial Economics, vol. 14, 71-100.

GOODHART, C. (1996), The transition to EMU, Second Annual Lecture delivered at the Scottish Economic Society/Royal Bank of Scotland, January.

GROS, D. (1996), Towards Economic and Monetary Union: Problems and prospects, CEPS Paper, no. 65, Centre for European Policy Studies, Brussels.

GROUP OF TEN (1993), International capital movements and foreign exchange markets - A report to the Ministers and Governors by the Group of Deputies, April, Rome.

GUILLAUME, D.; DACOROGNA, M.; DAVÉ, R.; MÜLLER, U.; OLSEN, R.; PICTET, O. (1994), From the bird's eye to the microscope: A survey of new stylized facts of the intra-daily foreign exchange markets, Olsen & Associates, Research Group Discussion Paper, DMG.1994-04-06, October, Zurich.

HANSEN, L. (1982), Large sample properties of generalized method of moments estimators, Econometrica, vol. 50/4, 1029-1054.

HARTMANN, P. (1994), Vehicle currencies in the foreign exchange market, DELTA Discussion Paper, no. 94-13, DELTA (Ecole Normale Supérieure), Paris, June.

_____ (1996a), Trading volumes and transaction costs - Evidence from daily dollar-yen spot data, LSE Financial Markets Group Discussion Paper, no. 232, London School of Economics, January.

_____ (1996b), Monnaies véhiculaires sur le marché des changes, unpublished Ph.D. thesis, Ecole des Hautes Etudes en Sciences Sociales, Paris.

JORION, P. (1994), Risk and turnover in the foreign exchange market, Paper presented at the NBER/CEPR/Banca d'Italia "Microstructure of Foreign Exchange Markets" Conference, July 1-2 1994 in Perugia.

JONES, R. (1976), The origin and development of media of exchange, Journal of Political Economy, vol. 84/4, 757-775.

KENEN, P. (1983), The role of the dollar as an international currency, Group of Thirty Occasional Papers, no. 13, New York.

KINDLEBERGER, C. (1993), A financial history of Western Europe (2nd ed.), Oxford.

KRUGMAN, P. (1980), Vehicle currencies and the structure of international exchange, Journal of Money, Credit, and Banking, vol. 12/3, 503-526.

_____ (1984), The international role of the dollar: Theory and prospect, in: Bilson, J.; Marston, R. (eds.), Exchange Rate Theory and Practice, Chicago, 261-278.

LYONS, R. (1995a), Tests of microstructural hypotheses in the foreign exchange market, Journal of Financial Economics, vol. 39, 321-351.

_____ (1995b), Foreign exchange volume: Sound and fury signifying nothing?, NBER Working Paper, no. 4984.

MEESE, R., ROGOFF, K. (1983), Empirical exchange rate models of the seventies - Do they fit out of sample?, Journal of International Economics, vol. 12/1, 3-24.

SHASTRI, K. (1992), Bid-ask spreads, in: Newman, P. et al. (eds.), The New Palgrave Dictionary of Money and Finance, vol. 1, 196f.

SWOBODA, A. (1969), Vehicle currencies and the foreign exchange market: The case of the dollar, in: Aliber, R., ed. (1969), The International Market for Foreign Exchange, 30-40.

TAVLAS, G. (1991), On the international use of currencies: The case of the deutsche mark, Essays in International Finance, no. 181, Princeton University.

_____ (1992), Vehicle currencies, in: Newman, P. et al. (eds.), The New Palgrave Dictionary of Money and Finance, vol. 3, 754-757.

TAVLAS, G., OZEKI, Y. (1992), The internationalization of currencies: An appraisal of the Japanese yen, IMF Occasional Paper, no. 90.

TYGIER, C. (1983), Basic handbook of foreign exchange - A guide to foreign exchange dealing, London.

UNITED NATIONS DEVELOPMENT PROGRAMME (1994), United nations common coding system, New York, March.

WEI, S.-J. (1994), Anticipations of foreign exchange volatility and bid-ask spreads, NBER Working Paper, no. 4737, May.

Comments on: Foreign Exchange Vehicles Before and After EMU: From Dollar/Mark to Dollar/Euro?

Emil-Maria Claassen

The paper by Philipp Hartmann reminds me of an old issue in monetary economics which concerns the concept of the neutrality of money. Wicksell was the inventor of the notions of "neutral" money and the "natural" interest rate. One condition for the neutrality of money was the equality of the market rate of interest with the natural rate of interest. However, general equilibrium analysis of the first generation (à la Walras) went even further. Money was neutral when the monetary economy was working like a barter economy. But which type of a barter economy?

It is an organized barter economy of the type Philipp Hartmann describes with his model of the "polar" forex market (figure C.1). He may be surprised that I assimilate his world markets for currencies with a primitive economy like a barter economy. However, this world money market with n currencies is a primitive money economy functioning *as if* it is a highly organized barter economy. Only a world economy with a single currency would deserve the epithet of a well-functioning money economy. However, one should not derive from this statement that I am a defender of a single world currency. There are simply more transaction costs with n currencies than with a single currency and from this point of view the world money market looks like a barter economy.

But this barter economy is a well organized one where "well-organized" means lower transaction costs. Assume a closed economy and the world economy is a closed economy with four physical goods (n = 4) called dollar, yen, mark, and franc. One type of organization for this barter economy would be to have n(n−1)/2 = 6 trading posts (figure C*.1).

Figure C*.1: Trading Posts in a World without a Vehicle Currency

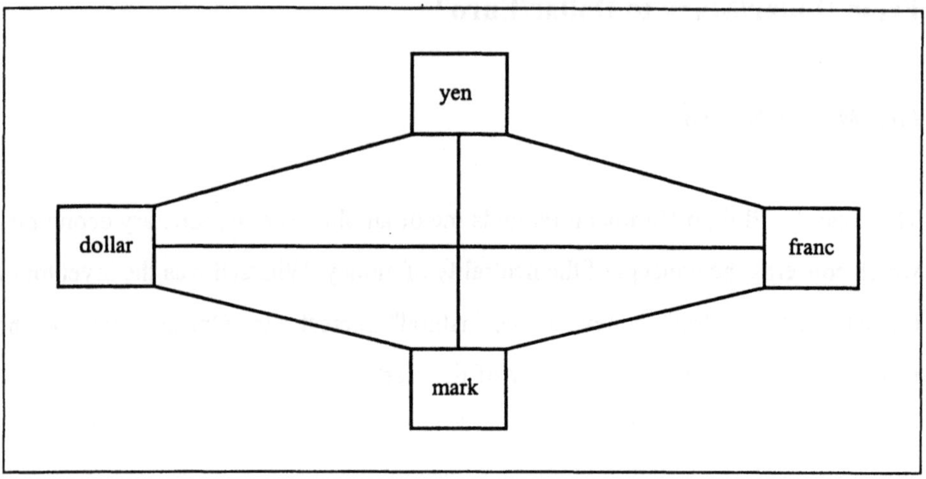

Another type of barter would imply the emergence of an intermediary good which is also considered as a generally accepted means of exchange ("vehicle currency"), e.g. the good dollar. In this case, the number of trading posts are reduced to n–1 = 3 (figure C*.2). In a world of 100 goods or 100 currencies, the number of trading posts decreases from 4950 to 99.

These 99 trading posts are also our foreign exchange markets which are treated in our textbooks on international monetary economics. However, textbooks often have the tendency to lag behind reality. Our figure C*.2 describes the dollar–vehicle–standard which was relevant until the early 1980s. Philipp Hartmann's figure C.2 illustrates the recent dollar–standard-cum-deutschmark-standard. Why did a second currency emerge as a vehicle currency in the world forex markets? At first sight, a second vehicle currency in the foreign exchange markets of the world economy is rather contradictory since the number of trading posts (or the size of transaction costs) increases.

This puzzle can be solved with the proper model of Philipp Hartmann which he elaborates on in his paper. One important element for the choice of the vehicle currency within the world economy is the volatility of its exchange rate. Since the 1980s, there was a block of floating exchange rates (including the exchange rate of the German mark) around the US dollar and a block of fixed exchange rates around the deutschmark (European Monetary System). The lower volatility of EMS currencies with respect to the deutschmark gave rise to the mark as the vehicle currency. Thus, in a world which pursues partly fixed and partly floating exchange rates, the emergence of two vehicle currencies is rather compatible. Once the euro has come into existence, the triangle dollar–euro–yen will dominate the international monetary system. Since no country in the world has fixed its exchange rate to the yen, the future single vehicle currency will be either US dollar, euro, or both? This we do not know yet.

Figure C*.2: Trading Posts in a World with a Vehicle Currency

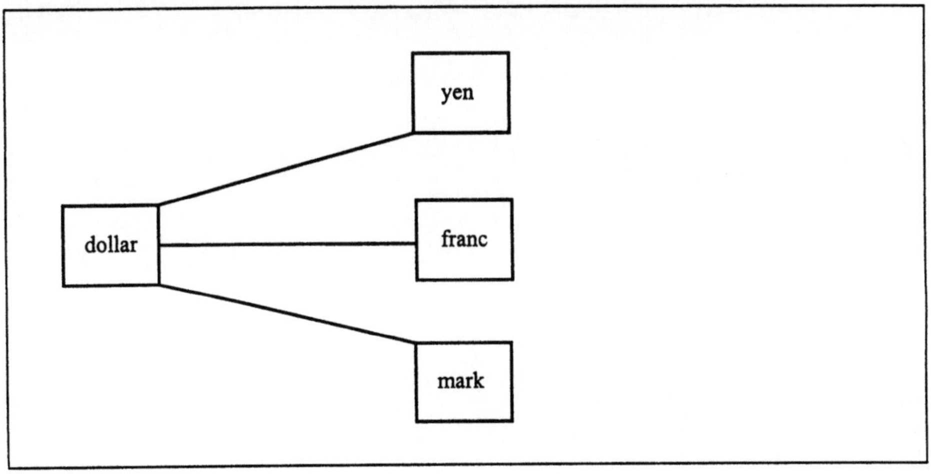

D. Does a Core-Periphery Regime Make Europe into an Optimal Currency Area?

Maria Demertzis, Andrew Hughes Hallett and Ole Rummel

1. Introduction

The argument for a two-speed regime in Europe is that a small number of countries have already achieved sufficient convergence in their structures to benefit from the advantages of a single currency without risking large adjustment costs. The periphery group would, by default, be those countries which are unable or unwilling to achieve sufficient convergence by 1999. That distinction is made on the basis of the theory of optimal currency areas, which specifies the conditions under which a single currency would be advantageous. In this paper we adapt a formal model of optimal currency areas to show how those conditions can be transformed into testable propositions on whether there is sufficient symmetry in shocks and transmission mechanisms to make the formation of a currency union worthwhile. This, it turns out, depends on rough equality of the size and positive correlations between shocks across the union; and on the equality in impact and timing of the transmission of policy changes or external shocks. We apply these results to ask if the core-periphery distinction is the appropriate response to the difficulty of creating a monetary union in Europe. Does Europe really have a better chance of achieving monetary union if it proceeds in two (or more) stages, with the periphery left to catch up in its own time? Or is the evidence for that so weak that we must assume that such a distinction is politically driven and likely to be a long-run state of affairs?

Several authors have attempted to gauge whether Europe as a whole is a optimal currency area using broadly similar techniques: *Eichengreen (1990)*; *De Grauwe and Vanhaverbeke (1993)* and *Bayoumi and Eichengreen (1994)* are probably the best known. But none, so far as we know, have developed a formal model of the required tests and then gone on to match those tests to the data. Nor has previous work attempted to determine whether Europe as a whole would be a suitable currency union, as opposed to a German-led economic zone. Nor, more importantly, have previous authors attempted to determine whether the core European economies would form a better currency area instead, with perhaps the periphery economies as a separate area, and whether there are important asymmetries between the two groups so that any attempt to form a single Europe-wide currency would, at this stage, prove counterproductive. If that is true, then the current *de facto* core-periphery distinction is justified and helpful.

Finally, according to the Maastricht treaty monetary union in Europe has one important special feature; it is founded on the presumption that an independent monetary policy and price stability must be the prime and leading objectives. Thus the construction of a monetary union, whether on a core-periphery basis or otherwise, and the tests of its suitability, must be conducted in terms of whether a single monetary policy would suffice; or whether such a policy would imply extra costs unless compensated by policies which support output and/or remove local disequilibria, or by coordinated but regionally differentiated monetary policies to account for the core-periphery distinction. Thus although the analysis is conducted almost entirely within the theory of optimal currency areas, it is really about the framework within which monetary policy should be set when monetary union arrives. Should monetary policy be set singly, or jointly but severally?

All those questions are the agenda for this paper, and we show how to apply standard econometric techniques to answer them. What we do not do, however, is to go beyond those standard techniques and question the methodology applied. But since our analysis uncovers a number of questions which remain unanswered (and unanswerable), it would clearly be important to do so. Nor do we question the accepted definitions of core and periphery countries. That we leave to future work. For the present, the key questions are as follows:

(a) Would EU countries have an interest in forming a currency union, either within a core group or EU-wide?

(b) Would they be suitable as members of a currency union? Are they sufficiently symmetric (converged) in shocks and structure?

(c) Are the core-periphery groups sufficiently distinct from each other?

(d) What evidence is there that a single monetary policy is suitable, or might an independent central bank not imply costs even in the core?

2. Theory: A Formal Model of Currency Unions

2.1 Theory

The literature on optimal currency areas tells us that a single currency will be desirable if the inability to change the value of the exchange rates does not make adjustments in the face of shocks, price rigidities or other disequilibria more difficult or more costly. *Mundell (1961)* argued that a single currency would reduce transactions costs and the degree of imperfect competition; but that having fixed exchange rates would prove costly in the face of asymmetric shocks or price rigidities. However, those costs would be small if labor and capital were sufficiently mobile. *McKinnon (1963)* stressed that openness to trade was also an important criterion because changes in exchange rates would, in that case, destabilize internal prices and would have few beneficial effects in terms of real wages or the terms of trade. In other words, a currency union would be beneficial if it were open to internal trade but relatively closed to the rest of the world. Finally, *Kenen (1969)* maintained that countries with a high product diversification would find it easier to maintain a currency union since canceling between shocks would make them better able to absorb disturbances to particular industries.

The theory of optimal currency areas therefore tells us that it will be beneficial to forsake flexible exchange rates and adopt a single currency if: (a) the countries are mutually open to trade; (b) there is a high degree of factor mobility between the different countries; (c) wages and prices are flexible in both directions; (d) there is a high degree of product diversification; and (e) the countries concerned do not display significant asymmetries in their shocks, or in their economic structures (whether institutional; or in supply, demand or policy preferences) so that even common shocks have asymmetric effects.

A number of recent papers[1] have reviewed these conditions and the extent to which they are satisfied in Europe. The conclusion that EU economies are sufficiently open to trade and that capital is highly mobile appears uncontroversial. Likewise the conclusion that labor is largely immobile for linguistic and cultural reasons, as well as because of the personal and social costs of migration, is probably accepted by all. Indeed, *Eichengreen (1990)* points out that labor mobility within the nation-states of the EU is probably two or three times lower than that within the US monetary union, and that is before we even consider the mobility *between* European countries.

Labor mobility, coupled with the fact that wages and prices (particularly wages and non-wage labor costs) are not flexible downwards in Europe, means that asymmetric shocks would lead to significant and persistent disequilibria under a common currency. Indeed, even symmetric shocks will generate persistent disequilibria if the degree of labor mobility or of wage and price flexibility varies across Europe. That will reveal itself in asymmetries of structure or asymmetries in the transmission of shocks or policy changes. By contrast, product diversification would imply symmetry in the time profile of the transmission mechanisms so that industry- or country-specific shocks would have rather similar impacts and would be rapidly absorbed everywhere. On the other hand, increasing regional specialization would imply asymmetric transmission mechanisms and disturbances that were more persistent. This trend towards regional specialization has been documented as a feature of the monetary unions formed in the last century (Italy, Germany, the US) and would be a natural consequence of the opportunities for exploiting the scale economies and wider range of comparative advantages which the single European market now offers *(De Grauwe and Vanhaverbeke, 1993)*.

The conclusion of the literature is therefore that Europe is not an optimal currency area on at least three counts: imperfect labor mobility, insufficient wage/price flexibility, and asymmetries in shocks and structures. It could also lose its regional diversification. But none of that says that Europe is so far away from being an optimal currency area that monetary union would be ill advised. For one thing there are the transaction costs, and information and competition benefits. Moreover, the impact of the failure to meet these currency area conditions will all come out in the incidence of asymmetric shocks, or asymmetric transmission mechanisms. Hence to test whether Europe, or any subset of it, could actually function as a single currency area we have to examine the symmetry of shocks and transmission mechanisms. Only if we wish to go further and discuss what policies would be necessary to make it function better as a currency union, do we have to examine the structure of the underlying shocks and transmission mechanisms.

2.2 A Formal Model

To link symmetry with the costs of forming a monetary union, we apply the model presented in *Bayoumi (1994)* in which the author derives the expected utilities for countries forming a currency union and staying outside it.[2]

The cost-benefit ratio between joining and not joining a currency union in the Bayoumi model depends on demand elasticities (β_{ji}), transactions costs (τ), the elasticity of the demand for labor (α), and the similarity or dissimilarity of the shocks in different regions, as denoted by their standard deviations, σ. Non-members will be worse off because adjustment difficulties in the Union spill over to cause disequilibria outside, without any benefits being created to offset those costs.

Thus a core monetary union will always impose costs on the periphery countries, but the periphery will impose no such costs on the core.[3] However, since the shocks are symmetrically distributed around zero, there will be times when $\varepsilon_j < \varepsilon_k$, and times when $\varepsilon_k > \varepsilon_j$, with a probability of one-half of either event occurring; where ε_j and ε_k are output disturbances with mean zero which are distributed independently of the exchange rate regime for two countries j and k. Specifically, the model contains equations for output, employment and wages under different exchange rate arrangements. Consumption is chosen to maximize utility levels in each region, subject to prices, relative prices and available income. Wages are sticky: they adjust up to provide full employment if there is excess demand at current exchange rates, prices and output. But they do not adjust down if there is excess supply: instead they stay at the equilibrium that would prevail at full employment when there are no shocks and exchange rate deviations from parity. Given that, Bayoumi derives the *ex ante* expected benefit for country j in joining a currency union with country k as

$$\begin{aligned} E(\Delta U_j) &= \beta_{jk}\tau - \beta_{jj}\gamma E(\varepsilon_j - \varepsilon_k | \varepsilon_j < \varepsilon_k) P(\varepsilon_j < \varepsilon_k) \\ &\quad - \beta_{jk}\gamma E(\varepsilon_k - \varepsilon_j | \varepsilon_j > \varepsilon_k) P(\varepsilon_j > \varepsilon_k) \\ &= \beta_{jk}\tau - \gamma(\beta_{jj} + \beta_{jk})\phi(0)\sqrt{\sigma_j^2 - 2\rho\sigma_j\sigma_k + \sigma_k^2} \end{aligned} \quad (2.1)$$

And for the non-members, here represented by country one, the welfare costs are

$$E(\Delta U_1) = -\gamma(\beta_{1j} + \beta_{1k})\phi(0)\sqrt{\sigma_j^2 - 2\rho\sigma_j\sigma_k + \sigma_k^2} \quad (2.2)$$

where E denotes the expectations operator, $\phi(0)$ is the density function of a standard jointly normal distribution of random variables, $\gamma = \alpha/(2(1-\alpha))$, and ρ is the correlation coefficient between ε_j and ε_k. Thus the expected costs of monetary union are minimized for members and nonmembers alike if $\rho \to 1$, but only if $\sigma_j \cong \sigma_k$. Hence a necessary condition for a low cost currency union is a high positive correlation between the shocks in regions j and k; but the necessary and sufficient condition is a high positive correlation *and* shocks of similar size. Only under those conditions are the gains unambiguously positive, and the costs negligible elsewhere. And when costs do appear they depend on the importance to consumption of the goods produced within the Union; the elasticity of labor demand in production; and on the adjustment problems in the core, not the periphery. The cost-benefit analysis of monetary union therefore depends on the impact and cost of absorbing disequilibria, not on the underlying equilibria.

Extending this analysis to a Union of several countries, 1 ... k, region i will evidently have full employment if its supply (or productivity) shock is above the average for the remainder of the Union; wages in the Union adjust up to give full employment if demand is above the level of the other members since, if wages did not adjust, labor would move to region i (not possible under our current assumptions) or wages would be bid down elsewhere (also not possible given inflexible labor costs). Hence the expected output loss in region j, without full employment, is

$$\begin{aligned} E(\Delta y_j) &= -\alpha E(\varepsilon_j - \bar{\varepsilon}_j \mid \varepsilon_j < \bar{\varepsilon}_j)\, P(\varepsilon_j < \bar{\varepsilon}_j) \\ &= -\gamma\phi(0)\sqrt{\sigma_j^2 - 2\rho\sigma_j\bar{\sigma}_j + \bar{\sigma}_j^2} \end{aligned} \tag{2.3}$$

where $\bar{\varepsilon}_j$, $\bar{\sigma}_j$ are the mean and standard deviation of the disturbances of the Union *excluding* region j respectively. Since each region will have this output loss, and the disturbances are symmetrically distributed so that each region has an equal chance of receiving a shock below or above the average of its partners, i.e. ($\varepsilon_j < \bar{\varepsilon}_j$ or $\varepsilon_j > \bar{\varepsilon}_j$ respectively) the expected welfare changes are:

$$E(\Delta U_j) = \sum_{k \neq j} \beta_{jk} \tau - \gamma \sum_{k \neq j} \beta_{jk} \phi(0) \sqrt{\sigma_j^2 - 2\rho\sigma_j \overline{\sigma}_j + \overline{\sigma}_j^2} \qquad \text{j, k} \in \text{Union} \quad (2.4)$$

for members, and

$$E(\Delta U_1) = -\gamma \sum_k \beta_{1k} \phi(0) \sqrt{\sigma_k^2 - 2\rho\sigma_k \overline{\sigma}_k + \overline{\sigma}_k^2} \qquad \text{k} \in \text{Union} \quad (2.5)$$

for nonmembers. The conclusion is the same; the costs inside and outside the Union diminish only if the shocks are of similar size and well correlated within the core.

3. Estimating Demand and Supply Shocks: The Methodology of Blanchard and Quah

3.1 The Effects of Shocks

This paper uses long-run restrictions on a simple VAR model to identify the fundamental demand and supply shocks that have driven output and prices in each member country of the EU. These in turn will allow us to calculate the sizes and correlations of the underlying demand and supply disturbances.

In such a structural VAR model, the fundamental shocks to the economy are not directly observable and have to be recovered. This is achieved by imposing some long-run restrictions on the short-run dynamics which are determined from the data. This technique was pioneered by *Blanchard and Quah (1989)* and has been used extensively by *Bayoumi and Eichengreen (1992, 1994)* and, more recently, by *Ahmed et al. (1993)*.

The starting point for the analysis is the aggregate supply and demand diagram as displayed in figure D.1, with a downward sloping aggregate demand curve (AD), an upward sloping short-run aggregate supply curve (SRAS). The long-run aggregate supply curve (LRAS) will be vertical for classical reasons.

Figure D.1: The Aggregate Demand and Supply Model

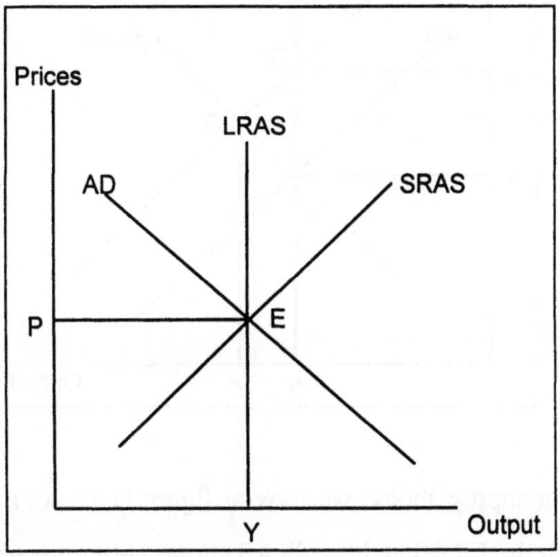

Figure D.2 shows the effect of a demand shock. The AD curve shifts from AD to AD' thereby moving the equilibrium point from E to D'. This raises both output and prices, but as the aggregate supply curve becomes more vertical over time, the economy gradually moves from its short-run equilibrium at D' to its new long-run equilibrium at D", thereby restoring the old level of output. The response to a permanent (positive) demand shock is thus a short term rise in output coupled with a permanent rise in prices at P". And so long as the size of the shock (AD to AD') and the transmission of the shock (P to P", depending on the slope of AD) are approximately the same in each country, a single monetary policy will entail few costs.

Figure D.2: The Effects of a Positive Demand Shock

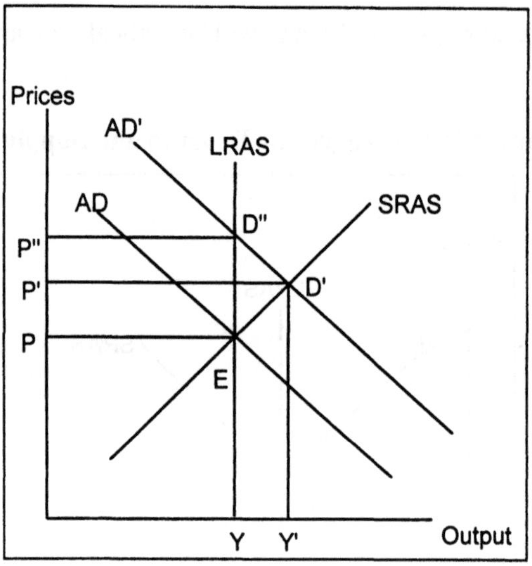

For the effect of a supply shock, we look at figure D.3. As a result of a positive supply shock, both the LRAS and the SRAS curves shift outwards. In the short run, this raises output and reduces prices, thereby shifting the equilibrium from E to S'. As the supply curve becomes increasingly vertical over time, the economy moves from S' to S''. This implies a further fall in prices and an additional increase in output respectively.

Unlike demand shocks, supply shocks result in permanent positive changes in output and negative changes in prices. But in this case, the transmission mechanisms are important. If the demand and supply curves are steep and if supply is price elastic in the long run, then most of the adjustment will take place through prices. The situation is as for demand shocks; symmetry in shocks and the transmission of shocks will imply a single monetary policy is appropriate. But if the demand and supply curves are flatter and/or supply price inelastic in the long run, then most of the adjustment will be made via output. In that case, additional policies (fiscal or supply side) will be needed if output is to be stabilized as well as prices, and if the supply shocks are as important as the demand shocks. And in either case, a single monetary policy will entail significant costs if countries differ either in the size of their shocks or in the transmission of those shocks (principally as a result of different demand and supply elasticities).

Figure D.3: The Effects of a Positive Supply Shock

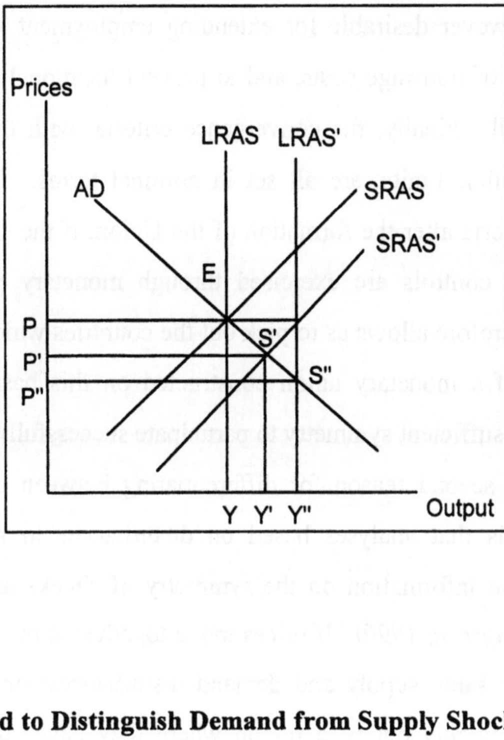

3.2 Why We Need to Distinguish Demand from Supply Shocks

This methodology relies on the ability to identify the two underlying shocks. We have already argued that this is important in the European context because price stability and the establishment of an independent central bank have been assigned prime position among the objectives of monetary union. If it is right to give monetary policy and price stability the dominant position in the Union's policy framework, then the Union's economies had better be dominated by price (demand) disturbances rather than price and quantity (i.e. supply side) disturbances. If that is not the case, then additional instruments will be needed to deal with the quantity movements which are not foreseen in the Maastricht treaty. On the contrary, fiscal interventions are to be limited - perhaps severely if the German "stability pact" is adopted. Moreover there is no obvious mechanism for coordinating those fiscal interventions. Similarly there are no particular mechanisms for encouraging wage flexibility or labor mobility between countries: on the contrary, the impact of the social chapter, however desirable for extending employment security, will be to extend the rigidity of nonwage costs, and to prevent locational competition (social "dumping") as well. Finally, the convergence criteria, with the exception of the fiscal debt and deficit limits, are all set in nominal terms. It will be easier to maintain those criteria after the formation of the Union, if the shocks are primarily to prices and the controls are exercised through monetary policy. Separating demand shocks therefore allows us to pick out the countries which are most suitable for membership of a monetary union constructed on this basis, and to examine whether they have sufficient symmetry to participate successfully.

There is a second reason for differentiating between demand and supply shocks, and that is that analyses based on disturbances in prices or quantities themselves conflate information on the symmetry of shocks and on the speed of adjustment *(Eichengreen, 1990)*. If prices move together, it may be either that both markets suffer the same supply and demand disturbances; or that the factors of production move quickly out of a region where they have started to rise, while demand shocks move in the opposite direction. Either way relative price variability would be minimized. That does not matter for the smooth functioning of a monetary union. But a problem arises if some price variability remains because you cannot distinguish whether it is asymmetries in the shocks, or rigidities in the quantity/price adjustments, which are causing difficulties. That matters very much for the chances of a smoothly functioning Union. Similarly if the quantity movements are large we cannot tell if that is because the shocks are not on the demand side, or whether the adjustment processes are just sticky (particularly in the labor markets), or whether the shocks are simply asymmetric. But again the successful functioning of the Union and the need for additional instruments depends entirely on distinguishing between asymmetries and the speeds of adjustment, and on distinguishing demand from supply shocks.

3.3 Estimating the Shocks

There are by now several excellent discussions of the Blanchard-Quah methodology. For a more elaborate derivation of the main results, the interested reader is referred to, *inter alia*, the original paper by *Blanchard and Quah (1989)*, the applied papers by *Bayoumi and Eichengreen (1992, 1994)*, and the discussions in *Lippi and Reichlin (1993)* as well as *Enders (1995)*.

In order to identify the structural innovations from a reduced-form VAR model, we start with the following representation of a vector x_t of stationary variables

$$A(L)x_t = e_t \qquad (3.1)$$

with $A(L) = I + A_1L + A_2L^2 + \ldots + A_kL^k$, where L is the lag operator and e_t has an independent multivariate normal distribution with mean zero and covariance matrix $\Sigma = E(e_te_t')$. This process has a dual vector moving average representation of the form

$$x_t = C(L)e_t = \sum_{i=0}^{\infty} C_iL^ie_t \qquad (3.2)$$

where $C(L)=A(L)^{-1}$ and the matrices C_i represent the impulse responses of x_t to shocks. However, identifying the structural innovations from (3.2) is problematic, since the elements of e_t are composites of the two structural innovations to output and inflation from the bivariate system (3.1). The unobservable and underlying shocks, ε_t, are therefore linear combinations of the observed error terms, e_t, and can be written as $\varepsilon_t=P^{-1}e_t$. The matrix P is obtained as follows. Since Σ is a positive definite matrix, there exists a lower triangular matrix P such that $\Sigma=PP'$. Using $e_t = P\varepsilon_t$, we can rewrite equation (3.2) as:

$$x_t = \sum_{i=0}^{\infty} C_i PP^{-1} e_{t-i} = \sum_{i=0}^{\infty} D_i \varepsilon_{t-i} \tag{3.3}$$

where $D(L)=C(L)P$. Thus $E(\varepsilon_t\varepsilon_t')=P^{-1}E(\varepsilon_t\varepsilon_t')P=I$, since $\Sigma=PP'$ and $P^{-1}=P'$ for an orthogonal matrix. Hence given estimates of e_t and Σ from (3.1), we can construct estimates of ε_t. But while the usual Choleski decomposition will give us an unrestricted decomposition, *Blanchard and Quah's (1989)* analysis requires us to identify P on the basis of structural relationships. This is done by imposing three restrictions:

(i) the two components of ε_t are orthogonal.

(ii) the components of ε_t have unit variances.

(iii) one of the components of ε_t has no long-run effect on one of the variables in x_t. Indeed, supply shocks have permanent effects on the level of output, while demand shocks have only temporary effects on the level of output and both shocks have permanent effects on the level of prices.

In view of figures D.2 and D.3, our model (3.3) then becomes

$$\Delta y_t = d_{11}(L)\varepsilon_{dt} + d_{12}(L)\varepsilon_{st}$$
$$\Delta \pi_t = d_{21}(L)\varepsilon_{dt} + d_{22}(L)\varepsilon_{st}$$

where $d_{11}(1)=0$, $d_{12}(1)>0$, $d_{21}(1)>0$, and $d_{22}(1)<0$ describe the long-run values of the impulse parameters. We are therefore interpreting the component of ε_t which has no long-run effect as a demand shock, ε_{dt}, while the other is a supply shock, ε_{st}.

Our data is described in an appendix. It incorporates all 15 members of the European Union, spans from 1960 to 1995, and is of quarterly frequency. Our classification of Europe into two groups is based on the commonly accepted definition of the core consisting of France, Germany, the Benelux, Denmark and Austria and the Periphery consisting of the remaining eight. This of course is a political (and orthodox) definition. We make no attempt to assess whether it is the right grouping, nor do we ask whether an alternative would be a better classification.

4. Results: The Symmetry of Shocks

4.1 The VAR Structure

In implementing the Blanchard-Quah decomposition, an important practical issue is the length of the lag to be used in the estimates of the underlying bivariate VAR equations. We select the shortest lag length such that adding extra lags adds nothing significant to the explanatory power (information content) of the model. The information criteria used are the Schwarz criterion (S), the Hannan-Quinn criterion (HQ), the Akaike criterion (A), and the F-version of the likelihood ratio test (F).[4] *Englund et al. (1994)* note that the Schwarz and Hannan-Quinn criteria are consistent in the presence of unit roots, but that the Akaike criterion is not.

Consequently, where there was disagreement between the criteria, we took the longer lag indicated by the Schwarz or Hannan-Quinn criteria on the argument that too many lags might yield inefficient estimates in the VAR equations, but too few would introduce misspecification biases. That is, a uniform lag is chosen to preserve the symmetry of the specification across countries, as recommended by *Bayoumi and Eichengreen (1994)*. The order of the lag we apply is 2, being the average of what the information criteria suggest.

Table D.1: Optimal Lag Lengths by Country

Core:	Austria	3	Periphery:	Spain	3
	France	3		Italy	1
	Germany	4		Portugal	2
	Belgium	4		Greece	4
	Denmark	2		Ireland	1
	Luxembourg	3		UK	1
	Netherlands	4		Finland	2
				Sweden	3

4.2 The Correlations With Group Averages

Previous work in this area, e.g. *Bayoumi (1992)*, has concentrated on the correlation coefficients between supply or demand shocks between pairs of countries. In the first instance, countries contemplating joining a single currency area should pay attention to the correlations between their shocks and those of any individual country within that group. However, a country would not necessarily be damaged if her shocks were poorly correlated with those of another member unless her shocks were also largely uncorrelated (or negatively correlated) with those of the group as a whole.

Table D.2: Correlation Coefficients, 1961:3-1995:1

CORE	With double counting						No double counting			
	Demand			Supply			Demand		Supply:	
	w Core Ave	w Ger	w EU	w Core Ave	w Ger	w EU	w Core Ave	w Peri	w Core Ave	w Peri
AU	.28*	.19*	.19*	.38*	.31*	.37*	.20*	.16	.30*	-.27*
F	**.48***	-.01	**.43***	**.65***	.29*	**.59***	.11	-.11	.32*	-.34*
G	**.57***	1.00	**.46***	.77*	1.00	**.67***	.02	-.09	.37*	-.30*
B	.11	-.07	.14	.35*	.29*	.36*	-.04	-.14	.31*	-.25*
DK	-.05	-.03	-.09	-.34*	-.24*	-.32*	-.02	-.00	-.31*	.18*
LU	-.10	.03	-.14	.20*	.25*	.25*	-.01	.11	.20*	-.20*
NL	-.24*	-.14	-.23*	**-.44***	-.23*	**-.42***	-.20*	.08	-.30*	.29*

(continued)

Sample Size = 135
Critical Value = 0.169
* denotes significance of the correlation coefficient at the 5% level
bold implies that we cannot reject H_0: $\rho=0.5$ in favour of H_1: $\rho<.5$.

Table D.2 (continued): Correlation Coefficients, 1961:3-1995:1

PERI-PHERY	with double counting						No double counting			
	Demand			Supply			Demand		Supply:	
	w Peri Ave	w Ger	wEU	w Peri Ave	w Ger	w EU	w Peri Ave	w Core	w Peri Ave	w Core
S	-.14	-.15	.10	-.16	.04	.04	-.05	.06	-.01	-.04
I	**-.45***	.06	.25*	**-.41***	.07	.32*	.01	.09	-.01	.21*
P	.16	-.17*	-.21*	.15	-.07	-.14	-.09	-.24*	-.10	-.11
GR	.04	-.01	-.00	-.12	.28*	.24*	.06	.08	-.12	.29*
IR	-.06	.03	.06	-.03	-.09	-.04	-.06	.09	-.00	-.08
UK	**.68***	.06	-.30*	**.76***	-.28*	**-.65***	.00	-.00	-.16	-.37*
FI	.10	-.08	.09	-.34*	.13	.28*	.13	.07	-.24*	.18*
SW	**-.45***	.10	.20*	-.37*	.20*	.31	-.05	-.01	-.08	.16

Sample Size = 135
Critical Value = 0.169
* denotes significance of the correlation coefficient at the 5% level
bold implies that we cannot reject H_0: $\rho=0.5$ in favour of H_1: $\rho<.5$.

Thus table D.2 has our main results; the correlations of each country's demand and supply shocks with the average shocks of its own group. This table reports the results for the full sample.

We include two further classifications. We report the correlations of each core country's demand and supply shocks with Germany's demand and supply shocks, on the argument that the core may become dominated by German policies. It would then be necessary for each core member to have similar shocks to Germany, if the core is to be sustainable. We also report the correlations of each country's shocks with those of the group to which it does *not* belong. This allows us to compare (i) within group correlations of the natural cohesion and sustainability of each group as single currency area, and (ii) between group correlations for the natural separation of the two groups because they do not have enough symmetry in common to form one larger common currency area. This amounts to a test of whether it is sensible and perhaps necessary to form a core monetary union first, and then allow the periphery countries to join when they have become more similar to the core.

Table D.2 also makes a distinction between correlations with and without double counting. One might expect to have to examine each country's correlations with the European or group average shocks, where the average includes the country in question (*Bayoumi, 1994*). But that is the wrong comparison. Equations (2.4) to (2.5) make it clear that the costs and benefits for each country must depend on the similarity of domestic shocks with the average of their partners' shocks, not the average of the group as a whole. The point, whether one is joining a common currency area or counting the cost of an existing membership, is to show sufficient convergence with one's partners. Correlations with the group average as a whole, if the country in question is a large player, will be much stronger due to double counting. Nevertheless it is still of interest to look at the difference between correlations with and without double counting in order to show where the important within group asymmetries lie.

Finally, statistical significance of correlation coefficients in table D.2 can be assessed using Fisher's z-transformation,

$$z = \frac{1}{2}\ln\left[(1+\hat{\rho})/(1-\hat{\rho})\right] \tag{4.1}$$

which is approximately normally distributed, with mean zero and standard deviation $\sigma=(n-3)^{-1/2}$ where n is the sample size.[5] The critical values are provided at the bottom of each table and the hypothesis examined is H_0: $\rho=0$ against the alternative H_1: $\rho>0$.

On this basis there turns out to be some evidence for symmetry between European countries, although more on the supply side than on the demand side. However, that evidence is fairly weak and clearly not uniform over countries. Moreover, and much more important, the evidence substantially vanishes (especially on the demand side, which represents the case where price stability and an independent central bank would be the appropriate policy framework) when the effect of double counting is removed. What is problematic here is the negative correlations appearing for both demand and supply shocks for Denmark and the Netherlands, and in certain cases for Belgium and Luxembourg. In the periphery group, however, the negative signs and the lower levels of significance are to be expected. Presumably that is why they have been, or should have been, allocated to the periphery.

The Core Countries and the Small Country Problem

When we look at the whole sample period for the core group, the demand correlations are mostly significant, but they are eliminated when double counting is removed - with the exception of Austria and the Netherlands. Moreover, the correlation is negative in the latter case. On the supply side, however, the correlations with the core averages show a much higher degree of significance (with and without double counting), but for Denmark and the Netherlands which have strong negative correlations in all subsamples examined. This unexpected behavior can probably be explained through the "small country syndrome". Being more closely tied to the impact of the policies of their larger neighbors, they are often obliged to accept policy changes which are not entirely suitable for their own circumstances. It might be, for example, that Germany expands at some point and that, as this increases prices, the Bundesbank raises interest rates to head off inflation. In the Netherlands or Denmark, monetary conditions are tightly linked to those in Germany, but output growth less so because of the effects of a nontradeables sector and a different pattern of trading links, Dutch and Danish prices will also be stabilized. But, in the absence of any other changes, their output levels will be depressed by the higher interest rates. And, in a second round effect, those deflations will tend to reduce Danish and Dutch prices while the conditions in Germany will not be affected again. Hence the supply side shocks will tend to show negative correlations for those countries most closely allied with German monetary policy. Demand shocks may show the same effect although this (being a second round effect) will naturally involve weaker negative correlations.

That would explain the apparently perverse results in table D.2. But what it is really signaling is a potential confusion between policy shocks and stochastic shocks (the former being an endogenous response by policy makers, the latter being exogenous to policy makers and to the economy). Our techniques of analysis cannot distinguish between the two although it obviously makes a difference both to our ability to correctly allocate countries to the different groups, and to our judgment of whether the groups could be regarded as having sufficient internal symmetry to make a currency union worthwhile and sustainable. To do that requires a different methodology and an examination of the dominant policy effects country-by-country. That is a subject for the next stage of research and lies beyond the scope of this paper.

When seen over different periods of time (tables D.3 to D.6), it is clear that the 70s and the 80s saw the greatest degree of symmetry, and that the 90s saw no significant correlations for *any* of the countries. Interestingly, Germany's demand correlations in the latter period are very significant (despite the small sample), but change sign and cease to be significant when she is removed from the group average. Similarly the supply correlations also drop and lose significance when double counting is taken out. This implies two things: firstly, the question of double counting in the case of big countries is very important. Secondly, the impact of German unification is also very important (we shall see this when we discuss the existence of a German zone in the next subsection). These results show how the pursuit of domestic interests by Germany at the beginning of the current decade has damaged the cohesion of the European economy and hence the attempts to forge a coherent monetary policy. This is to be compared to the 80s when Germany's shocks were very closely linked to those of its partners.

More generally this build up of correlations through the 70s and 80s, even when double counting is taken out, vanishes again in the 90s - back down to a level broadly similar to that of the 60s. But with double counting the significance pattern remains largely unchanged. So it is not just a matter of a smaller sample; it is genuinely a case of increasing asymmetries. Moreover, the correlations with the EU average do not die either, which implies that the divergence of the 90s may be leading to a weakening of the core-periphery distinction. Notice also that these remarks apply as strongly to France and Germany as they do to the smaller countries. The French and German correlations, which had been built up both between themselves and with the rest of the core during the 70s and 80s, all fall away in the 90s. The symmetry of the French-German axis therefore appears to be weaker than it was and possibly insignificant. Hence the overall problem is one of greater divergence within the core as a whole, rather than the emergence of an inner French-German axis in which the weaker brethren have got left behind.

Looking again at the changes when double counting is allowed, we find Denmark and the Netherlands to be negatively correlated with the rest of the core, while the Austrian, Belgian and Luxembourg supply disturbances are largely unaffected. So the major change is in the French and German correlations, unsurprisingly given double counting and the weight of those countries in the core. This shows that if a core monetary union were formed with policies directed at the French-German average, then the core might have a reasonable chance of success. Only the Netherlands and Austria would need some compensating transfers or regionally distinct policies to remove local disequilibria. However, in the absence of significant correlations on the demand side, the core's policies would still have to be directed at *both* prices *and* quantities. Price stability policies alone, under the control of an independent central bank, would generate significant costs even within the core; some attention must be paid to the real side if this core union is to survive. Growth and employment depend on that, as the current difficulties of the French and German economies demonstrate only too clearly.

Table D.3: Correlation Coefficients, 1961:3-1969:4

CORE	With double counting						No double counting			
	Demand			Supply:			Demand		Supply:	
	w Core Ave	w Ger	w EU	w Core Ave	w Ger	w EU	w Core Ave	w Peri	w Core Ave	w Peri
AU	.14	-.05	-.01	.29	.27	.27	.08	.22	.25	-.13
F	.47*	-.06	.36*	.85*	.33	.76*	-.03	-.03	.32	-.24
G	.55*	1.00	.66*	.68*	1.00	.49*	.07	.06	.37*	.02
B	-.07	-.07	-.18	.22	.40*	.27	-.08	-.14	.20	-.15
DK	-.18	-.34*	-.17	-.39*	-.41*	-.28	-.16	-.29	-.36*	.04
LU	-.18	.41*	.16	.20	.31	.26	.03	-.10	.20	-.23
NL	-.42*	-.38*	-.33	-.28	-.37*	-.16	-.37*	.03	-.24	-.04

Sample Size = 34
Critical Value = 0.339
* denotes significance of the correlation coefficient at the 5% level

(continued)

Table D.3 (continued): Correlation Coefficients, 1961:3-1969:4

PERIPHERY	with double counting						No double counting			
	Demand			Supply:			Demand		Supply:	
	w Peri Ave	w Ger	wEU	w Peri Ave	w Ger	w EU	w Peri Ave	w Core	w Peri Ave	w Core
S	-.34*	-.18	-.11	-.05	-.06	-.20	-.22	-.18	.26	-.29
I	-.40*	-.03	.05	-.40*	-.37*	.18	-.13	-.01	.05	-.03
P	-.14	.09	-.07	-.12	-.16	-.03	.12	-.19	.15	-.12
GR	-.15	-.27	-.17	.15	-.17	-.31	-.18	-.07	.15	-.31
IR	-.02	-.07	-.16	-.03	-.12	.02	.13	-.09	-.02	-.02
UK	.60*	.15	.00	.80*	-.31	-.77*	.09	.24	-.01	-.42
FI	.03	.15	-.03	.06	-.31	.06	.11	.12	.09	.16
SW	-.48*	.26	.46*	-.08	-.03	-.02	.07	.15	.15	-.08

Sample Size = 34
Critical Value = 0.339
* denotes significance of the correlation coefficient at the 5% level

Table D.4: Correlation Coefficients, 1970:1-1979:4

CORE	With double counting						No double counting			
	Demand:			Supply:			Demand:		Supply:	
	w Core Ave	w Ger	w EU	w Core Ave	w Ger	w EU	w Core Ave	w Peri	w Core Ave	w Peri
AU	.28	.15	.23	.35*	.33*	.24	.17	.25	.28	-.11
F	.37*	-.05	.35*	.54*	.41*	.55*	-.00	-.19	.39*	-.44*
G	.63*	1	.40*	.93*	1	.78*	-.11	-.14	.55*	-.38*
B	.14	-.07	.13	.45*	.38*	.50*	.03	-.26	.42*	-.42*
DK	-.11	.29	-.11	-.57*	-.48*	-.53*	.08	.02	-.56*	.32*
LU	-.14	.01	-.29	.39*	.45*	.35*	-.03	.35*	.39*	-.22
NL	.05	.05	.05	-.58*	-.29	-.51*	-.04	-.03	-.28	-.40*

Sample Size = 40
Critical Value = 0.312
* denotes significance of the correlation coefficient at the 5% level

(continued)

Table D.4 (continued): Correlation Coefficients, 1970:1-1979:4

PERIPH ERY	with double counting						No double counting			
	Demand			Supply:			Demand		Supply:	
	w Peri Ave	w Ger	wEU	w Peri Ave	w Ger	w EU	w Peri Ave	w Core	w Peri Ave	w Core
S	.03	-.46*	-.01	-.29	.01	.27	.01	-.14	-.22	.23
I	-.34*	.04	.11	-.41*	.08	.33*	.08	.15	.06	.23
P	.21	.05	-.03	.31*	-.14	-.25	-.14	-.00	-.27	-.18
GR	.17	-.19	-.22	-.16	.24	.23	.19	-.19	-.15	.24
IR	-.09	-.05	.00	.10	-.27	-.22	-.09	.02	.11	-.22
UK	.77*	.04	-.51*	.81*	-.42*	-.72*	-.03	-.13	-.11	-.40*
FI	.20	-.28	.03	-.33*	.13	.20	.24	.02	-.23	.04
SW	-.49*	.21	.24	-.25	.10	.24	-.11	.07	-.14	.18

Sample Size = 40
Critical Value = 0.312
* denotes significance of the correlation coefficient at the 5% level

Table D.5: Correlation Coefficients, 1980:1-1989:4

CORE	With double counting						No double counting			
	Demand			Supply:			Demand		Supply:	
	w Core Ave	w Ger	w EU	w Core Ave	w Ger	w EU	w Core Ave	w Peri	w Core Ave	w Peri
AU	.35*	.16	.24	.65*	.61*	.62*	.31	.04	.62*	-.49*
F	.73*	.26	.64*	.56*	.46*	.55*	.44*	-.20	.44*	-.51*
G	.36*	1	.41*	.94*	1	.92*	.38*	-.43*	.63*	-.69*
B	-.03	-.05	.03	.28	.25	.26	-.03	-.05	.25	-.16
DK	.08	-.18	.00	-.30	-.31	-.32*	-.02	.25	-.27	.23
LU	.05	.20	.16	.22	.23	.21	.22	.23	.22	-.19
NL	-.49*	-.07	-.52*	-.53*	-.32*	-.42*	-.33*	.29	-.38*	.22

Sample Size = 40
Critical Value = 0.312
* denotes significance of the correlation coefficient at the 5% level

(continued)

Table D.5 (continued): Correlation Coefficients, 1980:1-1989:4

PERIPH ERY	with double counting						No double counting			
	Demand			Supply:			Demand		Supply:	
	w Peri Ave	w Ger	wEU	w Peri Ave	w Ger	w EU	w Peri Ave	w Core	w Peri Ave	w Core
S	-.12	.16	.49*	-.29	.11	.22	.03	.53*	-.26	.20
I	-.71*	.39*	.57*	-.59*	.50*	.60*	-.03	.15	-.34*	.52*
P	.33*	-.44*	-.29	.13	-.01	-.16	-.20	-.25	-.08	-.16
GR	-.11	.18	.17	-.17	.25	.29	-.01	.22	-.17	.33*
IR	-.10	-.00	.17	-.01	-.12	-.05	-.09	.18	.03	-.07
UK	.48*	.20	-.22	.80*	.49*	-.64*	-.01	.05	-.56*	-.48*
FI	.00	.01	.21	-.31*	.11	.22	.02	.20	-.17	.17
SW	-.37*	.32*	.06	-.66*	.55*	.65*	-.06	-.06	-.47*	.58*

Sample Size = 40
Critical Value = 0.312
* denotes significance of the correlation coefficient at the 5% level

Table D.6: Correlation Coefficients, 1990:1-1995:1

CORE	With double counting						No double counting			
	Demand			Supply:			Demand		Supply:	
	w Core Ave	w Ger	w EU	w Core Ave	w Ger	w EU	w Core Ave	w Peri	w Core Ave	w Peri
AU	.34	.42	.27	.45*	.21	.58*	.28	-.05	.25	-.46*
F	.37	-.21	.30	.43*	.18	.54*	.02	.21	.31	-.45*
G	.69*	1	.53*	.68*	1	.52*	-.23	.11	.11	-.07
B	.23	-.07	.37	.46*	.21	.47*	-.06	-.15	.40	-.25
DK	-.05	.03	-.13	-.24	.01	-.31	-.03	.11	-.18	.19
LU	-.09	-.11	-.30	-.01	.09	.20	-.10	.06	-.01	-.20
NL	-.04	-.24	.16	-.21	.27	-.24	-.09	-.44*	-.10	.10

Sample Size = 21
Critical Value = 0.433
* denotes significance of the correlation coefficient at the 5% level

(continued)

Table D.6 (continued): Correlation Coefficients, 1990:1-1995:1

PERIPHERY	with double counting						No double counting			
	Demand			Supply:			Demand		Supply:	
	w Peri Ave	w Ger	wEU	w Peri Ave	w Ger	w EU	w Peri Ave	w Core	w Peri Ave	w Core
S	-.02	-.24	.01	-.42	.08	.44*	.17	-.03	-.38	.26
I	-.38	-.22	.09	.04	.01	.07	.12	-.08	.25	.17
P	.00	-.33	-.55*	-.09	.05	.16	.08	-.58*	.16	.17
GR	.24	.14	.27	-.10	.35	.53*	.13	.33	-.08	.65*
IR	.15	.27	.44*	-.35	.03	.21	-.15	.37	-.31	-.04
UK	.77	-.04	-.35	.36	.14	-.11	.01	-.06	.03	.04
FI	-.18	.02	.25	-.59*	.09	.65*	-.30	.06	-.46*	.40
SW	-.39	-.33	-.21	-.65*	.13	.47*	-.04	-.35	.19	.07

Sample Size = 21
Critical Value = 0.433
* denotes significance of the correlation coefficient at the 5% level

A German Economic Zone?

The estimated correlation coefficients *with* double counting display a much higher correspondence with the *Bayoumi and Eichengreen (1994)* anchor country results. Can we go further and conclude that a core union, where Germany sets the policies, is viable? From columns 2 and 5 we see that, just like in the previous section, there is greater symmetry in the supply shocks than in the demand shocks and only Austria has significant correlations on both accounts. When these correlations are examined through different sub-samples, the 70s and 80s again show closer links between Germany and the other core countries. Therefore, in periods when external constraints have affected the demand side (oil crises and the EMS respectively), the supply side of the economy had to react in very similar ways to compensate for the changes in demand. The 90s, however, found the core countries losing the few common features that had previously united them. Interestingly, France has demand shocks negatively correlated with Germany, which only become positively correlated during the period of the EMS when price stability was an objective common to both countries. This positive correlation is then reversed again in the next decade. Thus, a German economic zone might be viable, but it would be very limited. But any such arrangement would be less symmetric, and hence more costly, than a core union based on the average of Austria, France, Germany and Belgium. That in turn, would require *greater* co-ordination between the national fiscal policies and the common monetary policy, although a little more weight could be given to price stability and the independence of monetary policy.

The correlations presented here are therefore much smaller than their counterparts in *Bayoumi and Eichengreen (1994)*. There are two important reasons for this. First, Bayoumi and Eichengreen's sample finishes in 1988 whereas ours finishes in early 1995. As we have seen, the 90s was a period of increasingly asymmetric shocks and would therefore reduce the overall correlations. Indeed it is only too likely that the last 6 years of our sample would generate differential shocks in output, covering as they do the "hard" EMS regime up to 1992, the break up of the EMS regime and the 1991-94 recession. If at the same time prices were relatively steady, as they were, this would imply lower supply shock correlations while the underlying monetary convergence would have left the demand shock correlations largely unchanged. And this is exactly what we find when we compare table D.2 with Bayoumi and Eichengreen's results, all of which suggest that such symmetries as we find here are driven by policy intervention, or policy induced shocks, rather than by a convergence in the underlying (stochastic) shocks. A monetary union formed on this basis might prove extremely fragile when faced both by the limits of policy and by the capriciousness of policy makers' preferences.

Second, Bayoumi and Eichengreen use annual data, whereas we have quarterly data. That suggests that an important part of the asymmetries are also to do with the *timing* of the shocks, rather than with their size and incidence on average. If adjustments really are sticky, these timing differences could accumulate into serious costs for the members of a monetary union. We investigate that further by examining the differences, in timing and impact, between the transmission mechanisms within each country (section 6).

The Periphery Economies

The periphery economies show nothing of the same cohesion or internal symmetry. Italy and the UK, who must dominate the periphery economically, show some demand shock correlations with the rest of the periphery - but only when we allow double counting. That means such cohesion is illusory; take the double counting out and the significant correlations vanish. On the other hand their supply correlations with the core group are significant, this time negative for the UK[6] and positive for Italy. Rather surprisingly, Greece and Portugal also have significant correlations with the core, maintained for most sub-samples. On the whole, however, these results do not suggest that the periphery could successfully join the core or act as a "counter-union" of those countries left out; nor would there be much advantage in them trying to do so. They are simply too different and asymmetric in their shocks. This is not surprising. Whereas the core countries have been following a common monetary path over the past 10-15 years and have shown some convergence, the periphery is defined as the default group which either chose not to participate or at least showed less convergence. Their lack of correlation therefore reflects the pursuit of individual targets rather than a failed partnership. This is not to say, however, that the periphery could not act as a coalition or a co-operative bloc in opposition to the core, and benefit significantly from the experience. But it would have to be done on a discretionary basis with tailor-made and internally co-ordinated policies, *not* as a formal exchange rate union.

Is the Core-Periphery Classification Correct?

Table D.2 also shows the correlations between demand and supply shocks in the core countries with those in the periphery, and between the periphery countries' shocks and those in the core. On the demand side there is very little between group correlation. In fact, without double counting the demand shocks are no more correlated within groups than they are between groups.

On the supply side things are clearer. Here the correlations between core members and the periphery are all high and negative in sign (except Denmark and Luxembourg). This implies that objectives are quite different and, what is more, they are rigorously pursued. Similar conclusions hold when comparing the peripheral countries with the core average, Greece, Finland and Sweden apart. However, any significance of this results is coming from the period of the 80s and a little bit from the 70s, whereas it disappears in the other sub-samples. Indeed, the reversal of the expected sign patterns in the last two columns of table D.2 for Denmark and the Netherlands suggests that these two countries might function better if transferred to the periphery. Similarly, on this basis Sweden, Finland, Italy and Greece would be candidates for the core. Hence it would certainly be a good idea to re-examine the criteria for membership of the core before proceeding.

5. The Costs: Are They Small?

5.1 The Costs of Asymmetric Shocks

Section 2 showed that the cost of forming or joining a monetary union depends on two things: the degree of correlation between shocks in member countries, and the size of those shocks. For the costs to be small, the correlations must approach unity *and* the shocks must have approximately equal variances. From table D.2, the first condition is violated in every case in both the core and the periphery. In fact a simple one-tailed test shows every correlation coefficient is significantly less than 0.5 (the lower critical value being 0.36), where

$$z = \frac{1}{2}\ln\left[(1+\hat{\rho})/(1-\hat{\rho})\right] \sim N\left(0,(n-3)^{-1}\right)$$

under the null and n=135. Hence, in the absence of double counting, no country satisfies the first condition in this period.[7]

For the second condition, we have set out the standard deviations of the shocks in table D.7. To test the equality of the variances of the errors from different VAR equations, we can use the Wald test (*Hamilton, 1995*, p. 301):

$$\frac{n(\hat{\sigma}_i^2 - \hat{\sigma}_j^2)^2}{2\hat{\sigma}_i^4 - 4(\hat{\rho}\hat{\sigma}_i\hat{\sigma}_j)^2 + 2\hat{\sigma}_j^4}$$

which is distributed asymptotically as $\chi^2_{(1)}$, where $\hat{\sigma}_j = \overline{\sigma}_i$ in view of (2.3) to (2.5).

This test will have critical values of 3.8 and 6.6 at the 5% and 1% significance levels. But applying such a test to table D.7 shows that every single variance is significantly different from its group average at the 1% level, with the single exception of the Spanish demand shocks in the periphery. But that is exactly one of the cases where the correlation coefficient is both vanishingly small and negative. Hence, every single case that matters violates the second condition for low costs too. In particular that happens for each country in the core group.

Given this rather damning evidence, the costs will certainly not be small - not even within the core. Can we say anything more concrete about those costs? Notice that if $\rho \cong ½$ and $\sigma_j \cong \sigma_k$, then the last term of (2.1) becomes

$$\sqrt{\sigma_j^2 - 2\rho\sigma_j\sigma_k + \sigma_k^2} = \sigma_j .$$

In that case the cost becomes $\gamma(\beta_{ij}+\beta_{jk})\phi(0)\sigma_j$, which is just one standard error away from zero, the minimum cost under exactly symmetric shocks or no disturbances at all. But we have $\rho<½$ and $\sigma_j \neq \sigma_k$ in every case. Hence the costs for each country are *at least* one standard deviation larger than the adjustment costs which that country would have faced in a floating regime. And in many cases they will be considerably larger than that since $\rho=0$.

Table D.7: Standard Deviations of Aggregate Supply and Aggregate Demand Shocks by Country (Without Double Counting)

	Demand:	σ_i	$\bar{\sigma}_i$	Supply:	σ_i	$\bar{\sigma}_i$
Austria		.0117	.0042		.0156	.0065
France		.0075	.0045		.0128	.0063
Germany		.0077	.0002		.0086	.0001
Belgium		.0097	.0043		.0053	.0067
Denmark		.0084	.0042		.0095	.0066
Luxembourg		.0120	.0040		.0074	.0065
Netherlands		.0080	.0043		.0116	.0068
Core average		.0044	.0258		.0260	
Spain		.0074	.0067		.0093	.0072
Italy		.0098	.0072		.0102	.0080
Portugal		.0219	.0059		.0123	.0065
Greece		.0282	.0000		.0286	.0000
Ireland		.0087	.0060		.0105	.0064
UK		.0109	.0069		.0114	.0067
Finland		.0125	.0062		.0170	.0064
Sweden		.0218	.0059		.0207	.0065
Periphery ave.		.0064			.0256	
EU average		.0015			.0015	

5.2 The Size of Shocks: Who Would Want to Join a Currency Union?

According to table D.7, the periphery countries all have shocks which are larger than the group average on the demand side, but smaller than the group average on the supply side (Greece excepted). But the demand and supply shocks of individual countries are of roughly equal size. The core countries, by contrast, also have demand shocks which exceed their group average and supply shocks which are smaller than their group average; but in this case the demand shocks are smaller than the supply shocks (Belgium and Luxembourg excepted). Thus the periphery average shock is more stable than its component parts on the demand side, but less stable on the supply side. These countries would presumably wish to join a regime which offered this greater stability on the demand side - perhaps through better monetary policies and an independent central bank - provided it can be done without destabilizing the supply side. That would require additional policies to cater for stabilizing output levels over and above the independent monetary policy, so it is doubtful whether membership of a currency union on Maastricht lines could supply that stability.

The core likewise contains automatic stabilizers on the demand side (the aggregate is more stable than its constituent parts), but destabilizing mechanisms on the supply side. Hence the greater symmetry between the core countries has its own cost in making the differences between countries smaller, but the variability of the system as a whole larger. Countries may be less keen to remain in a regime with that property.

On the other hand, core countries individually have smaller shocks and a more uniform distribution of shocks than the periphery countries. In that respect core countries make better candidates for a common currency. But the fact that the supply shocks are much larger in aggregate than the demand shocks in that group also implies that the core is not well suited to (or in need of) a single monetary policy conducted by an independent central bank, *unless* it is actively supported by policies directed at stabilizing output at the same time.

6. Asymmetric Transmission Mechanisms

The symmetry or asymmetry of shocks is not the end of the story. Common shocks in economies which have asymmetric economic structures will have asymmetric impacts on the targets of policy and on welfare.

6.1 Impulse Response Analysis

We therefore have to examine the similarity and differences in transmission mechanisms within the core and periphery. This we do by estimating impulse response functions constructed from domestic variables and group aggregates. The results are presented in the form of the variance decomposition of the h-step ahead forecast error, indicating the percentage of forecast error variance of one particular variable due to the innovation in another variable, i.e. the proportion of the total forecast error variance of one variable caused by shocks to the moving average representation of another endogenous variable. The Choleski variance decomposition used here is, however, not invariant to the ordering of the variables in the system. This is because the variance-covariance matrix is unlikely to be nearly diagonal in practice. Different orderings can in fact lead to significantly different variance decompositions. We must therefore impose some kind of arbitrary decomposition of the covariance matrix of the residuals so that the errors themselves are orthogonal. If the residuals are uncorrelated, the ordering is immaterial and the order of factorization makes little difference. In the case of significant partial correlation coefficients, the usual procedure involves starting with a particular ordering and then reversing or changing the ordering to see if the results are changed. If they are, we have to appeal to economic theory in order to impose a structural interpretation.

In our case however, experimentation with different orderings of the variables (especially putting the interest rate before the money supply) did not substantially affect the outcome of the decompositions and the ordering - i.e. money → long-term government bond yield → CPI → industrial production - was retained. That particular ordering was derived by imposing a "semi-structural" interpretation on the model. This causal and temporal ordering implies that movements in money precede movements in the other three variables; interest rates, the price level and output. In addition, core and periphery aggregate variables appear before national European variables. This restriction results from the observation (section 5.2) that the aggregates as a whole are larger than any of the constituent parts and thus less likely to respond contemporaneously to shocks to individual European economies. In addition, given differences between the two aggregates and the national economies, the aggregation procedure involves a cancellation of the errors, making the aggregates less prone to contemporaneous shocks than the national economies.

6.2 Results: The Core Countries

The numerical results of this procedure, collected together, country by country, tell the following story:

Belgium: Core money supply exerts very little influence on the national variables. The core's long term bond yields, on the other hand, have a strong influence on Belgian long term interest rates, although the percentage of the latter's variance which is explained that way peaks at 37% after two years. For Belgian prices, the influence of core interest rates is also strong and persistent - it peaks at 26% after five years. The core price level also has a strong influence on Belgian prices, even though the percentage explained reaches its peak two years after any changes. Core output levels, on the other hand, have some influence on Belgian activity levels but not on much else. And if we use periphery aggregates in place of the core variables, we find the influences on Belgian variable become almost entirely domestic. Belgium is therefore a genuine core group country in its responses, with her focus almost entirely on her nominal targets.

Denmark: The picture here is rather different. While core money has rather little impact on Danish national variables, core interest rates have a considerable influence on both Danish money supply and Danish interest rates - explaining up to a quarter of the variance of the forecast errors. But those core interest rates take two to five years to exert their influence. Core price movements, by contrast, do not have much influence on Danish prices; and core output has only a weak influence on Danish output, and then only with a lag. This is at variance with the responses of a typical core country such as Belgium. Indeed, replacing core aggregates with periphery variables changes the picture radically. Periphery interest rates have a sizeable influence (up to 35%) on Danish money, interest rates and output. Otherwise things remain domestic. A nominally peripheral but marginally core country therefore, where the core influences take a long time to emerge.

France: By contrast again, core money appears to be very important for the French price level; and core interest rates completely dominate French interest rates and hence French prices. The former is an instantaneous influence, the latter emerges after two years. What is more, the pervasive influence of core interest rates on French interest rates declines only slightly from 75% to 73% after 5 years, whereas the percentages for French domestic interest rates falls from 34% to 18% over the same period. The influence of core interest rates accounts for nearly 40% of the variance in French prices. Core prices, on the other hand, have an immediate impact of 20%, declining to 6% after 5 years, while domestic price movements account for 76% to 50% of subsequent price movements. Finally, core output has a strong influence on French output, but is always lower than the influence of domestic activity levels. Just like Belgium, periphery aggregates are almost without influence. The rest of the explanation falls to domestic variables. Hence France appears to be completely dominated by the core, but only in monetary policy. On the real side the influences are domestic.

Germany: In Germany, the core variables play an even stronger role - not surprisingly given Germany's size within the core and the fact that we have double counting here. Core variables dominate the German money supply, German interest rates, prices and output. In fact domestic variables have only a minor influence on monetary conditions (30% or less), prices (15%), and output (15%). The rest of the explanatory power is provided by the core variables. With the strength of these figures, it is hard to avoid the conclusion that Germany *is* the core in terms of impulse responses. France and the other members are simply not important in comparison. That of course implies a radically different response pattern again, as does the *consistency* of core influences over time. No one has that constant a pattern of responses. The periphery variables never have any influence here - except in prices and output. But that is never more than 20% of the total.

The Netherlands: Dutch responses are closer to Germany, but not exactly the same. Core money again has no influence, but core interest rates have some influence on Dutch money supplies and prices (up to 30%). Domestic variables still have the largest influence, however. Core interest rates completely dominate Dutch interest rates, just as in Germany. But, contrary to Germany, core money has no influence on Dutch interest rates; and core interest rates take one year to play themselves in. Moreover, domestic output is independent of core influences (unlike Germany). Dutch prices also follow their core counterparts, but only to 20%. However, just as in Germany, the periphery aggregates do not influence Dutch variables to any extent; the activity that is not core driven is domestically driven. Hence this is a follower country. Given the build up of influence from core variables, the Netherlands is independent in the short run, but core dominated in the long run.

Austria is also a clear core member, but has some periphery influences on interest rates. Money is domestically determined, but interest rates are 50% core determined in the short run and core dominated in the long run. Again, prices and output are domestically determined at first, but are shared between core and domestic influences in the longer run. There are no periphery influences here.

6.3 Results: The Periphery Countries

Italy: Italy stands apart from the rest of the periphery and much of the core as well. One problem is that core interest rates play an important role in some of the Italian variables - especially Italian interest rates (up to 50% influence after 2 years). Core interest rates also explain more than a quarter of the variance in Italian prices, up to 20% for Italian output and 10% of Italian money supply. But the rest of the explanation (that is the majority) comes from periphery or domestic variables. In this, the Italian variables end up being influenced less by periphery variables than by core variables - except for the money supply, which is 30% periphery explained. But the periphery influences are nonetheless not negligible. For example, Italian interest rates are 40% periphery influenced and 50% influenced by domestic inflation, compared to 55% core inflation and 40% domestic interest rates. Similarly for the Italian price level. By contrast, Italian output is more influenced by periphery output (50%) as opposed to core output (15%). Italy really is a mixture of core and periphery responses, in contrast to the other large European economies. Domestic influences are relatively small.

The UK: Here again there are some core responses, but the influences are mainly from the periphery. Money supply is almost entirely set domestically, unlike its partners. Interest rates are 20% core driven, with the remaining influences divided between domestic interest rates and domestic money supply. The price level is driven by past domestic prices in the first instance; but after 2 years domestic money supply becomes the dominant influence. Output is almost entirely domestically driven. Of the remaining influences, the periphery influences UK money supply a little, and periphery interest rates influence UK interest rates quite a lot (up to 25%). If the core influences are removed, prices do follow periphery prices to some extent and output is influenced by periphery activity levels. But the picture is of a country which is quite different in its responses from all other countries, and where the economy's responses are mostly domestically driven.

Spain: The Spanish economic responses also appear to be fairly independent of core influences. Core interest rates have a weak influence on Spanish rates, but only after 4 years. Elsewhere domestic variables dominate changes in Spanish targets, except that core interest rates influence Spanish interest rates - but again only after 4 years. Periphery variables, by contrast, do play a significant role; as we see from the 20% contribution in the setting of the Spanish money supply, 60% in Spanish interest rates, 35% in the variation of Spanish prices, and 20% in Spanish output. Hence Spain is more periphery linked, and *less* domestically dependent than most countries. What is more, the domestic influences of all fade after 1 year. We do not observe that elsewhere.

Sweden: Sweden shows some influences from both the core and periphery, but more from the latter. Core money does not matter; periphery money (30%) and domestic money (50%) are the dominant forces on money supply. Swedish interest rates do follow core interest rates (30%) as well as past domestic interest rates. Swedish prices are predominantly a domestic affair; core monetary and interest rate policy has a weak influence, but only after a 4 year lag. Periphery monetary policy, however, is much more important (50%). Finally, Swedish output is domestically driven. This economy is therefore split between core, periphery and domestic responses.

Finland is another domestically driven economy, except that she appears to have begun to gear her monetary policy to activity levels in the core. Finnish interest rates are set domestically, with a little influence from the core. Prices are set domestically, and while output is a little sensitive to core monetary policy it is mostly domestically driven. Periphery variables appear to have very little influence in all this - a little influence on interest rates, prices and output perhaps, but domestic effects are large. An economy in transition to the core therefore?

Portugal: Core interest rates have some influence but only comparatively later on. This influence is fairly weak and appears in Portuguese interest rates and prices. The remaining influences on Portuguese targets are domestic. Indeed, the periphery only has an influence on Portuguese prices and output, and then only with a lag. This appears to be a periphery country but with substantial short run independence. That is rather different from other comparable countries such as Spain.

Greece, by contrast, shows almost *no* role for core variables. At most there is a weak (15%) and delayed (after 2 years) influence of core interest rates on Greek rates and of core prices on Greek prices. But the dependence on periphery aggregates is almost equally weak - with the exception of periphery interest rates on Greek rates. Everything else is domestic. This economy appears to be trying to follow an independent path on the real side, but to straddle the core and periphery monetary policies for nominal variables.

6.4 The Differences in Innovation Responses: Some Examples

The forecast error variance decompositions described above can be best illustrated graphically. Figures D.4 to D.7 show the percentage of forecast error variance decomposition for long-term interest rates and industrial production for two core countries (Germany and France), as well as two periphery countries (Italy and the UK). By no means exclusive, these - typical - examples serve to highlight the differences existing not only between, but also within, the two groups.

Figure D.4: Forecast Error Variance Decompositions: Innovations to Core and National Long-Term Interest Rates for France and Italy

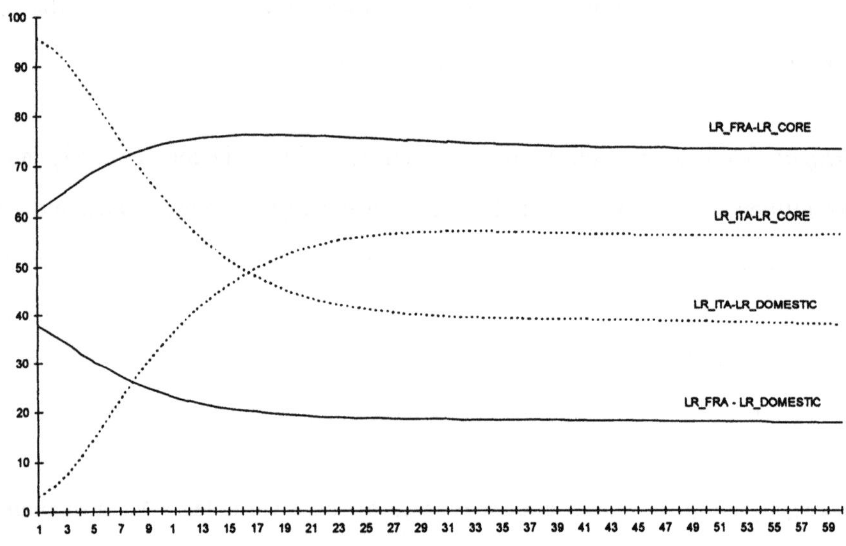

Figure D.5: Forecast Error Variance Decompositions: Innovations to Periphery and National Long-Term Interest Rates for France and Italy

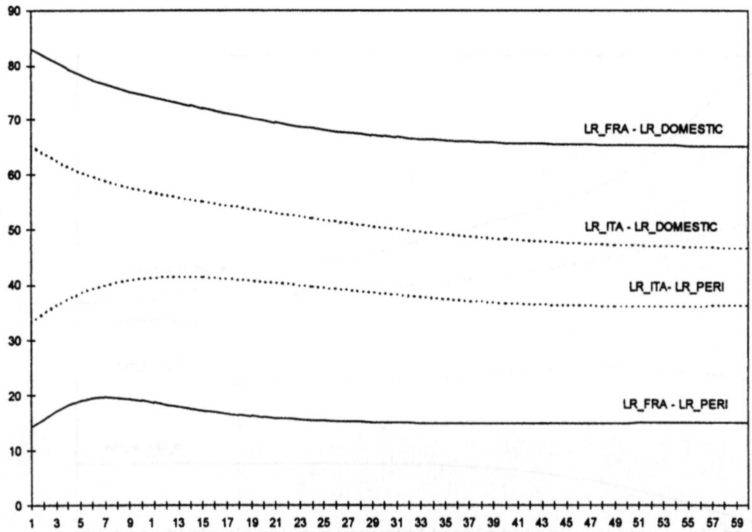

Figure D.6: Forecast Error Variance Decompositions: Innovations to Core and National Industrial Production Variables for Germany and the UK

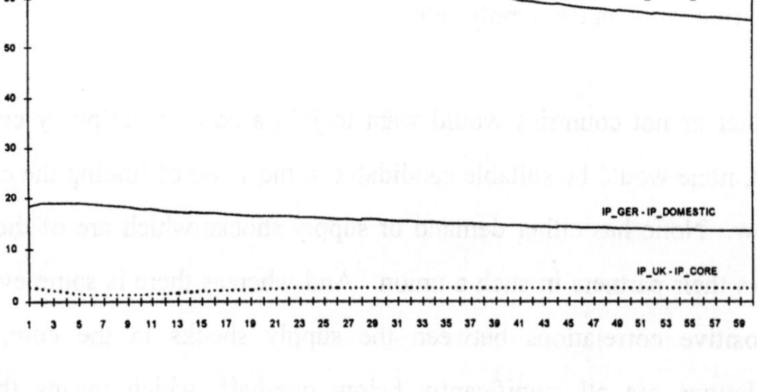

Figure D.7: Forecast Error Variance Decompositions: Innovations to Periphery and National Industrial Production Variables for Germany and the UK

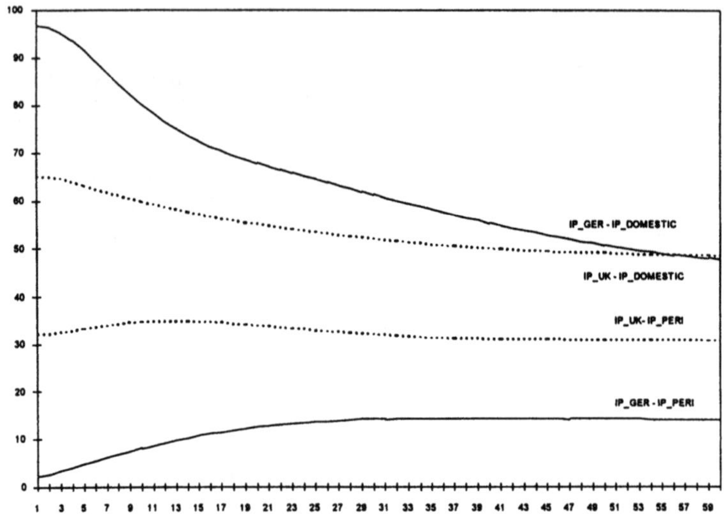

7. Conclusions

(a) In addition to the gains from lower transactions costs, all countries have some incentive to join a currency union in that the core and periphery aggregate shocks are smaller on average than their constituent parts. But this is true only on the supply side.

(b) Whether or not countries would want to join a core or periphery currency union, none would be suitable candidates in the sense of finding the costs to be low. None has either demand or supply shocks which are of the same size as their partners in such a union. And whereas there is some evidence of positive correlations between the supply shocks in the core, those correlations are all significantly below one-half, which means that the expected costs will be at least one standard deviation larger than what could have been achieved under floating. In addition, there is no evidence of positive correlations among the core demand shocks, or the periphery shocks of either kind.

(c) The distinction between core and periphery is well established however. The core disturbances are negatively related to their periphery counterparts, while the periphery disturbances are largely uncorrelated with those in the core.

(d) For all the attention paid in the literature to the asymmetries between shocks in the core countries, the greater asymmetries are actually in the strength and timing of the transmission mechanisms. Even common shocks would have asymmetric effects therefore.

(e) The time pattern of these correlations shows some convergence within the core during the 80s, but that that convergence has been completely lost during the 90s. That makes sticking to the Maastricht timetable a very risky enterprise.

Appendix A: Data

Quarterly data on real and nominal GNP in local currency for each of the fifteen member states of the EU were taken from the *Quarterly National Accounts* of the OECD over the period 1960:1-1992:4. The aggregates for the Core and the Periphery were constructed by first converting the national GNP's into ECU's on the basis of 1990 base-period bilateral exchange rates, and then aggregating the converted GNPs in ECUs across countries. The weights used in the aggregation procedure are GNP weights of the respective country in the desired aggregate.

The ratio of nominal to real GNP yielded the implicit GDP deflator, which was then used to construct GDP deflator inflation. Following *Bayoumi and Eichengreen (1992, 1994)* growth and inflation were calculated as the first difference of the logarithm of real GNP and the first difference between the ratio of the logarithm of nominal to real GNP respectively. These data are all seasonally adjusted.

In our study of the European transmission mechanisms the set-up of the estimation for each European country is as follows: the VAR systems include the narrow money supply (M) in index form, the long-term government bond yield (LR), the consumer price index (CPI), the industrial production index (IP) and the equivalent Core and Periphery aggregates of the foregoing. All data are monthly and taken either from the IMF's *International Financial Statistics (IFS)*, the OECD's *Main Economic Indicators (MEI)* or national sources. All variables, with the exception of the long-term interest rate, are in logarithms. Except for Denmark's industrial production, which ends in 1993:12, and Spain's long-term interest rate, which starts in 1982:1, all series run from 1979:1 to 1994:12. Core and Periphery aggregates for the four variables are constructed as weighted aggregates of their national counterparts. The weights used in the aggregation process are the quarterly GDP weights described earlier.

Appendix B: Dynamic Properties

To employ the Blanchard-Quah decomposition, both variables have to be in stationary form (*Enders, 1995*). In addition, the elements of the x_t vector cannot be cointegrated. Finally, the estimated VAR system has to be stable and hence invertible so that we can move from the standard VAR representation (3.1) to the orthogonalized VMA form (3.3). This appendix establishes those three points as a necessary preliminary step to the Blanchard-Quah variance decompositions. Detailed test results are available from the authors upon request.

(i) Stationarity: Unit Root Tests on x_t

On the basis of Augmented Dickey-Fuller (ADF) tests, the logarithm of real output is integrated of order one, while the logarithm of prices is integrated of order two. The latter makes inflation an I(1) variable. The stationary vector Δx_t of variables therefore consists of the growth rate of the logarithm of real output (Δy) and the rate of change of inflation ($\Delta^2 p = \Delta\pi$). Exceptions are Belgium, which has an I(2) real output; Luxembourg, for which prices appear to be I(1); and Greece, where prices are also I(0). The last two results for prices may be ascribed either to price controls in the case of Greece and the existence of the Belgian-Luxembourg Economic Union in the case of Luxembourg; or possibly to the weak power of the tests employed.

(ii) Cointegration Tests

The next step is to check on the cointegration of the price and output variables in our VAR models. If we rewrite (3.1) in error correction form, we get

$$\Delta x_t = \Gamma_1 \Delta x_{t-1} + \ldots + \Gamma_k \Delta x_{t-k-1} + \Pi x_{t-k} + v_t \qquad \text{(A1)}$$

where

$$\Gamma_i = -(I - \sum_{j=1}^{i} A_j) \text{ and } \Pi = -(I - \sum_{j=1}^{k} A_j).$$

The test for cointegration is now $\Pi=0$, or that $r(\Pi)<n$ where Π is a matrix of order n (=2 in our case) and r(.) denotes rank. The latter is of course definitive, but estimates of (A1) yielded Π matrices of full rank. We conclude, therefore, that our x_t vectors do not contain cointegrated variables.

(iv) Invertibility

To move from $A(L)\Delta x_t=e_t$ to $\Delta x_t=D(L)\varepsilon_t$, where $D(L)=[A(L)]^{-1}P$ as defined by (3.3), requires the roots of A(L) all to lie outside the unit circle. Direct tests from the estimated VAR models used in the main text showed the roots of $C(L)=[A(L)]^{-1}$ all lay within the unit circle. The largest roots being around 0.91 for Belgium and 0.92 for Luxembourg. Since P is an orthogonal matrix PP'=I and these tests are definitive. The VAR models are therefore all invertible.

Endnotes

1. *Masson and Taylor (1993); Tavlas (1993)*, provide general surveys. *Eichengreen (1992); Bean (1994); Eichengreen (1990); De Grauwe and Vanhaverbeke (1993);* and *Bayoumi and Eichengreen (1993)*, review the work on the nature of the underlying shocks and factor mobility.

2. A full development of this model will be found in *Demertzis et al. (1997)*. We pick only the relevant results here.

3. The periphery might impose other costs on the core however, for example if it indulged in *systematic* competitive devaluations designed to offset the output losses forced on it by the core's adjustment difficulties. But that would just come out in a higher probability of larger ε_k values and hence of $\varepsilon_k>\varepsilon_j$ rather than $\varepsilon_k<\varepsilon_j$. That in turn would simply lead to a probability weighted average of β_{ij} and β_{jk} replacing $(\beta_{ij}+\beta_{jk})\phi(0)$ in (2.1), and of β_{1j} and β_{1k} for $(\beta_{ij}+\beta_{1k})\phi(0)$ in (2.2). That would increase the costs in (2.1) and reduce them in (2.2), but *not* remove either entirely. Our analysis is unaffected, although the cost-benefit calculus will be less favorable to the core.

4. See *Schwarz (1978); Hannan and Quinn (1979)*; and *Enders (1995)*, respectively.

5. **For n≤50, the approximation can be improved using the first two moments given in *Kendall and Stuart (1967)*, pp.292-3. However we apply the following statistic $(n-2)\rho^2/\sqrt{(1-\rho^2)}^{-1}$ which is asymptotically distributed as F(1, n-2) and which we have found to provide close approximations to the true statistic. This is the test used in the smaller subsamples in tables 3 through 6.**

6. **Indeed the UK shows greater independence from either of the groups, especially during the 80s when both correlations become significantly negative.**

7. **Recall from equations (2.3) to (2.5) that double counting is not the appropriate set up for these tests.**

References

AHMED, S.; ICKES, B.; WANG P.; YOO, B. (1993), International Business Cycles, American Economic Review, Vol. 83, 335-359.

BAYOUMI, T. (1992), The Effect of the ERM on Participating Economies, IMF Staff Papers, Vol. 39, 330-356.

BAYOUMI, T.; EICHENGREEN, B., Shocking Aspects of European Monetary Unification, in: GIAVAZZI, F.; TORRES, F., eds. (1994), Adjustment and Growth in the European Monetary Union, Cambridge: Cambridge University Press.

BAYOUMI, T. (1994), A Formal Model of Optimum Currency Areas, CEPR Discussion Paper Series No. 968, London: Centre for Economic Policy Research.

BAYOUMI, T.; EICHENGREEN, B. (1992), Is There a Conflict between EC Enlargement and European Monetary Unification?, CEPR Discussion Paper Series No. 646, London: Centre for Economic Policy Research.

BEAN, C. (1994), European Unemployment: A Survey, Journal of Economic Literature, Vol. 32, 573-619.

BLANCHARD, O.; QUAH, D. (1989), The Dynamic Effects of Aggregate Demand and Supply Disturbances, American Economic Review, Vol. 79, 655-673.

DE GRAUWE, P.; VANHAVERBEKE, W. (1993), Is Europe an optimum currency area?: evidence from regional data, in: MASSON, P.; TAYLOR, M., eds. (1993), Policy Issues in the Operation of Currency Areas, Cambridge: Cambridge University Press.

DEMERTZIS, M.; HUGHES HALLETT, A. (1995), On Measuring the Costs of Labor Immobility and Market Heterogeneity in Europe, CEPR Discussion Paper Series No. 1189, London: Centre for Economic Policy Research.

DEMERTZIS, M.; HUGHES HALLETT, A., RUMMEL, O. (1997), Is a Two-Speed System in Europe the Answer to the Conflict between the German and the Anglo-Saxon Models of Monetary Control, in MOERSCH, M.; BLACK, S, eds., Which Way Ahead for the European Financial Markets? The German and the Anglo-Saxon Model, New York: Eltevier Science Publishers.

EICHENGREEN, B. (1990), Is Europe an Optimum Currency Area?, CEPR Discussion Paper Series No. 478, London: Centre for Economic Policy Research.

ENDERS, W. (1995), Applied Econometric Time Series, New York: John Wiley & Sons.

ENGLUND, P.; VREDIN, A.; WARNE, A, Macroeconomic Shocks in an Open Economy, in: BERGSTRÖM, V.; VREDIN, A., eds. (1994), Measuring and Interpreting Business Cycles, Oxford: Clarendon Press.

HAMILTON, J. (1994), Time Series Analysis, Princeton: Princeton University Press.

HANNAN, E.; QUINN, B. (1978), The Determinants of the Order of an Autoregression, Journal of the Royal Statistical Society, Series B, Vol. 41, 190-195.

KENDALL, M.; STUART, A. (1967), The Advanced Theory of Statistics, London: Griffin.

KENEN, P., The Theory of Optimum Currency Areas: An Eclectic View, in: MUNDELL, R.; SWOBODA, A., eds. (1969), Monetary Problems of the International Economy, Chicago: University of Chicago Press.

LIPPI, M.; REICHLIN, L. (1993), The Dynamic Effects of Aggregate Demand and Supply Disturbances: Comment, American Economic Review, Vol. 83, 644-658.

MASSON, P.; TAYLOR, M., Currency Unions: a survey of the issues, in: MASSON, P.; TAYLOR, M., eds. (1993), Policy Issues in the Operation of Currency Unions, Cambridge: Cambridge University Press.

MCKINNON, R. (1963), Optimum Currency Areas, American Economic Review, Vol. 53, 717-725.

MUNDELL, R. (1961), The Theory of Optimum Currency Areas, American Economic Review, Vol. 51, 657-665.

SCHWARZ, G. (1978), Estimating the Dimension of a Model, The Annals of Statistics, Vol. 6, 461-464.

TAVLAS, G. (1993), The 'New' Theory of Optimum Currency Areas, The World Economy, Vol.16, 663-685.

Comments on: Does a Core -Periphery Regime Make Europe into an Optimal Currency Area?

Hans G. Monissen[1]

1. Introduction

An important criterion for countries to either form or join a currency union is the symmetry of various monetary and real shocks and the similarity of the underlying transmission mechanism. A formal model for assessing these multi-country interdependencies has been presented by *Bayoumi (1994)*. The Bayoumi microeconomic model provides the theoretical structure for similar theoretical and empirical endeavors and is the starting point for an econometric study by *Demertzis, Hallett and Rummel (1996)*. The fundamental aggregate supply and demand shocks have to be derived from a theoretical model. The standard procedure here relies on a technique proposed by *Blanchard and Quah (1989)* who start from a Keynesian aggregate demand and supply model with some nominal wage rigidity.

The Bayoumi model itself is a pure numéraire model (cf. the appendix) and is therefore not directly related to the aggregate monetary model utilized by Blanchard and Quah. It will be the purpose of this paper to present a simple (monetary) alternative structure providing the micro-foundation of a standard macroeconomic model. To avoid the intricacies of capital formation and infinite horizons, aggregate demand is modeled within the perspective of a simple quantity theoretical frame. This structure of the proposed model is outlined in section II. Different from the research of Demertzis, Hallett and Rummel or others who analyze the stochastic properties of various aggregate shocks which could, of course, also be done with our model, interest is here directed on some strategic aspects of central bank behavior. After all, one strong argument for creating a currency union for Europe is the fact that such an institutional arrangement could prevent the welfare-reducing strategic behavior of dominant central banks. To evaluate the welfare effects of such behavior, the central bank's decision function is not an ad hoc postulated decision function, but the utility function of each country's representative agent. Focusing on this function is only meaningful if the macroeconomic structure has a consistent microeconomic foundation. Some of the welfare aspects of game theoretical interactions are discussed in section III. Section IV summarizes the main results. A short appendix illustrates the assertion that the Bayoumi model is a microeconomic model with numéraire money.

2. Outline of the Model

Efforts to model the economic foundations of incomplete nominal adjustments offer a broad menu to choose from (e.g. *Romer, 1996*). Our choice is determined by the intention to relate real output or employment to the monetary policy instrument of the central bank (i.e. base money) and to derive the expenditure structure for domestic and foreign goods from an independent subset of structural equations. The simple macroeconomic structure for country i incorporates the following equations (*Monissen, 1973*): The production function relates real output and labor input, where X_i is a productivity parameter which could be stochastic:

$$Y_i = X_i L_i^{\alpha_i}. \tag{1}$$

The labor demand function is derived from the profit maximization calculus of a representative competitive firm which sets the marginal product equal to the real wage rate:

$$\frac{W_i}{P_i} = \alpha_i X_i L_i^{\alpha_i - 1}. \tag{2}$$

The labor supply function is derived from the utility maximization calculus described below:

$$\frac{W_i}{I_i} = \gamma_i L^{\delta_i}. \tag{3}$$

I_i denotes a "true" price index for country i as a function of n commodity prices and n nominal exchange rates, including the country's own rate. E_{ij} defines the price of currency j in terms of currency i:

$$I_i = \prod_{j=1}^{n} (E_{ij} P_j)^{\beta_{ij}}. \tag{4}$$

Aggregate demand is described by a simple version of the quantity theory - perhaps supplemented by a loanable fund theory to determine the interest rate:

$$\frac{M_i}{P_i} = Y_i. \tag{5}$$

Under wage stickiness the monetary base, M, determines Y and L. The reduced forms are determined by solving equations (1), (2) and (4). Equation (3) remains excluded as long as the nominal wage rate is too high for full employment, given the monetary base and the foreign prices measured in domestic currency units:

$$Y_i = X_i \left(\frac{\alpha_i \overline{M}_i}{\overline{\overline{W}}} \right)^{\alpha_i}, \tag{6}$$

$$L_i = \frac{\alpha_i \overline{M}_i}{\overline{\overline{W}}}. \tag{7}$$

It will be shown that a central bank aiming at maximizing the utility of its representative agent will always operate along the labor demand function. If the monetary institution engages in the conventional endeavor to use a trade-off between employment and inflation, the labor market structure has to be modified accordingly. In the present paper we will analyze another important trade-off, the one between employment and "the" real exchange rate. A graphical illustration facilitates the understanding of the model's implications (figure D*.1).

Figure D*.1: Macroeconomic Equilibrium with a Fixed Nominal Wage Rate (Parameter values are defined below)

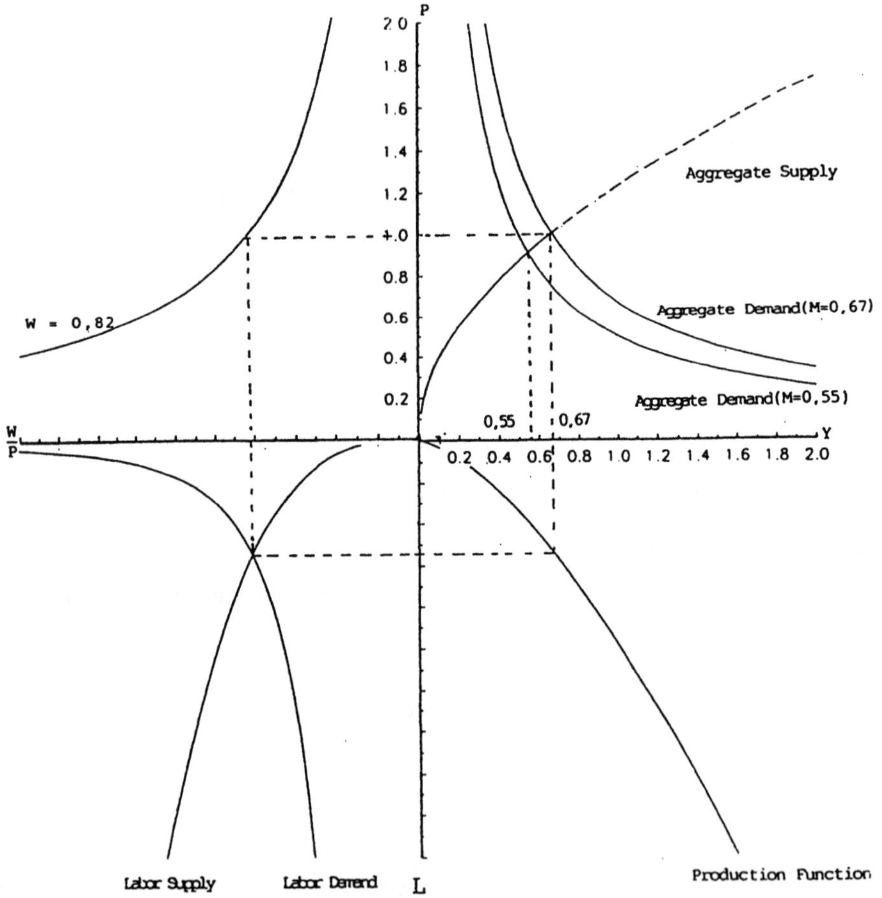

The utility calculus, on which the central bank will base its monetary policy, is embedded in a three-country model. Generalizing this case to the n-country case suggests itself without providing additional insight. The representative consumer in country 1 tries to maximize the following utility function including domestic consumer goods C_{11} and foreign goods from country 2 and country 3, C_{12} and C_{13}. L_1 indicates the planned supply of labor hours:

$$U_1 = A_1 C_{11}^{\beta_{11}} C_{12}^{\beta_{12}} C_{13}^{\beta_{13}} - h_1(L_1),\ for\ \beta_{11} + \beta_{12} + \beta_{13} = 1 \tag{8}$$

Because the labor supply function (3) excludes an income or wealth effect, the behavior of the representative consumer has to be based on a quasi-linear utility function (*Monissen, 1995c*). A further essential property of this functional restriction is the fact that a quantity restriction on the supply of labor does not affect the optimization calculus including the three consumption levels.

Equation (8) is to be maximized given the following budget constraint:

$$E_{11} P_1 C_{11} + E_{12} P_2 C_{12} + E_{13} P_3 C_{13} = E_{11} \Pi_1 + E_{11} W_1 L_1 = E_{11} P_1 Y_1 = E_{11} M. \tag{9}$$

Π_1 denotes non-wage income which remains excluded from the labor supply function due to the fact that the utility function is quasi linear.

The first order conditions, excluding the budget constraint, are:

$$A_1 \beta_{11} C_{11}^{\beta_{11}-1} C_{12}^{\beta_{12}} C_{13}^{\beta_{13}} - \lambda E_{11} P_1 = 0, \tag{10}$$

$$A_1 \beta_{12} C_{11}^{\beta_{11}} C_{12}^{\beta_{12}-1} C_{13}^{\beta_{13}} - \lambda E_{12} P_2 = 0, \tag{11}$$

$$A_1 \beta_{13} C_{11}^{\beta_{11}} C_{12}^{\beta_{12}} C_{13}^{\beta_{13}-1} - \lambda E_{13} P_3 = 0, \tag{12}$$

$$h_1'(L_1) - \lambda W_1 = 0. \tag{13}$$

Equations (9)-(13) allow one to determine the three consumption levels and the Lagrangian multiplier λ. The inverse of λ can be identified as the true price index deflating the domestic nominal wage rate. The solutions are:

$$C_{11} = \beta_{11} \frac{E_{11} P_1}{E_{11} P_1} Y_1, \tag{14}$$

$$C_{12} = \beta_{12} \frac{E_{11} P_1}{E_{12} P_2} Y_1, \tag{15}$$

$$C_{13} = \beta_{13} \frac{E_{11} P_1}{E_{13} P_3} Y_1, \tag{16}$$

$$\frac{1}{\lambda} = (E_{11} P_1)^{\beta_{11}} (E_{12} P_2)^{\beta_{12}} (E_{13} P_3)^{\beta_{13}} = I_1. \tag{17}$$

Equation (17) follows if the multiplicative term A_1 in the utility function is defined as:

$$A_1 = \beta_{11}^{-\beta_{11}} \beta_{12}^{-\beta_{12}} \beta_{13}^{-\beta_{13}}. \tag{18}$$

This yields from equation (13) the general form of the labor supply function stated above:

$$\frac{W_1}{I_1} = h_1'(L_1) \equiv \gamma_1 L_1^{\delta_1}. \tag{3}$$

The structure of the balance of payments equations for the three countries are conveniently measured in the currency units of country 1. The left-side of the equations indicate the monetary value of exports and the right-side indicate the corresponding value of imports. Symmetry suggests that one includes the home consumption of the respective domestically produced goods on both sides of the balance equations:

$$E_{11}P_1C_{11} + E_{11}P_1C_{21} + E_{11}P_1C_{31} = E_{11}P_1C_{11} + E_{12}P_2C_{12} + E_{13}P_3C_{13}, \qquad (18)$$

$$E_{12}P_2C_{12} + E_{12}P_2C_{22} + E_{12}P_2C_{32} = E_{11}P_1C_{21} + E_{12}P_2C_{22} + E_{13}P_3C_{23}, \quad (19)$$

$$E_{13}P_3C_{13} + E_{13}P_3C_{23} + E_{13}P_3C_{33} = E_{11}P_1C_{31} + E_{12}P_2C_{32} + E_{13}P_3C_{33}. \qquad (20)$$

Given the price levels and the consumption levels which are independently determined, equations (18) - (20) clearly define a homogeneous linear system in the nominal exchange rates E_{11}, E_{12}, E_{13}. This homogeneous system of three unknowns has a non-trivial solution if and only if the linear equations are linearly dependent. This expresses the economic fact that only n-1 of n balance of payments equations are independent. If we use the fact that E_{11} is equal to one by definition, we may solve for the remaining nominal exchange rates E_{12} and E_{13}.

The structure of the three country model incorporates not only the operation of the law of one price, but also relies on the standard arbitrage conditions for currencies, i.e. consistency conditions equalizing the direct and indirect exchange rates:

$$E_{ij}E_{ji} = 1 \text{ , and } E_{ij}E_{jm}E_{mi} = 1.$$

Substituting from (14)-(16) for each of the three countries under consideration gives:

$$E_{11}P_1\beta_{11}\frac{E_{11}P_1}{E_{11}P_1}Y_1+E_{11}P_1\beta_{21}\frac{E_{22}P_2}{E_{21}P_1}Y_2+E_{11}P_1\beta_{31}\frac{E_{33}P_3}{E_{33}P_1}Y_3=$$

$$E_{11}P_1\beta_{11}\frac{E_{11}P_1}{E_{11}P_1}Y_1+E_{12}P_2\beta_{12}\frac{E_{11}P_1}{E_{12}P_2}Y_1+E_{13}P_3\beta_{13}\frac{E_{11}P_1}{E_{13}P_3}Y_1, \tag{18a}$$

$$E_{12}P_2\beta_{12}\frac{E_{11}P_1}{E_{12}P_2}Y_1+E_{12}P_2\beta_{22}\frac{E_{22}P_2}{E_{22}P_2}Y_2+E_{12}P_2\beta_{32}\frac{E_{33}P_3}{E_{32}P_2}Y_3=$$

$$E_{11}P_1\beta_{21}\frac{E_{22}P_2}{E_{21}P_1}Y_2+E_{12}P_2\beta_{22}\frac{E_{22}P_2}{E_{22}P_2}Y_2+E_{13}P_3\beta_{23}\frac{E_{22}P_2}{E_{23}P_3}Y_2, \tag{19a}$$

$$E_{13}P_3\beta_{13}\frac{E_{11}P_1}{E_{13}P_3}Y_1+E_{13}P_3\beta_{23}\frac{E_{22}P_2}{E_{23}P_3}Y_2+E_{13}P_3\beta_{33}\frac{E_{33}P_3}{E_{33}P_3}Y_3=$$

$$E_{11}P_1\beta_{31}\frac{E_{33}P_3}{E_{31}P_1}Y_3+E_{12}P_2\beta_{32}\frac{E_{33}P_3}{E_{32}P_2}Y_3+E_{13}P_3\beta_{33}\frac{E_{33}P_3}{E_{33}P_3}Y_3. \tag{20a}$$

Simplifying yields:

$$\beta_{21}E_{12}P_2Y_2+\beta_{31}E_{13}P_3Y_3=\beta_{12}P_1Y_1+\beta_{13}P_1Y_1, \tag{18b}$$

$$\beta_{12}P_1Y_1+\beta_{32}E_{13}P_3Y_3=\beta_{21}E_{12}P_2Y_2+\beta_{23}E_{12}P_2Y_2, \tag{19b}$$

$$\beta_{13}P_1Y_1+\beta_{23}E_{12}P_2Y_2=\beta_{31}E_{13}P_3Y_3+\beta_{32}E_{13}P_3Y_3. \tag{20b}$$

Two of these three linearly dependent equations allow to solve for the two nominal exchange rates:

$$E_{12}=\frac{P_1Y_1}{P_2Y_2}\frac{\beta_{12}\beta_{31}+\beta_{12}\beta_{32}+\beta_{13}\beta_{32}}{\beta_{21}\beta_{31}+\beta_{21}\beta_{32}+\beta_{23}\beta_{31}}, \tag{21}$$

$$E_{13} = \frac{P_1 Y_1}{P_3 Y_3} \frac{\beta_{13}\beta_{21} + \beta_{13}\beta_{23} + \beta_{12}\beta_{23}}{\beta_{21}\beta_{31} + \beta_{21}\beta_{32} + \beta_{23}\beta_{31}}. \tag{22}$$

If the three countries have identical magnitudes, the same production potential, and the three representative consumers are characterized by the same preferences, the exchanges rates are equal to one, as they should be.

3. Some Game Theoretical Implications of the Model

In comparison to Bayoumi or Demertzis, Hallett and Rummel and others who extensively investigate the success of an optimal currency area based on symmetries of demand and supply shocks, the following analysis focuses on strategic behavior. An independent argument for the advantage of a currency union is the fact that it might reduce the welfare losses of strategic interdependencies.

To elaborate the argument we restrict the analysis to two countries and introduce some simplifying assumptions. If a central bank is in a position to exercise influence on the real exchange rate a trade-off exists between this rate and the level of employment. There will be a tendency to focus on a solution with less than full employment. Only if the central bank behaves competitively in the game, a notion which will be soon explained, the equilibrium will be characterized by full employment. A currency union will operate in this way: In addition to the admittedly vague notion of transactions costs savings, the above mentioned trade-off will disappear.

If a central bank is a non-selfish agent of its representative consumer (the principal), the goal is, of course, to maximize the latter's utility function. The utility function of the representative agent in the home country is

$$U_1 = \beta_{11}^{-\beta_{11}} \beta_{12}^{-\beta_{12}} C_{11}^{\beta_{11}} C_{12}^{\beta_{12}} - h_1(L_1). \tag{22}$$

We use the concept of the real exchange rate Z_{12} and write the balance of payments equations as follows:

$$P_1\beta_{12}Y_1 = P_1Z_{12}\beta_{21}Y_2,\ \text{for } Z_{12} = \frac{E_{12}P_2}{P_1}. \tag{23}$$

Equations (14), (15) and (1) allow one to substitute directly for the employment level:

$$U_1 = \beta_{11}^{-\beta_{11}}\beta_{12}^{-\beta_{12}}(\beta_{11}X_1L_1^{\alpha_1})^{\beta_{11}}(Z_{12}^{-1}\beta_{12}X_1L_1^{\alpha_1})^{\beta_{12}} - h_1(L_1), \tag{22a}$$

respectively,

$$U_1 = X_1Z_{12}^{-\beta_{12}}L_1^{\alpha_1} - h_1(L_1). \tag{22b}$$

Equation (22b) captures the complete structure of the two-country model. It is interesting to note that, given the real exchange rate, maximizing U_1 via the effect of the monetary base on Y_1 and L_1 will produce the conditions for neoclassical full employment equilibrium:

$$\alpha_1X_1L_1^{\alpha_1-1} = h'_1(L_1)Z_{12}^{\beta_{12}}.$$

Eliminating the real exchange rate by substituting from equation (23) amounts to

$$U_1 = X_1\left[\beta_{12}\beta_{21}^{-1}X_1L_1^{\alpha_1}X_2^{-1}L_2^{-\alpha_2}\right]^{-\beta_{12}}L_1^{\alpha_1} - h_1(L_1). \tag{24}$$

The term in the brackets summarizes the result of the substitution. This term in the domestic employment level becomes a "parameter" if the central bank behaves competitively as a price taker. This feedback effect incorporates an important component of strategic behavior. Simplifying yields

$$U_1 = \beta_{12}^{-\beta_{12}} \beta_{21}^{\beta_{12}} X_2^{\beta_{12}} L_2^{\alpha_2\beta_{12}} X_1^{1-\beta_{12}} \left[L_1^{-\alpha_1\beta_{12}}\right] L_1^{\alpha_1} - h_1(L_1). \tag{24a}$$

Maximizing U_1 gives

$$\frac{\partial U_1}{\partial L_1} = \beta_{12}^{-\beta_{12}} \beta_{21}^{\beta_{21}} X_2^{\beta_{12}} L_2^{\alpha_2\beta_{12}} X_1^{1-\beta_{12}} \alpha_1(1-\beta_{12}) L_1^{\alpha_1(1-\beta_{12})-1} - \gamma_1 L_1^{\delta_1} = 0. \tag{25}$$

h' in equation (25) was replaced by its concrete functional form (3). Equivalent equations for the foreign country allow to derive two reaction functions in the employment levels of the two countries:

$$L_1 = \left\{ \frac{\alpha_1(1-\beta_{12})}{\gamma_1} \beta_{12}^{-\beta_{12}} \beta_{21}^{\beta_{21}} X_2^{\beta_{12}} L_2^{\alpha_2\beta_{12}} X_1^{1-\beta_{12}} \right\}^{\frac{1}{\delta_1+1-\alpha_1(1-\beta_{12})}}, \tag{26}$$

$$L_2 = \left\{ \frac{\alpha_2(1-\beta_{22})}{\gamma_2} \beta_{22}^{-\beta_{22}} \beta_{12}^{\beta_{12}} X_1^{\beta_{21}} L_1^{\alpha_1\beta_{21}} X_2^{1-\beta_{21}} \right\}^{\frac{1}{\delta_2+1-\alpha_2(1-\beta_{21})}}. \tag{27}$$

If both central banks behave competitively as price-takers, which means they ignore the above mentioned feedback effect, the two reaction functions will be modified as follows:

$$L_1 = \left\{ \frac{\alpha_1}{\gamma_1} \beta_{12}^{-\beta_{12}} \beta_{21}^{\beta_{21}} X_2^{\beta_{12}} L_2^{\alpha_2\beta_{12}} X_1^{1-\beta_{12}} \right\}^{\frac{1}{\delta_1+1-\alpha_1(1-\beta_{12})}}, \tag{28}$$

$$L_2 = \left\{ \frac{\alpha_2}{\gamma_2} \beta_{22}^{-\beta_{22}} \beta_{12}^{\beta_{12}} X_1^{\beta_{21}} L_1^{\alpha_1 \beta_{21}} X_2^{1-\beta_{21}} \right\}^{\frac{1}{\delta_2 + 1 - \alpha_2 (1-\beta_{21})}} . \qquad (29)$$

To give a simple graphic illustration (see figure D*.2), we specify the parameters of the model as follows:

$$\alpha_1 = \alpha_2 = \frac{2}{3};\ \beta_{11} = \beta_{12} = \beta_{21} = \beta_{22} = \frac{1}{2};\ \gamma_1 = \gamma_2 = 1;\ \delta_1 = \delta_2 = \frac{1}{3};\ X_1 = X_2 = 1.$$

The reaction curves of the standard Cournot case based on equations (26) and (27) are marked by RC_C. The competitive case based on equations (28) and (29) is denoted by RC_K. The corresponding reaction curves and the equilibria are shown in figure D*.2. The underlying reaction functions for the Cournot case are

$$L_1 = \frac{1}{3} L_2^{1/3} \text{ and } L_2 = \frac{1}{3} L_1^{1/3}.$$

The multiplicative term for the competitive case will be 2/3 instead of 1/3.

Elementary game theory teaches us that the two cases do not exhaust the given strategy set. The home central bank might maximize its representative consumer´s utility function, which is subject to the foreign bank´s reaction function: The home bank behaves as a "von Stackelberg leader" expecting that the foreign bank will be the follower. However, there are two different reaction functions, one for the competitive case and one for the Cournot case. Together this defines 16 different strategy constellations.

To illustrate some of the game theoretical constellations we superimpose on the reaction curves in figure D*.2 a set of indifference curves from equation (24) for the representative actor in the home country. The displayed points 1 to 6 indicate the following menu of strategic interactions: Point 1 identifies the Cournot equilibrium. The diagram shows that the indifference curves for the agent in the home country depict zero slope along his reaction curve. In point 2 the domestic agent is a Cournot leader in the von Stackelberg sense with the foreign agent playing the role of a Cournot follower. Point 6 describes the situation where the domestic agent is a competitive leader and the foreign agent accepts the role of a competitive follower. Point 3 reverses the roles of the domestic and foreign agents in the Cournot game of leader and follower and point 5 respectively for the competitive game. Finally, point 6 indicates the competitive neoclassical full employment equilibrium which implies a Pareto optimum for the two agents.

Figure D*.2: Reaction Curves under Cournot and Competitive Behavior

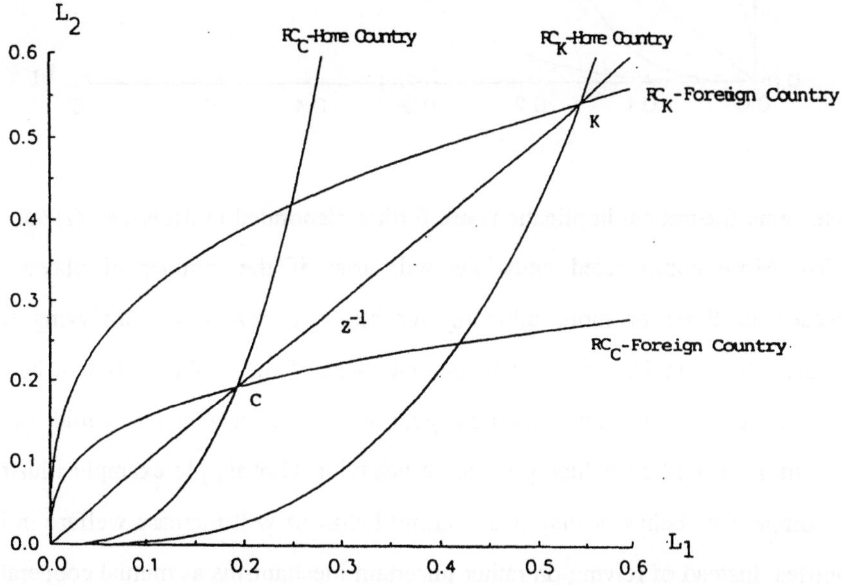

Figure D*.3: Reaction Curves and Indifference Curves for the Domestic Actor

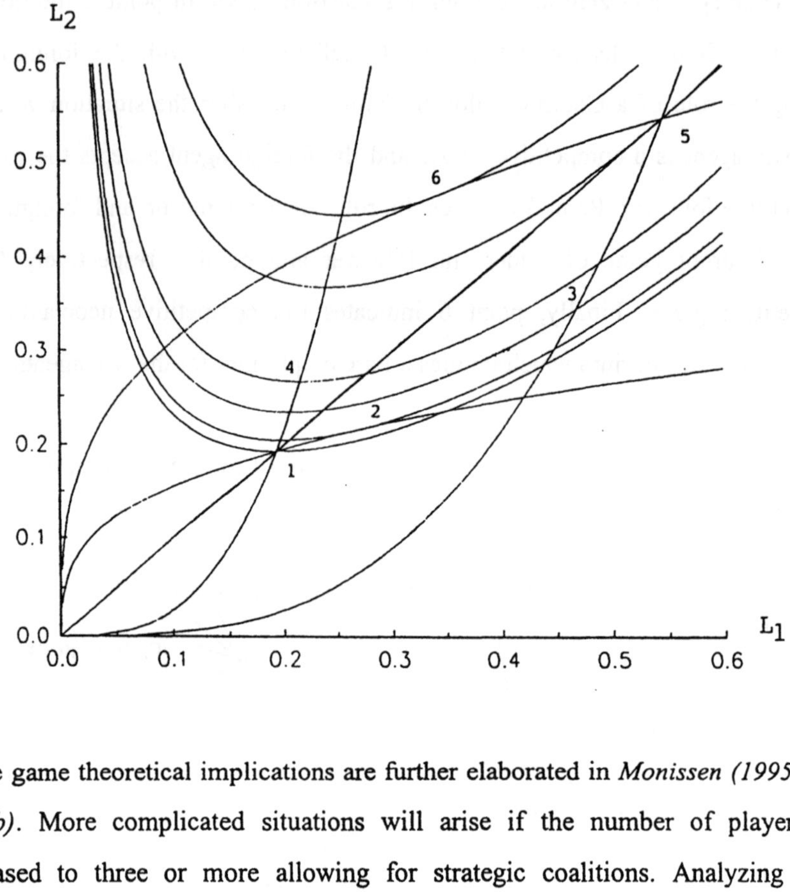

These game theoretical implications are further elaborated in *Monissen (1995a* and *1995b)*. More complicated situations will arise if the number of players are increased to three or more allowing for strategic coalitions. Analyzing these strategic interdependencies extends the statement of our problem. It will become intuitively clear that one important goal of a currency union could be the elimination of welfare reducing strategic behavior. Our simple example illustrates that competitive behavior vis-à-vis Cournot behavior will increase welfare in both countries. Instead of relying on rather uncertain mechanisms as mutual cooperation, binding a priori contract arrangements, trigger mechanisms and so forth, a currency union has the advantage that competitive behavior will be automatically induced.

4. Summary

One important strand of arguments to delimit the domain of an optimum currency area relates to the symmetry or asymmetry of the various shocks impinging on the various countries involved and thereby affecting the cost-benefit calculus for either forming or joining a currency union. The reference model here is the one proposed by Bayoumi. In that paper, it is argued that this model, which analyses multi-country interdependencies, is based on a numéraire economy and therefore not well suited to be linked to the standard macromodels. The identification of various demand and supply shocks follows the decomposition proposed by Blanchard and Quah. The model proposed in the paper, tries to reconcile the two disparate approaches by providing a simple microeconomic foundation to the standard macroeconomic model.

Instead of analyzing the stochastic properties of the model, which could be easily done along the lines of Demertzis, Hallett and Rummel, the focus is directed on the strategic interdependencies of the central banks involved. To evaluate the welfare properties of various strategic endeavors and capture benefits from the trade-off between the employment level and the terms of trade, the behavior focuses on the utility function of each country's representative agent. A Pareto-optimal equilibrium with neoclassical full employment will exist, if and only if, the actors involved refrain from strategic considerations and engage in a competitive behavior. Reducing the welfare cost of strategic interactions by forming a currency union could be a strong independent argument in the current policy debate.

Appendix: Two Country Case for a Numéraire Economy

The Bayoumi model for the two country case could be restated as follows:

Country 1 (numéraire region):

$$U_1 = C_{11}^{\beta_{11}} C_{12}^{\beta_{12}},$$

$$P_1 C_{11} + P_2 C_{12} = \Pi_1 + W_1 L_1 = P_1 Y_1.$$

The price of good 2 is measured in units of good one (numéraire).

Country 2:

$$U_2 = C_{21}^{\beta_{21}} C_{22}^{\beta_{22}},$$

$$P_1 C_{21} + P_2 C_{22} = \Pi_2 + E_2 W_2 L_2 = P_2 Y_2.$$

Profit maximization in country 2 yields:

$$\frac{\partial Y_2}{\partial L_2} = \frac{E_2 W_2}{P_2},$$

or in logs

$$w_2 - p_2 + e_2 = \ln MPL_2.$$

The nominal exchange rate is trivially determined. Pareto-efficiency is realized if the following condition prevails:

$$\frac{MPL_1}{MPL_2} = \frac{P_2}{P_1}.$$

This condition is, of course, violated if labor does not freely migrate between countries.

Endnotes

1. The author acknowledges helpful comments by John S. Chipman, Günter Krause, and Ute Schmidt.

References

BAYOUMI, T. (1992), The Effect of the ERM on Participating Economies, IMF Staff Papers 39 (June), 330-356.

BAYOUMI, T.; EICHENGREEN, B. (1992), Is There a Conflict Between EC Enlargement and European Monetary Unification? CEPR Discussion Paper Series No. 646, London. Centre for Economic Policy Research, May.

BAYOUMI, T.; EICHENGREEN, B. (1994), Shocking Aspects of European Monetary Unification, in: GIAVAZZI, F., TORRES, F. eds. (1994), Adjustment and Growth in the European Monetary Union, Cambridge and New York. Cambridge University Press.

BLANCHARD, O. J., QUAH, D. (1989), The Dynamic Effects of Aggregate Supply and Demand Disturbances, American Economic Review, Vol. 79 (September), 655-673.

BLANCHARD, O.J., QUAH, D. (1993), The Dynamic Effects of Aggregate Supply and Demand Disturbances: Reply, American Economic Review, Vol. 83 (June), 653-658.

DEMERTZIS, M., HALLETT, A.J.H., RUMMEL, O. (1996), Monetary Policies Set Jointly But Severally or Does a Core-Periphery Regime Make Europe into an Optimal Currency Area?, this volume.

MONISSEN, H.G. (1973), Preise, Löhne und Beschäftigung in dynamischer Betrachtung, Kyklos Vol. 26, 545-558.

MONISSEN, H.G. (1995a, b), Monetary Policy Interdependence of Central Banks with Endogeneous Objective Functions, in: von COLLANI, E., ed. (1995a), Proceedings of the Third Umea-Würzburg Conference in Statistics, Kronlund. An extended version is published with the title "Monetäre Interdependenz von Zentralbanken bei endogenen Zielfunktionen", Kredit und Kapital, Supplements to Vol. 13 (1995b), 139-162.

MONISSEN, H.G. (1995c), Quasilineare Nutzenfunktionen: Einige Verallgemeinerungen, Jahrbücher für Nationalökonomie und Statistik, Vol. 215, 1-13.

ROMER, D. (1996), Advanced Macroeconomics, New York: McGraw-Hill.

E. Competitive Neutrality of Monetary Policy Instruments for EMU

Lukas Menkhoff[1]

1. Introduction

According to the time-schedule for the European Monetary Union, the issue of monetary policy instruments is on the agenda for the year 1996. So far, no official document exists which gives any indication of the future instruments which may be expected. On the contrary, this area remains wide-open for debate.

From a theoretical point of view, however, many economists may prefer an instrumental concept which could be labeled as "lean" (*Menkhoff, 1995*). Ideally the *lean concept* rests on three elements: refinancing consists mainly of open market operations and some marginal refinancing and there are no minimum reserves. Such a concept would be as simple and as market-oriented as possible. Furthermore, it would fulfill the criterion of efficient monetary policy instruments, as open market operations are most suitable for steering the money market and the need for reserve requirements is very questionable. The lean concept is, finally, more than an academic idea: it actually occurs in the United Kingdom (see e.g. *King, 1994*).

From a conservative point of view, one may prefer a quite different solution for future monetary policy instruments of the European Central Bank (ECB). The goal may be to imitate a highly reputed central bank. Consequently, the instruments used by the Deutsche Bundesbank may be seen as an example for this solution (see *Cukierman, 1995*). Compared to the Bank of England the German instruments are quite different. The reason is lending facilities below market rates receive a high proportion of the refinancing volume and reserve requirements (see *Issing, 1994*).

To label the reasoning behind this instrumental set, it may be called a "*cautious concept*".

Although these concepts are competitive approaches, some areas of consensus can be identified:

- Following the characterization of *EMI (1995)*, the use of open market transactions from the type of reverse transactions in domestic securities is common to all 14 EU-countries under review.
- 12 countries use the interest rate tender as auction procedure.
- 13 countries use at least one of the three distinguished types of standing facilities.
- Looking at underlying trends in the evolution of instruments it becomes obvious that the importance of minimum reserves is declining. Either they are abandoned completely as monetary policy instrument or the burden is eased as in the German case.

In summary, a pragmatic approach would describe the following basis for monetary policy instruments in EMU. First, refinancing can rely mainly on open-market transactions, processed as reverse transactions and interest rate tenders. Second, the burden of minimum reserves should be at least low, in comparison to the past (see also *Jarchow, 1995*). This basis hints, however, at the same issues of disagreement as the short comparison between the United Kingdom and Germany:

- Is there any role for lending facilities applied in six EU-countries? This point gains relevance because Germany is among the present users of lending facilities.
- How low could the burden of minimum reserves become, which is presently between 0% and about 3% of GDP in the 14 EU-countries, and roughly 1.1% in the German case?[2]

A graphical presentation of the current disagreement in Europe is given in Figure E.1. At first glance, the situation gets even more complicated as there is no obvious relationship between the two dimensions. The divergence in Europe suggests the probability of different costs of adjustment in the respective countries when monetary policy instruments will be unified in the monetary union (see also *Kasman, 1992*). This gives the policy goal of competitive neutrality particular relevance.

Figure E.1: EU-Differences in Reserve Requirements and Lending Facilities

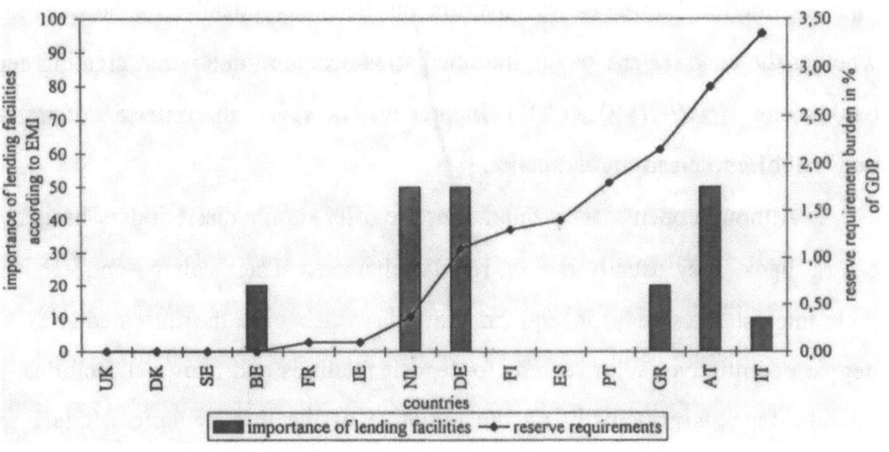

- lending facilities (importance): high: 100%; intermediate: 50%; low: 20%; close to market-rates calculated as 50% "discount" on the importance
- remuneration: close to market rate: 10% burden; partly: 50% burden; no remuneration: 100% burden

Source: EMI (1995), p. 128f.

The following sections discuss the above mentioned core issues of disagreement for monetary policy instruments in a EMU. Sections 2 and 3 consider refinancing instruments and, in particular, the appropriateness of lending facilities with respect to competitive neutrality and alternative arrangements. This pattern of neutrality and arrangement is repeated with regard to minimum reserves in sections 4 and 5.

Resulting from these discussions, in section 6 a decentralized concept for monetary policy instruments is developed that contrasts the lean and a cautious concept.

2. Refinancing Instruments and Competitive Neutrality

2.1 Open Market Operations versus Lending Facilities

Refinancing facilities for financial intermediaries, as they are provided by a central bank, can be distinguished in open market operations and standing facilities. The main distinction between these instruments lies, theoretically, in the question of whether the central bank or the intermediaries become initiative in creating central bank money (*EMI, 1995*, p.123). In practice, however, the criterion of initiative does not offer a clear-cut distinction.

Although open-market operations are offered on a discretionary basis by the central bank, they usually have a regular character. Their volume and even more their interest rates may depend on the bids which give the intermediaries some degree of initiative. With regards to deposit facilities and marginal facilities, their volume depends principally on the initiative of the intermediaries. It is limited, however, by unattractive low and high rates respectively. Thus, the initiative is of minor importance in this case. With regards to lending facilities, the central bank will take provisions to avoid any unwelcome elasticity in the money supply, such as the quotas for the distribution. Thus, no relevant room for intermediaries' initiative exists.

Overall, it is the central bank which determines the broader volume of money supply and it is the market - through financial intermediaries - which influences the conditions of this supply to a certain degree. This holds for both, open market operations as well as standing facilities. Under the present institutional circumstances and central banks' strategies it would be surprise to expect anything else.

Regardless of this similarity, there is a clear-cut advantage of the typical open market operations over lending facilities, since they are more flexible and, therefore, better suited to steer the money market under more turbulent conditions. The goal of efficiency reveals a serious disadvantage for lending facilities. Therefore, does the goal of competitive neutrality offer a justification for using this instrument?

2.2 Neutrality towards Different Financial Systems

The financial systems of the European countries have each grown over long periods of time and are not at all identical. Some examples of national peculiarities will be illustrated:

- Regarding the *organization* of the financial sector, the United Kingdom provides the classical case of a market-based system, whereas Germany usually provides a bank-based system. *Breig (1994, 1996)* demonstrates forcefully, however, that even the bank-based systems of continental Europe are quite different to each other.
- The typical *maturity* of financial contracts can be expected to vary depending on the degree of insecurity of expectations in the economy. Thus, high-inflation countries tend to have shorter maturities than low-inflation countries, as Italy and Germany demonstrate (*Bockelmann, 1996*).
- It is a common feature in most economies that retained earnings is the dominant *source of financing* for investment (*Frankel and Montgomery, 1991*). The degree of dominance differs, however. France provides an example where the remaining financial needs are not met by the financial sector but by trade financing to a large degree.
- Finally, the ways in which financial transactions are performed can be different. This has consequences e.g. for the *velocity of money*.

It is obvious that the characteristics demonstrated by national financial systems influence the monetary transmission mechanism (e.g. *Bockelmann, 1996; Cottarelli and Kourelis, 1994; Kneeshaw, 1995*). Other things being equal, it can be expected that the power of the central banks' actions on the money market is stronger, if the financial system is market-based, has shorter-term maturities, a high quantitative share of financial sector financing and a high (and stable) velocity of money.

There is no mandate for the ECB to influence the shape of the national financial systems. Furthermore, there is no clear evidence of the pros and cons of the diverse characteristics of financial systems which would justify a centralized reform of several aspects.[3] Thus, from the viewpoint of competitive neutrality, the set of monetary policy instruments should be constructed in a way that enables it to fit into a broad array of financial systems and their respective characteristics.

An obvious link exists between system and instruments. The system influences the available kind of asset which underlies the instruments, such as money market papers in the UK, trade bills in Germany or credits in France (*Icard, 1994*). The consequence is to allow for as much diversity as possible, in particular with regard to admissible assets. It can be imagined that there exists, in principle, only one category of assets underlying the monetary policy instruments regardless of the specific kind of refinancing instrument. In this category money market paper, bonds, trade bills, credits and so are found.

One might expect that, in the long-run, this problem of neutrality may get less dramatic as the financial systems become similar. With a unified monetary policy - by and large - expectations of financial developments will become homogeneous in the member countries which will influence the maturity of financial contracts. The same may apply to the payment transfer technology which would influence the velocity of money. Also in the field of bank-based versus market-based organization of the financial sector, some observers state this, e.g. a growing market orientation in Germany.

In the short-term, however, institutional adjustments seem to be necessary if one does not want to wait for markets to enforce them. The possible risks of adjustment problems (see here e.g. *Jerger and Menkhoff, 1995*) can be limited by a policy which gives the national central banks some discretion on the exact path for adjustment.

2.3 Neutrality towards Various Financial Centers

Unification implies almost the necessarity of centralization. The former national financial centers will become only subcenters of the monetary union and the former subcenters will fall further behind etc. Therefore, the problem of neutrality exists with the smaller financial places whose existence may be questionable. Since it is not the objective of the ECB to predetermine any such developments, its policy should be neutral towards the location and size of financial centers. The major implication affects the way of distribution of central bank money. The national central banks and their regional offices should be involved here.

2.4 Neutrality towards Various Admissible Assets

Whatever assets are qualified to be used for refinancing purposes, it will be an advantage for their issuers in comparison to the others. As some assets have to be taken, the first consequence is, from a neutrality point of view, to define the range of admissible assets as widely as possible. The possibility is, however, limited from an efficiency point of view. The second consequence is a preference for repurchase transactions instead of outright transactions (*Monticelli and Viñals, 1993*).

Besides the issuers, the asset structure of banks may also be relevant. The asset structure varies depending on the specialization of the bank and allows the banks respective access to admissible assets. For example, banks with an emphasis on business loans have easier access to trade bills, whereas banks with an emphasis on retail business often invest their surplus deposits in securities which give them a broader basis for bidding in open market auctions.

2.5 Neutrality towards Money Market Engagement of Banks

In the same way that the refinancing policy should be competitively neutral towards different assets it should also be so towards the different types of financial intermediaries or shorter banks. This applies to characteristics such as wholesale or retail banks, universal or merchant banks etc. A further interesting difference with banks is whether they are actively involved in the market in which the central bank operates or not. To keep the further discussion simple, we will distinguish between money market active banks (MMA) and money market inactive banks (MMI). Competitive neutrality means, in this respect, that refinancing instruments are operated in a way which does not favor MMAs over MMIs.

It is a clear consequence of this policy goal that all instruments or procedures which channel central bank liquidity exclusively through a smaller group of banks should be abandoned. Examples of such exclusive positions are discount houses in the UK, certain money market maker banks in France and principally the small amount of addressed banks with German short-notice tenders (Schnelltender). The less obvious but possibly more important question is whether the money market activity of banks favors their ability to participate in open market operations.

This issue has been addressed in prior research for Germany (see recently *Menkhoff, 1995*, in particular *Jerger and Menkhoff, 1995*). It is a prerequisite for an empirical examination that there are many heterogeneous banks in a country, as is the case in Germany with about 3,900 banks and a median balance sheet volume of only 250 million DM. No statistical information exists about money market activity, and therefore the size of a bank measured by its balance sheet volume may serve as a reasonable proxy.

The general relationship between the money market activity of a bank and open market operations is that the later involve some risk for the participating institution and that the MMIs may be less able to bear this risk. This risk has two dimensions, the volume and price, whose outcome can be uncertain in auctions: First, MMIs do not have a regular money market desk which would enable them to easily sell excess central bank money or to buy the missing amount. Second, MMIs do not have the same amount of information which would enable them to bid at auctions on a fair basis with the MMAs. It can be tested, whether these considerations, or the implicitly converse assumptions of competitively neutral open-market auctions, are more realistic. The following hypotheses are formulated based on the present status quo.

Generally, one might expect from functioning money markets that the banks' own money market activity does not influence their choice of various refinancing instruments. In Germany, the lending facility is offered with a price discount. Although this is justified to some degree by higher operating costs, the discount still gives a strong incentive to use this instrument. However, the refinancing volume offered this way only satisfies about one third of the banks′ needs, leaving more than enough room for open-market auctions.

Hypothesis 1: The number of banks using lending facilities and open-market auctions for their refinancing needs is the same.

If the previously mentioned risk is not relevant for the participation decisions of banks, then there should be no difference between the volume tenders which inhibit a gradual volume risk and the interest rate tenders which inhibit an absolute volume risk at a slight price risk.[4]

Hypothesis 2: The number of banks participating at volume tender auctions and interest tender auctions is the same.

To test these hypotheses, all tender auctions of the Deutsche Bundesbank have been examined for the period from August 1988, when the Bundesbank switched from the Dutch style to American style interest tender auctions until January 1996. As an influence from maturity of tender auctions on participation of banks exists, the analysis concentrates on tender auctions with a "regular" maturity, i.e. presently a period of about two weeks. Finally, the EMS-crisis in the autumn of 1992 led, among other things, to a change of the regular maturity of tender auctions from about four to two weeks. Therefore, the whole period of examination is also broken down in two subperiods. Results of the analysis can be seen from table E.1.

Table E.1: Participation at Open Market Auctions in Germany

data period	kind of events	number of events [n]	average number of participating banks [n]	median number of participating banks [n]	average ratio of banks participating and receiving [%]	average sum of liquidity demanded [bn. DM]	average ratio of liquidity supplied and demanded [%]
8.1988-	total	480	633,2	593,5		80,2	44,60
1.1996	volume tender	129	814,3	758,0	100,00	140,6	35,51
	interest rate tender	351	568,3	544,0	48,07	58,0	48,07
8.1988-	total	292	667,2	626,5		105,7	45,45
1.1996	volume tender	101	747,3	694,0	100,00	153,9	38,48
regular*	interest rate tender	191	624,8	589,0	77,39	80,1	49,13
8.1988-	total	124	868,7	824,0		60,3	33,13
9.1992	volume tender	29	1139,5	1265,0	100,00	87,3	20,69
regular*	interest rate tender	95	786,0	790,0	69,32	52,1	43,47
	*v.t./i.t.-Wilcoxon w***			*5,53*			
10.1992-	total	168	518,4	477,5		139,1	54,54
1.1996	volume tender	72	589,4	604,0	100,00	180,8	45,65
regular*	interest rate tender	96	465,2	451,0	85,37	107,9	61,21
	*v.t./i.t.-Wilcoxon w***			*5,24*			

* Regular auctions are those of 27-29 days maturity until 9.1992 and 13-15 days maturity thereafter.
** Significance at 1%-level needs w>2,3263.

The evidence is not in favor of the hypotheses. The first one is quite clearly rejected, because the majority of German banks, i.e. more than 2,000, borrow via the discount facility compared to the roughly 300 - 700 participating at tender auctions during the last few years. The second hypothesis is also rejected because the average number of participating banks is significantly lower for interest rate tenders than for volume tenders. Depending on the subperiod and whether the average or median participation is regarded, interest rate tenders receive a lower response rate of 20% or more. A Wilcoxon rank sum-test shows this difference to be highly significant for both subperiods (see table E.1).

There is, however, the question whether this supposed effect of more risky interest rate tenders is independent of the respective prices or vice versa: Are volume tenders more popular because the price advantage for participants is bigger than with interest rate tenders? This leads us to the last hypothesis:

Hypothesis 3: The number of banks participating at tender auctions increases with the price-advantages of the (expected) offers.

To test this hypothesis, the realized repo rates have to be compared to the alternative refinancing rates for banks. Although the overnight rate is often seen as a close substitute for the central bank offer, interviews with banks showed that they regard the equivalent maturities as more appropriate. For the first subperiod we have therefore chosen the market rate for one month as the closest matching alternative. For the second subperiod, when the tender maturity was only about two weeks, there was no published market rate available. Thus, a market rate for 14-day-money is estimated by using the information from the overnight, one month and three months rates (see Annex 1 for the procedure).

The result of the subperiods and the kinds of auctions can be seen from table E.2. It becomes obvious that hypothesis 3 is supported by the data. This holds true for the kinds of auctions, because more price-attractive auctions, i.e. volume tenders receive a higher participation. This holds also true over time, as during higher price-attractiveness, i.e. from 1988 until 1992, the participation was markedly higher than thereafter.

Table E.2: Deviation of Repo Rates versus Money Market Rates

data period	kind of tender	number of events*	average repo rate	average money market rate	difference (repo-market)
8.1988-9.1992	volume tender	29	6,716%	7,251%	-0,535%
	interest tender	95	8,026%	8,212%	-0,186%
10.1992-1.1996	volume tender	72	5,771%	5,918%	-0,147%
	interest tender	96	5,943%	6,022%	-0,079%

* Only "regular" tender auctions are considered

Interestingly enough, even after the Deutsche Bundesbank changed its policy and set the repo rates closer to the market, there is still an advantage for the recipients compared to normal market rates. In the critical discussion of standing facilities this used to be called a subsidy. Although this subsidy element is low in percentage terms, it is recognizable in absolute terms. From our data it should be about 60 - 90 million DM p.a. This depends on the ratio of volume and interest rate tenders in the respective year, which are distributed exclusively among the participants of open market auctions (see table E.3).

Comparing the price advantage over time, reveals another interesting result: Contrary to the expectation of declining subsidies, since the repo rates came closer to the market, the increasing volumes overcompensated the declining price advantage and caused even higher absolute subsidies as a result (see table E.3).

Finally, the higher absolute advantage was concentrated on a smaller number of banks than before, resulting in an increase of the absolute advantage per successfully bidding bank by about 100% between the first and the second subperiod (the figures in the last column of table E.3 are calculated per event, i.e. in the second subperiod there have been roughly twice as many events as before). As this advantage requires heavily increased volumes, the distribution of subsidies is skewed towards the bigger banks.

Table E.3: Absolute Advantage of Open Market Auctions

data period	kind of regular events	average sum of liquidity demanded [bn. DM]	average ratio of liquidity supplied and demanded [%]	average number of assigned banks [n]	interest rate advantage [%]
8.1988-	vol. tender	87,3	20,69	1139,5	0,535
9.1992	int. rate tender	52,1	43,47	544,9	0,186
10.1992-	vol. tender	180,8	45,65	589,4	0,147
1.1996	int. rate tender	107,9	61,21	397,1	0,079

data period	kind of regular events	abs. average advantage p.a. [mill. DM]	abs. average advantage per event [mill. DM]	abs. average advantage per event and bank [thd. DM]
8.1988-	vol. tender	96,6	7,4	6,5
9.1992	int. rate tender	42,1	3,2	5,9
10.1992-	vol. tender	121,3	4,7	7,9
1.1996	int. rate tender	52,2	2,0	5,1

Comparing the evidence regarding hypotheses 2 and 3 reveals a possible rivalry since the price effect might also be the explanation for the supposed risk effect. Any judgment would need further examination.

In summary, the analysis raises serious questions as to whether open-market auctions are really as neutral towards the money market activity and the size of banks as is often assumed. It has to be acknowledged, however, that the evidence does not lead to a compelling conclusion to the failed competitive neutrality of the present German open market auctions. First, the number of banks participating does not demonstrate that a *certain group* of banks, such as MMIs or small banks, is to some extent hindered from participating. Instead participation decisions may be made independently of the institutional characteristics of the banks. Second, non-participation might *not* be dis*crimination* since these banks make-up for their MMI-status by joining a co-operation with a MMA. This was the case for the German co-operative banks and savings banks.

Preliminary evidence, however, does not support these theoretical possibilities. Regarding systematic discrimination, qualitative information from interviews reveals that there is probably a positive correlation between participation and money market activity, and the size of the bank. Regarding equivalent organizational arrangements of direct or indirect participation the fact remains that banks seem to prefer direct versus indirect participation.

2.6 Summary

The previous sections showed some consequences for the goal of competitive neutrality for refinancing instruments. They included the preferences for a broad variety of admissible assets, for the liquidity distribution involving regional offices of the ECB, or for repurchase agreements. So far, there is no principal difference between open-market auctions and lending facilities. The critical issue seems to be whether auctions stop many banks from participating against their preference which seems to be a point in favor of lending facilities.

3. Alternative Arrangements of Lending Facilities

Assuming that the use of lending facilities has some rationale, there is still a debate on whether this advantage justifies the other disadvantages. Presently lending facilities are offered with a discount compared to the market rate and because of this attractive discount the lending volume has to be administratively distributed. The reason is to prevent unwanted endogeneity in the supply of central bank money. Nevertheless, from an economic point of view there is strong skepticism towards non-market elements such as subsidy and quota which contradict the goal of competitive neutrality.

It is, therefore, the aim of this section to analyze different existing and proposed arrangements for lending facilities to find out to what degree these arrangements are compatible with neutrality. Since Germany is the biggest user of this instrument and the Deutsche Bundesbank is a relevant supporter, Germany may serve again as the object to be studied.

Under the present regulations the German arrangement for lending facilities, in the *model I,* can be described as follows: The admissible assets are restricted to trade bills of highest quality, the interest rate is fixed for longer periods (discount rate) and are considerably below market rates and the distribution of the volume is organized by contingents. These contingents are mainly determined by the absolute equity capital of the bank and the share of short-term and medium-term credit to total credit.[5] This arrangement was sometimes heavily criticized, e.g. by the savings banks which thought to be at a disadvantage and from academics, e.g. by *Issing and Rudolph (1988)*. The latter criticized in particular the structural component, as an isolated increase of the longer-term credit volume would cut the contingents. Instead they proposed to integrate the absolute volume of short-term and medium-term credit into the calculation of contingents (model Ia). Another criticism regards the restriction of trade bills which seem to be "produced" only to serve as an asset for lending facilities. *Hesse and Braasch (1996)*, who otherwise forcefully defend lending facilities close to the German model (*Hesse and Braasch, 1994*), now propose to enlarge the admissible assets to non-financial transactions in related papers of the highest quality (model Ib).

If one tries to minimize competitive distortions within the present German framework, more general adjustments could be imagined (*Menkhoff, 1996*). The admissible assets could be opened as indicated in section 2 (see also *Issing, 1996*; *Remsperger and Angenendt, 1995*). This requires, of course, that a minimum quality standard for admissible assets exists. The discount rate shows quite different discounts to the repo rate over time which could be minimized by making the discount rate more flexible. A minimizing rule could be, to always keep this rate a certain amount of basis points below the prevailing repo rate. Regarding the distribution of contingents the connection with credit volume of whatever kind is never fair to the variety of banks. If one tries to minimize the distortion by subsidies it seems to be more appropriate to distribute the advantages only according to the equity capital of banks (*model II*, see also table E.4).

Table E.4: Alternative Models of Lending Facility Arrangements

model		distribution of volume	interest rate	admissible assets
I	present German arrangement	credit-related contingents	fixed, below market	trade bills of highest quality
II	modified German arrangement	equity capital-related contingents	flexible, below market rate (repo rate minus discount)	broad variety of qualified assets
III	volume tender arrangement	auction with given interest rate and proportional repartiation	= model I	non-financial transactions related papers of highest quality
IV	interest tender arrangement	Dutch style auction	bids are given as repo rate plus / minus margin	= model II

Although the proposed alternative arrangements for lending facilities probably reduce the distortions, the non-market elements regarding a price subsidy and volume distribution remain. Since the distribution via contingents would be even more problematic in Europe than in Germany alone, *Hesse and Braasch (1996)* discuss the alternative of volume tenders which would leave the problem of intercountry and interbank distribution to the bids of the single banks (*model III*). Assuming that an attractive interest rate is offered to avoid a shortage in bids, the required liquidity will be much higher than the volume supplied. This causes two problems regarding the competitive neutrality:[6] First, repatriation is a relevant source of uncertainty which discourages the MMIs. Second, volume tenders may repeatedly lead to the situation where the amount of admissible assets available to a single bank restricts the respective amount of a bid.

The subsidy element of the interest rate would still exist and be disruptive. Even if one proposes lending facilities to improve competitive neutrality, the question arises whether this offer, considering the needs of MMIs, should not have a positive price instead of a discount:

- To leave this decision to the market the interest rate can be found through a separate auction.
- To avoid any speculative element and arbitrage between these longer-term lending facility auctions and the "normal" open market auctions, it seems advisable to organize the bids in the form of plus or minus margins compared to the average repo rate of the identical period of time. Using this facility is similar to banks issuing a short-term floating note.
- This link to the repo rate ensures that the difference between the auctions is restricted to the perceived level of information: For MMIs it is attractive to realize a rate similar to the market, and for MIAs it will be attractive to try to gain a lower rate.
- The mark-up for lending facility auctions can be expected to be restricted by the present difference between the rep rate and the respective price in the money market which is - according to several sources - often in the range of 5 to 20 basis points (see also table E.2).
- To address the volume risk, it may be acceptable to organize the auctions in the Dutch style (*model IV*). What is usually regarded as a problem, the unrealistic high interest rate bids by smaller banks which do not influence the market, could now be interpreted as an advantage.
- These considerations, from the viewpoint of competitive neutrality, can be easily combined with other justifications for a lending facility, such as longer-term refinancing, private issuers for admissible assets (*Issuing, 1996,*

p.19)[7] or some connection to the real sector of the economy (*Hesse and Braasch, 1994, 1996*). There may be even a positive side-effect through the broader participation of lending facilities, as the central bank gets insights into the liquidity management of more banks.[8]

It is already a long way to change from model I to model II and even a longer way to switch to auction models for lending facilities. There is no doubt, however, that e.g. the German model I is not unproblematic from a competitive neutrality point of view (*Issing, 1988*) and would be even more problematic in other financial environments. So, a reform of the present German model seems helpful even if one favors lending facilities. This reform should erase administrative elements as much as possible.

4. Reserve Requirements and Competitive Neutrality

4.1 Reserve Requirements and Efficiency

Besides lending facilities, the existence and kind of reserve requirements is the second major issue of debate about a future European set of monetary policy instruments. At the moment, reserve requirements are used as monetary policy instruments in 10 of the 14 ECU-countries (excluding Luxembourg). That four ECU-countries operate without reserve requirements is a clear demonstration that this instrument is not absolutely necessary. This does not mean, however, that reserve requirements would not be helpful. There are at least three major justifications given (see e.g. *Rich, 1995, or Menkhoff, 1996*, for a more extensive discussion):

- Reserve requirements may be useful in rare situations by restricting an economy that is expanding too quickly, in particular, if there is an enormous inflow of liquidity.
- They might be useful in the longer run, if technological innovations allowing transactions without using any, or extremely little money, whose creation is based on central bank money.
- Reserve requirements may be useful in stabilizing the demand for central bank money, especially if they come with averaging provisions which give the banks the possibility to internally smooth their demand fluctuations.[9]

The consequence of these justifications seems to be heterogeneous. The first one, under normal circumstances needs no reserve requirement, but the possibility exists to introduce one with high ratios whenever feasible. The second one, requires a provision to introduce one, which then should be permanent with a low ratio. The last one leads to a permanent, but low ratio of reserve requirements, which are noticeable.

The major objection against reserve requirements is that they work as a kind of tax on certain liabilities, which would lead to the abandoning of this instrument completely.

Thus, there is no easy conclusion about efficiency. The key to any satisfying solution seems to be that the tax-effect is reduced as much as possible. This would keep the benefits and minimize the costs (see section 5).

4.2 Neutrality towards Financial Centers

From the viewpoint of financial centers, the concern with reserve requirements is their tax effect on liabilities, which distorts competition between these places. The goal of competitive neutrality leads to a simple conclusion: Whatever happens with the reserve requirements, the ratios should be identical in EMU.

4.3 Neutrality towards Systemic Risk

The case is similar with systemic risk. It has been argued that countries which operate reserve requirements increase the stability of their financial system (see justifications above). Within a monetary union, this implies that they also provide a public good to those countries which skip these requirements. The consequence should be again very clear: A competitive neutrality suggests identical regulations in all countries.

4.4 Neutrality towards Types of Banks

As banks have different structures of liabilities, competitive neutrality leads to the conclusion that the eligible basis on which the reserve requirements are calculated should be broad. Furthermore, different types of banks are affected indirectly. As mentioned above, averaging provisions help to stabilize the demand for central bank money. Provided that the central bank wants to smooth money market rates, certain reserve requirements allow the central bank to intervene less often in the money market and this equalizes the relative competitive position of the above-discussed MMIs with the position of MMAs.

4.5 Summary

There is an obvious contradiction in the EU between countries with and without reserve requirements. As costs and benefits seem to exist, the "solution" should be in the direction of minimizing the burden of this instrument. Further results of the neutrality analysis, which will be not discussed in section 5 again, suggest that the reserve ratio should be identical in the EMU. The eligible basis of the reserve requirements should be broad and averaging provisions are favorable.

5. Alternative Arrangements of Minimum Reserves

The discussion above has revealed some quite undisputable results and presented an open question. This section concentrates on the latter, i.e. arrangements to keep the burden of reserve requirements low. In principle, there are four elements to influence this burden: the ratio, the eligible basis, remuneration and vault cash satisfying the requirements. Leaving the last element aside and assuming a broad basis, covering e.g. sight, time and savings deposits, reduces the parameters to two, namely the ratio and the remuneration.

- The lower limit of the ratio is determined, assuming a given basis, by the amount of reserve requirements which should be higher than the working balances necessary for the banks to settle their payment transfers. The problem is to determine the working balances: Their volume depends on process efficiency, technology and share of transfers in the central bank network. To give an example, the Deutsche Bundesbank regards the present burden of roughly 1% of GDP as the lowest limit realizable whereas the Banque de France operates with one tenth of that burden.
- The upper limit for remuneration is the money market rate as there should be no incentive for banks to shift any money to central bank accounts for an attractive interest rate. In practice, the rate offered by Ireland and the Netherlands is slightly lower than the market rate to avoid any unwanted portfolio shifts.

As a result, these considerations shape an arrangement for reserve requirements which minimizes the burden. In comparison to the existing German arrangement, (*model I*, see table E.5), there may be still some room for lowering the ratio and an appropriate remuneration (*model II*). Although the latter slightly reduces the interest dependency on the money demand, it is an effective way to reduce the remaining burden. Considering competitive neutrality, remuneration seems even more advisable as a radical reduction of the ratio might be for many banks a way to reduce their reserve requirements below their voluntary working balances. In contrast to arguments of the Deutsche Bundesbank and others, *Bofinger (1996)* questions the theoretical considerations of whether there are any relevant working balances.

Table E.5: Alternative Models of Reserve Requirement Arrangements

model		gross burden in % of GDP	eligible basis	remuneration
I	present German arrangement	~ 1	sight, time, savings	no
II	minimizing arrangement	0.1 - 1.0	= model I	yes
III	voluntary arrangement	?	= model I	yes, if preannounced
IV	functional split arrangement	a) =II / III	= model II / III	= model II / III
		b) 0+X	e.g. additional credit volume	no
V	transactions oriented arrangement	> II	volume of payment transfers as basis	partially

More radical is the suggestion to switch from required to voluntary "reserves" (*Remsperger and Angenendt, 1995*). The remuneration should be restricted to those reserves which have been preannounced by the banks to the central bank (*model III*). This provides an incentive to disclose the unknown working balances and may help the central bank in adjusting its policy on setting reserve requirements and offering remuneration.

In addition to models II and III further alternatives may be worth discussion. To begin with the justifications for reserve requirements, there were two which did not call for a permanent and present positive ratio. Here the Dutch model may be useful (*Wellink, 1994*), to split the reserve requirements according to their different functions: One line would exactly follow model II but a second line would be a kind of safety net in case of unexpected liquidity problems (*model IV*, see in this direction also *Remsperger and Angenendt, 1995*). The ratio of this second line would normally be zero and in certain circumstances would be much higher than the first line ratios. For this purpose any remuneration would be unnecessary. Regarding the basis, one may consider the Dutch prototype when choosing the additional credit volume.

Regarding the model II arrangement, it has been the standard to use liabilities as the basis for calculating the reserve amounts. The discussion above has demonstrated, however, that the interesting value is the working balance which is related to the transaction volume. Thus, it could be useful to examine whether there is any direct link between reserve requirements and the payment transfer volume (*model V*). This perspective also raises the question of whether the total amount of reserves should be remunerated, or possibly, only that share which goes beyond the voluntary working balances.

6. Towards a "Decentralized Concept" of Monetary Policy Instruments

This paper started with a short description of two competing concepts for monetary policy instruments: a lean concept and a cautious concept. They would be close to the present UK and German instruments. The discussion revealed an area of instruments and instrument characteristics which can be expected to be a consensus, as a whole:

- The essential instrument of monetary policy should be open market operations, (usually) performed as interest rate tenders and being based on repurchase agreements.

- Further reasonable instruments are a deposit and a marginal facility, guarding the market and softening bigger shocks.
- It seems reasonable to define one single broad set of admissible assets which would form the underlying basis for refinancing operations.

More interesting is the disputed area, being related to the instruments of lending facilities and reserve requirements. Here, the complement of the policy goal "efficiency" through "competitive neutrality" leads to a certain emphasis:

- There seems to be a case for lending facilities, as they give MMIs a chance for direct refinancing from the central bank.
- The critical issues of lending facilities are their typical elements of subsidy and quota which exist, however, to a smaller degree also with open market auctions. Proposals have been made regarding how to minimize the distortions or to introduce a market model for lending facilities.
- Regardless if there is a justification for reserve requirements from an efficiency viewpoint, competitive neutrality would favor this instrument for the group of MMIs.
- Again, there is the issue of how the costs of this instrument could be minimized. Proposals show some potential for this.

The main concern for a concept which focuses on competitive neutrality are those institutions which do not automatically benefit from an international monetary union and internationalized money markets because they are more regionally oriented. Although, such typically small institutions may sometimes look old-fashioned in a world of globalization, thorough examinations of their performance do not suggest any systematic backwardness. Rather international and regional banks reveal different patterns of specialization which should be treated fair by the ECB.

The proposal of introducing lending facilities and reserve requirements into the ECB's toolbox suggests only at first glance to be a duplication of the German instruments. Although this similarity has valid reasons because of the Deutsche Bundesbank's reputation and the federal structure of Germany, the proposed modifications incorporate the experiences of European countries. In fact, they would make the lending facilities more similar to open market operations rather than to the German discount facilities, and the reserve requirements would be a new mixture of several countries' present regulations.

Appendix: Description of the Interest Rate Data Used

The data source for the overnight, one month and three months money market rates are data from the Deutsche Bundesbank. The rates are daily average rates. The first day of the tender is the reference date for determining the market rate.

The calculation of the 14-days interest rates has been conducted as an interpolation based on the mentioned three interest rates. It follows the supposition that the interest rate structure depends on the superposition of absolute, normal and inverse contributions. The interpolation corresponds with the solution of a linear equation system. For each date the parameters a, b and c of the equation system

$$i(t) = a + b\frac{1}{\sqrt{t}} + c\sqrt{t} \quad \text{with } t = 1,\ 30,\ 90\ \mathit{days}$$

are computed.

Endnotes

1. The Deutsche Bundesbank kindly supplied data on daily interest rates. Norbert M. Tolksdorf provided useful research assistance. I would like to thank Jürgen Jerger and conference participants for helpful suggestions, in particular Heinz Herrmann for his comment.

2. According to *EMI (1995)* the burden in Germany was 1.3% but the lowering in 1995 has decreased this to about 1.1%.

3. An exception is probably an emerging consensus on advantages of a universal banking system.

4. The price risk here is the uncertainty to pay more than competitors in American style auctions.

5. Precisely, there is a third component for determining the individual contingents of banks, which may be described as a discretionary right by the Deutsche Bundesbank to adjust the contingent if it is not used.

6. Hesse and Braasch have other objections which do not regard the issue of competitive neutrality.

7. Sometimes, the acceptance of privately issued assets is questioned because this would need some kind of rating which is not in every case available. In fact, however, this problem is neither insurmountable, as the case of German rediscount facility shows, nor decisive, as the quality of many private assets ranks above some public assets.

8. This could be a reason why members of the Deutsche Bundesbank board have shown a preference for broad participation in refinancing procedures.

9. If one regards this as the only convincing justification under present circumstances and questions the need for smoothing money market rates (see *Goodhart, 1996* for an interesting discussion), reserve requirements would be superfluous (*Bofinger, 1996*).

References

BOCKELMANN, H. (1996), Unterschiede in den nationalen Finanzstrukturen und ihre makroökonomische Bedeutung, in: DUWENDAG, DIETER, ed. (1996), Finanzmärkte, Finanzinnovationen und Geldpolitik, Schriften des Vereins für Socialpolitik No. 242, Berlin: Duncker & Humblot, 11-39.

BOFINGER, P. (1996), Mindestreserve und Feinsteuerung des Geldmarktzinses, in: Bofinger,Peter; Ketterer, Karl-Heinz, eds. (1996), Neuere Entwicklungen in der Geldtheorie und Geldpolitik, Festschrift für Norbert Kloten, Tübingen: J.C.B. Mohr, 295-324.

BREIG, H. (1994), Bank Lending and Corporate Finance in Major Industrial Countries: Are France and Germany Really Similar?, Institut für Finanzwissenschaft, University of Freiburg, Discussion Paper No.27.

--- (1996), Financial Regulation and the Banks' Role in European Economies, in: TILLY, R.; WELFENS, P.J.J., eds., European Economic Integration as a Challenge to Industry and Government, Contemporary and Historical Perspectives on International Economic Dynamics, Berlin et al.: Springer, 325-347.

COTTARELLI, C.; KOURELIS, A. (1994), Financial Structure, Bank Lending, and the Transmission of Monetary Policy, IMF Staff Papers, Vol.41, No.4, 587-623.

CUKIERMAN, A. (1995), How Can the European Central Bank Become Credible?, Paper presented at the CEPR/Irving Fisher Society-Conference on "What Monetary Policy for the European Central Bank?", Frankfurt/M.

DEUTSCHE BUNDESBANK, Monthly Report, Frankfurt/M., various issues.

EUROPEAN MONETARY INSTITUTE (EMI) (1995), Annual Report 1994, Frankfurt/M.

FRANKEL, A.B.; MONTGOMERY, J.D. (1991), Financial Structure - An International Perspective, Brookings Papers on Economic Activity, No.1, 257-310.

GOODHART, C. (1996), Why Do the Monetary Authorities Smooth Interest Rates?, LSE Financial Markets Group Special Peper No.81, London.

HESSE, H.; BRAASCH, B. (1994), Zum "optimalen" Instrumentarium der Europäischen Zentralbank, in: GAHLEN, BERNHARD; HESSE, HELMUT; RAMSER, H. J., eds., Europäische Integrationsprobleme aus wirtschaftswissenschaftlicher Sicht, Tübingen: J.C.B. Mohr (Paul Siebeck), 161-183.

--/-- (1996), "Standing facilities" - als geldpolitisches Instrument einer europäischen Notenbank verzichtbar?, in: BOFINGER, P.; KETTERER, K.-H., eds., Neuere Entwicklungen in der Geldtheorie und Geldpolitik, Festschrift für Norbert Kloten, Tübingen: J.C.B. Mohr, 275-293.

ICARD, A. (1994), Experience Gained with Monetary Policy Instruments in France, Deutsche Bundesbank, Auszüge aus Presseartikeln, 13.6.1994, 2-6.

ISSING, O. (1988), Das geldpolitische Instrumentarium unter dem Aspekt der Wettbewerbsneutralität, in: EHRLICHER, WERNER; SIMMERT, DIETHART B., eds., Wandlungen des geldpolitischen Instrumentariums der Deutschen Bundesbank, Beihefte zu Kredit und Kapital No.10, Berlin: Duncker & Humblot, 219-240.

--- (1994), Experience Gained with Monetary Policy Instruments in Germany, Deutsche Bundesbank, Auszüge aus Presseartikeln, 13.6.1994, 22-28.

--- (1996), Bedingungen für stabiles Geld in Deutschland und Europa, Deutsche Bundesbank, Auszüge aus Presseartikeln, No.6, 31.1., 16-22.

---; RUDOLPH, B. (1988), Der Rediskontkredit - Die geldpolitische Bedeutung und der Einfluß des Rediskontkredits der Deutschen Bundesbank auf die Wettbewerbssituation im Bankensektor, Stuttgart: Deutscher Sparkassenverlag.

JARCHOW, H.-J. (1995), Zur Strategie und zum Instrumentarium der Europäischen Zentralbank, Aussenwirtschaft, 50.Jg., No.3, 423-442.

JERGER, J.; MENKHOFF, L. (1995), Refinancing Policy Options of the European Central Bank, Paper presented at the CEPR/Irving Fisher Society-Conference "What Monetary Policy for the European Central Bank?", Frankfurt/M.

KASMAN, B. (1992), A Comparison of Monetary Policy Operating Procedures in Six Industrial Countries, Federal Reserve Bank of New York Quarterly Review, Vol.17, No.2, 5-24.

KING, M. (1994), Monetary Policy Instruments: the UK Experience, Bank of England Quarterly Bulletin, 268-276.

KNEESHAW, J.T. (1995), A Survey of Non-financial Sector Balance Sheets in Industrialized Countries: Implications for the Monetary Policy Transmission Mechanism, BIS Working Paper No.25.

MENKHOFF, L. (1995), Offenmarkt- oder Refinanzierungspolitik für Europa?, Wirtschaftsdienst, Vol.75, No.6, 313-319.

---- (1996), Geldpolitische Instrumente der Europäischen Zentralbank, Eine Analyse unter den Aspekten Effizienz, Wettbewerbsneutralität und Dezentralität, Stuttgart: Deutscher Sparkassenverlag; 2.ed; as revised and enlarged edition forthcoming: Monetary Policy Instruments for European Monetary Union, Berlin et al.: Springer.

MONTICELLI, C.; VIÑALS, J. (1993), European Monetary Policy in Stage Three: What Are the Issues?, CEPR Occasional Paper No.12.

REMSPERGER, H.; ANGENENDT, U. (1995), Zum Instrumentarium des Europäischen Systems der Zentralbanken, BHF-Bank Diskussionsbeiträge, Frankfurt/M., November.

RICH, G. (1995), Does the European Central Bank Need Minimum Reserves?, Paper presented at the CEPR/Irving Fisher Society-Conference "What Monetary Policy for the European Central Bank?", Frankfurt/M.

WELLINK, A. (1994), Experience Gained with Monetary Policy Instruments in the Netherlands, Deutsche Bundesbank, Auszüge aus Presseartikeln, 13.6.1994, 6-15.

Comments on: Competitive Neutrality of Monetary Policy Instruments for EMU

Heinz Herrmann

The monetary policy debate in the run-up to monetary union has many aspects. Several of the points under discussion are very much in the public eye. Other issues lead a more obscure existence outside the central banks. Belonging to the second category is the debate on the correct set of monetary policy instruments - something that is often neglected in the academic world, as well. Many regard it as a matter of purely technical interest. Professor Menkhoff has performed the service of bringing this subject to greater public attention.

The impression that this is a topic of concern only for bank specialists is in fact inaccurate. Anyone studying the problems involved in the workings of monetary policy will come across a number of interesting facets.

The connection between monetary policy strategy and monetary policy instruments has recently received a fair amount of attention. Even if the link is not always a strict one, there are nevertheless some indications that several monetary policy instruments have a certain affinity with particular monetary policy strategies. A monetary policy that has itself set the objective of defending a given exchange rate parity, for example, must always have the instrumental capability of reacting to any potential disturbance in a speedy and flexible manner. This has influenced the instruments of many European central banks.

A further aspect of the instrument debate is the link between the array of instruments and the nature of the financial markets. The disappearance of credit controls, the general rejection of administrative methods for influencing international capital flows - through the cash deposit requirement, for example - or the triumphant progress of open market policy are the result of the rapid growth and deepening of the financial and foreign exchange markets. The link may also be a reverse one, i.e. that instruments influence the markets. Menkhoff points to the connection between the trade bill and rediscount policy in Germany, for example.

It is a third aspect, in particular, that Menkhoff has turned his attention: The question of the relationship between the array of monetary policy instruments and competition in the financial sector. This is not an issue which has been publicly discussed in any great detail in the past. That was probably due to the fact that under normal circumstances, changes in the array of instruments in one country are not dramatic enough to generate noticeable competitive effects. This situation has been altered somewhat with the clash of different cultures in the European countries' financial systems.

A crucial difference between countries concerns the number and type of credit institutions which act as partners of the central bank in the individual countries and, on the other hand, are involved in funding the economy. Whereas almost 4,000 credit institutions are business partners of monetary policy in Germany - in open market operations their number is today almost 1,000 - the figure for their counterparts in several other Community countries is less than 20.

It is obvious that the large number of small banks have a less sophisticated money market management than do the handful of large banks that exist in Germany, as is the case in other countries. In the past, the German discount facility offered a simple and cheap way of obtaining central bank money. This was particularly important for small banks. On the other hand, for many of those small banks the provision of central bank money in the open market is linked to the fear of suffering a disadvantage because they are less sophisticated.

This fear is probably not universally justified for all types of open market operations. Certainly, a distinction has to be made between the different ways in which open market policy provides central bank money. It is understandable that small banks prefer simple lending facilities to complicated open market operations. It is not always easy to judge, however, which method of open market policy puts which type of banks at a disadvantage or at an advantage. Contrary to initial appearances, the Dutch auction method with high offers and low allotments, for example, may put small banks at disadvantage if they have difficulties in obtaining the necessary collateral.

The minimum reserves instrument, too, has competitive aspects in this regard. Minimum reserves that are to be held on an average of one period serve the purpose of smoothing money market rates since the maintenance of these reserves acts as a buffer against liquidity shocks. But small banks which do not have a sophisticated money market management are the ones likely to benefit the most from lower interest rate volatility. In addition, lower volatility of this kind favors an approach to an open market policy that forgoes a permanent central bank presence in the money market and provides central bank money for somewhat longer periods. This, also prevents small banks from suffering serious setbacks.

The question now arises of why so much consideration should be given to the smaller banks in restructuring the set of instruments for the ECB. Is it not natural to expect that the less sophisticated institutions will not be competitive enough and will have to disappear?

An initial argument against this is that monetary union is a shock caused by the government - which must not interfere with competitive relationships. This point is made by Menkhoff.

There is another aspect that would seem to be even more important, however. The diversity of the German banking environment has far-reaching implications extending into the real economy. Small banks occupy niches and, in Germany, form a major element of the house-bank relationship. There are indications that the relationships between savings banks and credit cooperatives and their customers are closer than those between large banks and their business partners.

That has wide-ranging implications for the propensity to grant loans when times are difficult, for example. Credit rationing does not play such an important role for small banks as it seems to play for a large bank. That is not without a good reason, of course. The interest on loans charged by small banks is likely to be higher and geared less to the market rate. This may be the price for increasing the chance of obtaining a loan even in times that are difficult. It would be possible to debate for a long time whether such close relationships strengthen the competitiveness of an economy in the long-term or whether they result in inefficient enterprises being kept afloat longer than necessary.

It is not possible to give an answer to all these questions today. What is important, however, is the finding that the efficiency of the financial system, and the monetary transmission process depend more than originally thought on the structure of the financial sector. Bearing that in mind, it is justified to give consideration to the competitive effects of an array of monetary policy instruments. Finding a balanced answer to all the problems mentioned is not easy, especially since the situation is changing from country to country.

III. Fiscal Aspects of the Maastricht Treaty and Political Economy of Transition

F. Self-Fulfilling Public Debt Crises

Daniel Gros[1]

1. Introduction

This paper will show that under certain conditions highly indebted countries could fall into a low credibility trap. This occurs when a government is judged to be not credible by financial markets. It then has to pay a risk premium through higher interest rates. The higher debt service burden that results, if inflation is kept low, makes it even more likely that the authorities will abandon their attempt for stabilization and try to reduce the real value of the debt through a inflation. As a result, this further increases the risk premium demanded by financial markets and could possibly lead to a spiral of increasing interest rates until the government caves in.

However, the debt trap is not the only equilibrium. The same country could also end-up with low interest rates by starting a virtuous circle of high credibility and low interest rates. All that is needed to reach this equilibrium is for markets to think *a priori,* that the government will be tough on inflation. It will then pay lower interest rates and thus, at the same inflation rate have a lower debt service burden to carry. This could then validate the initial assumption. Hence, there could be two equilibria in financial markets and a mere shift in expectations leading to a bad equilibrium would have to be validated even in the situation of a hard-nosed government.

The current crisis in Italy is a good illustration of the bad equilibrium. It is often argued that the Banca d'Italia cannot tighten monetary policy because the increasing interest rates further increase the fiscal deficit. However, it seems that the national bank of Belgium does not have this similar problem. Belgium and Italy can be compared because they have a similar public finance problem. The debt to GDP ratio is somewhat higher in Belgium than in Italy (140 versus 125) whereas the Belgian deficit is somewhat lower. But Belgium seems to be in a good equilibrium because their interest rates are closer to German levels. However, Italy seems to be stuck in a bad equilibrium because its government pays 5 to 6 percentage points more for public debt, although its inflation rate is only about 2 percentage points higher than in Belgium.

This paper differs from previous models on public debt crises because it emphasizes feedback from the initial assumption prevailing in the market to the eventual choice of the government. In the framework of *Giavazzi and Pagano (1990),* the public does not know the preferences of the government in terms of the fraction of the deficit that should be monetized. In this paper the preferences of the government are known and the government can act in the (short term) interests of the country.

The problem is, that if it is well known, a government that cannot bind its hands, could end up in a bad equilibrium. The novelty of the paper is that it shows that there is also a good equilibrium which is locally stable. However, once financial markets are far away from the good equilibrium they make it very difficult for the government to stabilize.

2. The Model

The starting point is a standard social loss function, L_t, given by:

$$L_t = [\alpha q_t^2 + p_t^2] \qquad \alpha \geq 0 \tag{1}$$

where p_t stands for the inflation rate and q_t stands for tax revenues as a percentage of GDP, which is equivalent to the average tax rate. High taxes and high inflation create distortions which are thus costly in social terms. The parameter α indicates the *relative* weight of taxes in the social loss function. A high α could be interpreted to mean that the tax collection system is not efficient, i.e. that it causes high distortion costs for a given revenue, or it could be interpreted to mean that the politicians in power dislike high taxes (e.g. high marginal tax rates in households).

The aim of the authorities, as usual no distinction is made between the central bank and the ministry of finance, is to minimize this loss subject to the budget constraint :

$$d(b_t) = g_t + b_t(i_t - p_t) - q_t - p_t\sigma \tag{2}$$

where b_t is the public debt/GDP ratio and g_t represents the (non-interest) expenditure relative to GDP. The last term in this budget constraint represent seigniorage revenues under the assumption of a constant velocity demand function for money with velocity equal to σ. Real growth is for simplicity assumed to be zero. Government expenditures could be made endogenous, as in a number of other contributions on the optimal choice of taxes and inflation. However, this is not done here because it would not affect the main results of the paper, which concentrates on the incentive to use inflation as a method to reduce the value of the public debt.[2]

The crucial point about the budget constraint (2) is that *ex-post* real interest payments, given by $b_t(i_t - p_t)$, are a function of the difference between the nominal interest rate and inflation. This formulation implies that all government debt has the same maturity, equal to the length of the period of this model. Another interpretation would be that b represents only the government debt that matures in this period. Interest payments on other government debt would then be subsumed under general government expenditure. This is not a serious limitation of the model since some countries such as Italy have a relative short average duration period of debt (and some long term debt is indexed on short term interest rates).

The nominal interest rate, i_t, can be written as the sum of the real interest rate, ρ, and expected inflation, $E_{t-1}(p_t)$. The real interest rate demanded by financial markets is here assumed (as usual) to be constant. The budget constraint can then be re-written as:

$$d(b_t) = g_t + b_t(\rho + E_{t-1}(p_t) - p_t) - q_t - p_t\sigma \tag{2'}$$

The authorities determine inflation after the financial markets have formed their expectations and set their interest rates.

The F.O.C. for a minimum of the loss (1), subject to the constraint (2)' are :

$$\partial L_t/\partial q_t = 0 = 2\,[\,\alpha q_t - \lambda_t\,] \tag{3}$$

$$\partial L_t/\partial p_t = 0 = 2\,[\,p_t - \lambda_t(b_t + \sigma)\,] \tag{4}$$

where λ_t is the shadow price associated with the budget constraint (2)'.

In order to simplify the notation only the steady state will be considered, with a constant debt/GDP ratio, denoted as b.[3] Conditions (3) and (4) yield a simple relationship between inflation and tax revenues (as a percentage of GDP):

$$p_t = (b + \sigma)\,\alpha q_t \tag{5}$$

This can be substituted into the budget constraint (2)' to obtain an expression for the steady state 'tax rate'. If one assumes that the public anticipates inflation correctly (i.e. the public knows the incentives of the government and has rational expectations), the debt to GDP ratio remains constant only if :

$$0 = g_t + bp - q_t - \sigma(b + \sigma)\alpha q_t \tag{6}$$

If the expenditure is constant at $\breve{g}$ the optimal tax ratio also becomes a constant given by:

$$q = [\,\breve{g} + bp\,] / [\,1 + \sigma(b + \sigma)\alpha\,] \tag{7}$$

The loss under discretion L_d would then be given by :

$$L_d = \alpha \{[\breve{g} + b\rho] / [1 + \sigma(b + \sigma)\alpha]\}^2 +$$

$$\{[\breve{g} + b\rho] [(b + \sigma)\alpha] / [1 + \sigma(b + \sigma)\alpha]\}^2 \qquad (8)$$

In order to highlight the role played by the interest burden on public debt, it will be assumed from now on that $\sigma = 0$. This elimination of seigniorage from the model could be justified through the fact, that over the last years seigniorage has not played a major role in EU public finances as shown by *Gros and Vandille (1995)*. The tax basis for seigniorage is the monetary base which is below 10% of GDP in most countries. In contrast the debt/GDP ratio is above 100% in a number of countries.

Suppressing seigniorage, as a source of revenues has the advantage that the social optimum (for the government) would be to announce that it will set inflation to zero. If this believed by the markets, this would lead to a lower loss because it would imply the same tax ratio as is under discretion. This model would yield the same result as in literature that stresses an incentive for governments to engineer surprise inflation which leads to an increase in employment or output. The problem, again as usual, is that the announcements of zero inflation in reality are not credible.

Examination of equation (8) (and (2)) shows that the sum $\rho b + g$ is all that is of importance. Hence $\breve{g}$ from now on can just be interpreted as representing the sum of the non-interest expenditure plus (*ex ante*) real interest payments on the public debt. The loss under discretion then is reduced to :

$$L_d = \alpha \breve{g}^2 + (\breve{g} b\alpha)^2 = \alpha \breve{g}^2 (1 + b^2\alpha) \qquad (9)$$

It is clear that the loss under the social optimum, i.e. under a credible stabilization plan, is lower than this, since the second term would then just fall away. This is a standard result.

What happens if the government does keep inflation stable, but it is not believed *ex ante* by financial markets? In this situation the *ex post* real interest rate will be higher. This means that the size of the social loss under a stabilization plan that is only partially credible *ex ante*, but is actually implemented, is determined by the budget constraint. This implies, in turn, that taxes have to be increased to pay for the higher *ex post* real interest rates :

$$q = \breve{g} + b\,E_{t-1}(p_t) \tag{10}$$

Assuming risk neutrality in financial markets the expected inflation rate is given by the product of the probability that the stabilization fails and the inflation rate expected in case the government gives up in their attempts. The subjective belief of the market concerning the probability that the government will give up in their attempt to stabilize is denoted by π_s. It will be determined in a model consistent with section IV. The next section determines the inflation rate that the government should create given the value of π_s that has been incorporated into a nominal interest rate.

3. Giving Up

What would the optimal inflation rate be if the government were to give up their plans to stabilize? Designating this case with the subscript '$_{gu}$' one can start with the budget constraint which yields:

$$O = \breve{g} + b\,(\pi_s\, p_{gu} - p_{gu}) - q_{gu} \tag{11}$$

where it was assumed that the rate chosen in case the government gives up, p_{gu}, is equal to the one anticipated by the market.

The relationship between taxes and inflation calculated from the F.O.C. for loss minimization under given expectations of inflation is still valid in equation (5). It implies that $p = b\alpha q$. Using this relationship (5), in equation (11) yields a solution for the tax rate that becomes optimal when the government wants to abandon their attempts to stabilize and minimize the one period loss:

$$q_{gu} = \breve{g}\ [1 + (1-\pi_s)\, b^2\alpha]^{-1} \tag{12}$$

Using equation (5) marginal incentives to use inflation or taxes also yields the solution for the optimal inflation rate to chose if the government gives up:

$$p_{gu} = \breve{g}\, b\alpha[1 + (1 - \pi_s)\, b^2\alpha]^{-1} \tag{13}$$

It follows that the loss resulting if the government gives up 'in an optimal manner' can be written as:

$$\begin{aligned} L_{gu} &= \alpha[1 + (1 - \pi_s)\, b^2\alpha]^{-2} + (b\alpha)^2\, [1 + (1 - \pi_s)\, b^2\alpha]^{-2} \\ &= \breve{g}^{\,2}\, [1 + (1 - \pi_s)\, b^2\alpha]^{-2}\, [\alpha + (b\alpha)^2] \\ &= \alpha\, \breve{g}^{\,2}\, [1 + (1 - \pi_s)\, b^2\alpha]^{-2}\, [1 + b^2\alpha] \end{aligned} \tag{14}$$

By abandoning their attempts to stabilize (in other words by fooling the markets) the government can actually achieve a lower social loss (at least for one period) as becomes apparent if one compares equation (14) to equation (9).

Giving up also yields a smaller loss than stabilizing. This is a well-known result in the context of the general time inconsistency approach. It can be shown to hold true in this model as well. Under stabilization the need for taxes is determined by the budget constraint with actual inflation equal to zero (but expectations of inflation are positive):

$$q_{stab} = \breve{g} + b\pi_s p_{gu} = \breve{g} + \alpha\, b^2\, \pi_s \breve{g}\ [1 + (1 - \pi_s) b^2\alpha]^{-1} \tag{15}$$

The loss under stabilization then becomes:

$$L_{stab} = \alpha \breve{g}^{\,2}[1 + \alpha b^2\pi_s / (1 + (1 - \pi_s)\, b^2\alpha)]^2 \tag{16}$$

which can be written as:[4]

$$L_{stab} = \alpha \breve{g}^2 [1 + (1 - \pi_s) b^2\alpha]^{-2} [1 + b^2\alpha]^2 \tag{17}$$

Is it always better to stabilize? The answer could be no if the stabilization plan is not fully credible *ex ante*. Equation (17) shows that the loss under stabilization with only partial credibility is larger if $[1 + (1 - \pi_s) b^2\alpha]^{-2} [1 + b^2\alpha]$ exceeds one. This will be the case if π_s equals one. If the government only has a very low credibility with the markets it would do its country a favor, if it did not even try to stabilize. However, a perfectly credible stabilization ($\pi_s = 0$) always leads to a lower loss. The borderline subjective probability that leads to the same welfare loss under discretion and under stabilization can be determined from the condition:

$$2 (1-\pi_s) + (1 - \pi_{s2}) b^2\alpha = 1 \tag{18}$$

A comparison of equations (17) and (14) also shows that as long as b and α are positive the loss under stabilization is larger than under 'giving up'. The difference in welfare under the two policies is:

$$\begin{aligned} L_{stab} - L_{gu} &= \alpha \breve{g}^2 [1 + (1 - \pi_s) b^2\alpha]^{-2} \{(1 + b^2\alpha)^2 - (1 + b^2\alpha)\} \\ &= \alpha \breve{g}^2 [1 + (1 - \pi_s) b^2\alpha]^{-2} (1 + b^2\alpha) b^2\alpha \end{aligned} \tag{19}$$

which is always positive, as argued above. Of course, the gain from fooling people cannot often be reaped, but the temptation certainly exists. A number of studies have concentrated on the game theory implications of the fact that giving up creates a lower social loss, at least for one period. This paper does not follow this route. Instead it would like to show that more than one model consistent equilibrium could exist if the decision of the government is uncertain.

4. When to Give Up

The less than perfect credibility *ex ante* makes it costly for the government to stabilize because it has to pay a risk premium on its debt. But so far this lack of full credibility, i.e. a positive value of π_s has only been assumed. The crucial innovation proposed in this paper is that the probability that the government does give up should be a function, at least *inter alia*, of the difference in the loss. This is an intuitively attractive assumption because the larger the welfare loss, even if only for one period, the more likely the government should be able to override other considerations that would induce it to attempt stabilization against the odds. A similar idea is contained in a series of papers by Ozkan and Sutherland who pursue a slightly different approach. In their framework (e.g. *Ozkam and Sutherland (1994)*) there are external stochastic shocks that can drive the economy away from a politically acceptable equilibrium and the government abandons their attempts to stabilize with certainty once it pays to do so. The decision of the government is based on expectations of stochastic variables, but the rule is perfectly known by the public and the decision criterion is clear. This can also create self-fulfilling speculative attacks.

The probabilistic approach of this paper seems to be closer to reality in that financial markets can never be entirely certain about what course of action the government will eventually chose because other considerations (e.g. reputation effects) also play a role. Hence it will now be assumed that the decision process of the government is such that the *probability* that it abandons the attempt to stabilize is an increasing function of the difference in the loss.

In order to obtain a simple solution it is assumed that the 'objective' probability, π_o, that the government gives up depends on the square root of the difference in loss as in[5]:

$$\pi_o = \gamma\,[L_{stab} - L_{gu}]^{0.5} + \Gamma \tag{20}$$

where γ and Γ are two arbitrary constants. Equation (20) is, of course, only defined over the range $0 \leq \pi_o \leq 1$. If the RHS of equation (20) is negative, π_o must be set to zero, and if the RHS exceeds one, then π_o must be set equal to one. Assuming these restrictions are observed this equation implies that the probability of not implementing zero inflation is equal to Γ when implementing zero inflation were to lead to the same social loss as the high inflation discretionary equilibrium. Γ thus represent other factors that influence the choice of whether to stabilize or not, it could be zero or it could even be positive if the country is in political turmoil. A country that attaches great importance to achieving zero inflation (over and above the effect operating through the social loss function for the current period), for example because it wants to participate in EMU at some point in the future, would imply that Γ is negative. In this case the probability of abandoning the stabilization attempt might be zero even if the social loss is greater than under discretion (as usually the case here). Henceforth it will be assumed that Γ is negative.

The parameter γ indicates the impact of an increase in the net cost of stabilization on the probability of failure. The higher the value of γ the more important the cost/benefit analysis becomes in influencing the decision of whether to stabilize against the odds which are set by the market.

The sequence of events in this set-up could be described as follows: The economy starts in the discretionary equilibrium. The government makes a plan to stabilize and announces it. The public then forms its subjective probability, π_s, that the plan will actually succeed. The reaction of the public determines (through equation (12) the level of expected inflation (i.e. interest rates) which then determine the gain (or loss), *ex post* the government would make (or have to bear) if it actually implemented the plan. This, in turn, determines the objective probability, π_o, that the government will actually implement the plan (equation (13)). The public knows this and hence a model consistent equilibrium can hold only if the belief about the probability of failure by the public is equal to the objective probability of failure ($\pi_s = \pi_o = \pi$). Equations (12) and (13) can then be used to determine the probability of failure, and hence the expected inflation rate (equal to the nominal interest rate here).

The implicit solution for the model consistent probability of failure is then (using equation (19) in equation (20)):

$$\pi = \gamma \; [\,[1 + (1 - \pi)\, b^2\alpha]^{-2}\, \breve{g}^{\,2}\, \alpha\, (1 + b^2\alpha)\, b^2\alpha]^{0.5} + \Gamma$$
$$= \gamma\, \breve{g}\, b\alpha\, [1 + (1 - \pi)\, b^2\alpha]^{-1}\, (1 + b^2\alpha)^{0.5} + \Gamma \tag{21}$$

This implies a quadratic solution for π.[6] If one defines the composite term on the RHS as $\cap \equiv \gamma b\alpha \breve{g}\, (1 + b^2\alpha)^{0.5}$ this can be rewritten as:

$$\pi^2\, \alpha b^2 - \pi\, [1 + \alpha b^2(1 + \Gamma)] + \cap + \Gamma(1 + \alpha b^2) = 0 \tag{22}$$

The solutions to this quadratic expression are given by:

$$\pi_{1,2} = 0.5[\;[1+\Gamma+(\alpha b^2)^{-1}] \pm [(1+\Gamma+(\alpha b^2)^{-1})^2 - 4(\alpha b^2)^{-1}(\cap+\Gamma(1+\alpha b^2))]^{0.5}] \tag{23}$$

It is apparent from equation (21) that if either b or α are equal to zero the only equilibrium is the one where the probability of giving up is zero. The reason for this is that if α is zero, the government does not have an incentive to use surprise inflation, the lower taxes it can impose are worth zero. If b is zero the government does not gain from surprise inflation.

The intuition behind the two solutions in equation (23) can be seen more clearly if one analyses equation (21) graphically through a numerical example. The value of the RHS of equation (21) can be displayed on the vertical axis as a function of the probability of failure assumed by financial markets (π_s). The equilibrium is then determined by the intersection between this curve and the diagonal as in figure F.1. Initially it was assumed that b, the debt/GDP ratio is equal to one, that γ is also equal to one, and that the expenditure ratio $\breve{g}$ is equal to 0.5.

Figure F.1 shows two cases: the first case is the line labeled 'alpha = 1, gamma = -0.33' which shows the value of the right hand side when α equals 1 and Γ

= - 0.33. In this case there is only one equilibrium, namely at the point A where the probability of failure assumed by financial markets is equal to the one that results from the incentives for the government. This equilibrium is stable in the sense that if the private sector were to initially guess a lower value of π it would find that the incentives for the government would imply a higher probability (and vice versa). For this parameter constellation a non negative value of Γ would imply that the only equilibrium is at zero.

Figure F.1: Two Cases: i) One Internal Equilibrium, and ii) Two Internal Equilibria

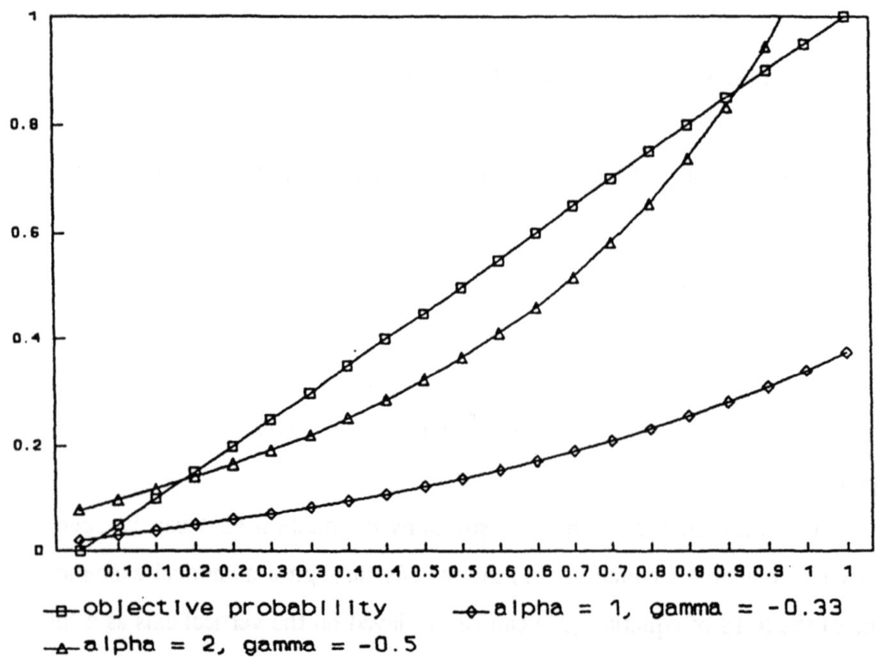

To illustrate the potential of two internal equilibria, the second line in figure F.1 is based on the value $\alpha = 2$. For this value of α a low expected inflation equilibrium and a high expected inflation equilibrium can exist inside the interval (0, 1), depending on the value of Γ. The curve shown in this figure intersects the diagonal twice, because Γ was set equal to -0.5. A lower value Γ would shift the curve downwards (at a certain point π=0 zero becomes the only equilibrium) and vice versa for higher values of Γ (until π=1 becomes the only equilibrium).

However, the potential for two equilibria exists also in a more general formulation of the link between the welfare gain from giving up and the probability that it actually happens. Instead of the square root assumed in equation (20) one could just postulate that the objective probability is a more general function of the gain from cheating:

$$\pi_o = \gamma\, [L_{stab} - L_{gu}]^{\varepsilon} + \Gamma \quad \text{with } \varepsilon > 0 \tag{24}$$

If one again substitutes for the expression of the welfare loss from equation (19) one obtains the generalized equivalent to equation (21):

$$\pi = \gamma\ [\,[1 + (1 - \pi)\, b^2\alpha]^{-2}\ \breve{g}^{\,2}\, \alpha\, (1 + b^2\alpha)\, b^2\alpha]^{\varepsilon} + \Gamma \tag{25}$$

The right hand side of this equation is a convex function of π since the second derivative is always positive in the region (0, 1).[7] Hence the potential for two solutions always exists when the RHS of equation (25) is positive at π = 0. Figures F.2 and F.3 show the numerical results for the same parameter constellations as before but with different values for ε. The only difference is that the values for Γ were in some cases adjusted to ensure that the curves were in the range between zero and one.

Figure F.2 shows the case of ε = 1 and figure F.3 shows the case of ε = 2. A comparison of these two figures with the first one shows that even these wide variations in ε do not affect the nature of the results. For low values of α (which are equivalent to low values of b) only one equilibrium is possible whereas in the case of α = 2, it always gives the potential for two equilibria. (The value of Γ determines the position of the curve and hence whether there are actually two equilibria in the interval (0, 1).)

Figure F.2: Linear Relationship between Welfare Gain and Objective Probability

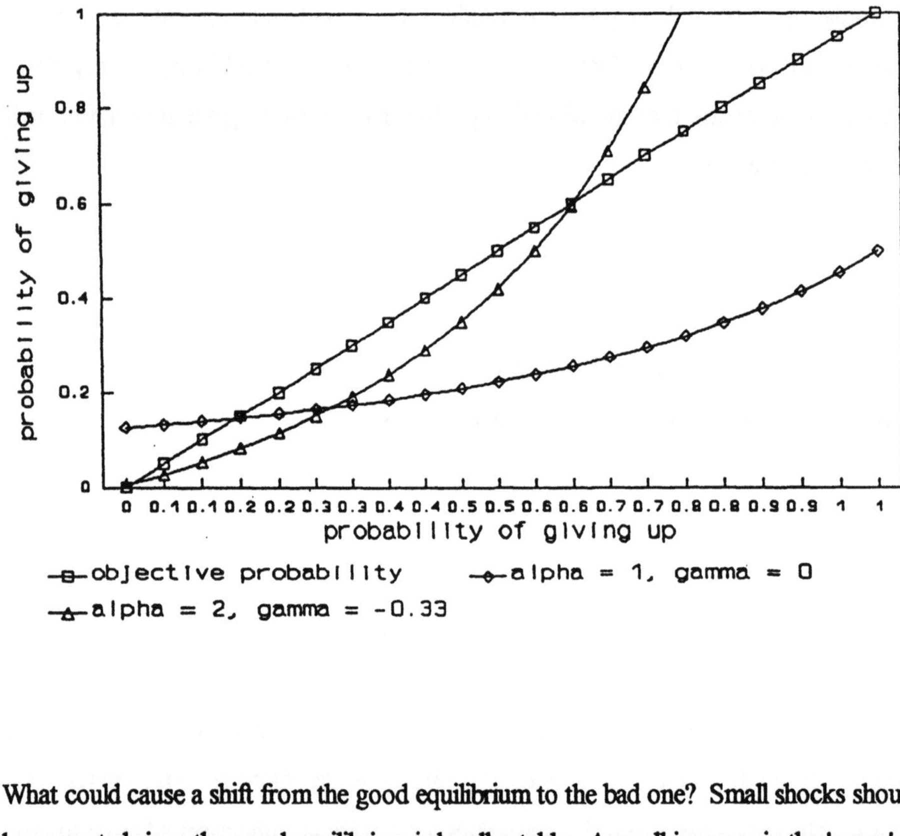

What could cause a shift from the good equilibrium to the bad one? Small shocks should be corrected since the good equilibrium is locally stable. A small increase in the 'guess' of financial markets would increase the incentive by the government to only give up very little. To the right of point A (within a finite neighborhood) the objective probability would be below the subjective one as guessed by the market. One would normally assume that the market adjusts the initial guess downwards if it exceeded the objective probability. If this is the case the good equilibrium is stable and a large shock is needed to drive the economy far away from the good equilibrium. Once the economy has reached the bad equilibrium (point B) the situation changes dramatically. In the neighborhood of this point the (ex post) real interest rate is very high and the marginal cost of further tax increases needed to finance the large primary surplus needed to stabilize the debt/GDP ratio are also very high. A one unit increase in the subjective probability of failure assumed by the market leads to an increase, at this point, in the objective probability of failure that is larger than one unit. Hence the bad equilibrium is not stable.[8] An economy that has reached the bad equilibrium could thus be driven to a corner solution where the risk premiums demanded by financial markets are so high that the government gives in with the probability of one and the economy effectively is stuck at the discretionary equilibrium.

Figure F.3: Quadratic Relationship between Welfare Gain and Objective Probability

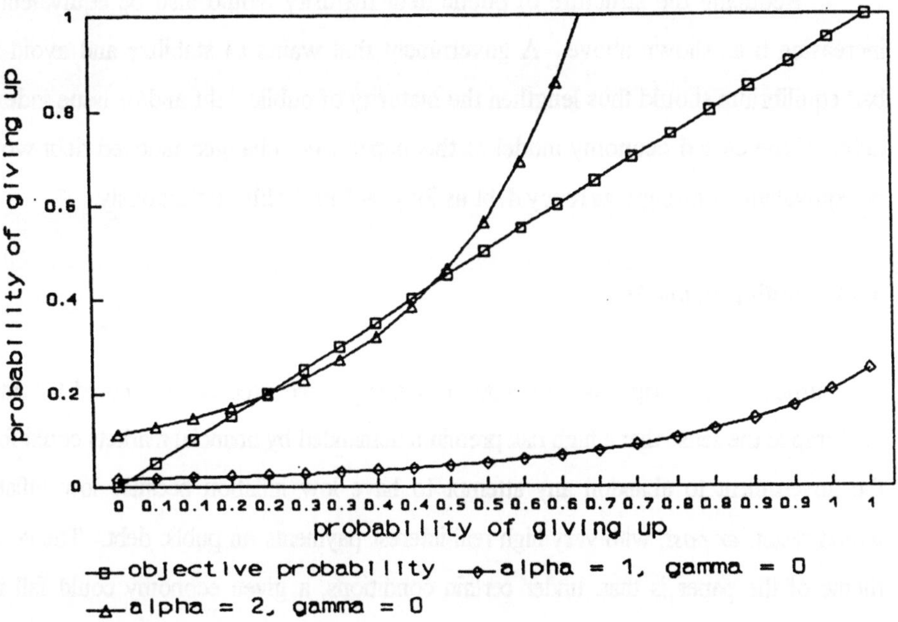

An example of a shock that was not large enough to lead to the bad equilibrium could be the example of Belgium after the 1993 ERM crisis. The central bank did not hesitate to increase short-term interest rates once the crisis had started. The result after several months of uncertainty was that interest rates and the Belgian Franc to DM exchange rate returned to their pre-crisis equilibrium.

However, a small discrete change in the parameters could also mean that the good equilibrium is no longer possible. For example, if a new government comes into power that has different preferences than the previous regime. The Berlusconi government in Italy made it clear in 1994 that it would not levy new taxes. This could be viewed as being equivalent to an increase in α. Another possibility is that the equilibrium *ex ante* real interest rate increases. As mentioned above this would be equivalent to an increase in $\breve{g}$.

Reducing the structure of public debt maturity would also be equivalent to increasing b as shown above. A government that wants to stabilize and avoid the bad equilibrium should thus lengthen the maturity of public debt and/or issue indexed debt. If the closed economy model of this paper were changed indexed debt would be equivalent to foreign currency debt as long as PPP holds continuously.

5. Concluding Remarks

The purpose of this paper was to show how a highly indebted country could fall into a debt trap in the sense that a high risk premium demanded by financial markets could force the government to abandon any attempt to have low inflation because low inflation would result, *ex post*, with very high real interest payments on public debt. The central theme of the paper is that, under certain conditions, a given economy could fall into either one of two equilibria: The bad equilibrium, which could be called a 'debt trap', and a virtuous equilibrium with good credibility and low interest rates. It is obviously more attractive to stabilize the economy under the good equilibrium. The debt trap could actually be worse than not even attempting to stabilize.

Once a country is in the debt trap small changes in policy instruments (e.g. increasing the discount rate a bit) might not have any effect. What is needed to get out of the debt trap, is a discrete change in any one of the parameters which is large enough to push the economy to the left of the debt trap or even eliminate the possibility of a debt trap. If the minimum threshold of action has been reached the rewards would be large enough for the economy to get to the good equilibrium.

Table F.1: Debt Levels and Yields on Public Debt

	Debt/GDP	Yield on public debt	Savings at German yield	inflation	Savings at German real yield
Germany	35.8	7.0		2.4	
Belgium	130.0	7.9	1.2	1.7	2.1
Netherlands	60.1	7.2	0.1	2.4	0.1
Italy	117.9	13.0	7.0	4.3	4.8
Spain	42.2	12.0	2.1	4.8	1.1
Sweden	20.2 (80.0)	11.0	0.8 (3.2)	2.6	0.8 (3.2)

Source : The Economist April 1-7, 1995 for yields on public debt, OECD Economic Outlook, 56, December 1994, for net financial obligations (net government debt). For Sweden the net debt is given at 20 % of GDP but gross debt is given at 80 %. This is the only country with such a large difference between net and gross debt.
This table intends only to give an idea on the order of magnitude for the problem. A more detailed empirical analysis would have, first of all, to take into account the average maturity structure of public debt.

How important is the mechanism modeled in this paper? Table F.1 below shows the debt level and yields on public debt of some highly indebted countries in comparison to Germany. The most striking feature in this table is that the early 1995 Italian government debt yields are almost 6 percentage points higher than German public debt. There is still a considerable amount of debt with lower interest rates outstanding, but this table calculates what would happen if present yields were to persist and became incorporated into the entire amount of public debt. The fourth column of this tabl shows that given the high level of the (net) public debt in Italy the Italian government could save almost 7 % of GDP in interest expenditure if it had German interest rates.[9] Even if Italy were to 'only' reach Belgian interest rates the savings would still be in the order of 5 to 6 % of GDP. For Belgium, the interest rate differential with Germany is much lower, hence the gain from having German interest rate would also be limited. For the Netherlands there seems to be absolutely no problem of credibility. Sweden and Spain also seem to have a credibility problem, but since their debt levels are so much lower than that of Italy their debt trap is much less severe.

Endnotes

1. Center for European Policy Studies (CEPS), Brussels and the University of Frankfurt. Tobias Adrian provided useful research assistance. Participants at a seminar at the Banco de Espana provided stimulating comments.

2. See for example *Gros (1990)* and the references cited therein.

3. *Gros (1990)* shows that this should not affect the conclusions.

4. Equation (16) can be rewritten as

$$L_{stab} = \alpha \breve{g}^{2}[1 + (1 - \pi)b^2\alpha]^{-2} [1 + (1 - \pi) b^2\alpha + \alpha b^2\pi]^2,$$

   the step to equation (17) is obvious.

5. If one were to assume a linear relationship (for example: $\pi = \gamma [L_{stab} - L_{gu}] + \Gamma$ the solution would not change qualitatively, but would be more complicated. The solution with the "objective" probability (as a function of the difference in the loss) equal to the subjective probability assumed by financial markets, would be:

$$\pi = \gamma\alpha \breve{g}^{2}[1 + (1 - \pi) b^2\alpha]^{-2} (1 + b^2\alpha) b^2\alpha + \Gamma$$

   This yields a cubic equation in π, for which no general solution exists. All one can do is to perform some numerical simulations. This is done in figure F.2.
   [One can also calculate the extreme values for: i) $\pi = 0$, which implies that the RHS becomes

$$\gamma\alpha \breve{g}^{2} b^2\alpha / (1 + b^2\alpha) + \Gamma, \text{ or i) } \pi = 1$$

   which implies that the RHS becomes

$$\gamma\alpha \breve{g}^{2} b^2\alpha (1 + b^2\alpha) + \Gamma.$$

   But since one cannot say whether these expressions are larger or smaller than one this does not help.]

6. Equation (21) implies

$$\pi(1 + (1 - \pi)\, b^2\alpha) = \gamma b\alpha\, \breve{g}\, (1 + b^2\alpha)^{0.5} + \Gamma\, \pi(1 + (1 - \pi)\, b^2\alpha).$$

7. This can be proven by noting that the part of this expression that depends on π, namely

$$[1 + (1 - \pi)\, b^2\alpha]^{-2\varepsilon}$$

is convex. The first derivative (with respect to π) of this expression is equal to:

$$2\varepsilon(b^2\alpha)\, [1 + (1\text{-}\pi)\, b^2\alpha]^{-2\varepsilon-1}$$

and the second derivative is equal to:

$$2\varepsilon(b^2\alpha)^2(2\varepsilon + 1)\, [1 + (1\text{-}\pi)\, b^2\alpha]^{-2\varepsilon-2}.$$

As long as π is between zero and one (and ε is positive) these expressions are always positive.

8. A more sophisticated '*tatonnement*' process would lead to different conclusions regarding the stability of the two equilibria: one could also assume that when at two consecutive '*trials*', i.e. subjective probabilities, (the absolute value of) the difference between the subjective and the objective probability increased, the next guess should be lower (and vice versa if the (absolute value of the) difference had diminished). If the signs of the difference had changed the new guess should be in between. Under this tatonnement process both internal equilibria are stable. The dividing line would be the point of maximum distance between the diagonal and the line representing the objective probability.

9. It is very difficult to obtain reliable data on actual interest payments on public debt. The figures published by the European Commission for 1994 give Italy an 'effective' interest rate of 9.2 % and predict (as of March 1995) that for 1995 it should go down to 8.7 %. These numbers are too low to be believable.

References

DAVIES, G.;VINES, D. (1995), Equilibrium Currency Crises: Are Multiple Equilibria Self-Fulfilling or History Dependent?, CEPR Discussion Paper, No. 1239, September.

DE GRAUWE, P. (1995), The Economics of Convergence Towards Monetary Union in Europe, University of Leuven and CEPR, April.

FLOOD, R. P.; GARBER; P. M.; KRAMER; CH., Collapsing Exchange Rate Regimes: Another Linear Example, NBER Working Paper Series, Working Paper No. 5318.

GIAVAZZI, F.; PAGANO, M. (April 1989), Confidence Crises and Public Debt Management, NBER Working Paper Series, Working Paper No. 2926.

GROS, D. (1990), Seigniorage and EMS discipline, chapter 7 in DE GRAUWE, P.; PAPADEMOS, L. (eds.), The European Monetary System in the 1990s, Longman, London, 162-177.

GROS, D.; VANDILLE, G. (1994), Seigniorage and EMU: The Fiscal Implications of price Stability and financial Market Integration, An update, (with Guy Vandille) Brussels, Centre for European Policy Studies, CEPS Working Document No. 89, Journal of Common Market Studies.

OBSTFELD, M. (1986), Rational and Self-fulfilling Balance of Payments Crisis, American Economic Review, No. 76, pp. 72-81.

OBSTFELD, M. (1995), Models of Currency Crises with Self-Fulfilling Features, NBER Working Paper Series, Working Paper 5285.

OZKAN, G.; SUTHERLAND, A. (1994), A Model of the ERM crisis, CEPR Discussion Paper No. 879.

Comments on: Self-Fulfilling Public Debt Crises

Helmut Wagner

This is a very interesting paper. It illuminates the danger of highly indebted countries that try to stabilize their economies and get into a debt crisis when they do not implement institutional precautions. This topic is highly relevant in the light of current EMU plans. The paper works out the following idea:

Highly indebted countries can fall into a low credibility trap. If a government is judged by financial markets to be not credible, it has to pay a risk premium in terms of higher interest rates. A resulting higher debt burden, may force the authorities to abandon their attempt to stabilize and instead try to reduce the real value of the debt through surprise inflation. This further increases the risk premium demanded by financial markets, leading to a spiral of increasing rates until the government caves in. One can draw two different conclusions from this story with respect to Monetary Unions. Either highly indebted countries are not able to enter a Monetary Union with less highly indebted countries, or quite the contrary, the highly indebted countries should be let into a Monetary Union with less indebted countries in order to increase the credibility of their stabilization or fiscal consolidation policy. Gros does not reveal his conclusion from the story but he only emphasizes "all that is needed" to avoid this trap is to get "markets think *a priori* that the government will be tough on inflation". I am going to concentrate my remarks on 3 subjects:

1. the "innovation" character of the model

2. the empirical part of the paper

3. institutional implications of the model results.

1.) Gros uses a standard-time or dynamic inconsistency approach for his modeling as indicated above.

In such a standard-time inconsistency approach of the Barro/Gordon-type, one can usually derive the following: If the announcement of a government to stabilize the price level is credible, it can be realized. If it is not credible, the economy will end-up with a positive inflation rate in a discretionary regime.

Even if an announcement to stabilize the price level is done honestly, it often cannot be realized in practice - at least within a single-period game as assumed in this paper - because government is viewed to have an incentive to produce surprise inflation in order to reduce either unemployment or real debt service burden. The public - in Gros's terminology as the financial markets - will recognize or anticipate this and adopt its inflation expectations in relation to the discretionary level of inflation.

If the public does this, it is not worth it for the government to stick to its announcement, even if it tries to maximize the common welfare as assumed in this paper. In Gros' words, the loss, when stabilizing, is bigger than the loss, when giving up (or "fooling the markets"). In other words, producing the discretionary level of inflation (i.e. monetarily accomodating the increased inflation expectations) is the only Nash equilibrium (which is subgame-perfect).

The "innovation" proposed in this paper is "that the probability that government does give up should be a function, at least inter alia, of the difference in the loss." This assumption is undoubtedly "intuitively attractive", but I am not sure whether this "innovation" has been given an appropriate theoretical and/or empirical basis in this paper. The real problem with this "innovation" is the missing microfoundation. It seems that the choice of the rational solution is dependent upon the size of losses here. Moreover, it is unclear how the crucial assumption of a $\pi_S<1$ in accordance with rational expectations assumed elsewhere in the paper can be achieved. The above "innovation" seems to be only convincing if there are opportunity costs for the government when it gives up. It is important to work these opportunity costs out in detail to microfound the above "innovation".

Moreover, instead of assuming the functional forms of equations (20) and (24), other functional forms could be used. It is assumed in the model that the probability to cave-in increases with the expected inflation rate. It is also meaningful to assume that the probability decreases. The reason for this may be that an expected rising inflation symbolizes the increasing costs of giving-up the attempts to stabilize the price level. Suppose, for example:

$$(*) \quad \pi_0 = 1 - c(p^e) \geq 0 \qquad c'(p^e) > 0.$$

Adopting a linear function, e.g. $c(p^e) = \gamma p^e$, the objective probability decreases in the subjective belief of the market which determines p^e. One can show that this produces only one equilibrium in the interval (0,1).

Another passage in the paper says: "The novelty of the paper is that it shows that there is also a good equilibrium (with low inflation and low interest rates) that is *locally stable.*" However, as long as there is an incentive to produce inflation as argued above, one is inclined to assume that this equilibrium tends not to be stable or not to even exist -- at least not in a one-period-game as assumed in Gros' paper.

By extending the model to a more-than-one-period-game, the above assertion, however, may be valid or reasonable - based on reputation mechanisms and dependent upon the time preference rate and the punishment strategy . One could argue that the paper (over-)simplifies the presentation of an interesting idea.

Finally in reference to the theoretical part of the paper, one could indicate that the process leading to the debt crisis is not modeled concretely enough; it seems to be introduced only in a way of plausibility.

In the rest of this discussion, I shall say only some words (in 2.) to the very short empirical part and (in 3.) to the institutional implications.

2.) Gros indicates how the situation in Belgium is a good illustration of the good equilibrium whereas he regards the situation in Italy as a good illustration of the bad equilibrium. However, I wonder why Belgium has not succeeded in the last years in reducing its public debt rate below that of Italy. Or, in other words, I wonder whether one can really catch the empirical differences in inflation and interest rates in countries such as Belgium and Italy with this rather simple model structure which eliminates not only seigniorage but also all other institutional specialties.

Furthermore, when examining the empirical data and regarding not only distinct points of time but also time series, the empirical "proof" is hardly convincing. As figure F*.1 shows the Italian inflation rate has substantially declined since the beginning of the 80s. It is hard to believe that this reduction can be reconciled with the idea of a debt and credibility trap. Furthermore, the Italian real interest rate was below the Belgian rate until the end of the 80s and is estimated to be one or two percentage points above the Belgian real interest rate until 1997 (see figure F*.2).

Figure F*.1: Inflation (GDP-Deflator)

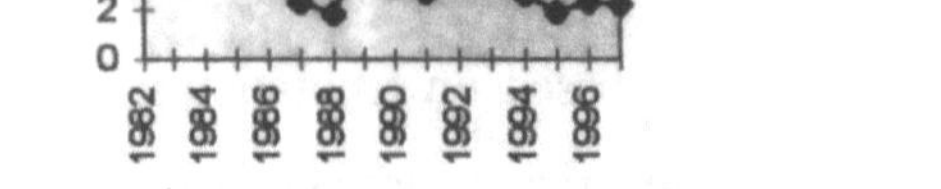

Figure F*.2: Long Term Real Interest Rates

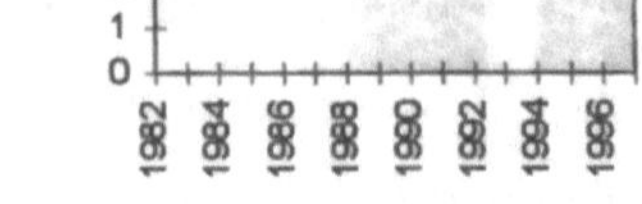

Source: OECD, Economic Outlook, 58, December 1995. The data for 1995-1997 are estimations.

3.) *Firstly*, I see the value of the paper in emphasizing that crises can be self-fulfilling despite the good intentions to stabilize, and, *secondly*, in deducing the model-based determinants of the "objective" probability that the government gives up in its attempt to stabilize the price level. This may give important hints regarding to what - economic-politically - should be done in order to avoid such a self-fulfilling debt crisis. Beyond this (and this paper), one can deduce from the arithmetics of the public budget restriction that fiscal consolidation and the speed of convergence is the more fostered the lower the real interest rate is and the higher the real GDP-growth rate is.

Hence, it is particularly important to work out the necessary political measures for reducing real interest rate and increasing real GDP growth rate. Gros also emphasizes the first, by pointing at institutional measures to increase the credibility of the announcement of price-level stabilization as a precaution to reduce real interest rate. He concretely proposes to lengthen the maturity of public debt and/or issue indexed debt.

As well, one should also look at the supply- and demand-side political measures in accodance with the EC-White Paper of Dec. '93 as well as at improving conditions of location competition ("Standortwettbewerb") by restructuring institutions as a means to increase the real GDP growth rate. One could in particular think of labor market policies (such as improvement of labor market flexibility), the tax policies (reform of taxation for firms income taxation), the infrastructure (including R&D) and deregulation policies.

G. EU Labor Markets Inside and Outside the Monetary Union

Richard Jackman

1. Introduction

This paper looks at the question of the impact of membership of the European monetary union (EMU) on the labor market and in particular on unemployment. It examines both the role of exchange rate flexibility as a mechanism for offsetting the effects of labor market rigidities and the implications of monetary union on the feasibility and effectiveness of structural reforms to reduce unemployment within Europe.

It is written at a time when rather old-fashioned short term Keynesian problems appear to be dominating the political agenda. The worry is that countries outside the EMU can obtain a competitive advantage as against the EMU members through exchange rate depreciation. EU finance ministers appear ready to propose a revised ERM regime for the currencies remaining outside the monetary union. The governments of countries outside EMU would be expected to maintain their exchange rates against the Euro, with exchange rate adjustments permitted only with the consent of the European Central Bank.

The history of the past thirty years has taught policy-makers that in general devaluations bring not competitive advantage but only higher inflation. But the most recent experience, that of the collapse of the ERM in 1992, appears to suggest on the contrary that nominal wages and prices are rather insensitive to exchange rate movements, and that exchange rate changes can therefore have lasting real effects.

In the first part of the paper I offer an interpretation of this change in behavior, leading to the conclusion that old-fashioned Keynesian concerns may need to be taken more seriously now than in the recent past. The adoption of inflation targets by governments and the consequence of slower and more stable inflation, has led to a greater degree of nominal rigidity which in turn gives a greater role for macroeconomic factors in affecting real activity.

Even so, the main causes of unemployment are, and will remain, structural. Probably the most important factors can be grouped under four headings. First are the incentives and opportunities facing unemployed people - the level, duration and conditionality of unemployment benefits and the assistance with search or employment or training opportunities provided by active labor market policies. Second are the institutional arrangements for wage-setting, the coverage of collective bargaining, the powers of the trade union movement and the degree of coordination in wage bargaining. Third are structural imbalances in the labor market, in particular the growing demand for skills and its reflection, high unemployment rates of people without skills. Finally, there are the non-wage costs of employment, which include taxes on employment, employment protection legislation and other "social" obligations on employers.

While it is clear that the obligations of countries as members of the European single market may well impose constraints on national policies in these areas, it is less evident that the choice of the currency unit has any necessary relevance. From a labor market perspective, the most obvious factor is the increased transparency of wage comparisons across countries, and the stimulus this may be expected to give to comparability across countries as an influence on wage setting.

Finally, while much theoretical discussion is couched in terms of whether a group of countries will do better by adopting a single currency or by maintaining separate currencies, it seems only realistic now to envisage the EU as consisting post 1999 of two groups of countries: an inner group (Germany, France, the Netherlands, Benelux and perhaps one or two others) which have replaced their national currencies by the Euro, and an outer group of countries unwilling to join or excluded from membership by failing to meet the criteria (Italy, Spain, Portugal, Greece, Sweden, Denmark and the UK).

2. Conceptual Issues

Economic theory supposes that equilibrium in the labor market, and hence the allocation of labor across sectors and the relative wages of each activity, will reflect only real forces, that is households' preferences and endowments, the technology and capital stock of firms and policy and institutional factors such as taxes and bargaining arrangements. The units of measurement of the money stock are in principle irrelevant to optimizing decisions by firms or households, and hence to equilibrium in the labor market. Yet very clearly much of the concern about monetary union arises from the belief that it will have real effects in the labor market, on wages and competitiveness and above all on unemployment. Invoking the neutrality of money, whatever its textbook appeal, does not do much to calm the fears of firms or workers who worry their markets or jobs may be at risk.

Why then might the units of measurement of the money stock impinge on the labor market? There are perhaps two critical dimensions, both harking back to *Keynes' (1936)* notion that workers were in general more concerned about their wage relative to other workers than their wage relative to the price of goods. The main reason for such concern lies in the absence of perfect mobility in the labor market, so that the labor market is not a market at all in the conventional sense of the word. Prices are not set by market traders - rather firms set wages which to some extent are affected by the availability of labor. Firms have the opportunity in the short and even perhaps in the long run to exploit monopsony power and wage bargaining arrangements, in particular the emphasis on wage relativities, are a mechanism for countering such tendencies.

It is well-known that concern over relative wages can introduce stickiness in nominal wage rates (*Phelps, 1978; Taylor, 1980*). The reason is that where wage-setting is decentralized no one group of workers is able to cut its money wage without at the same time reducing its relative wage. If there is an exogenous cut in the money stock of 10% (or equivalently, in a fixed exchange rate system, an exogenous reduction in the external price level of 10%), equilibrium can be restored by a fall in all nominal wages and prices of 10%. But if these wage and price reductions cannot be made simultaneously (because they are uncoordinated), the group to cut its money wage first suffers a relative (and indeed a real) wage cut. This leads to opposition to nominal wage cuts in the face of a reduction in aggregate demand. By contrast, in some circumstances, a depreciation of the exchange rate can achieve the required adjustment simultaneously, and thus overcome the coordination problem.

Whilst nominal rigidities provide scope for macroeconomic policies to assist in the adjustment to macroeconomic shocks, they also create the potential for manipulation of the economy for short term political gain, with the consequence of permanent economic loss. With nominal rigidities, an expansionary boost to an economy already in equilibrium can create output gains in the short run at the expense of permanently higher inflation and no gain in output in the longer term. Nor is it sufficient simply for governments not to indulge in such short term behavior: it may be necessary for them to convince private sector agents, firms and workers, that they cannot or will not so indulge. A long-standing argument for a fixed exchange rate regime is that it prevents monetary policy (though, as we note below, not fiscal policy) being used to manipulate economic activity by creating unsustainable boosts to demand.

There is however a second possible concern raised by the issue of relative wage comparability, and this is the question of the comparator group. Normally it is assumed that workers concern themselves with wages paid to other workers within their own country. Such a limitation makes good sense, in part because international labor mobility is much lower than mobility within countries and in part because numerous variables, from labor productivity to retail prices, tax rates, social benefits and working conditions, differ across nations. But there is no doubt that international comparisons of wage rates are further clouded by the existence of separate national currencies. A single currency will expose the differences in contract wages across nation states which may in turn lead to pressures for greater uniformity of wage rates for people doing the same jobs across countries. This can be envisaged as the regional problem writ large. Many countries suffer large variations in economic conditions including in particular unemployment rates across their regions, which are large relative to the variations in unemployment rates across countries. This is in a way surprising in that most of the structural determinants of unemployment are common across regions within nation states. It suggests that differences in productivity across regions tend not to be fully reflected in wage differences whereas across nations they are.

If the single currency leads to pressure for greater harmonization of nominal wage rates across member states, there is likely to be pressure for harmonization both of non-wage labor costs and of social benefits. But even a complete harmonization of non-wage labor costs cannot overcome the problem of differences in productivity resulting from differences in capital intensity, transport costs or agglomeration effects.

This may then impinge on the labor market in two ways. First, if workers and their employers become more conscious of wages paid to workers in similar jobs in other countries than of the wages of other workers in their own country, the within country coordination of wage setting will become increasingly problematic. (*Freeman and Gibbons, 1993*, offer an account of the stresses on wage coordination in Sweden along these lines.) Second, wage bargaining may need to become more "flexible", in the sense of taking more account of local labor market conditions. In the past, wage coordination has been a powerful force for wage moderation, and hence for sustaining full employment in many European countries. This mechanism may be expected to operate with more difficulty in countries linked by a single currency. I turn now to more detailed discussion of these issues.

3. Nominal Inertia: The Adjustment to Shocks

We have noted that wage-setting procedures may be subject to nominal inertia, and that where there is nominal inertia, exchange rate changes can offer a less costly mechanism of adjustment, in particular to adverse real shocks, than relying on changes (in particular, reductions) in nominal wages. Thus discussion has focused on two issues:

i) Are nominal rigidities important in practice - how much unemployment is required to achieve some given reduction in wages and prices?

and

ii) To what extent are economies subject to real as opposed to monetary shocks - the latter as already noted being best accommodated in a fixed exchange rate regime?

In this section, I first outline some of the evidence on these issues starting from the 1992 experience. Concluding that there are important nominal rigidities and that economies are subject primarily to real shocks, the section proceeds to a discussion of the types of labor market reforms that might alleviate these difficulties.

3.1 The Lessons of 1992

The most remarkable macroeconomic event of recent years has been the non-appearance of inflation following the collapse of the ERM in September 1992. Five countries (Italy, Portugal, Spain, Sweden and the UK) effectively abandoned the ERM peg, and as a result their exchange rates fell by, on average, around 30% against the remaining ERM members. Yet, during the past three years, the countries with depreciated currencies have experienced not a resurgence but, on average, a decline in their inflation rates. More remarkably, as recently noted by *Gordon (1996)*, the decline in inflation in these countries has actually been more rapid than the decline in inflation in the countries remaining in the ERM.

How is this experience to be explained? A change in the nominal exchange rate might in principle affect domestic prices (as measured by the GDP deflator) through three channels: the cost-of-living effect on wages, the effect on demand and the effect on expectations. (If one uses a price index other than the GDP deflator, such as the CPI or the TFE deflator, there will also be direct effects on the index of the higher prices of imported foreign goods.)

i) a "cost-of-living" effect resulting from a rise in consumer relative to producer prices leading to higher money wage claims. Higher money wages would then feed through into higher producer prices and thus into the GDP deflator. There appears however to have been only a very small relative price effect - in the three years since September 1992, in the depreciating countries the average rate of increase of the GDP deflator was 3.8% and of the consumer price index 3.9%.

ii) a demand effect, resulting from the greater competitiveness of domestic goods in international markets. International competitiveness is of course only one of many factors influencing the overall pressure of demand. If demand is already low, a real depreciation may raise demand but leave it still below the (non-inflationary) equilibrium level of output. There is thus no reason why real depreciation, even in the absence of other changes, need lead to rising inflation. If the real depreciation takes place at a time when other components of demand are declining, it may serve only to slow down, rather than reverse, the rate of decline in activity. In fact, of the countries which left the ERM in 1992, all except one (the UK) have suffered increasing unemployment.

In conventional Phillips Curve terms there is thus no mystery as to why the countries which left the ERM have experienced continuing declines in inflation. Their unemployment rates have remained high, and, in most cases, rising. The depressed demand in the domestic economy may also have limited the extent to which import prices could be raised. The situation in the UK, of low inflation in conjunction with falling unemployment, is atypical, but may reflect the effects of various supply-side reforms on the NAIRU.

With regard to Gordon's comparison with the countries remaining in the ERM, it may be noted that they also typically experienced declining inflation, and also suffered increasing unemployment. In absolute terms the gap in inflation rates between the two groups of countries closed a little, but in proportional terms it was unchanged, and if anything slightly widened. If one were to allow that it is more difficult to achieve a given percentage point reduction in inflation when it is already low than when it is high, the behavior of inflation might be held to be fully consistent with unemployment in both groups of countries. (If one regresses the proportional reduction in inflation on the proportional excess of unemployment over trend from end 1992 to end 1995, and a dummy for whether the country left the ERM in 1992, for these countries, the unemployment differential has the expected negative effect (t=-1.8), while the dummy variable is negative but insignificant (t=-0.6)).

iii) an expectations effect, according to which prices rise in response to a rise in the expected equilibrium price.

It is the third of these channels which is perhaps the most perplexing. Hitherto, the relatively rapid adjustment of domestic prices to an exchange rate change has often been attributed to the idea that it has affected expectations. By contrast, this recent experience suggests that inflation behavior can be explained entirely in terms of domestic demand pressures with no role for expectations.

A possible explanation of this change of behavior could be rooted in a changed policy perspective. Arguably, in the past, policy was directed towards real targets: growth, full employment and so on, and financial policy was accommodating and permitted a high level of demand in pursuit of these targets. Under a fixed exchange rate, high domestic demand led not so much to inflation as to balance of payment problems. If the exchange rate was then devalued, the excess domestic demand was redirected into the domestic economy leading to immediate upward pressure on wages and prices. On this interpretation the main pressure on domestic prices would have been excess demand rather than any direct feedthrough of foreign into domestic prices.

By contrast, in the current policy climate real targets have been abandoned and the prime objective of policy is price stability. Countries left the ERM in September 1992 because they found it impossible to make the reductions in their price levels necessary to achieve equilibrium at the given nominal exchange rates. To put it another way, the exchange rate anchor had become inconsistent with their projected domestic inflation rates. As a result the abandonment of the exchange rate anchor did not materially alter market expectations about equilibrium prices, since the government's policy objectives with regard to inflation had not changed.

In sum, the evidence appears to suggest that the post-1992 macroeconomic experiences of the EU countries can be adequately represented by a domestic inflation/unemployment trade-off of the standard form.

3.2 Nominal Rigidities are Important

I turn now to magnitudes. It is sometimes argued that the evidence of estimated wage and price equations demonstrates that nominal inertia is unimportant in many European countries. Many studies find that wages respond quite quickly to price increases, and also that prices respond quickly to wages. The relatively short mean lags in the wage and price equations have led some economists (e.g. *Branson and Rotemberg, 1980*) to the conclusion that nominal variables are flexible in Europe as compared to say the US. But the cost in terms of percentage point years of unemployment of a unit reduction in the inflation rate (nominal wage rigidity, or the "sacrifice ratio") depends on the interaction of the coefficient on unemployment in the wage (and price) equation and the mean wage-price lag (*Grubb et al., 1983; Layard et al., 1991*). Even if the mean wage-price lag is short, if inflation is not very responsive to unemployment the sacrifice ratio may still be high. One recent estimate, *Alogoskoufis et al. (1995)*, finds a Phillips Curve coefficient of -0.87 for European countries, so that an unemployment rate one percentage point above the NAIRU for one year will allow a permanent reduction in the inflation rate of 0.87 per cent.

This might suggest a reasonably high degree of flexibility of nominal wages but, to put matters in context, it may be noted that the 1992 devaluation achieved a 30% reduction in relative costs. If this were to be achieved through unemployment, one would require say of the order of an extra two percentage points of unemployment for four years, followed by unemployment two percentage points lower than otherwise for four years, to achieve the desired outcome. Competitiveness could be achieved more quickly by a sharper initial increase in unemployment but at the expense of greater disruption.

More importantly, the historical evidence may well seriously underestimate of the magnitude of the problem. There is little doubt that the variability of inflation is directly related to the inflation rate. When inflation is high it is also volatile, and quite large percentage point changes in the inflation rate can be achieved by restrictive demand policies often without great effects on output or employment. By contrast, when inflation is low it is very much more stable, and restrictive demand policies tend to have a greater effect on output.

To illustrate this point, if one takes the period from 1968 to 1995, over which these estimates were calculated, and divides it into two, the variance in unemployment rates relative to trend of the G7 countries in the first half of the period (1968-1981) was only one-third as high in the second half (1982-1995) while the variance in inflation rates was twice as high in the first half of the period than in the second. At the same time the average level of unemployment was almost twice as high in the second half of the period as in the first, while the average inflation rate was less than half. This suggests that a given percentage point increment in unemployment has a much smaller effect on inflation when unemployment is high or when inflation is low. In recent years inflation has been stable and subdued in most countries while unemployment has remained abnormally high. It seems plausible to think that recent unemployment fluctuations are variations around the NAIRU having relatively little impact on inflation rather than that the NAIRU itself has taken to wandering around with actual unemployment clinging closely to it.

Thus it might be better to measure the sacrifice ratio in proportional rather than in percentage point terms. Over the period as a whole the average unemployment rate and the average inflation rate for the G7 countries were about the same (5.7%), but to reinterpret the estimated coefficient (of approximately -1) in proportional terms would mean that one would need a doubling of the unemployment rate (in the EU from 11% to 22%) to achieve a halving of the inflation rate (i.e. a reduction from 3% to 1.5%). The percentage point sacrifice ratio is then about 7, almost ten times as high as the conventional estimate.

In some countries inflation is so low as to have practically disappeared, and to reduce it further may be possible only by cuts in money wage rates. Such adjustments would be without precedent in post-war history, but of course the downward rigidity of money wages in the face of extremely high unemployment rates was a major factor in contributing to the persistence of the Great Depression of the 1930s.

To be specific, we may return to the 1992 experience. The French inflation rate in 1992 was about 2.5%. Even the currently very high French unemployment rate has been able to reduce inflation by at maximum one percentage point, to 1.5%, and this appears to be something of a floor. This inflation rate is around 2 percentage points below the average inflation rate of the devaluing countries, so that on present trends it will take about 15 years for the French economy to re-establish the competitive position it had before September 1992 in relation to the devaluing countries. Even if France were able to reduce its inflation rate to zero, it would still take 8-9 years.

In Appendix A, I set out an example of a model in which wages feed through into prices within a year and likewise prices are fully reflected in wages within the year. Nonetheless, even with a standard value (-0.1) of the responsiveness of wages to unemployment, the response of the economy to a foreign price shock can involves long lags. Consider, for example, the effects of a 10% fall in the foreign price level.

This will require a corresponding reduction of 10% in the domestic price level to reestablish equilibrium. But in this example even after 8 quarters wages have made only 12.5% and prices only 7.5% of the requires adjustment. The unemployment rate rises by 10 percentage points, and by the end of the eighth quarter it is still 9.75 percentage points above equilibrium.

The final matter of concern in this context is whether the degree of nominal wage flexibility would itself be affected by monetary union, on the grounds that cross-national wage comparability would be facilitated by a common currency. I return to this question in section 4(a) below.

3.3 Real Shocks are Important

We next consider the extent to which economies are subject to real as against financial shocks. The basic argument here can be most simply formulated within the standard Mundell-Fleming framework of an open economy subject to perfect capital mobility, taking the price level as given. This allows an investigation of how aggregate demand fluctuates in response to shocks under different policy regimes. It is however appropriate to think of economies with large trading sectors, which are therefore substantially affected by external trade as well as capital mobility. The textbook results in this framework are:

i) If the economy has a fixed exchange rate (or, *a fortiori*, is part of a single currency union), aggregate demand is affected by real expenditure shocks. The magnitude of the effect of domestic shocks is to some extent diminished by the openness of the economy (so that much of the shock is absorbed by imports) while the economy is more exposed to external real shocks because of the size of the trading sector. The impact of real shocks is also increased by international capital mobility which prevents a rise in interest rates and hence any financial crowding out. On the other hand, any changes affecting the demand for money or the financial sector have no effect on demand. With perfect capital mobility, the supply of money adjusts automatically to changes in the demand for it through flows across the exchanges and there is no effect on interest rates. Changes in world interest rates do affect demand, even in the absence of any effects on foreign expenditures, since some components of domestic expenditure are interest-sensitive. In a regime of fixed but adjustable exchange rates, changes in expectations concerning the possibility of future changes in the exchange rate have to be compensated by corresponding adjustments in domestic relative to world interest rates, which again affect domestic demand. In principle, however, this last type of shock will not exist with a single currency.

ii) If the economy has a predetermined monetary target, and allows its exchange rate to float freely, then the level of economic activity is unaffected by real (domestic or external) shocks, which are in principle fully offset by changes in the exchange rate. Only to the extent that exchange rate changes change consumption relative to output prices and thereby affect the demand for money will there be any net demand effect from real shock. An increase in demand will lead to an appreciation of the exchange rate which will reduce consumer relative to output prices and thus reduce the demand for money and thus stimulate demand. Leaving aside this monetary effect, demand in a flexible exchange rate economy is insulated from external shocks. By contrast, shocks affecting the demand for money do affect economic activity, and the direct effect of such shocks is amplified by movements in the exchange rate. Changes in world interest rates also affect demand, but the (e.g.) contractionary effect of an increase in the world interest rate is more than offset by the induced depreciation of the exchange rate, so that perversely interest rate increases are expansionary and decreases contractionary under this regime. Shifts in exchange market confidence likewise have perverse demand effects - worries for the future of a currency can lead to its immediate devaluation with expansionary demand effects.

iii) In practice, monetary policy is no longer operated in most countries on the basis of a rigid target for some predetermined monetary aggregate, but more commonly by adjusting interest rates in relation to some target for forecast inflation. Such a regime can in principle substantially insulate an economy against both real and financial shocks. It is sometimes thought that it is impossible to use interest rates as a target variable in conditions of perfect capital mobility, since interest rates are set in world markets. But if a move in domestic interest rates is made solely for the purpose of stabilizing inflation, and is thus expected to be temporary, it will lead to a jump in the exchange rate such that the expected return of the exchange rate to its equilibrium will exactly compensate the interest rate differential. The analytics of this system are set out in Appendix B. Real shocks can be instantaneously offset by exchange rate adjustments while financial shocks, including world interest rate and confidence shocks, require also temporary deviations of the interest rate from the world level.

The orthodox view is that flexible exchange rates are better where economies are subject to real shocks but fixed exchange rate systems work better where there are financial shocks. The above discussion suggests that where monetary policy is conducted on some procedure more sophisticated than a money stock target, a fixed rate system no longer has any advantage in terms of absorbing financial shocks.

The question remains however as to whether real shocks are important. There seems little doubt that industries are becoming increasingly sensitive to international economic developments. Changes in technology and in relative factor prices alter the comparative advantage of nations in different sectors. Where a particular development has an adverse effect on some particular economy, the equilibrating adjustment requires a depreciation of its real exchange rate. This can of course be brought about either by a change in the nominal exchange rate or by a reduction in domestic relative to world prices. If there are nominal rigidities in the economy, clearly the former will be easier. This comes back to the standard optimal currency area question of whether the shocks hitting the member states of the group are common or different.

It would go beyond the scope of this paper to review studies of the similarities of industrial structure across the EU countries (*Bean, 1992*). The general conclusion is that the "core" EU countries (Germany, France, Benelux, Netherlands, Denmark) do have a similar industrial structure, but the EU as a whole does not. In particular, countries like Greece or Portugal have a much larger agricultural sector than the core countries, and generally rather different industrial specialization. (The UK differs slightly from the main core countries because of North Sea oil.) This suggests that a monetary union confined to the core countries could function successfully, in that most economic shocks would hit member nations in a similar manner and could be offset by adjustment of the Euro relative to other currencies. An important corollary is that in this context it would be in the interests of the EMU countries to encourage, rather than attempt to prevent, flexibility of the Euro in relation to the remaining national EU currencies.

3.4 Credibility and Reputation

Since the publication in 1983 of the Barro/Gordon paper on the positive theory of inflation, a commitment to a fixed exchange rate (and, hence, *a fortiori*, membership of a monetary union) has been seen as a powerful mechanism for making policies for low inflation or price stability credible. The argument was that governments always had an incentive to indulge in inflationary policies in order to boost output, albeit temporarily, and as a result people would base their expectations on the assumption that the economy would be inflated irrespective of the government's policy pronouncements. These adverse expectations would make the pursuit of low inflation policies excessively costly. The only way of avoiding this problem would be to institute a policy regime in which governments did not have the power to manipulate demand in the short term. Clearly, as a member of a single currency union, a government gives up an independent monetary policy.

While membership of a monetary union prevents the exercise of opportunistic monetary policy, the same cannot be said with regard to fiscal policy. On the contrary, resort to expansionary fiscal policy could be encouraged because there need be no offsetting costs in terms either of higher interest rates or of exchange rate depreciation. Will there not be a temptation for national governments to borrow to excess with their credit ratings under the protection of the European Central Bank? The proposal that member states of the monetary union restrict their fiscal deficits to a target of 1% of GDP, with automatic fines on those exceeding 3%, under the Waigel plan, would clearly counter this risk. But it is not clear that a plan as inflexible as this would be credible (a country in economic difficulties might prefer to leave the EMU than pay the fine), or whether a more flexible scheme would be effective in preventing opportunistic behavior.

As far as wage setting behavior is concerned, there seems in any event little evidence that the unemployment cost of reducing inflation is affected by credibility considerations of this type. In the UK for example, inflation fell rapidly as unemployment rose following the decision to join the ERM in 1990. But inflation had fallen even more rapidly with high unemployment following the advent of Thatcherite monetarist policies in the early 1980s when the exchange rate was floating. Nor has the French economy, with its particularly striking commitment to the Franc fort policy, appeared to benefit from a favorable unemployment/inflation trade-off. We have already noted that the inflation/unemployment trade-off for the countries leaving the ERM in 1992 was no different from that of those which stayed in.

4. The Monetary Union as a Regional Labor Market

Within a nation state, wages of workers doing essentially the same work tend to be the same across regions. The tendency is for uniformity in nominal terms, but where there are large differences in the cost of living, there are often pay supplements. The uniformity of wage rates within a country appears to be largely a product of national wage-setting arrangements. This is not to say that wages are wholly insensitive to local labor market conditions, but rather that the degree of responsiveness is insufficient to prevent the emergence of large and persistent regional unemployment differentials (*Layard et al., 1991*, chapter 6; *OECD, 1990*).

There are also of course large and persistent differences in unemployment rates across countries, but these can generally be explained in terms of differences in institutions and policies. What is striking is the absence of any systematic relationship between productivity and unemployment across countries. It is by contrast typically the case within countries that peripheral regions, with low productivity associated with high transport costs and the absence of agglomeration economies, have higher unemployment rates than more central regions.

It is clearly a matter of guesswork whether monetary union would significantly add to the pressure for comparability of wage rates across countries. If one looks at the inner group of likely EMU members recent EU data suggests that productivity per worker is about 10% higher in Belgium and in France than in Germany, while in the Netherlands productivity is about 7% lower. Some of this will reflect compositional factors, but to the extent it does not, one would expect wage rates to reflect the productivity differentials and hence be higher in France or Belgium than in Germany or the Netherlands. Standardization of wages would then raise wage rates in the Netherlands and reduce them in France and Belgium, which would tend to reduce unemployment inequality. Even so, the differences are not enormous, and the effects would probably not be large.

Very much more serious adjustment problems would arise however in a wider currency grouping. Productivity levels in Greece and Portugal are only half the EU average and any attempt to equalize wages in these conditions would run into problems comparable with those of the assimilation of the East German labor market.

5. Monetary Union and the Quest for Jobs

Finally, would monetary union impede the efforts of member states to tackle unemployment and to create more jobs? This section is of necessity somewhat speculative since economic theory provides no firm basis for linking real structural developments with the choice of a monetary unit. But if the greater transparency of wage rates across member states leads to pressures for greater harmonization of other elements of the employment contract, it will affect policies to reduce unemployment.

At a strategic level, there is view, supported by much evidence, that there are two possible successful models for the labor market - one deregulated and non-unionized where market forces rule (as exemplified by the USA), the other operating through consensus and collective decision-making by the social partners (as exemplified by the Nordic countries). According to this view, whatever the relative merits of these alternative models, one has the worst of both worlds by attempting to operate with some mixture of the two. This view was perhaps first popularized by *Calmfors and Driffill (1988)* with their picture of a hump-shaped relationship between unemployment and the degree of centralization of wage bargaining. It has many recent reaffirmations, for example *Bertola and Ichino (1995)*, who, writing about the Italian labor market, compare deregulation to crossing a river, where the objective is to get to the other side rather than getting stuck half way across.

The EU countries, with some noted exceptions, have tended more to the corporatist than to the free market approach. Equally, however, there has been an increasing acceptance of the case for increased flexibility and labor market deregulation in many countries, which has been encouraged by the relative success of free market economies within the EU (in particular, the UK) and the collapse of full employment policies in Sweden. Wage comparability across countries will in any event make more difficult the maintenance of centralized wage bargaining arrangements within countries. Given that there differences between member states on these questions, it might be better to let each choose its own route towards labor market reform.

6. Conclusions

i) Monetary union matters only because there exist nominal rigidities in the economy. In the absence of nominal rigidities there would be no real consequences of the exchange rate regime save those connected with the inflation tax and the optimal quantity of money. However, this does not mean that real rigidities (or other real features of the economy) are irrelevant to the effects of monetary union. This is because, in the presence of nominal inertia, the real consequences of a nominal shock depend on the interaction of real and nominal factors.

ii) However, the evidence is that nominal rigidities are important and are becoming more important in conditions of low and stable inflation. The belief that nominal inertia is unimportant in many European countries is based on evidence drawn from historical episodes characterized by rapid and volatile inflation, and this experience is not relevant to the present very different inflationary environment, as shown by the effects of the 1992 exchange rate realignments.

iii) Even in the presence of nominal rigidities, it is sometimes argued that there can be no presumption that nominal exchange rate flexibility is necessarily helpful: in the standard model, real shocks are neutralized by a flexible exchange rate, but monetary and financial shocks are more effectively neutralized by a fixed exchange rate, or single currency, system. However, in the paper it is argued that this assumes the flexible exchange rate regime must entail fixed money stock targets. With a more sophisticated monetary policy rule, the flexible exchange rate regime can neutralize both real and monetary shocks.

iv) There appears no evidence that the macroeconomic policy regime affects the output or unemployment costs of reducing inflation.

v) Should there be any tendency of the single currency to lead to greater wage comparability across countries, the outcome would be high and persistent unemployment in low productivity countries. Amongst the "core" EU countries, however, productivity differentials are not enormous, so this problem will be a matter for concern only if the EMU is widened to include countries with lower productivity such as Greece or Portugal.

vi) Even so, cross-country wage comparability may undermine centralized wage bargaining within countries. This has perhaps been one of the most valuable elements of the corporatist approach to economic management, and its loss may further tilt the balance towards relying more on market forces in wage determination.

Appendix A: A Model of Wage and Price Adjustment

Let the wage equation be

$$w_t = 0.25\sum_{i=1}^{4}(p_{t-i} + q_{t-i} - 0.1\,U_{t-i}) \tag{1}$$

and the price equation be

$$p_t = 0.25\sum_{i=1}^{4}(w_{t-i} - q_{t-i}) \tag{2}$$

where w is the log wage, p the log price, q log labor productivity and U the log of the unemployment rate. The wage equation assumes that there are annual wage contracts and the wage set in each contract depends on the economic situation in the previous quarter, so that the prevailing level of wages at any point in time is the average of wages set in the current and three previous quarters. The price equation assumes the current price embodies vintages of unit labor costs going back over four quarters. Labor productivity grows at an exogenous rate g

$$q_t = q_0 + g_t \tag{3}$$

The unemployment rate is determined by international competitiveness according to

$$U_t = -e\left(0.25\sum_{i=1}^{4} p_{t-i}^{*} - p_{t-i}\right) \tag{4}$$

where p* is the foreign price measured in terms of domestic currency and e is the elasticity of the unemployment rate with respect to the relative price (real exchange rate).

Initially we assume stable domestic and international prices, with p=p*=0.00, so that U is zero and w(t)=q(t). We consider a once and for all drop in p*, say from 0.00 to -0.10 at time t=1. We also assume for simplicity that e=1.

The effect of lower foreign prices is to cause demand to shift to foreign goods, and unemployment rises by 0.025 per quarter, reaching a peak of 0.10 after four quarters. The higher unemployment leads to a fall in wage settlements which in turn feeds through to a lower level of wages. Lower wages in turn feed through to lower prices, which also feed back into lower wages. At the same time lower prices improve competitiveness which causes unemployment to fall. But all this takes time. Even after two years (8 quarters), prices are at .9926, that is they have made only 7.5% of the required adjustment, wages have made only 12.5% of the required adjustment, and the unemployment rate has fallen from its peak of 0.10 to 0.0973.

Appendix B: Adjusting to Shocks With an Interest Rate Rule

This appendix attempts no more than to offer a very simple model of an open economy subject to shocks where the authorities conduct monetary policy according to a rule linking the interest rate to the behavior of the price level. The economy can thus be described by four equations:

i) Uncovered arbitrage

$$\dot{e} = r - r_w - q \tag{1}$$

where e is the exchange rate (Euros per dollar), r is the domestic interest rate, r_w the world interest rate and q the risk premium.

ii) The policy reaction function (interest rate rule)

$$r = r_w + b(p_c - p_c^*) \tag{2}$$

where p_c is (the log of) the actual, and p^*_c (the log of) the target, price level. The rule is here formulated in levels rather than of rates of change. The two are basically equivalent, up to a constant of integration, in that differentiation of (2) leads to the rate of change rule (assuming r_w constant) if there is no "base drift".

iii) Demand

$$y = z + g(e - p) \tag{3}$$

where y is output, z incorporates all exogenous components of demand, p is the output price index (GDP deflator) and g(e-p) the effects of the real exchange rate.

iv) Phillips curve

$$\dot{p} = a(y - y^*) \tag{4}$$

where y* is equilibrium output. Finally the consumer price index is defined as $p_c=(1-s)p+se$, where s is the share of imported goods in the consumer price index. The fundamental dynamic equations for this system are thus:

$$\dot{e} = b(se + (1-s)p - p_c^*) - q \tag{5}$$

and

$$\dot{p} = a(z + g(e - p) - y^*) \tag{6}$$

The phase-plane diagrams show the response of this system to a shock in real expenditure, z (figure G.1), and a shock to confidence, q (figure G.2). In the case of real shocks, there is an immediate jump in the exchange rate. If the inflation target were formulated in terms of the GDP deflator the exchange rate would jump immediately to the new equilibrium. But with a CPI target the exchange rate change itself affects the price level and the GDP deflator has to adjust to bring the CPI back on target. For example, a deflationary demand shock will lead to a rise in the interest rate and consequently a less than full immediate depreciation of the exchange rate, so that demand will not be immediately fully restored and the GDP deflator will decline until the CPI is back on target. (This is the counterpart to the problem of the demand for money depending on the CPI rather than the GDP deflator where there is a fixed money supply target.)

An increase in world interest rates, or an adverse confidence shock (a rise in q), also leads to a jump depreciation of the exchange rate. This raises domestic demand and hence the domestic price level, leading the government to raise interest rates and this in turn serves to sustain the new lower value of the exchange rate.

There is no need to examine demand for money shocks as these are automatically neutralized by the interest rate rule.

It therefore seems possible to conclude that in dealing with real, financial or world interest rate shocks, the interest rate rule dominates either a fixed exchange rate system or a fixed money stock target. The only type of problem where the interest rate target is not best is in regard to exchange market confidence shocks, which might in principle disappear altogether if there were a single currency.

Figure G.1: An Adverse Real Shock

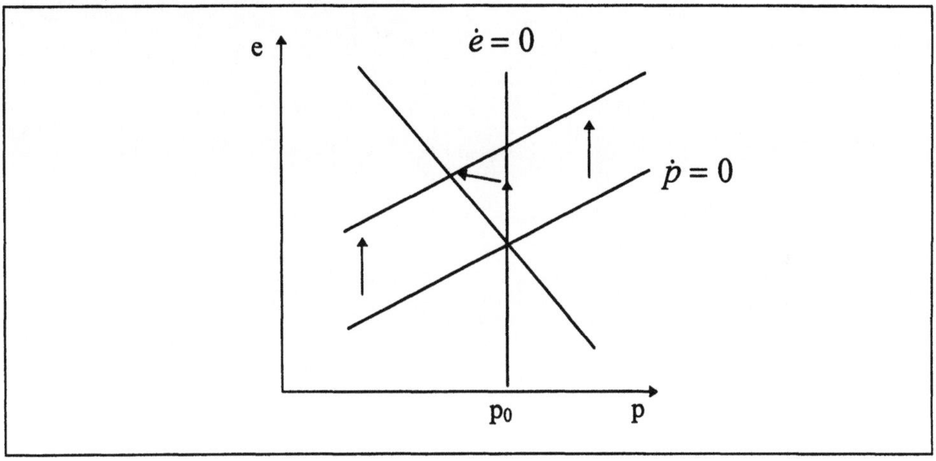

Figure G.2: A Loss of Confidence Shock

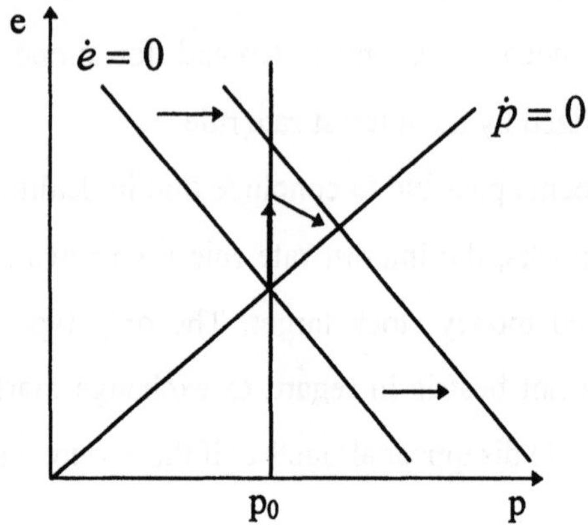

References

ALOGOSKOUFIS, G.; BEAN, C.R.; G. BERTOLA, G; COHEN, D.; DOLADO J.; SAINT-PAUL, G. (1995), Unemployment: Choices for Europe, Monitoring European Integration, 5, CEPR, London.

BARRO, R.; GORDON D. (1983), A Positive Theory of Monetary Policy in a Natural Rate Model, in: Journal of Political Economy, 91, 589-610.

BEAN, C.R. (1992), Europe 1992: A Macroeconomic Perspective, in: Journal of Economic Perspectives, 6, 31-52.

BERTOLA, G.; ICHINO, A. (1995), Crossing the River: A Comparative Perspective on Italian Employment Dynamics, in: Economic Policy, 21, 361-415.

BRANSON, W.; ROTEMBERG, J. (1980), International Adjustment with Wage Rigidity, in: European Economic Review, 13, 309-32.

CALMFORS, L.; DRIFFILL, J. (1988), Bargaining Structure, Corporatism and Macroeconomic Performance, in: Economic Policy, 6, 13-61.

FREEMAN, R.; GIBBONS, R. (1993), Getting Together and Breaking Apart: The Decline of Centralised Collective Bargaining, NBER Working Paper no. 4464.

GORDON, R. (1996), Macroeconomic Policy in the Presence of Structural Maladjustment, Paper presented to OECD Conference on "Interactions between Structural Reform, Macroeconomic Policies and Economic Performance", Paris, January, 1996.

GRUBB, D.; JACKMAN, R.; LAYARD, R. (1983), Wage Rigidity and Unemployment in OECD Countries, in: European Economic Review, 21, 11-39.

KEYNES, J.M. (1936), The General Theory of Employment, Interest and Money, Macmillan.

LAYARD, R.; NICKELL, S.; JACKMAN, R. (1991), Unemployment: Macroeconomic Performance and the Labor Market, Oxford University Press, Oxford.

OECD (1990), Employment Outlook, Paris.

PHELPS, E.S. (1978), Disinflation without Recession: Adaptive Guideposts and Monetary Policy, in: Weltwirtschaftliches Archiv, 114, 783-809.

TAYLOR, J. (1980), Aggregate Dynamics and Staggered Contracts, in: Journal of Political Economy, 88, 1-23.

Comments on: EU Labor Markets Inside and Outside the Monetary Union

Michael C. Burda

Just as the optimists begin to wrest control of the agenda, Richard Jackman has provided us with a number of new arguments for skepticism towards European Monetary Union. As usual, he has shown his ability to wear several hats. Wearing his British hat, he argues that EMU can indeed cripple a government's ability to deal with idiosyncratic macroeconomic shocks. Doffing his LSE hat, he justified this argument by showing that labor markets -- specifically the interaction of real and nominal rigidities in price and wage determination -- are central in understanding what is going on. Nor did Jackman leave his new-Keynesian hat in London: he reminds us that the great irony of the EMU debate is that it puts the burden on the monetarists such as Alan Walters, Patrick Minford, and Manfred Neumann as well as less conventional "real business cycle" advocates to show us why, after all, the choice of monetary unit really *does* matter. If it doesn't, as they have argued all along, then we are left wondering what the big fuss about a monetary union really is. If on the other hand, if nominal rigidities -- appropriately interacted with real rigidities -- are important, then a monetary union takes away a potential weapon for stimulating a sagging economy via competitive devaluations.

The discussion is thus intimately related to the nature of nominal and real rigidities. Two decades ago, Robert Gordon, Bill Branson, Julio Rotemberg and Jeffrey Sachs were arguing *uni sono* that Europe was macroeconomically different from the US. They claimed, with good reason, that nominal wages and prices were not rigid in European economies so attempts at demand expansion would simply result in higher inflation; unemployment was a real wage problem. This in itself is good reason to believe that EMU is neutral. The interesting evidence supplied by Jackman in the present paper, however, seems to suggest that the Branson-

Rotemberg-Gordon-Sachs regime has been replaced in Europe by one with rigid nominal prices. Jackman has made a point that has not gone unnoticed by many observers: despite massive nominal devaluations on the order of 30-40% in the UK, Italy, and Spain, inflation remains stable, increasing only moderately in Italy and falling in other countries. While one could argue that these countries were in severe deflationary modes, this argument seems strained. Reality seems far removed from the late seventies and early eighties, when devaluations quickly were translated into domestic price increases.

To understand how this might be is possible, consider the following standard aggregate supply-aggregate demand framework in inflation-output space presented below. The long run capacity "speed limit" value of output is given by trend output $\bar{Y}$, and the long-run aggregate supply schedule is vertical, expressing the long-run neutrality of demand as a working hypothesis. The downward sloping demand curve -- which can be thought of a transformation of the textbook curve in (p,Y) space -- expresses the depressing effect of higher inflation on aggregate demand at given policy parameters, including the nominal exchange rate or growth rate of nominal money. The supply curve expresses a positive relation between inflation and goods supplied by firms and their employees. It is upward-sloping either because firms will supply more output only if prices rise faster given wages or their expectation of wages, or workers will supply more labor only if wages rise relative to their price expectations or prices themselves, or both . The AS curve is conditioned on the "core inflation rate" which is associated with inertial price and wage setting in the economy or expectations of future wage and price inflation, or some combination of the two.

The Gordon/Branson/Rotemberg/Sachs hypothesis is that European macroeconomies are more "neoclassical" than "Keynesian" due to wage and price flexibility, implying that they spend most of their time at the "equilibrium" or natural rate of output. This can hold for two reasons. First the AS curve might be very steep. This corresponds to the hypothesis that unemployment has a very swift impact on nominal wages and prices. A second possibility is rapidly (and correctly) adjusting expectations. Recall that deviations of output from its capacity or trend level are only possible when the inflation rate which conditions the supply curve differs from the actual inflation rate. If expectations dominate core inflation, the AS curve will shift to reflect the monetary policy and exchange rate regime and not simply the past (adaptive weighted averages). Therefore the issue is the slope of the AS versus speed at which AS shifts.

Both panels below show two different outcomes for the same parallel outward shift in aggregate demand. In the first panel the conditioning inflation rate rises rapidly with the demand expansion (note that rational expectations is not necessary for this argument). In the second inflation rises due to tension in labor markets, while core inflation remains unchanged. Note that without additional information both explanations are plausible, and unless more information is brought to bear, observationally equivalent.

Figure G*.1: Standard Aggregate Supply-Aggregate Demand Framework

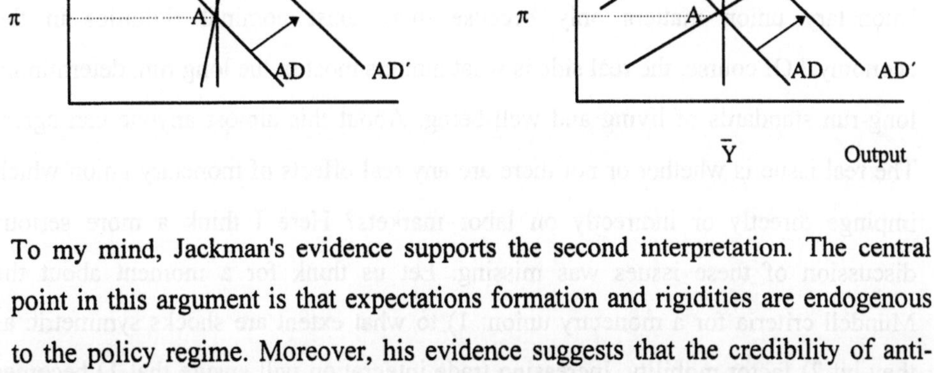

To my mind, Jackman's evidence supports the second interpretation. The central point in this argument is that expectations formation and rigidities are endogenous to the policy regime. Moreover, his evidence suggests that the credibility of anti-inflation policies has less to do with government statements regarding fixed versus flexible exchange rates than with public perceptions of inflation-fighting attitudes. In the history of the ERM and EMS, we have seen very credible anti-inflation fighters which have stayed in while others have dropped out. It is certainly instructive that, once out, the outsiders let their monetary reins loose, hardly the same behavior observed in France, Belgium or Denmark. The Robert Gordon fact -- to my mind -- is proof that ERM membership in itself is neither necessary nor sufficient for establishing credibility.

Despite agreeing with Jackman, I doubt that this tradeoff is either exploitable or should be regretted if left unexploited and forsaken. My argument is similar in spirit to one made by Fischer and Summers, who show in a Barro-Gordon framework that measures which render inflation less costly actually *worsen* inflation outcomes. By reducing the cost of inflation, the government increases its own net temptation to do wrong (inflate by surprise). In the present case, the logic applies in reverse: by increasing the cost of inflation by adopting painful sanctions and exposure to political embarrassment, governments have revealed their type over the past decade. Yet, one should beware of the Lucas critique: the more the policy option is employed, the less likely it is to be successful. In the limit, European Monetary Union would rule out devaluations and inflationary policy, and workers would adjust their behavior accordingly. The rather poor fit of Jackman's regression lends support to the instability of the inflation-output tradeoff, even now.

Turning to the labor market, I think that it is a mistake for to claim that "monetary union matters only because there exist nominal rigidities in the economy." Of course, the real side is what matters most in the long run, determining long-run standards of living and well-being. About this almost anyone can agree. The real issue is whether or not there are any real effects of monetary union which impinge directly or indirectly on labor markets? Here I think a more serious discussion of these issues was missing. Let us think for a moment about the Mundell criteria for a monetary union: 1) to what extent are shocks symmetric as they hit 2) factor mobility. Increasing trade integration will ensure that 1) becomes increasingly important on the demand side. Factor mobility will also be important. Labor mobility is low in Europe and will remain so for some time. Intra-European mobility is remarkably low and between countries it is much smaller. In my view, capital mobility may be much more important in its effects on labor markets, exerting an important disciplining pressure on labor markets, as long as capital is complementary to labor in the production process.

The argument goes as follows. In the absence of currency risk, firms will scale down operations in high wage, high regulatory-regime countries and move to cheaper, less-regulated ones. The best recent evidence of this is continued Japanese FDI activity in Britain, as well as the widely publicized losses of German jobs to Central European production sites. Within EMU, this means that capital will move from countries with high labor costs like Germany Denmark and Belgium to Holland and France. Restructuring, which has been postponed due to the option value of waiting will be undertaken. Short term, wages will rise in lower wage countries and unemployment will rise the high wage, high regulation countries.

All is not lost however, reacting to or even anticipating this, Cournot competition among countries on the dimension of regulation regimes should emerge. Some evidence on this is available from the US, where right to work spread rapidly from the South into most other states in some form or another. There is really a danger of over-*de*regulation which might remove the social protection so highly valued by Europeans. Of course it is in this context which a social charter should probably be assessed.

A couple of final remarks will conclude my comments. First, the importance of radical supply-side deregulation cannot be ignored. One might call it Maggie's last laugh. As much as it pains me to say so, recent evidence from Britain indicates that Patrick Minford was probably right: the potential for an inflation-free expansion of demand was greater than one thought in early 1990s, made possible by supply-side reforms undertaken in Britain during the 1980s. One can only hope that, should a supply side reform occur some day on the continent, there will be some demand around to put the capacity to good use. My last remark is to compliment the author for his particularly clear refinement of the sharp dichotomous Mundell-Fleming results to account for a third policy alternative which has become increasingly popular over time: an interest rate rule pegging the price level, which can outperform either of the traditional extremes of a fixed money supply or a fixed nominal exchange rate.

H. Political Economy of EMU and Stabilization Policy

Paul J.J. Welfens and André Jungmittag

1. Introduction

The Maastricht way to European Monetary Union is another attempt by the Community to achieve full monetary integration. An earlier approach was the Werner plan as envisaged in 1970 where within a decade the exchange rate would be irreversibly fixed and capital controls be abolished, while an EC central bank system would pursue monetary policy; the fiscal policies would be decided at the EC level by an authority that would be responsible to the European Parliament. Facing two oil price shocks in the 1970s the EC countries gave up their plans to proceed with monetary union for some time. The Maastricht approach to EMU is different and suggests that there will be a common monetary policy, while fiscal policies will remain at the national level. It is constrained by the fiscal convergence criteria.

European Monetary Union will be a complex and a fragile transition process which raises many issues (e.g. *Kenen, 1995; Welfens, 1996*). It could bring major benefits for the EU and the rest of the world under certain conditions. The EU may expect five benefits from monetary union:

- savings on transaction costs;
- lower inflation rates as compared to the average inflation rates of the period from 1957-95 thus creating positive wealth effects;
- lower long term real interest rates that might, however, require specific steps beyond simple monetary integration;

- higher investment and growth that would partly reflect a higher marginal product of capital in the monetary union;
- a real exchange effect vis-à-vis the US and Japan which is uncertain to predict.

There are also risks related to credibility problems of the new ECB, the mechanisms in achieving a consistent policy mix of monetary and fiscal policy in the Euro area and problems in achieving improved market clearing dynamics in the new regime, which eliminates parity changes within EMU. European monetary union, will bring a new monetary regime for Western Europe. Such a historical transition should be carefully planned, where appropriate national and supranational policy reforms should be taken into consideration.

For EMU to start a qualified majority decision in the EU will be necessary to determine which countries should form the starting group in 1999 or later. The success of EMU will be judged in terms of its durability, its inflation and interest rate record and the general welfare gains that can be achieved. Interestingly, moving towards EMU and the Euro raises some new core issues in the monetarist debate, e.g. the neutrality of money or the relative merits of fiscal and monetary policy. The analysis is organized as follows. In Section 2 theoretical aspects and some empirical issues are highlighted. In Section 3 the focus is on the political economy of monetary union and stabilization policies. The final Section offers some conclusions.

2. Theoretical Aspects of Economic and Monetary Union

Main theoretical aspects with respect to EMU concern (figure H.1):

- the link between the nominal volatility of exchange rates (and money supply growth) and investment growth and employment;

- the real exchange rate effects of EMU and the induced changes of foreign direct investment inflows into the EU;
- the welfare effects of EMU and the associated income and wealth effects;
- the problem of fiscal policy coordination in the absence of political union and the consequences for the efficiency of stabilization policy;
- the appropriate fiscal and monetary policy mix in the EMU area and the overall effectiveness of a stabilization policy;
- the need for national and supranational policy reforms as a means of improving market-clearing mechanisms.

Figure H.1: Strategic Issues of the Creation of EMU

Nominal Volatility	Investment and Growth
Real Exchange Rate Effects	FDI Developments
Welfare Effects	Income and Wealth Effects
Fiscal Policy Coordination	Efficiency of Stabilization Policy
Monetary and Fiscal Policy Mix	Effectiveness of Stabilization Policy
National Policy Reforms	Improving Shock Absorption Capacity
Supranational Reforms	Encouraging Market-Clearing

While the first three topics are more theoretical in nature, the last four refer to the political economy of EU integration.

The switch to EMU raises several important issues, however, only the strategic ones can be addressed here. One important issue is the exchange rate volatility, given that investment and growth are known to be influenced by uncertainty and volatility. EMU will reduce this exchange rate volatility and hence encourage investment. Since foreign direct investment became increasingly more important in OECD countries after 1985, an emphasis to the link between the real exchange rate (of the DM or the euro) in the context of EMU should be made. This already points to the welfare effects as higher (lower) net EU FDI inflows will contribute to higher (lower) employment and income after 1999. Clearly, there are also critical policy issues which mainly concern the assignment of fiscal policy to the national and supranational layers and the coordination of fiscal policy in a new regime - including aspects of the stability pact. These issues naturally are subject to conflicts between governments, trade unions and employer federations.

2.1 Investment Growth and Nominal Volatility

The theoretical argument that uncertainty (volatility) affects investment and output can be found in the literature, e.g. *Mascaro and Meltzer (1983)* - as well as in the monetarist debate (survey: *Neumann, 1996*) arguing that the monetary policy variance which can be influenced by the central bank will have output effects. In an empirical analysis there is a problem with standard measures of exchange rate variability, e.g. the variance or the coefficient of variation. Due to theoretical reasons, one may expect that they are high in a period of exchange rate disequilibria. Hence if one tests for the impact of exchange rate variability on investment (or employment) a negative coefficient could indeed reflect the impact of currency overvaluation. This is relative to purchasing power parity, and such periods of overvaluation or undervaluation might indeed last for several years. Exchange rate movements can be influenced over extended periods by medium term stock market bubbles. as well as by financial market impulses whose impact on the exchange rate can counter purchasing power parity. Finally, a strong nominal devaluation as occurred in 1992/93 where bilateral exchange rates were changing by up to 30% will have a distinct and long-term impact. Strong nominal exchange rate changes are impossible to anticipate and thus lead to a situation where rational expectations are not very meaningful since disturbance terms are assumed to be distributed with white noise patterns. Secondly, such changes occur in a world of sticky prices and wages so that strong negative real effects are likely in EU partner countries that suffer from a strong real appreciation and induced stagnation. There will, of course, be negative repercussions for the depreciation countries from depressed output growth in the major EU trading partners with an appreciation.

It is clear that the monetary policy of a future European Central Bank should be less volatile than the average EU monetary policy prior to 1999 (the assumed starting date of the Euro) if one assumes that national monetary policy will react to national business cycles. As an ECB monetary policy for a larger starting group of EMU countries will focus on the EMU business cycle (or the EU business cycle) this policy should be less volatile - unless business cycles of EU countries prior to 1999 are perfectly synchronized. A future ECB monetary policy could in principle be less volatile than that of the Deutsche Bundesbank. It has adopted for various reasons a rather volatile monetary policy course in terms of M3-growth rates (official intermediate target) and M1-growth rates in the 1980s.

Monetary union in the EU will mean a transition towards a common monetary policy. In the large Euro area there will be improved long-term opportunities to adopt a smooth and stable monetary policy, since EU monetary demand is expected to be more stable than the demand functions for national money in the EU (*Lane et al., 1991*). In this section, empirical analysis of the impact of monetary variability on investment growth in EU countries shows a significant negative coefficient. A greater stability of monetary policy - requiring adequate monetary policy instruments and the absence of foreign exchange market shocks - in continental Europe should therefore stimulate investment and employment growth in the EMU area.

Empirical evidence on the impact of monetary and exchange rate variability - implying the non-neutrality of money - were obtained in the following analysis: Exchange rate variability affects investment growth as is shown by the following tables. Both the variability of the ECU exchange rate for ERM member countries and the variability of the dollar exchange rate negatively affect investment growth in several EU countries. Since EMU eliminates nominal variability within the EMU area, it is expected that the monetary union will increase investment and output growth. It is unclear whether the EU's external exchange variability will be reduced after the adoption of EMU: Reduced variability could be expected if EMU facilitates monetary cooperation between the US and Europe and if the monetary policy that is pursued will be less discretionary and unstable than in the EMS I period. It is an old monetarist belief that monetary policies that are less unstable will bring a development of output which is less volatile.

Data and Methodology

When examining the question of whether relationships exist between the investment and the variability of money supply growth, the ECU exchange rate variability and the U.S. dollar exchange rate variability, a number of different investment variables and other measures of variability can be constructed. By using nonoverlapping measures of variability in the empirical analysis, the yearly growth rates of real gross fixed capital formation in eight EU countries, were employed as investment data. A limitation of eight countries was necessary because the data for the capital market interest rates of the other EU countries was not available for the analyzed period of 1960 to 1992. Due to the construction of growth rates of real gross fixed capital formation the sample is then limited to the 32 year period from 1961 to 1992.

The series for the measures of variability were constructed on the basis of monthly data. Four measures were constructed. On the one hand, the twelve monthly values of each year were used to calculate the yearly standard deviations (SD1) and the yearly coefficients of variation (CV1). By means of calculating coefficients of variation, it was taken into account that large observed values often involve larger variations than small observed values. Due to the use of a relative measure of variation, better comparability within a series of one or more trends is achieved. The one year standard deviations and coefficients of variation are nonoverlapping measures of variability since every value of the variable is assigned a value of a measure of variability with a different amount of information. On the other hand, 24 monthly values of two years were used to calculate the two year standard deviations (SD2) and the two year coefficients of variation (CV2). These measures can be interpreted as a longer-term measures of variability. At the same time, they are also overlapping measures of variability because a part of the information which is assigned to the actually observed value could have already affected the observed value of the previous period. Furthermore, each of the four measures of variability were used with a lag period of one year to make allowances for possible adjustment processes. In detail, the measures of variability were constructed on the following three variables:

- the growth on a percentage base of the money supply M1 with respect to the same month of the previous year (international definition of M1 by the IMF),
- the ECU exchange rate (national currency/ECU) and
- the U.S. dollar exchange rate (national currency/U.S. dollar).

While the measures of variability for the growth of money supply show varying values in the entire sample period, the measures of variability for the exchange rates show variations of zero in the periods of fixed exchange rates. Furthermore, for the growth of money supply, the absolute values of the coefficients of variation were used because some countries showed a negative means rate of growth rates for limited periods of time. Thus, meaningful values for these measures of variability could not have been obtained.

Besides the measures of variability, two classical variables which can help explain investment spending were considered:

- the difference between the actual real interest rate and the real interest rate of the previous period and the real interest rate is approximated by the nominal interest rate minus the change on a percentage basis of the gross fixed capital formation price deflator,
- the difference between the real interest rate of the actual and the previous year multiplied by the gross fixed capital formation price deflator.

In the first step, simple correlation coefficients were calculated for the relationships between the growth rates and each measure of variability as well as for the relationships between the growth rates and the capital market variables. This facilitates the ability to judge the influence of the measures of variability on the growth rates of gross fixed capital formation. In the second step, the obtained statistical findings were compressed to a SURE model with one equation for each country under consideration. SURE models are appropriate in this context because they take the temporal correlations of the error terms for individual equations into account that result from the common influences affecting the endogenous variables. This model also includes some additional explanatory variables, namely the real gross fixed capital formation with a lag period of one year, the yearly change of the long-term real interest rate, and the growth rate on a percentage basis of the relative unit labor costs (the national unit labor costs to U.S. unit labor costs). Additionally, the effects of German unification were approximated by a dummy variable (DGU). As a further test, a second SURE model was used to explain the ration of gross fixed capital formation to gross domestic product. Now the ratio of gross fixed capital formation to GDP with a lag period of one year, the real interest rate and unit labor costs as well as relative unit labor costs and again the dummy variable DGU were employed as additional explanatory variables. In both cases the problem arose that quite high collinearities between the different measures of variability as well as between the measures of variability and the additional explanatory variables make the estimation of meaningful multivariate regression models more difficult.

Empirical Analysis

The simple correlation coefficients for the relationships between the growth rate of real gross fixed capital formation and the measures of variability of the growth rate of money supply are summarized in table H.1. It is obvious that the strength of the relationships for the individual countries under consideration is quite different. Only the one year coefficient of variation, with a lag of one year, is significantly smaller than zero for Belgium. Significant relationships exist for the actual coefficients of variation for West Germany and for those with a one and two-year lag period. However, there is no significant relationship between the growth rates of gross fixed capital formation and the measures of variability of the growth rate of money supply for France and the United Kingdom. On the other hand, the relationships for Italy and especially for the Netherlands are very unambiguous. Clearly, the fewer measures of variability indicate that relationships exist between the considered variables. This is the case for Denmark and Ireland. The one and two year coefficients of variation are relevant in this case.

As expected, there are significantly fewer relationships between the growth rates of real gross fixed capital formation and the measures of variability of the ECU exchange rate. This is due to the fact that these variables are not approximating the variability within the EMS very well because it is the aim of the EMS to ensure a relative high stability of exchange rates. The results are summarized in table H.2. It is not possible to present results for Belgium because the time series for the ECU exchange rate is not available for the whole sample period. Nevertheless, there are a number of significant results for France, Italy, the Netherlands and Denmark. The relationship for West Germany turned out to be weaker. In the case of the United Kingdom and Ireland, no significant relationships could be established.

Table H.1: Simple Correlation Coefficients for the Relationships between the Growth Rates of Real Gross Fixed Capital Formation and the Measures of Variability of the Growth Rates of Money Supply

Measure	Growth rate of real gross fixed capital formation							
of variability	Belgium	West Germany	France	Italy	Nether lands	Denmark	United Kingdom	Ireland
SD1	-0.0908	0.2814	-0.0107	-0.1034	-0.3212**	-0.0708	0.1536	-0.1210
SD1 (-1)	-0.1102	0.1665	-0.0567	-0.5724***	-0.2435*	0.0374	0.1730	-0.1525
CV1	0.0284	-0.3624**	0.2960	-0.2250	-0.5167***	-0.2756*	0.0956	-0.4042**
CV1 (-1)	-0.5847***	-0.3712**	0.0303	-0.4952***	-0.4606***	-0.1349	-0.0259	-0.2032
SD2	-0.1194	0.2055	0.0645	-0.2101	-0.3166**	-0.2051	0.2351	-0.2841*
SD2 (-1)	-0.1512	0.0504	-0.0722	-0.3359**	-0.2455*	-0.0862	0.1730	-0.1337
CV2	0.1474	-0.4447***	0.2055	-0.3676**	-0.5925***	-0.4338***	-0.0522	-0.3469**
CV2 (-1)	-0.1556	-0.2527*	0.0103	-0.1103	-0.4505***	-0.1196	0.0653	-0.0785

* for $\alpha = 0.1$ is $\rho < 0$
** for $\alpha = 0.05$ is $\rho < 0$
*** for $\alpha = 0.01$ is $\rho < 0$

Table H.2: Simple Correlation Coefficients for the Relationships between the Growth Rates of Real Gross Fixed Capital Formation and the Measures of Variability of the ECU Exchange Rates

Measure of variability	Growth rate of real gross fixed capital formation						
	West Germany	France	Italy	Nether lands	Denmark	United Kingdom	Ireland
SD1	-0.1231	-0.3666**	-0.2500*	-0.3620**	-0.0374	-0.1554	0.0791
SD1 (-1)	-0.2483*	-0.1440	-0.2199	-0.2076	-0.3693**	-0.1923	-0.1376
CV1	-0.1637	-0.3224**	-0.2130	-0.4161***	-0.0255	-0.1498	0.1316
CV1 (-1)	-0.2827*	-0.0896	-0.1729	-0.2292	-0.3643**	-0.1805	-0.0997
SD2	-0.1654	-0.2993**	-0.2966**	-0.2598*	-0.2703*	-0.2188	-0.0136
SD2 (-1)	-0.2387*	-0.2554*	-0.2978**	-0.2693*	-0.5350***	-0.2036	-0.0648
CV2	-0.2233	-0.2374*	-0.2162	-0.3060**	-0.2584*	-0.1949	0.0630
CV2 (-1)	-0.2603*	-0.1995	-0.2685*	-0.2795*	-0.5284***	-0.2150	0.0068

* for $\alpha = 0.1$ is $\rho < 0$
** for $\alpha = 0.05$ is $\rho < 0$
*** for $\alpha = 0.01$ is $\rho < 0$

For a lot of EU countries, stronger correlations exist between the growth rates of gross fixed capital formation and the variability of the U.S. dollar exchange rates. The individual results are given in table H.3. In the case of France, Italy, the Netherlands and Ireland almost all measures of variability are highly significant. For Belgium, five out of the eight measures of variability show significant relationships. The result of the evidence for West Germany and Denmark turned out to be obviously slighter. Surprisingly, in the case of the United Kingdom, almost no significance for the considered variables could be established. This result is astonishing because traditionally close economic relations between the USA and the United Kingdom existed.

Considering the relationships between the capital market variables and the growth rates of gross fixed capital formation significant relationships can be established in the case of West Germany, Italy, the Netherlands and the United Kingdom. In the case of Belgium there are almost none. In the case of France and Denmark there are no significant relationships. For Ireland, the correlation coefficients show unambiguously the wrong sign. If the relationships are significant, then the second capital market variable (ΔCR) dominates the real interest rate variable (ΔIR) in all cases. Also, it can be shown that the measures of variability often outperform the capital market variables at the level of simple correlations.

The obtained statistical findings provide a basis for the specification of a SURE model to explain the growth rates of real gross fixed capital formation in each country under consideration. The inclusion of additional explanatory variables in such a model, are of particular interest, in this context since additional explanatory variables can possibly overlap the influences of the measures of variability. This would be the case if the measured variabilities are only an expression and/or a result of the development of other economic variables. The results for this SURE model are summarized in table H.5. All multiple coefficients of determination show acceptable values for a model with growth rates as endogenous variables.

Table H.3: Simple Correlation Coefficients for the Relationships between the Growth Rates of Real Gross Fixed Capital Formation and the Measures of Variability of the U.S. Dollar Exchange Rates

Measure of variability	Growth rate of real gross fixed capital formation							
	Belgium	West Germany	France	Italy	Netherlands	Denmark	United Kingdom	Ireland
SD1	-0.3338**	-0.1 819	-0.4901***	-0.3216**	-0.3142**	-0.1236	-0.1822	-0.4887***
SD1 (-1)	-0.1840	-0.2776*	-0.3727**	-0.2743*	-0.3494**	0.0240	-0.1334	-0.4095***
CV1	-0.3460**	-0.0976	-0.5462***	-0.3744**	-0.3935**	-0.3174**	-0.2879*	-0.4338***
CV1 (-1)	-0.2505*	-0.2176	-0.4561***	-0.3528**	-0.4421***	-0.1573	-0.1937	-0.3431**
SD2	-0.3002**	-0.2824*	-0.5283***	-0.3049**	-0.3470**	-0.0309	-0.1235	-0.3419**
SD2 (-1)	-0.0801	-0.2934*	-0.4659***	-0.2325	-0.3626**	-0.1321	-0.0281	-0.4934***
CV2	-0.3690**	-0.2100	-0.6188***	-0.3697**	-0.4246***	-0.2060	-0.2338	-0.2679*
CV2 (-1)	-0.1432	-0.1923	-0.5987***	-0.3181**	-0.4145***	-0.2446*	-0.1221	-0.4767***

* for $\alpha = 0.1$ is $\rho < 0$
** for $\alpha = 0.05$ is $\rho < 0$
*** for $\alpha = 0.01$ is $\rho < 0$

Table H.4: Simple Correlation Coefficients for the Relationships between the Growth Rates of Real Gross Fixed Capital Formation and the Capital Market Variables

Variable	Growth rate of real gross fixed capital formation							
	Belgium	West Germany	France	Italy	Netherlands	Denmark	United Kingdom	Ireland
ΔIR	-0.2050	-0.3066**	-0.0491	-0.3385**	-0.2480*	0.1101	-0.3481**	0.4141
ΔCR	-0.2813*	-0.3497**	-0.2141	-0.3538**	-0.3349**	0.1308	-0.4968***	0.2875

* for $\alpha = 0.1$ is $\rho < 0$

** for $\alpha = 0.05$ is $\rho < 0$

*** for $\alpha = 0.01$ is $\rho < 0$

The DW statistics indicate in almost all cases the absence of first order autocorrelation. It can be seen that the change in long-term real interest rate is a relevant additional explanatory variable for West Germany (weakly significant), the Netherlands and the United Kingdom. Changes of relative unit labor costs significantly affect the growth rates of real gross fixed capital formation in France, Italy, Denmark, the United Kingdom and Ireland. Variability of money supply growth has negative effects on investment in Belgium, West Germany, Italy, the Netherlands and Ireland. The negative effect of the ECU exchange rate variability is limited to Denmark. However, variability of the U.S. dollar exchange rate affects the growth rates of investment in almost all countries under consideration. The only exceptions are Italy and, as expected, the United Kingdom based on the results of the simple correlations.

A second SURE model for the investment/GDP ratio was specified in order to gain additional insight into the effects of variability on investment spending. The results are summarized in table H.6. The displayed multiple coefficients of determination for the individual equations are adequate. The Durbin H statistics indicate the absence of first order autocorrelation for each equation. It can be seen that the long term real interest rates for almost all countries under consideration are highly significant. The only exception is Denmark. Unit labor costs or relative unit labor costs show effects on France, Italy, the Netherlands, Denmark, the United Kingdom and Ireland. In this model, the variability of money supply growth only affects the investment/GDP ratios of West Germany and the Netherlands. A negative influence of the ECU exchange rate variability could only be established for West Germany. The effects of the variability of the U.S. dollar exchange rates are again very strong. Only France and Ireland are not affected by a measure of this variability.

Table H.5: SURE Model for Explaining Growth Rates of Real Gross Fixed Capital Formation

Expl.	Growth rates of real gross fixed capital formation							
variables	Belgium	West Germany	France	Italy	Nether lands	Denmark	United Kingdom	Ireland
Constant	6.0401	7.2837	14.7980	21.4106	9.5314	21.4512	9.0652	13.7482
	(5.7876)*	(7.5045)	(9.1972)	(6.8431)	(7.6195)	(4.2026)	(2.6697)	(6.0794)
DGU		21.3979						
		(8.9312)						
IREAL(-1)			-0.0106	-0.0001		-0.1290	-0.1186	
			(-5.1378)	(-4.7713)		(-2.3543)	(-1.9421)	
Real interest rate								
ΔIR		-0.2759			-0.8901		-0.6488	
		(-1.5554)			(-3.0201)		(-2.7198)	
Relative unit labor costs								
ΔULCR	-0.3385		-0.9144	-0.5307		-1.4054	-0.9673	-0.9822
	(-1.3082)		(-4.5701)	(-2.3093)		(-2.9760)	(-2.7124)	(-2.2267)
Variability of money supply								
SD1(-1)				-1.5678				
				(-6.2487)				
CV1								-7.7831
								(-1.7904)
CV1(-1)	-0.8781							
	(-5.0706)							
CV2		-8.8030			-11.0799			
		(-5.2612)			(-4.9784)			

Table H.5 (continued)

Expl. variables	Growth rates of real gross fixed capital formation							
	Belgium	West Germany	France	Italy	Nether lands	Denmark	United Kingdom	Ireland
Variability of ECU exchange rates								
SD2(-1)						-39.7469		
						(-2.8639)		
Variability of U.S. dollar exchange rates								
SD1	-1.2828							
	(-2.6326)							
CV1						-55.0819		
						(-1.2041)		
SD2(-1)		-12.8030						-185.1733
		(-2.8418)						(-4.3640)
CV2			-34.6128		-38.6965			
			(-3.0529)		(-2.5788)			
$R^2_{adj.}$	0.4540	0.7518	0.5643	0.5756	0.4667	0.5088	0.2974	0.4432
DW	1.4851	1.5107	1.1010	1.9179	1.7981	1.6106	1.5083	1.7707

* empirical t-values in parentheses

Table H.6: SURE Model for Explaining Gross Fixed Capital Formation/Gross Domestic Product (I/Y)

Expl.	Gross fixed capital formation/GDP (I/Y)							
variables	Belgium	West Germany	France	Italy	Nether lands	Denmark	United Kingdom	Ireland
Constant	0.0864	0.0685	0.1277	0.2317	0.1575	0.3697	0.2026	0.1838
	(6.1026)*	(8.0272)	(6.4407)	(7.1970)	(5.0726)	(4.5787)	(6.7594)	(2.9472)
DGU		0.0218						
		(6.2676)						
I/Y(-1)	0.6283	0.7698	0.8181	0.8928	0.6029	0.8500	0.6056	1.1328
	(9.8838)	(22.1222)	(15.3343)	(10.3705)	(8.1805)	(11.1314)	(7.6196)	(9.1903)
Real interest rate								
IR	-0.0013	-0.0027	-0.0006	-0.0011	-0.0018		-0.0013	-0.0012
	(-3.7171)	(-9.7957)	(-2.3852)	(-4.4504)	(-3.3608)		(-5.1362)	(-2.2869)
Unit labor costs								
ULC							-0.0021	-0.0040
							(-4.2394)	(-2.4763)
ULC(-1)					-0.0009			
					(-2.0701)			
ULCR			-0.0989	-0.2596		-0.3693		
			(-6.2208)	(-5.4043)		(-4.1901)		

Table H.6 (continued)

Expl. variables	Gross fixed capital formation/GDP (I/Y)							
	Belgium	West Germany	France	Italy	Nether lands	Denmark	United Kingdom	Ireland
Variability of money supply								
SD2					-0.0022			
					(-3.2511)			
SD2(-1)								
CV2		-0.0060						
		(-2.3948)						
Variability of ECU exchange rates								
CV2(-1)		-0.1643						
		(-3.5207)						
Variability of U.S. dollar exchange rates								
SD1(-1)				-0.0001				
				(-3.4317)				
CV1						-0.1396		
						(-1.6347)		
CV1(-1)		-0.1142			-0.2254			
		(-3.5554)			(-3.7426)			
SD2	-0.0032						-0.1629	
	(-4.5608)						(-3.4295)	
$R^2_{adj.}$	0.9242	0.9732	0.9375	0.8768	0.9263	0.8835	0.7578	0.8803
Durbin-H	-0.7560	1.2898	1.5355	0.2138	0.6559	1.7605	1.3587	-1.5057

* empirical t-values in parentheses

Summarizing the empirical analysis, the results provide a lot of indications that variability of money supply growth and exchange rates have a role in the determination of investment spending. This cannot be ignored. They suggest that the ability to explain and predict investment spending can be improved through the explicit inclusion of measures of variability. However, this analysis is based on highly aggregated investment data and further research with less highly aggregated data is necessary to affirm these findings.

2.2 Foreign Direct Investment Aspects

In Germany, many proponents of monetary union expect that switching from the EMS to EMU will eliminate the real appreciation pressure. This temporarily impaired export growth and job creation in the FRG in the 1980s and early 1990s. This is only one aspect of the problem of upward pressure on the DM. It was particularly high in periods of doubts in the viability of the EMS and the EMU project, respectively. Hence, the expectation that failure to achieve EMU would cause a massive DM appreciation (a similar reasoning holds true for the Dutch florin and the Austrian schilling which were closely linked to the DM for more than a decade).

Since the 1980s Germany has been suffering from a massive foreign direct investment outflow and from stagnating or modest inflow. As shown by *Froot and Stein (1990)* - in a study focusing on the US - changes in the real exchange rate affect (de-trended) foreign direct investment flows. In imperfect capital markets a real appreciation of an investor's currency will facilitate multinational companies investment abroad: the investor's equity capital, evaluated in the depreciating currency of the host country has increased which thus facilitates borrowing in order to take over a company abroad; it becomes easier to win a merger and acquisition battle. A continuing appreciation of the DM would reinforce the outflow of foreign direct investment which reached a record level of DM 58 billion in 1995. In this perspective, an appreciation of the DM would facilitate German firms' attempts to take over firms abroad in the long-run. From this new perspective EMU could prevent political tensions that are related to the fears of German dominance - i.e. strongly rising German FDI stimulated by DM appreciations - that otherwise could occur in the EU in the long-run. A similar reasons holds, of course, with respect to the otherwise continued dominance of the Bundesbank which is perceived to be conducting monetary policy with EU spillover effects, while not being subject to political accountability at the EU level.

Depending on the Eurodollar exchange rate the EU stands to gain or to lose in transatlantic foreign direct investment inflows. If there would be a real depreciation of the Euro (the ECU) the US foreign direct investment going to the EU would increase; a real appreciation of the Euro will stimulate EU foreign direct investment towards the US and the wider dollar area. In a transatlantic context rising foreign direct flows could have positive regional and global welfare impacts because foreign investment flows are the main avenue of international technology transfer. Given the fact that in the technologically advanced OECD area both the host country and the multinational companies benefit from the inflow of capital. Their foreign subsidiaries can adopt new technologies in the host countries and transmit it to the parent company. There is a positive sum game to be expected if foreign direct investment flows increase. This holds especially true because a considerable amount of transatlantic foreign investment is taking place in an oligopolistic market setting so that investment flows in one direction trigger investment flows of rivals going into the opposite direction. If EMU facilitates Europe's return to high investment and full employment monetary union would generate external benefits because there will be induced trade and foreign investment creation.

2.3 Transaction Costs, Network Aspects and Interest Rate Effects

Monetary union will reduce transaction costs in all markets which will create direct economic benefits as well as indirect potential benefits that stem from increased competition in markets with improved price transparency. The direct economic benefits were estimated by the EC Commission to reach up to 0.5% of Community GDP. For most voters saving transaction costs will be hardly visible - except in the context of tourism in EMU countries. While for most firms doing international business there could be considerable savings since EU banking transactions will become cheaper and currency exchange costs would be avoided. Multinational firms can be expected to favor monetary union. European oriented and global banks from EU countries also are likely to favor EMU because a functional EMU will reinforce the options to exploit economies of scale or scope and "thick market externalities" in larger financial markets.

Monetary union will reduce transaction costs in all financial markets of the EMU area: Interest rates paid by borrowers will be reduced and the net rate accruing to lenders will increase. In the situation prior to EMU the gross rate paid by borrowers is r'_0, while lenders receive a net rate (r'_0 minus transaction costs) of r_0 (figure H.2). Ideally, switching to monetary union eliminates transaction costs so that the new interest rate r_1 and a higher loan volume Q_1 are realized. Figure H.2 shows the gross credit demand curve (GCD) and the net credit demand curve (NCD) The latter excludes transaction costs. Monetary union means that the wedge between the two curves is reduced so that the interest rate will fall which in turn should stimulate investment and support budget consolidation in EMU countries.

The real interest rate will be further reduced if foreign demand for EMU denominated bonds would increase; „foreign" here means investors from non-EMU countries. Such an increase in foreign demand can be expected, however, only if the ECB's future monetary policy is credible and effectively oriented towards price stability because non-EU central banks and private economic agents in financial markets would otherwise substitute Euro denominated assets for other currencies.

Controlling a larger (EMU) monetary aggregate will be easier in the long term than controlling national monetary aggregates in the EMS European Union. This advantage in monetary policy control under monetary union could be offset initially by the practical problems of monetary policy effectiveness. They are due to imperfections of instruments and a lack of knowledge about behavioral changes in new EMU financial markets. Therefore, the issue of choosing a proper mix of policy instruments is crucial. The choice of policy instruments applied will certainly be shaped by the initial group of EMU countries. This should be an advantage for Germany and France with their respective financial centers - in contrast to London and the UK.

Figure H.2: Monetary Union and Interest Rate

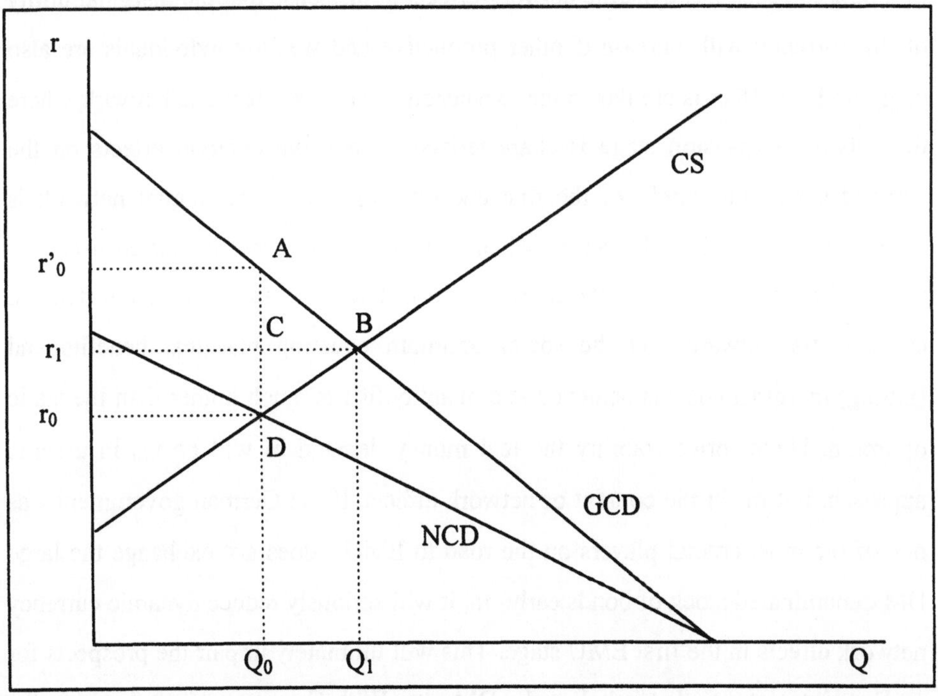

The benefits of a new currency, which is used as a means of transaction, is a store of value and a unit of account depends on the strength of the financial system. The central bank's ability to achieve a low inflation rate and the liquidity of assets is denominated in the currency. The decision of governments in the EMU area to exchange the stock of bonds denominated in national currency into new Euro bonds certainly will affect the liquidity of Euro markets. If the German government - as it has stated so far and in contrast to France - is not exchanging the stock of DM denominated bonds into Euro early, this would certainly impair the liquidity of the Euro bond markets and foster London's position as a leading financial center of DM bonds trade.

From an individual investor's perspective the usefulness of a new currency in goods and assets markets depends heavily on others also using the same currency. A thin Euro bond market implies m^d_0, while a broader bond market with high turnover figures implies an Euro money demand m^d_1 (figure H.3). The introduction of a new currency has dynamic network effects in the sense that the marginal utility of the currency will increase if other productive and wealthy individuals are also using it. This effect is similar to the expansion stage of a telephone network where the network expansion stage is characterized by positive external effects on the demand side. The benefit of the first and only user of a new digital network is obviously quite limited. However, when more and more other interested users are switched onto the network, the marginal benefit will increase. Thus, the demand curve shifts outward and the social optimum equating marginal benefits and (falling) marginal costs is achieved at a quantity that is much higher than the static optimum. Under price stability the real money demand m will be m_0 in a static approach, but m_1 in the context of network effects. If the German government - as one of the most crucial players on the road to EMU - does not exchange the large DM denominated stock of bonds early-on, it will seriously reduce dynamic currency network effects in the first EMU stage. This will ultimately impair the prospects for an Euro interest rate that is below the DM rate. With Germany not exchanging the stock of its bonds for Euro early-on, there will be a welfare loss equivalent to the triangle ACD. The higher the stock of real balances the higher will be the demand for real capital K, following the portfolio theory. A higher demand for K implies a reduced marginal product of capital and hence a lower real interest rate as well. In a non-inflationary Euro area, the real rate r will fall to r_1 and real balances will increase to m'_1. Since with an exogenous nominal money supply M real balances can only increase if the price level P of the Euro area falls. Either the prices of tradable and nontradables would have to fall or the Euro exchange rate has to appreciate.

Figure H.3: Euro Currency Demand Without and With Network Effects

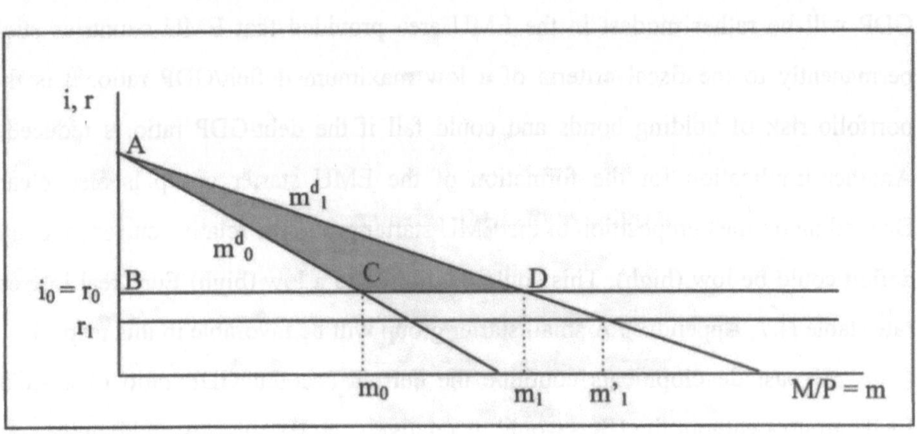

Real interest rate perspectives

In the highly integrated OECD world the real interest rate is not determined simply on the national market. Rather, savings and investment in the G-3 countries strongly influence real interest rates. In a new approach, *Orr, Edey and Kennedy (1995)* explained the low frequency (i.e. long term) real interest rate in each country as being a function of the slower moving fundamentals related to savings and investment as well as indicators of any risk premium required by private investors:[1]

$$r_{it} = \alpha_1 z_{it} + \alpha_2 d_{it} + \alpha_3 \beta_{it} + \alpha_4 CA_{it} + \alpha_5(\pi-\pi^e)_{it}$$

where r is the low frequency long-term real interest rate in country i,

z is the rate of return on capital,

d is the government deficit relative to GDP

ß is a measure of the domestic portfolio risk of holding bonds

CA is the current account balance relative to GDP (using a 5 year moving average)

π is a long term average of past inflation

π^e is the Hodrick-Prescott measure of expected future inflation.

Assuming that EMU is neutral with respect to the rate of return on capital one may address the other influences on the interest rate: Government deficits relative to GDP will be rather modest in the EMU area provided that EMU countries stick permanently to the fiscal criteria of a low maximum deficit/GDP ratio. ß is the portfolio risk of holding bonds and could fall if the debt/GDP ratio is reduced.[2] Another implication for the formation of the EMU starter group is also clear: Depending on the composition of the EMU starter group the relative current account deficit could be low (high), This could contribute to a low (high) Euro real interest rate (table H.7, Appendix). A small starter group will be favorable in this respect.

If past developments continue the current account GDP ratio of a small EMU group - without the UK - would be relatively modest. This would help to keep real interest rates low. Similarly, an ECB monetary policy that provides small inflation errors will contribute to low real interest rates.

3. Political Economy of Monetary Unification

Since EMU reduces uncertainty, with both money demand and money supply being more stable than in the EMS-I regime, and thus favoring investment dynamics, there is a clear reason why major firms and exporters in almost all countries favor the monetary union. If transfers have to be increased in the EMU area, mobile multinational companies are unlikely to contribute to its financing. Such firms increasingly escape the tax man at the national level. A wide starter group would reduce the risk of competitive devaluations within the EU; a risk which still would persists as long as Italy, Spain and the UK are among the outsiders. Therefore, a part of the industry in the EU is favoring a larger starter group. The arguments in favor of a small starter group are its advantage in terms of credibility and hence its favorable impact on interest rates. This is, of course, also crucial to the business community.

Assuming that there will be at the most seven countries which will be starting candidates for EMU, the question arises whether a small group of countries is a good basis for a functional EMU. Applying the *Buchanan and Tullock (1962)* approach to decision-making in EMU within the clubs and standard analysis from game theory, one may argue that efficient decision-making can be expected if the number of club members is small, if the interdependency is high among them (i.e., free rider strategies are a minor problem), and if the problems to be resolved represent repeated games; i.e. similar situations have to be tackled over several periods. The latter aspect suggests that the initial group of countries should enjoy several years where no further EMU members will be considered. This clearly creates a special problem because the UK and Denmark could decide on their own about the date of their joining EMU, provided that the convergence criteria are met. Moreover, according to the Treaty, every two years outsiders are to be reviewed with respect to convergence and inclusion into EMU. The main problem here clearly is the UK since London is a leading global financial center. Therefore, it would be quite helpful for the liquidity of the Euro currency if the sophisticated network of the UK's financial industry could be soon fully-integrated into the EMU financial market system.

Graduation for EU Outsiders

EU outsiders which cannot join EMU in the first round face two mayor disadvantages. It is unclear on what future date they could join the EU. Moreover, being left behind in a slim EMS (II) will bring about higher nominal and real interest rates unless there are strictly fixed parities with the Euro. For achieving long-term convergence, parities with wide margins could be useful (*Bender, 1994*). However, such wide margins could cause a high variability of the exchange rates moving within the band width, raise interest rates and hence impair growth and the consolidation of the government budget.

3.1 Stabilization Issues

With the creation of a single market, new economic structures are developing in Western Europe. EU innovation dynamics, exchange rate shocks, national fiscal and monetary policy impulses as well as external shocks and shifts influence economic development in the EU. Given the enormous increase in capital mobility in the EU after 1990, national monetary policy became less powerful in terms of stabilization, except in the case of Germany's monetary policy, which induces other central banks to shadow its policy for the sake of maintaining the exchange rate. This avoids a real appreciation and thus a loss of competitiveness vis-à-vis Germany and achieves higher credibility that leads to lower real interest rates and a reduced sacrifice ratio in anti-inflation policies.

Behind the political pressure for EMU at the Maastricht Conference, there was concern from Germany's partners about its economic dominance after unification which reinforced its role as the No. 1 export destination for almost all EU partner countries (see table H.8, Appendix). In a system of fixed exchange rates Germany's strict monetary policy enforced some EU monetary dominance through the pro-competitive impact of low inflation policies and the additional competitive advantage from relatively low nominal and real interest rates which allowed

German firms to finance modernization investment at favorable conditions; Germany will lose this latter advantage with the switch to EMU.

There was particular concern about the Deutsche Bundesbank's dominance in Western Europe. On the one hand it is not welcome for political reasons. A supranational monetary policy could restore some political influence to each EU country in matters of monetary strategies and policy stance (even with EMU this is not quite true given the fact that national central banks and the ECB are politically independent). On the other hand, German dominance is an economic problem if business cycles across EU countries are not harmonized, as the Bundesbank policy stance is fully-guided by its domestic policy priority. Indeed, if e.g. France and the Benelux countries were facing a recession, while Germany was facing a boom with inflationary pressures, the Bundesbank would have to adopt a restrictive monetary policy. This would be in order to achieve its primary goal as stipulated by German law, namely price stability. Such a German monetary policy would not take into account Germany's own economic interest in stabilizing its major partners' economic growth for the sake of Germany's own long term economic growth (this includes helping to avoid renewed protectionism). The only way to remedy this problem - i.e. take into account policy repercussion effects from abroad - would be to modify the Deutsche Bundesbank Act and add to the price stability goal economic growth as a second goal. Such a reform, however, would be bound to compromise the EU wide appreciated credibility of the Deutsche Bundesbank in terms of anti-inflationary policy. Moreover, this would amount to a watering-down of the responsibility of trade unions, employer organizations and the government in the pursuit of strategies in line with international competitiveness and economic growth.

The only way to solve the repercussion problem as mentioned before, namely to internalize negative external effects of monetary policy of a big country is to adopt some form of common EU monetary policy which takes into account a larger relevant policy area. With the formation of the ECB the problem of how monetary policy should deal with a combination of a recession in France and a boom in Germany is not really solved. However, there are two advantages provided by an ECB that is modeled on the Deutsche Bundesbank, which clearly is the case: (1) The whole EU will benefit from the switch from a D-Mark to an E-Mark because the Euro will reduce the EU inflation rate below the previous EU average of national inflation rates. (2) Assuming that monetary policy impulses are contributing to economic cycles - especially if the national banks are subject to political interference in democracies - the combination of a recession in France (country I) and a boom in Germany (country II) is becoming less likely in the presence of a joint monetary policy. (3) Since there are no longer national central banks subject to government interference for the sake of national reelection, the ECB monetary policy could be less discretionary than EU monetary policies before - this will contribute to a smoothening of the business cycle. The argument would be not valid if the Bundesbank's monetary policy had never been subject to political pressure and if the Bundesbank had in fact fully dominated monetary policy of EU partner countries.

With a common EMU wide monetary policy there is, however, a new risk in the field of fiscal policies if the combination of recession and boom in France/Germany is emerging: France is more likely to request from Germany that it should pursue an expansionary fiscal policy. To be sure the situation could also occur in a reversed assignment, namely with Germany pressing for expansionary French fiscal policy (also, after German unification Germany has surprisingly become the third largest recipient of EU structural funds in the 1990s). Expansionary fiscal policy typically will cause sustained undesirable increases of the government expenditure/GDP ratio and a higher debt/GDP ratio. The German government is no longer facing a politically risky conflict with the Deutsche Bundesbank could be more likely to accommodate the partner country's pressure. While this gives a worse government to Germany, the Maastricht Treaty gives a blueprint for a quasi-Bundesbank at the EU level without incentives for cooperation between the (European) Central Bank and government: *Kösters (1995)* convincingly argues that the Bundesbank's successful anti-inflation record was partly driven by the Bundesbank's desire to reinforce its position by gaining a reputation in the public - gaining public support for potential conflicts with the German government and parliament, respectively. One could have changed the Bundesbank Act with a simple majority but this option has never seriously been considered because of the strong policy record of the Bundesbank. Comparing the ECB's political position with that of the Bundesbank in this respect, the ECB is too strong: Only if a qualified majority vote of the European Parliament (or a similar mechanism) triggered deliberations of the European Council on the ECB's statute, there would be an endogenous mechanism for encouraging the ECB strongly to build up an anti-inflationary reputation. This holds all the more true because the ECB's board member remuneration is - in comparison to New Zealand - not linked to the inflation record of the central bank.

Five conclusions are to be drawn here: (1) Small countries who give up their respective national monetary policy through joining the EMU, are relatively powerless when they want to press a big partner country to adopt a change in its fiscal policy stance. (2) EU fiscal policies could become more discretionary as governments that effectively lose the monetary policy instrument will resort more often to changes in the fiscal policy stance. (3) Accommodating fiscal policies could become a major problem for the EMU. Given the limited possibilities to reduce tax rates this would always mean higher government consumption and higher deficit GDP ratios. In this respect, credible rules for limiting the deficit/GDP ratios are useful since they amount to tying one's own hand. They should have the positive side effect of encouraging governments to pursue national policy and labor market reforms that reinforce the flexibility and shock absorption capacity of markets. Rules for deficit/GDP ratios should be allowed to be waived in a period of massive adverse shocks. This, according to a new rule, might have to be identified by an independent scientific EU policy advisory committee. One never can rule out shocks such as the OPEC price shock, international financial shocks as in 1929 and 1987 or adverse regional shocks like those suffered by Finland in 1990/91 when the USSR and the CMEA collapsed. (4) National governments with a desire to raise expenditures, but facing a national deficit problem could exert mounting pressure on the European Investment Bank, in order to extend soft loans for investment projects that are in effect part of an expansionary fiscal policy. To the extent that this would help to restrict the growth of net indebtedness of governments such a development might not be unwarranted. (5) Countries facing structural problems and recession are increasingly likely to press for raising EU structural funds. Each EU country i in effect can aim for appropriate higher EU funds at the expense of j's taxpayers. Since voters' control at the level of the European Parliament is weaker than at the national level, national policymakers could indeed favor such a development in most EU countries. This poses a major policy failure problem, given the rather modest EU regional policy record. This problem could be avoided by stipulating that no country in the wider EU mean income bracket (at PPP values) is allowed to receive gross transfers of more than 1% of GDP, except twice the amount during a maximum of three years per decade if such years are in an economic recession with a serious regional decline in industrial unemployment. A slightly more (less) generous rule for poorer (richer) countries could be adopted.

3.2 Labor Markets and Stabilization Policy

The EMU is an institutional innovation with some risk but there are also major anticipated benefits if the transition is well organized. If both the national and the supranational policy levels adopt appropriate reforms that allow the EU member countries to cope with their core problem, which is unemployment. In the EU there is sustained high unemployment, including a high share of long term unemployed. Part of the high budget deficits in some countries is related directly to high unemployment figures. It is difficult to imagine that a switch to EMU will be sustainable if the unemployment rates cannot be reduced.

Solving the unemployment problem is of paramount importance since high and diverging unemployment rates in the EU will create divergent national policy stances and possibly undermine the public acceptance of EMU which is often considered as causing further problems in the labor market. The unemployment problem in the EU consists of an overhang of unemployment which dates back to the 1970 and a high rate of structural unemployment. To eliminate the overhang a transitory spurt of economic growth with wage increases below productivity growth is necessary. To cope with structural unemployment qualification measures and a wave of creating new firms are necessary; moreover, since redundancies mostly affect unskilled workers and occur mainly in industries with high capital intensity with high labor productivity and real wages, a market-driven shift to the service sector which is less capital intensive but more skill intensive - is often blocked. To avoid this, workers who accept a less well-paid job could be paid a temporary bonus from the national government. Such a rule could be incorporated into national tax laws. An expansion of the service industry, which offers specialized services at low prices, is still a valid option for the creation of jobs in most EU countries, especially in Germany. The argument that the percentage of services jobs in Germany (*DIW, 1996*) - disregarding whether such jobs are in industry or in specialized firms - are similar to the US is not addressing the point. Namely that only explicit outsourcing of services brings specialization gains and allows the opportunity to provide innovative and relatively cheap services as valuable inputs to industry, which therefore, can more easily continue to grow in absolute terms.

However, the main key to higher employment is a surge of productivity growth and appropriate national and supranational innovation policies. In this respect, the EU has so far neglected adequate initiatives. Facing increasing import competition from low wage countries in transforming Eastern European countries and the global excess supply of unskilled labor (from Asia), the EU countries have to move up the technological ladder. German, British, French and Dutch R&D expenditures-GDP ratios fell after 1989. This points to strategically inadequate approaches in the field of innovation policy (in the US civilian R&D/GDP ratios increased as did those of Asian NICs in the period from 1989 to 1995).

The European employment problem could be aggravated by EMU which will bring about an unprecedented degree of capital mobility and financial market transparency. Since the 1990s there is increasing pressure in stock markets to achieve competitive returns across countries. This tendency is reinforced by EMU and rising capital mobility, respectively. Managers' traditional bias to the overexpansion of firms and employment, will no longer be tolerated in stock markets, that are embedded in a system of free capital flows in OECD countries.

Privatization of companies in many EU countries will add to the problem. Therefore, the creation of new firms is all the more important. *Audretsch (1996)* finds in his analysis that since the mid-1980s there are OECD-wide trends in corporate downsizing, while the bulk of new employment is in small and medium sized firms. The EU compares poorly to the US in regards to the creation of new firms.

Structural employment becomes a persistent problem if incentives to avoid unemployment are weakened. EU structural funds sometimes effectively act in such a way. From an economic perspective the transition to EMU not only requires a focus on the deficit problems at the national level and required policy reforms. There is also a need to raise the question of reforms at the supranational level that are consistent with EMU. Since EMU imposes budgetary discipline at the national level it is all the more important to prevent politicians from trying to substitute higher EU outlays for national government expenditures.

Finally, to maintain full employment it would be necessary to introduce an unemployment insurance reform that operates on the basis of regionally and possibly sectorally differentiated contribution rates (*Welfens, 1994*): In regions with high unemployment rates and a high share of long-term unemployed, contribution rates to employment insurance should be rather high, whereas in full employment areas effective contribution rates would be very low. This will create incentives for regional government, employers and trade unions to avoid measures that raise the unemployment rate. Given the likely resistance in high unemployment regions against such a reform it is obvious that such a reform could be only introduced if full employment has been achieved before.

Stabilization Issues and Labor Markets

Stabilization policy in EMU will be rather difficult regardless of the composition of the initial EMU core group. Assuming that centralized monetary policy will focus mainly on the goal of price stability, there are five main options, disregarding fiscal policy, to cope with asymmetric shocks as well as with EMU wide shocks (figure H.4).

(1) Increased cost flexibility could help to absorb adverse shocks. Cost flexibility has somewhat increased through the process of outsourcing and corporate downsizing in the 1980s and early 1990s. However, the long-term development into a high-technology society with many skilled personnel and high R&D costs which are often fixed costs, means that cost flexibility can hardly be increased very much.

(2) Higher wage flexibility obviously could help to absorb shocks. Without special tax incentives and tax reforms there are no prospects to achieve higher intertemporal or higher regional wage differentiation, including higher wage dispersion. Tax reforms and labor market reforms are needed to achieve such higher flexibility.

(3) Rising labor mobility could be achieved within EU countries, certainly less so across EU countries. New tax incentives for regional mobility and removing impediments for mobility could help to achieve higher mobility. This still

would leave the EMU area far behind the US in regards to overall labor mobility.

(4) Increasing supranational EU transfers could be used to compensate regions with a declining demand. Such a policy would, of course, be highly undesirable because it raises EU budget costs at the expense of the EU taxpayer. EU taxpayers face extreme difficulties in controlling the effectiveness and efficiency of EU regional policies. Compared to local, regional or national elections the marginal impact of an EU voter is even more limited so that the incentive to be well-informed when voting is very small. Following this reasoning, one should raise the transparency of regional policies as well as other policy fields through mandatory standardized reporting procedures, which include a policy summary report for all citizens (similar to a company report to its shareholder. Furthermore, rising EU transfer funds could indeed be limited by new rules for a maximum amount (relative to GDP) which a country of a certain income group - evaluated at PPP level - could receive as transfers. Based on NUTS-2 regions the analysis of the *European Commission (1996)* points to the limited success of regional policy: Between 1983 and 1993, the Gini coefficient increased slightly from 0.149 to 0.153. However, at the national level, cohesion increased, since per capita GDP of Spain, Portugal, Greece and Ireland increased from 66% of community average in 1983 to 74% in 1995.

(5) Higher price flexibility could help to absorb demand shocks. In the single market including a monetary union, price transparency is increased and higher price flexibility can indeed be expected in a more competitive setting - as long as intra-EU mergers and acquisitions are not restoring previously high market shares of large firms (then in the relevant national markets).

Taking into account the pro-competitive effects of increased price transparency price flexibility will increase in the EMU area in the medium term. In fully integrated EMU markets there will be an erosion of market power for internationally oriented firms. The crucial question is whether wage flexibility will increase to a similar degree as price flexibility.

Figure H.4: Absorption Possibilities in the Case of Demand Shocks

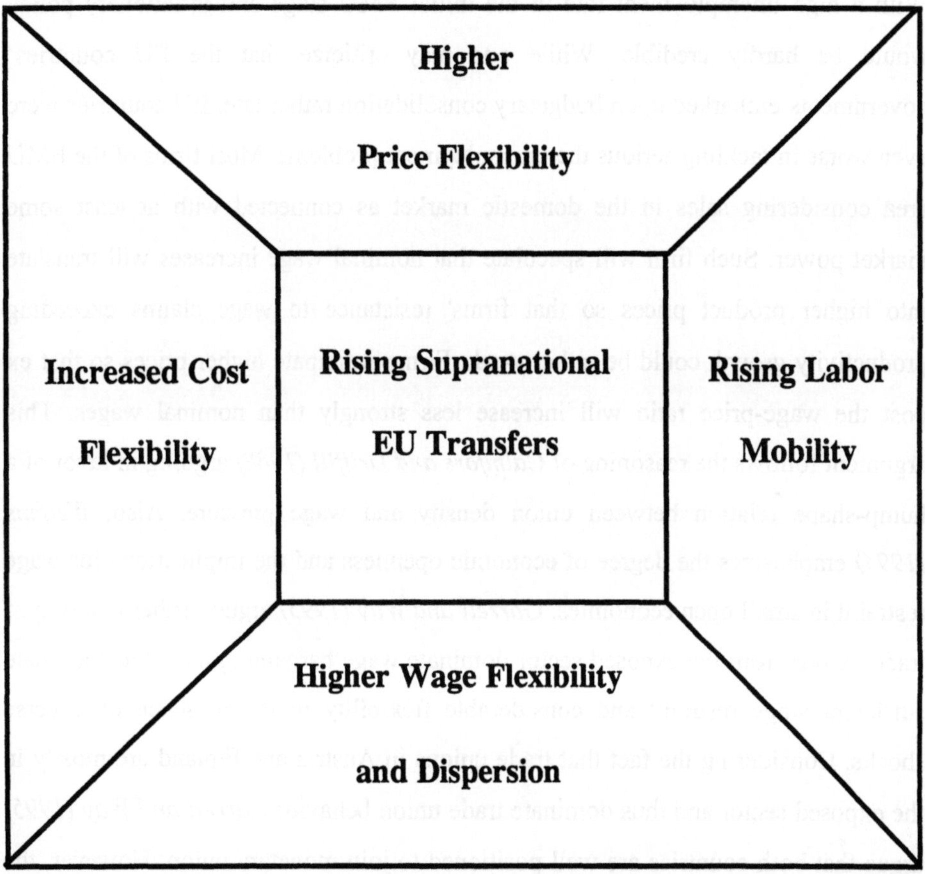

The EMU area will mean for all countries involved, that they can no longer be considered as small open economies whose firms are pricetakers in international markets; the EFTA countries were typical in such a position, which implied heavy resistance by firms from the tradables sector to accept wage increases above productivity gains. The larger the initial EMU group is, the bigger will be the market power of firms in the tradables sector. There is a risk that the switch to EMU will entail higher nominal wage pressure since wage transparency is increasing, while trade unions in low wage EMU countries will press for strongly rising wages. An accommodating monetary policy could then lead to rather high inflation rates. With a high unemployment rate in the initial EMU stage anti-inflationary policy would be hardly credible. While one may criticize that the EU countries' governments embarked upon budgetary consolidation rather late, EU countries were even worse in tackling serious the unemployment problems. Most firms of the EMU area considering sales in the domestic market as connected with at least some market power. Such firm will speculate that nominal wage increases will translate into higher product prices so that firms' resistance to wage claims exceeding productivity growth could be rather weak: Firms anticipate higher prices so that ex post the wage-price ratio will increase less strongly than nominal wages. This argument follows the reasoning of *Calmfors and Driffill (1988)* arguing in favor of a hump-shape relation between union density and wage pressure. Also, *Welfens (1994)* emphasizes the degree of economic openness and the implications for wage restraint in small open economies. *Garrett and Way (1995)* argue further that only if trade unions from the exposed sector dominate wage bargaining may one anticipate sufficient wage restraint and considerable flexibility in the presence of adverse shocks. Considering the fact that trade unions in Austria and Finland are mostly in the exposed sector and thus dominate trade union behavior *Garrett and Way (1995)* argue that both countries are well positioned to join monetary union. However, the wage pressure in Sweden in the 1990s dominated by the tradables sector, showed that insufficient productivity growth of the non-tradables sector can be a serious problem, too.

In the long run there could be problems with unions which will tend to organize themselves more on a pan-EMU level, and this might be more easy to achieve in the nontradables sector. The European Commission's pressure on the EU countries' liberalization of network industries (telecoms, energy and railways) which stimulates privatization and economic opening up of these industries is not only economically beneficial in its own right it also reduces the scope of the sheltered nontradables sector. With an ongoing move towards a service dominated economy, the EU nevertheless is facing a problem to the extent that the single market directives only stimulate trade in services to a limited degree. Rising intra-EU foreign direct investment - which has been strong in the service sector in the late 1980s and the first half of the 1990s - is contributing to competition in this sector. However, it is only an imperfect substitute for tradability. For EMU countries it will be crucial to strictly adhere to liberal import competition which will help to keep wages in line with productivity growth.

Wages will increase in the EMU area because trade unions in low wage countries will press for higher wages. Thus the wage gap between Germany and other EMU countries is reduced. This argument would hardly be valid if the initial EMU group consists only of a small group of high wage (and productivity) countries. Facing serious wage pressure in a larger EMU group, however, could confront the problem of a lack of political union. With rising EU unemployment most EU member countries are likely to call for increasing supranational transfers.

Rising supranational transfer programs were a major problem in the EU in the early 1990s when 52% of the EU population benefited from EU structural funds which are mainly designed to help poor regions and areas with declining industrial output (*European Commission, 1994*). About 1/3 of the EU budget was spent for regional policies, i.e. structural funds, another 50% for agriculture. This policy is often counterproductive, and employment growth in objective 1-areas (per capita income below 75% of EU average) was indeed weaker than in the EU average in the 1980s (*IWD, 1995*). Regions that anticipate that rising EU funds can be obtained under declining economic conditions have poor incentives to avoid these conditions.

3.3 The Transition Process Towards EMU

The transition process for monetary union consists of three stages which raise important politico-economic issues, especially in stage A. Stage A will be devoted to the preparation of EMU. In mid-1998 the participating countries will be selected, the starting date be fixed. The ECB and the ESCB will be established. EU member countries will pass legislation for the switch to the new currency. Production of Euro notes and coins will start and the banking sector will complete its preparations for EMU. Outsiders will be linked to EMU via a new European Monetary System (EMS II) which will be based on fixed parities and, most probably, asymmetric interventions in exchange markets.

The decision by the members of the starting group has to be taken with a qualified majority. Thus the number of members in the first wave is unlikely to be very small. 26 out of 87 votes (table H.9, Appendix) can block entry of a country in the EMU starter group. Italy which has a serious debt problem is likely to remain outside and the UK has an opting-out clause. Since the UK and Italy each represent 10 votes it is not unlikely that Spain, one of the EU latecomers, would join the starter group. This would have the advantage that EMU citizens on vacation in Spain - Europe's holiday destination No. 1- could enjoy first hand advantages from monetary union; a benefit which is rather insignificant economically, but could help to convince ordinary citizens about the virtue of monetary union. Spain and France are the EU's top two holiday destinations. They are also ideal to show visitors from outsider countries that the Euro is working beyond the commercial sphere. Given the high debt-GDP ratio of Belgium its inclusion into the EMU starter group could only be justified because of the falling deficit-GDP ratio, while Italy's deficit ratio is making slow progress. The really important difference between Belgium and Italy is that the former is a small country with small effects on the Euro interest rate while Italy's 10 per cent deficit ratio would alone account for a EMU deficit-GDP ratio of 2-3% - exposing the Euro area at G-7 meetings to allegations about fiscal negligence. If the UK and Italy really remain outside the starter group, Germany would face the fact that two of its top three trading partners are outside the EMU area. This would seriously reduce the attractiveness of EMU for Germany unless EMS II would be constructed in a way which prevents sharp competitive devaluations in EU member countries. France has called for sanctions against countries that strongly devaluate.

Determining the outsiders will be critical since these countries are likely to be those with a high debt-GDP ratio and therefore could suffer from a increase in real interest rates reflecting high devaluation risks after the establishment of the EMU group. The fiscal convergence criteria could become more difficult for the outsiders to meet immediately after the first wave of EMU participants has been fixed. *Gros (1995)* and *de Grauwe (1996)* emphasized that EMU membership would facilitate fiscal consolidation in high debt countries since EMU interest rates could fall closer to the former low German level. This economic argument does, however, not consider the credibility and consistency problem of the early membership of highly indebted countries whose high (net) debt-GDP ratio points to past social and political conflicts over financing public expenditures and which could reemerge after the introduction of EMU: Excessive national government deficit spending in EMU would face neither the sanction of currency devaluation and high interest rates nor of short average bond maturities which normally reflect fear of inflation. Short average maturities that are typical of a high inflation-high debt country strongly expose the country to adverse external interest rate shocks which will quickly feed into the government budget constraint. Short bond maturities lead to short term government financing decisions, reduced economic growth and an ad hoc political management under short lived governments with poor efficiency in decision-making ("policy failure"), where remedies are mainly internal reforms in the political system. Since there is no EU political union malfunctions of the national political system cannot be corrected from above, i.e. by supranational policy reform initiatives.

EMU membership reduces the pressure for political reforms. Instead national governments could be inclined to accommodate distribution conflicts by trying to raise EU structural fund expenditures and appropriating a increasing share of supranational transfers. For the leading contributors to the EU budget this is an unwelcome political risk: In terms of net per capita contributions the Netherlands, Germany and France are the leading countries.

There is a strong incentive in high debt countries to join EMU - possibly before 2002 - because anticipated membership will bring down long term interest rates and effectively lead to a more long term average maturity. However for an existing EMU starting group the membership of a country like Italy could bring a union-wide once-and-for all adjustment problem because a large stock of short term Italian bonds will be converted into Euro bonds, while the Italian government has every incentive to refine its debt structure with long term bonds. Such a temporary constellation could bring an excess supply of long term bonds, a sharp fall in bond prices and hence a sharp increase in long-term interest rates in EMU.

Stage B could start at the beginning of 1999 with the fixing of conversion rates between the participating currencies and the Euro. The ESCB will provide its TARGET system which allows real-time gross settlements in Euro; new government bonds denominated in Euro will be issued, where the conversion of the existing stock of bonds remains an open question; e.g. France prefers immediate conversion, while Germany prefers it only in 2002. Future contracts will be difficult to fulfill if DM-denominated bonds are circulating in parallel to Euro bonds (can DM-bonds be used to deliver a Euro future contract?). The liquidity of the Euro bond and the DM bond market would be impaired and higher interest rates than otherwise could result. To strengthen London's position as a global financial center the UK, even if it is not a member of the EMU, might decide to issue a large amount of Euro denominated debt. If the UK abstained from EMU membership for the long term the paradox situation of EMU creating major benefits for Britain as an outsider is bound to cause political tensions within the Community.

In stage B monetary policy control will be shifted to ECB, and the ESCB will carry out money market transactions in Euro and convert accounts held by its counterparts. The remaining switch in the non-cash field to the Euro will take place in a market-driven process. Germany's option to maintain the existing stock of DM bonds until 2002 also implies the problem that DM denominated bonds could have lower yields than the Euro which could raise the issue of falling DM bond prices (wealth losses) at the time of conversion and hence cause political conflicts in stage B in Germany and, furthermore, undermine the credibility of the whole transition scenario.

Stage C is the completion of the currency switch and the replacement of notes and coins: Euro notes and coins will circulate by January 1, 2002. Firms, private households and government agencies in EMU countries will switch to the Euro. Completion of EMU is scheduled for July 2002. Europe's big banks which target the whole EU market can be expected to contribute actively towards a wider use of the Euro. Banks which are present in all EMU countries stand to benefit from the type of network effects described earlier. Small savings banks might be among the losers of a transition to EMU.

3.4 Fiscal Issues and Political Union

In a monetary union fiscal discipline could be rather loose - as argued e.g. by *Issing (1996)* - since high debt countries are not facing the sanction of currency depreciation. Moreover, one may add that a successful Euro monetary union which achieves price stability could bring about low interest rates which encourage increasing government indebtedness. While one may argue that credit rating agencies will generate some market-imposed discipline, experience shows that credit rating is an imperfect instrument to restrict government indebtedness (the 1994/5 Mexico crisis being one extreme case). Furthermore, the bail-out clause of the Maastricht Treaty is itself not really credible since excessive deficits of a major trading partner (C) of an affluent EMU member (A) would naturally induce country A's government to bail out the indebted partner C if this would really prevent a collapse of the C-economy and hence of trade relations. One may note that this bail-out problem is not necessarily less prevalent without monetary union as was emphasized by *de Grauwe (1996, p. 20)*. If A is a major source country of foreign direct investment there would be an additional incentive to launch a rescue operation for the indebted country facing default which in the absence of a bail-out it will witness a sharp fall in asset prices and, probably, industrial and political unrest. From a German point of view the no-bail-out clause of the Maastricht Treaty would be difficult to implement for internal consistency problems, too: Within Germany the federal government is required by Germany's Basic Law - calling for the equalization of living standards within the country - to provide extra transfers to poor regions ("Laender").

The more comprehensive the EMU political union would be, the more difficult it will be for rich union members to deny bail-out measures for highly indebted partner countries; at the same time political interference across EMU countries could be more easily organized which might help to avoid excessive debt problems. Those which argue that monetary union should be coupled with political union should take into account this two-pronged bail-out problem. From this perspective a limit on the debt-GDP ratio is sensible, while it remains unclear which ratio is appropriate. A reasonable way to encourage fiscal solidity at the national level is, however, to rely on appropriate incentives. Since high private and public debt GDP ratios imply an increased systemic risk for the whole of financial markets in the EMU area supranational transfers could be negatively linked to the rating of government bonds issued; moreover, as soon as the three leading rating agencies downgrade government bonds to a grade below top quality the country's central banks governor could only have a dormant vote in the ESCB. In order to encourage optimal banking supervision this rule could also apply after a major national banking crisis.

De Grauwe (1996) shows in his analysis of the convergence criteria that identical debt-GDP ratios, regardless of the absolute figure, create a common interest among EMU member countries with respect to the maximum tolerable inflation rate; this holds as long as the national preferences for inflation are identical. While this points to a rationale for a debt-GDP convergence criterion it is quite unclear why the maximum ratio should be 60%. The theory of optimum government financing does not provide a rationale for this figure.

Another economic argument for imposing a limit on the debt-GDP ratio is that it implicitly restricts the deficit GDP ratio to rather low figures. This in turn ensures that public investment/GDP ratios are not falling below critical levels. Empirical analysis (*Lane, 1995; Haan, Sturm and Sikken, 1996*) shows that high deficit-GDP ratios cause government capital formation to decline. Given the high unemployment rates in the EU a long term reduction of government capital formation is undesirable.

3.4.1 Stability Pact, Optimum Growth and Lobbying

Based on the proposals of the German minister of finance, Theo Waigel, the European Council adopted a stability and growth pact - thus adding the aspect of growth. The rules adopted in early 1997 are as follows: If a country's deficit exceeds 3 % of GDP the Commission will consider this as related to an exceptional economic decline if the fall in GDP is at least 2 per cent p.a.; natural disasters or other exceptional events also qualify for an excuse. An exception clause could also hold if special reasons for an excessive deficit can be identified (e.g. a sudden and cumulated output decline) - output within a year must have fallen by at least 0.75%. If the Commission should qualify a deficit above 3% not as excessive it will inform the Council in writing on this and the respective reasons. The countries introducing the Euro will introduce stabilization programs which indicate prospective public deficits over the medium term. Member states will publish stabilization and convergence programs. Countries which are no adhering to the Euro group will have to present only convergence programs and face no sanctions in the case of excessive deficits. EMU countries are expected to have a balanced budget or a minor deficit in the long run.

Economic sanctions for exceeding the 3% deficit threshold are 0.2% of GDP as a lump sum payment and 0.1% per deficit point above the 3% figure - with the maximum upper limit of 0.5%. Payments have to be made as a deposit on which no interest will accrue. If excessive deficits continue the deposit will become a fine. Extra revenues thus accruing to the EU will be distributed to EMU member states which have stayed within the deficit limit.

While the wording of the stability and growth pact is not always clear from an economic point of view the idea of sanctions is useful. However, for a federal country - such as Germany, Austria or Belgium - there is the problem that an internal fiscal stability pact is required to the extent that regional authorities are allowed to run a budget deficit. Instead of an internal stability pact the central government could assume full responsibility for the country's deficit position if regional states were not allowed to run a deficit (the rule applied with modest rigor in the US). At the bottom line one may consider the EMU deficit threshold of 3 % as reasonable only if one would add the requirement that structural deficits must reflect public investment or subsidies for innovations. This then points to the need to distinguish between a net debt and a gross debt GDP ratio. In Sweden the net ratio is much lower than the gross figure.

The literature on the optimum public debt problem does not provide to a clear critical debt GDP ratio or an optimum deficit ratio but from an economist's point of view the use of borrowed funds is always important. One might derive optimum fiscal ratios from the optimum growth theory which requires as a standard result that $r=n+\beta$ (r=real interest rate, n= growth rate of population, β=rate of technological progress). A higher permanent deficit ratio will raise r and lower the rate of technological progress if borrowed funds are used for public consumption thus requiring higher income taxes which impair growth and encourage mobile production factors to go abroad. If extra government funds raised through borrowing instead go to public investment (including higher education) and R&D subsidies the rate of technological progress will increase - the equality sign in the above equation could then hold even at a deficit ratio above 3% where appropriate refinements could also include aspects of the new growth theory. Such considerations were not taken into account in the Delors Report and other EU deliberations on fiscal limits for EMU member countries. This also points to a limitation in the relevance of most optimum debt models which cannot cover the distribution aspects associated with alternative transition paths to a new steady state or a new permanent growth rate.

Social Security Aspects and Capital Markets

Rather high public deficits in Germany and some other countries are - disregarding special aspects of unification in the case of Germany - related to high unemployment rates and demographically induced deficits in poorly designed social security systems. The implicit debt GDP ratio of the pension system in Germany and France reached about 110 % in 1995 (higher than in Italy and much higher than in the UK) and therefore was higher than the official debt GDP ratio (*IMF, 1996*).

High social security contribution rates in Germany, the Netherlands, France and Italy have caused high labor costs which in turn reinforce unemployment - unless social security contributions are financed to a major extent by value-added taxes (the case of Denmark) which will not impair exports under current EU tax rules. Given the high unemployment rates in the EU and the intensified international competition, i.e., the globalization of the economy - with a sharp quest for mobile capital (MNC's investment) worldwide - one wonders why EU countries have such a strong focus on deficit criteria while few discuss the urgent need for labor market reforms in Western Europe as well as the need to improve the efficiency of capital markets. The fact that capital productivity in Germany and France is only about ¾ of that of the US (*McKinsey, 1996; 1997*) points to serious problems in continental

EU capital markets where capitalization of stock markets is significantly lower than in the US, the UK and Switzerland or Sweden. The introduction of the Euro could improve the situation in the long term since it will increase the transparency of capital markets for EU insiders as well as outsiders - say, e.g. US venture capital firms with a focus on Europe.

With rising capital flows in the world economy and important regional convergence processes (*Welfens and Wolf, 1997*) the EMU group might particularly benefit if a low inflation track record can be established early on. Prospects are favorable in this respect as long as the initial starting situation is one of very low inflation rates in all EMU countries. From this perspective even a large EMU starter group could be viable. However, a small EMU starter group would not only be easier in accordance with the fiscal convergence criteria but it would also face lower costs of political consensus building in the early stages of speculative attacks or adverse shocks. Even if countries are hit by the same shock the ability to cope with it differently, would make countries prefer different adjustment paths which can cause damaging delays and inadequate policy measures in policymaking.

Continental EU firms suffer, compared with their US counterparts, from insufficient equity capital which is urgently needed to finance risky innovations which has increasingly become important in the global high technology race of the late 1990s. Equity capital is crucial for financing innovations in a world of asymmetric information: While the innovator knows the most about the technical and commercial side of the innovation, the bank - and thus credit financing - naturally is at a disadvantage. While loan officers will critically check the innovator´s project once, i.e., before extending the loan, the alternative financing of innovations - via the stock market - means that the firm is constantly monitored by analysts and thus will strive to acquire reputation as a successful innovator.

Per Capita Income and Wage Centralization

From a political economy point of view trade unions are likely to be in favor of a compact EMU starting group with a similar per capita income and technology level, because this should facilitate the EMU-wide cooperation of trade unions. This would also reduce the probability of major policy conflicts within the EMU group. In regards to additional unemployment risk, much will depend on the degree of bargaining centralization and other institutional aspects of the EU and the EMU group, respectively (*Calmfors and Driffill, 1988; Fitzenberger and Franz, 1994; Fitzenberger, 1995; Schweickert, 1996; Addison and Welfens, 1997*) as well as the EU's response to the global high technology race (*Welfens, Addison, Audretsch and Grupp, 1997*). Since EMU reinforces the integration of product markets the effective degree of bargaining centralization is reduced so that trade unions and employer organizations are likely to come up with a more differentiated wage bargaining patterns in the medium term; this should stimulate employment. More uniform patterns will, however, hold in the long term, i.e., after trade unions of EU countries have learned to better cooperate among themselves. With weaker and more responsible trade unions the employment situation could improve, but the EMU could face reduced productivity growth as lower wage pressure slows down rationalization investment. An important question is whether in a future period of high inflation disinflation can be achieved at lower costs than previously in the EU because the ECB in fact amount to saying that a central bank à la Deutsche Bundesbank rules everywhere in the EMU area and that trade unions and employers' federations recognize the credibility of the ECB.

Prospects for higher (capital) productivity growth could, however, be improved by more integrated capital markets in the EMU area. With a higher capital productivity the EMU should benefit from massive net capital inflows in the long term which could, assuming that investment inflows were dominated initially by short term capital inflows, result in a rather steep yield curve. At the same time nominal interest rates in the EMU area could fall as intra-EMU capital flows are no longer subject to exchange rate risks. In the EMU area interest rates should mainly reflect the rating of firms and countries, respectively.

Many trade unions will detest the deficit limit since it undermines the options of a Keynesian type of fiscal policy which could partly remedy excessive real wage pressure or insufficient wage dispersion (between skilled and unskilled labor). Moreover, trade unions will be afraid that the gains from EMU and globalization accrue mainly to capital owners which form a small share of the population except in Sweden and in the UK. Germany's trade unions have supported the EMU project because it promises reduced future risks in real currency appreciations which have often undermined Germany's export position in the early 1990s. Trade unions in France are openly hostile in part to the Euro project because they fear that future French political autonomy will be lower than in the EMS-I-regime. Employer federations in most EU countries are dominated by big companies which are major exporters and thus favor EMU since it reduces exchange rate risks and transaction costs in EU business. In the mid-1990s, the majority of voters in each EU member country, except German, British, Danish and Swedish voters, was in favor of the Euro project, which is no surprise; disregarding Austria and the Netherlands which have effectively shadowed the Deutsche Bundesbank's policy since the 1970s, other EU member countries which had high inflation rates in the 1980s can expect a lower inflation risk in a future Euro area. Since a qualified majority is required for determining the EMU starter group one may anticipate that Spain could be included in the starter group; and for political reasons it will hold that if Spain is in the starter group, Italy will also demand its starting ticket; the same then holds mutatis mutandis for Portugal because of its strong economic links with Spain.

The Maastricht Treaty suffers from one serious deficit, namely that latecomers - which qualified for EMU but choose the option out position initially - can enter after three years or even earlier. Latecomers should be allowed to enter only after a decade since that type of sanction is the only way to avoid free-rider strategies of EU countries. Without such a clause the UK and Denmark effectively takes a free-rider position with respect to institutional monetary innovation (the Euro), i.e., it can observe the costs of the early starter group and then can join fairly early at reduced marginal entry costs if it wants to do so. If EMU would face massive problems, monetary union could be the starting point for EU disintegration, but a successful monetary integration could reinforce the single market and create positive welfare effects. The EMU could become - at least after the UK joining - a major net exporter of financial services as well as a net exporter of capital. Thus, sustained EU trade balance deficits could occur.

A successful Euro will cause the City to put maximum pressure on the UK government to finally join the EMU club. Even if the Euro should be weak the British government is likely to face pressure to join in the medium-term as the UK could face a problem similar to that of Germany with its appreciating DM in the first half of the 1990s: A weak Euro will imply a strong dollar and a strong pound, and the latter can hardly be welcome by the British government which attracted under the Thatcher and Major governments many multinational companies by pointing to British (labor) cost advantages. Whether the Swiss Franc will benefit from EMU is doubtful. A massive appreciation - in periods of speculations against the Euro - will further erode the competitiveness of Swiss exports, a depreciation thus might be more welcome. Hence it is clear that the EMU project could create many political and economic adjustment pressures.

A positive external effect of EMU could be easier crisis management in the triad as fewer actors have to be coordinated. A negative internal effect might be that remedying high unemployment in the EU countries could become more difficult as political conflicts of the stability and growth pact absorb „political consensus capital" to a large extent, leaving national political systems incapable of adopting important labor market reforms. High and sustained unemployment rates could in turn undermine the political support for EU integration and cause a dangerous revival of economic nationalism in Western Europe. This might be the biggest difference between de facto US monetary integration of more than 100 years ago - it was also a hard political integration that allowed to cope with even extreme adverse economic shocks. Whether EMU will facilitate any kind of closer political integration in the EU is an open question.

3.4.2 Coordination Problem in the EMU

Except for international spillover effects (in border areas) and in the case of transeuropean infrastructure networks there is no economic reason for supranational regional policies and EU transfers, respectively. For EU agricultural policies there is absolutely no economic justification, except when it comes to health and safety standards. There are, however, economic reasons for raising the share of supranational EU expenditures, namely in fields which represent an EU international public good: infrastructure expenditures, part of R&D expenditures, environmental programs with cross border effects and defense outlays could amount to about 5% of Community GDP. This would also generate a critical mass for supranational EU fiscal policy in the sense that in recessions and booms a consistent countercyclical policy could be pursued. Here lies indeed one risk related to lack of EU political union - a functional union would certainly establish supranational expenditures that exceed the current 1.24% of EU GDP. Conversely, at the national level government expenditures would have to be reduced by more than 1:1 for every increase in expenditures at the supranational level. This holds true to the extent that from an efficiency perspective government consumption-GDP ratios are excessive in EU countries.

Raising expenditures at the EU level, while trimming the expenditure structure in a way that is consistent with economic reasoning, could be useful for achieving a consistent mix of fiscal and monetary policy. Since there is no proper coordination of fiscal policies at the EU level - except for an unclear outcome at the ECOFIN - a critical mass of EU outlays would indeed be a useful starting point for a consistent EU fiscal policy. If the European Parliament would chose a fiscal policy coordinator for the ECOFIN (from possibly a short list of candidates prepared by the European Commission to remedy the democratic deficit in at least one policy field) for a long term period there also would be an institutional starting point for a consistent EU fiscal policy that could be based on flexible rules allowing the coordinator to raise EU outlays by a maximum of x percent during a recession and cutting outlays by a maximum of x (or z) percent in an EU boom period. This approach is superior to the uncertain outcome of an ad hoc coordination under the present regime which implicitly assumes that 15 country representatives can achieve consensus about important fiscal policy issues.

The political economic problem related to fiscal policy reform is two-fold: National governments will be unwilling to reduce national government outlays and to give up national economic power, respectively. At the same time it will be difficult to implement regional policies in member countries in a way that is conducive to an efficient structural adjustment.

A remedy against excessive government GDP ratios could be the intensification of locational competition with a higher responsibility by political players: Each layer of government - whether local, regional or national - should have its own sources of tax revenue. Both the responsibility for financing expenditures at the respective government level will be strengthened and locational competition be intensified. The latter will help to reduce overall government expenditures. Finally, by applying the principle of subsidiarity in EU member countries in the field of public transfer policies would require that the regions would develop a system in which economically strong areas support in a strictly horizontal equalization scheme the poorer ones. There should be an effective no-bail-out clause at the regional level which can be implemented in such a way that regions unable to financially manage their affairs lose their political independence: clear indicators for assessing financial viability and a warning threshold would have to be defined before imposing political merger. If such fiscal responsibility reforms were applied in all EMU countries the non-bailout clause of the Maastricht Treaty, which refers to the relations between EU member countries, would become much more credible. Political moral hazard at the national level can hardly be avoided if not strict incentives discourage unsustainable debt strategies in an endogenous process.

3.5 EMU as Scapegoat and as a Challenge for Policy Reform

Once EMU has been created the nonsupporters of EMU are likely to blame all kind of their problems on the formation of monetary union, regardless whether these problems are actually caused or aggravated by such a union or whether related to other causes. It should be clear at the outset that EMU will have an easy scapegoat function, if the European Commission takes not stock of the existing economic and social problems in all EU countries prior to EMU. Without EMU as well as with EMU problems will continue to exist and certainly there will be policy options to remedy such problems. Taking the Maastricht Treaty into account, there are, however, new fiscal policy restrictions which could impair an efficient flexible policy mix and an optimal policy assignment.

With fiscal policy facing restrictions it is important that price flexibility as well as wage flexibility increase, so that adverse - symmetric or asymmetric - shocks and shifts cannot cause persistent macroeconomic disequilibria. Without a stability pact that involves trade unions and employer organizations one cannot hope to achieve the required change in wage regime: higher wage flexibility and a rule that restricts (with an escape clause for sustained excess demand situations) wage increases of unskilled labor to a percentage increase that is below the average increase as well as greater wage dispersion at the expense of unskilled labor. The fact that unskilled workers would have to accept lower gross wages, might be mitigated by lower income tax rates for unskilled labor or by special government bonus payments for income accruing from additional investment income based on new employee ownership programs and other special investment savings plans (possibly including voucher privatization).

From the perspective of a risk-averse voter or politician, the switch to EMU which is perceived as a risky change in regime, should be undertaken ideally when general economic conditions are favorable and, hence, overall risks are limited. Favorable conditions means high economic growth or a boom period. Eurobarometer opinion polls show support for European integration - a risky business in most voters' perception - to depend indeed upon the economic growth rate. Therefore, political prudence suggests that EMU be implemented in an economic upswing period. If the European Council or the European Commission would anticipate 1999 to be a year of economic stagnation it would be worthwhile to consider postponement by about two years. With economic stagnation the deficit convergence criteria will also not be fulfilled by many EU countries. EMU is an enormous challenge to government, industry and its citizens.

Appendix A: Tables

Table H.7: Trade Balance (without Internal Trade) for Alternative EMU Starter Groups as a Percentage of GDP (1985-1994)

D, F, NL, B/L, DK:	1.27
D, F, NL, B/L, DK, I:	1.00
D, F, NL, B/L, DK, UK:	0.21
D, F, NL, B/L, DK, I, UK:	0.18
D, F, NL, B/L, DK, I, E, P:	0.25
D, F, NL, B/L, DK, I, UK, E, P:	-0.37
EUR 15:	-0.49

Note: B/L = Belgium plus Luxembourg; D = Germany; DK = Denmark; E = Spain; EUR 15 = current EU member countries; F = France; I = Italy; NL = Netherlands; P = Portugal; UK = United Kingdom

Source: European Commission

Table H.8: Top Three Export Destinations (Percentage of Total Exports)

EU-Countries	1.	2.	3.
Germany	France (11,97 %)	Great Britain (7,99 %)	USA (7,90 %)
Great Britain	Germany (13,08 %)	USA (12,79 %)	France (10,11 %)
France	Germany (17,15 %)	Great Britain (9,91 %)	USA (7,02 %)
Italy	Germany (19,01 %)	France (13,08 %)	USA (7,76 %)
Spain [1]	France (22,60 %)	Germany (14,11 %)	Portugal (9,26 %)
Netherlands	Germany (28,09 %)	France (10,46 %)	Great Britain (9,34 %)
Belgium/ Luxembourg	Germany (20,73 %)	France (18,83 %)	Great Britain (8,40 %)
Sweden	Germany (13,31 %)	Great Britain (10,16 %)	Norway (8,14 %)
Finland	Germany (13,42 %)	Sweden (10,96 %)	Great Britain (10,33 %)
Denmark	Germany (21,67 %)	Sweden (9,90 %)	Great Britain (8,26 %)
Austria	Germany (38,10 %)	Italy (8,12 %)	Swiss (6,36 %)
Greece [2]	Germany (22,66 %)	Italy (14,51 %)	Great Britain (6,57 %)
Portugal	Germany (18,71 %)	France (14,72 %)	Spain (14,64 %)
Ireland	Great Britain (27,47 %)	Germany (14,10 %)	France (9,20 %)

[1] September 1994
[2] June 1994

Source: OECD (November 1995) Monthly Statistics of Foreign Trade

Table H.9: Political Economy of Coalition Building

Country	Votes	Share in EU-GDP in % (1993)	Share of EU Structural Funds Received (1993-98)
Germany	10	25.2	12.89
France	10	18.1	7.98
United Kingdom	10	16.5	6.45
Italy	10	17.1	12.94
Spain	8	8.7	25.55
Belgium	5	3.3	1.16
Greece	5	1.9	11.06
Netherlands	5	4.5	1.31
Portugal	5	2.0	11.02
Austria	4	2.6	1.01
Sweden	4	2.5	0.88
Denmark	3	1.7	0.48
Finland	3	1.3	1.06
Ireland	3	0.8	4.57
Luxembourg	2	0.2	0.05
Total	**87**	**100.0**	**100.0**

Appendix B: Problems with Estimating the Demand for Money

Monetary policy will face some short-run policy uncertainties in the EMU since the handling of the new set of instruments could cause technical problems - compounded by uncertainty about the demand for Euro money - as well as a credibility problem. The latter will be serious if the ECB set a strict short term inflation goal and then fails to achieve it.

Estimating the Demand for Money:

While traditional money demand theory has largely focused on the role of income and interest rates a refined modern approach in societies with high ratios of wealth to income must take into account both output and asset markets. In terms of a modified Fisher equation one would have to focus on:

$$M\,V = PY + p^{A} ø A \text{ or}$$

where p^{A}:= price of assets, P= price level of goods, ø =turnover rate of assets, A:=real stock of assets. With a stock market boom (or strong effects in asset market turnover volumes) in the EMU area it will be difficult to assess whether the ECB's monetary policy is expansive or contradictionary. *Field's (1984)* analysis for the US in the 1920s showed that transactions in the stock markets absorb about 1/5 of liquidity for an equal amount of nominal transaction volume in the goods markets.

Endnotes

1. High frequency (short run) explanatory variables included first the differences of the low-frequency determinants mentioned, in addition to a lagged dependent variable, quarterly inflation changes and proxies of the stance of fiscal and monetary policy.

2. More precisely, ß is the beta coefficient, defined as a 12 month moving average of the covariance between the ex post bond yield and the return on a domestic portfolio, divided by the variance of the ex post return on the domestic portfolio (including bonds and equities); in calculating the capital gains on domestic bonds an average effective duration of 6.5 years is assumed by the authors.

References

ADDISON, J.; WELFENS, P.J.J., eds. (1997), Labor Markets and Social Security in Europe, Heidelberg and New York: Springer (forthcoming).

AUDRETSCH, D. (1996), New Firms and Creating Employment, Paper presented at the international conference "European Labor Markets and Social Security (II)", EIIW, Potsdam, 04.04.1996.

BENDER, D. (1994), EWS-Bandbreitenerweiterung, Konvergenz und Währungsunion, in Hamburger Jahrbuch für Wirtschafts- und Gesellschaftspolitik, Vol. 40, 39-57.

BUCHANAN, J.M.; TULLOCK, G. (1962), The Calculus of Consent. Logical foundations of constitutional democracy, Ann Arbor: University of Michigan.

CALMFORS, L.; DRIFFILL, J. (1988), Bargaining Structure, Corporatism and Macroeconomic Performance, Economic Policy, Vol.3, 13-61.

DE GRAUWE, P. (1996), The Economics of Convergence: Towards Monetary Union in Europe, Weltwirtschaftliches Archiv, Vol. 136, 1-27.

DE HAAN, J.; STURM, J.E.; SIKKEN, B.J. (1996), Government Capital Formation: Explaining the Decline, Weltwirtschaftliches Archiv, Vol. 136, 55-74.

EUROPÄISCHE KOMMISSION (1996), Erster Kohäsionsbericht, Brüssel.

EUROPEAN COMMISSION (1994), Europa 2000+, Europäische Zusammenarbeit bei der Raumentwicklung, Brussels.

FIELD, A.J. (1984), A New Interpretation of the Onset of the Great Depression, Journal of Economic History, Vol.44, 489-498.

FITZENBERGER, B. (1995), Zentralisierungsgrad von Lohnverhandlungen und Lohnbildung in Ländern der Europäischen Union, in: Oberender, P. and M.E. Streit (eds.), Europas Arbeitsmärkte im Integrationsprozeß, Baden-Baden: Nomos, 77-112.

FITZENBERGER, B.; FRANZ, B. (1994), Dezentrale versus zentrale Lohnbildung in Europa: Theoretische Aspekte und empirische Evidenz, in: GAHLEN, B., HESSE, H. und RAMSER, H.J., Hg., Europäische Integrationsprobleme aus wirtschaftswissenschaftlicher Sicht, Tübingen: Mohr, 321-353.

FROOT, K.A.; STEIN, J.C. (1990), Exchange Rates and Foreign Direct Investment: An Imperfect Capital Markets Approach, Quarterly Journal of Economics, November, 1191-1217.

GARRETT, G.; WAY, C. (1995), The Sectoral Composition of Trade Unions, Corporatism, and Economic Performance, in: Eichengreen, B.; Frieden, J. and J. von Hagen, eds, Monetary and Fiscal Policy in an Integrated Europa, Heidelberg and New York: Springer.

IMF (1996), World Economic Outlook, May 1996.

ISSING, O. (1996), Europe: Political Union through Common Money?, Occasional Paper No. 89, London: Institute for Economic Affairs.

KENEN, P.B. (1995), Economic and Monetary Union in Europe. Moving Beyond Maastricht, Cambridge University Press.

KÖSTERS, W. (1995), Probleme der europäischen Währungsunion, Vortrag beim Institut für europäische Integrationsforschung, Bonn, 10.11.1995.

LANE, T. (1995), High Public Debt: Consequences for Investment and Growth, Paper presented at the international conference "Banking, International Capital Flows and Growth in Europe", EIIW, Potsdam, 12.-14.10.1995.

MASCARO, A.; MELTZER, A.H. (1993), Long- and short-term interest rates in a risky world, Journal of Monetary Economics, 12, 485-518.

McKINSEY (1996), Capital Productivity, Washington D.C.

NEUMANN, M.J.M. (1996), Geldpolitik und Stabilisierung, in: von HAGEN, J.; WELFENS, P.J.J.; BÖRSCH-SUPAN, A. (eds.), Springers Handbuch der Volkswirtschaftslehre, 2. Wirtschaftspolitik und Weltwirtschaft, Berlin et al.: Springer, 81-122.

ORR, A.; EDEY, M.; KENNEDY, M. (1995), The Determinants of Real Long-Term Interest Rates: 17 Country Pooled-Time-Series Evidence, OECD Working Papers, No. 155.

SCHWEICKERT, R. (1996), Harmonisierung versus institutioneller Wettbewerb, in: Maastricht II - Entwicklungschancen und Risiken der EU: Erweiterung, Vertiefung oder Stagnation, Beihefte der Konjunkturpolitik, No. 44, Berlin: DIW/Duncker & Humblot, 181-212.

WELFENS, P.J.J. (1994), Growth and Full Employment in the European Union, Discussion Paper No. 201, Westfälische Wilhelms-Universität, Münster.

WELFENS, P.J.J. (1996), European Monetary Integration, 3rd revised and enlarged edition, Heidelberg and New York: Springer.

WELFENS, P.J.J.; ADDISON, J.; AUDRETSCH, D.; GRUPP, H. (1997), Research and Development (R&D) Policy and Employment, Study for the European Parliament, DG IV, Luxembourg.

WELFENS, P.J.J.; WOLF, H., eds. (1997), Banking, International Capital Flows and Economic Growth, Heidelberg and New York: Springer (forthcoming).

Comments on: Political Economy of EMU and Stabilization Policy

Willem Molle

The paper by Welfens and Jungmittag (further abbreviated as W&J) is an interesting one. I would like to make two types of *preliminary remarks*. On the one side, the shiny side, one notes that the empirical work reported on in the first part of the paper is skillfully done and makes an important contribution to our understanding of an aspect of EMU. In the same vein one notes that the broad ranging political economy discussion of the second part of the paper gives some new insights in EMU and makes many interesting and creative suggestions for the design of policy both by the European institutions and by national governments. On the other side, the more shady side, one observes that the linkages between the two parts of the paper are not very clear and that the width of the political economy discussion implies a certain lack of focus of the paper in general and of the conclusions in particular.

A paper that addresses such a large spectrum of relevant questions invites reactions to a large number of questions too. I will restrict myself to a few comments on elements that in my personal view are particularly important in the whole debate on EMU.

My first major point is on the *fundamentals*. W&J present in their general introduction a list of the benefits and risks of the EMU. These are the ones that can in general be found back in all major textbooks now. However, the developments in preparing for EMU have made that we have passed that stage of the discussion. For understanding the present dynamics of monetary integration in Europe we have to look principally at some other aspects in more detail: in practice the behavior of political and corporate decision makers.

Most *politicians* think, that the main advantages of EMU are of a rather qualitative nature, and will appear only in the long run. Apparently politicians have considered that these benefits are so important that they should guide their short term actions. Quite some economist consider that this political decision does not stand up to scrutiny. However, before economists start sermonizing politicians on this point they might consider that the history of European integration suggest modesty instead of indignation. Indeed, in the past decades most important steps on the road to integration have been taken by statesmen at a moment that the economics profession was very divided on the best course to follow. Different schools had different views because of insufficiencies in the development of realistic theories, sufficient data bases and adequate research methods. During a recent conference on the lessons from 40 years of integration since the signing of the treaty of Rome I interrogated many key persons who had been involved in decisions on major advances in the EU integration process such as the customs union, the cohesion policy, the internal market etc. The question I asked was, "on what grounds have you taken your decision given so many warnings". The answer was invariably of the same kind: "because we believed in it". This is very akin to the answer you get from successful entrepreneurs, who had decided to launch a new product although their marketing specialist were divided as to its chances of success in the market. Often with hindsight economist have been able to prove why such decisions had been beneficial all the same.

As far as the *corporate sector* is concerned detailed studies by branch of activity have shown that the benefits of the EMU can be quantified in terms of direct savings on cost of transactions, hedging, bookkeeping and treasury management. For many branches, notably those trading internationally, the expected savings are so significant, that the one time cost of the change-over to the Euro will be earned back in two to three years. These earn-back periods are longer for the financial sector and the branches that trade mainly nationally like retail. On top of these direct benefits many firms expect important indirect benefits due to increased price transparency, lower capital cost, and a larger market. Although these benefits are less clear cut than the former category, they have in common that they shorten the pay-back periods for all branches. On the basis of such calculuses many firms have decided to get prepared as soon as possible for EMU and have started to invest in machines, software, communication and human capital (the same is true for many public institutions). These actors will be penalized for their long term views in case the project is canceled or delayed. These cost of the corporate sector increase with each additional investment that is now made.

My second major point is *employment*. All surveys show that the prime preoccupation of the European public and of politicians now is (un)employment (see for a substantiation of this point several issues of the Eurobarometer). W&J are right in their section 3.2 to stress that the (un)employment effects of EMU will be paramount in the public debate on EMU. Hence it is a task for the economist to clarify the issues involved. Let us see the *pros and cons*:

- On the pro side some argue that there is not much reason for concern. EMU will enhance competitiveness of European firms, this will stimulate growth, which in turn will have a positive effect on employment.
- On the con side others argue that EMU can have a negative effect due to several factors, the most important of which are :

1) Maastricht criteria force governments to pursue deflationary policies;

2) asymmetric shocks cannot be cushioned by national fiscal measures (and by definition no longer with exchange rate changes);

3) fairness principle brings countries to accept higher wages than justified on the basis of productivity;

4) enhanced competition among rules in the EU erodes the tax basis on mobile factors (capital) and increases the pressure on the immobile base (labor);

5) usual adaptation mechanisms such as migration and transfer payments do not provide a sufficient answer in the EU context.

I agree with much of the things W&J say about these issues. They rightly stress that realizing the positive effects and mitigating the negative effects is not only constrained by the lack of policy instruments but also by institutional factors.

So in order to cope as well as possible with the major problem of unemployment other policy solutions, not addressed in the W&J paper, need to be found. Labor market policies are obvious candidates. We discuss two groups in some detail.

Active labor market policies (ALMP). Active labor market policies are designed to improve the matching of workers to jobs and to keep the unemployed in contact with the labor market. They improve the prospects for poorly qualified job seekers by improving their skills. Given their nature, they are rather in the national than in the European domain. However, the EU can play an important role as well. The EU could stimulate countries to improve the effectiveness of their present ALMP's, which would improve flexibility, reduce hysteresis and enhance employability. The European Social Fund's rules could be adapted to give the EU a more effective instrument to stimulate member states to adapt their policies in this respect.

Reform of labor market institutions. One of the most important institutions in this respect (also mentioned in the W&J paper) is the wage bargaining process. We would like to add to the suggestions for adaptation of this institution made by W&J the reinforcement of the EU wide coordination in order to prevent wage setting detrimental to employment growth. Such coordination should be oriented towards behavioral changes of the most important actors (*Torsten, 1995; Grahl and Teague, 1992*). This can be done by the promotion of: 1) public discussion about the changed responsibility of economic agents in a new framework; 2) legal measures; for instance coordinated actions at EMU level to tax excessive wage increases; 3) an intensified social dialogue at the EU level, which could serve as a source of conventions (objective points of reference) for decentralized bargaining; 4) exchange of results of experiments about institutional and regulatory change in member states.

My last major point is on the rationale for *structural policies*. Improving cohesion is a task that the treaty bestows on the institutions of the EU. As I have outlined elsewhere (*Molle, 1997*), there are sound economic and social reasons for pursuing an EU cohesion policy. The creation of EMU makes that a number of adaptation mechanisms are no longer available to national governments to improve their position. This may lead to higher imbalances in the EU. Hence an increased need to keep an instrument for improving the cohesion. The present set up of transfers through the structural Funds is not very favorably judged by W &J in section 3.2. I can agree with much of their judgment. However, I feel that the proposals they make to improve the situation are insufficient. Improving the transparency and accountability on one hand and reducing the percentage aid in modulation with the wealth level will not increase enough the effectiveness and efficiency of the operations of the structural funds. In view of the increased need to make the best of scarce resources under tight EMU budget rules this is of primary importance. It presses even more if we consider that new partners will put forward their legitimate demands such as the CEECs.

My *proposals* for a reform of the Structural Funds go thus much further. Applying the principle of subsidiarity I plead for a considerable trimming of the system (see *Molle, 1997*). Indeed, I consider that the transfers to all regions in industrial decline and to rural development areas do not pass the subsidiarity test. Even some negative effects that might occur as a consequence of the creation of EMU would in my opinion not constitute a justification for the involvement of the EU. The structural adaptation of such regions should be a normal task of the member states. The EU would then only have to concentrate on two EU problems; and a fund might serve each of these objectives. The first Fund would be concentrated geographically and be active only in the major backward areas (limited to some 20 % of population for instance). The second Fund would concentrate its resources on project for the improvement of social problem groups in particular unemployed. Acknowledging the paramount importance of human capital, this Fund might then provide help in labor market adaptation in areas al over the EU that seem to be particularly affected by negative developments, including those stemming from the introduction of the Euro.

To conclude, many of the aspects of EMU addressed by W&J and their suggestions for the improvement of policy as many incentives for the discussion about the best way to frame the historical event that is the creation of the European Monetary Union. I have made my contribution to this discussion by picking up three of the points they had brought up. I think that many others will in a similar way be stimulated to discuss the propositions. If that happens, the W&J paper will have achieved its aim.

References

GRAHL, J.; TEAGUE P. (1992), Integration theory and European labour markets, British Journal of Industrial Relations, december, 515-527.

MOLLE, W.T.M. (1997), The Economics of European Integration, Theory, Practice, Policy (third revised edition), Dartmouth/Ashgate, Aldershot.

TORSTEN, P. (1995), European Monetary Union and Labour markets, What to expect? International Labour Review, Vol. 134.3, 315-332.

Panel I:
Necessary Amendments for a Functional EMU

Deficits, Debts and the Stability Pact

Stefan Collignon[1]

Twenty-seven months before the start of European Monetary Union (EMU), national efforts to meet convergence have already resulted in major achievements. Today, already 9 or 10 countries satisfy the criteria for inflation, interest and exchange rates. Despite these positive results, uncertainties remain about the EMU starting on schedule because of insufficient convergence with regard to the fiscal criteria. This view is not only wrong, but also dangerous. Due to inappropriate communication from authorities, financial markets may have renewed doubts about the timing of EMU and these speculative turbulences could then destroy the convergence results that have been already achieved. In order to prevent this unfavorable evolution, a credible stability pact is needed to strengthen popular and financial market confidence.

1. Margins of Interpretation for the Fiscal Criteria in the Maastricht Treaty

EMU will not necessarily have to fail because of the fiscal criteria. The Maastricht treaty clearly provides margins of interpretation for these criteria[2]. EMU can start even if the reference values of 3% and 60% are not achieved.

The public debate often ignores these reasonable margins of interpretation. The authorities wish to preclude the misrepresentation that the convergence criteria might be weakened in order to realize Monetary Union at all costs and that its principal objective, namely the creation of a stability community, may not be attained. To maintain public confidence in the stability of the Euro and the success of EMU, they insist on a strict and rigid application of the convergence criteria without mentioning the margins of interpretation. However, this approach is counterproductive by its radicalism. It must be emphasized, that interpreting the fiscal criteria, within the framework of the Maastricht Treaty, does not impose a threat to the Euro. The behavior in financial and exchange markets during the last few months clearly indicates that market agents expect a political decision for EMU and not a rigid adherence to the reference values. This is proven by long-term interest rates converging even in those countries where deficits and debts are still far away from the reference values provided that inflation rates are low and exchange rate stability is assured while reasonable, fiscal consolidation is pursued. The Netherlands, Austria, Belgium and France are examples of this. If rigid dogmatism gained the upper-hand, implying a rigid application of the reference values, confidence in financial markets would quickly be lost. This would be followed by speculative attacks against the D-Mark and other currencies.

Moreover, achieving the reference values of 3 percent and 60 percent for deficits and debt at a particular date does not guarantee fiscal discipline thereafter. On the other hand, exceeding the reference values does not threaten the stability of the Euro, if this is caused by a bad business cycle and provided that the other criteria are convincingly and durably met.

2. Reasons for the Difficulties of Fiscal Consolidation

Against widespread opinion, the difficulties some countries are facing in meeting the fiscal criteria can no longer be blamed on lax budgetary policies. The performance of the structural primary budget of all member states clearly shows the efforts already undertaken since the Maastricht Treaty was signed. The reason why the expected success has not been achieved yet, is often due to aggregate demand and the development of interest and growth rates. Therefore, the interaction of monetary, income and budgetary policies has to be taken into account[3] .

The current situation in Europe is peculiar. The monetary policy of the Deutsche Bundesbank dominates monetary policies in nearly all the other EU countries, although it is optimally designed for Germany. Yet, budget consolidation in some of the neighboring countries requires relaxing monetary policy beyond what is considered to be appropriate for Germany. This explains why France, Austria and Belgium, although far advanced in stability, have great difficulty in reducing their deficits. In France, for example, the structural deficit has been lowered significantly, while the economic recession has stabilized the observed deficit.

The external determination of monetary policies prevents the above mentioned countries from choosing the optimal policy-mix, which would be required to reduce the deficit significantly. From a demand management point of view it can be shown that German monetary policy leads to recessive and deflationary tendencies in the stability-oriented neighboring countries. This is especially dramatic in France.

The reduction of public deficits requires simultaneous reductions in interest levels below the levels set by the Bundesbank. In practice, this task is impossible given the fully integrated financial markets. In EMU, interest rates would be set by the ECB with a view to preserving price stability for the whole Euro area. The resulting demand effects are spread out over the whole Euro market area, once the exchange risk has disappeared. Monetary demand stimulation would allow countries in a recession growth, without inflationary side effects. In this regard, voices coming from countries with high deficits and low inflation requesting to start EMU at an earlier date are not surprising.

3. Confidence and Acceptance of EMU by the Population

The acceptance of EMU stands and falls with the credibility of its stability. For this reason, it should be pointed out in the public discussion that the success of EMU depends on the following:

- adequate application of the interpretation of the margins in the Maastricht Treaty so that EMU can start on time.
- Second, a convincing concept of how a stable Euro can be guaranteed in a stable growth environment after the start of Stage III.

The key to a convincing communication strategy is the stability pact which will reassure public opinion (requesting stability) and the financial markets (expecting a start of EMU in 1999).

Precautions guaranteeing budgetary discipline for the time after the introduction of the EMU are more convincing than a single qualifying condition for participation in EMU[4].

The Maastricht Treaty already provides some rules for budgetary policy. However, they are generally not thought to be sufficient.

4. The Stability Pact Suggested by the German Government

The perceived insufficiencies led to the idea of a stability pact proposed by Finance Minister Theo Waigel. The reference values for the deficit ratio of the EU-Treaty are to be tightened to 1 %, and automatic sanctions, including fines, are to be imposed.

The basic idea of this stability pact was well received. At the end of 1996 the European Council will adopt a final version. However, three points in the German proposal can be questioned. First, it does not sufficiently cover the increased necessities for monetary and fiscal co-operation between the independent ECB and the autonomous EU member states. Second, the exclusive insistence on budget discipline may prevent the needed flexibility when confronted with economic shocks. Finally, the automaticity of administrative fines is problematic.

The greater necessity for co-operation results from the fact that the independent ECB will set monetary data. This would have to be taken into account by each member country when elaborating its budgetary policy, if the stability of the economic and monetary Union is to be preserved in the long run. This necessity for co-operation does not question the principle of subsidiarity (art. 3 EC Treaty), but requires its practical implementation.

The differences in economic business cycles and their consequences for deficits also needs attention in order to avoid monetary and fiscal stability turning into employment instability. Empirical research has found evidence that the cyclical responsiveness of deficits is in some countries such as the Netherlands and Sweden is twice as high as in others such as Germany and France. Given the fact that cyclical shocks hit countries to different degrees, greater flexibility is required when fixing the criteria for excessive deficits (and not further tightening). This is provided that it is consistent with the primary objective of price stability. A successful stability pact requires an answer to this problem.

Automatic sanctions in the form of fines, in the case of excessive deficits after the criteria have been tightened, are hardly compatible with the principles of an open market economy with free competition (art. 3 of the EU-Treaty). They may even be counterproductive and politically problematic. In fact, if the proposed fines had already been applied in the past, half of the EC income would have been financed by fines - in some years even more (as can be seen from the enclosed graphs). Such a discriminatory tax cannot be justified in the long run. The fact that deficits depend not only upon parliaments and governments, but also upon structural and macroeconomic conditions minimizes the deterring effects of sanctions. A tightening of the reference values (from 3% to 1%) even reinforces these problems. A successful stability pact requires credible sanctions whenever the stability criteria are not met.

The European Commission has made suggestions of how to put the idea of a stability pact into secondary legislation attached to the Maastricht Treaty. The following proposal for a Pact for Stability and Co-operation is meant to provide additional "food for thought".

5. A Pact for Stability and Co-operation

The Pact for Stability and Co-operation could be viewed as an extension of the German stability pact. In essence, it provides a set of coherent rules for co-ordinating the ECB's monetary policy with the different national fiscal policies.

The pact must prevent the stability orientation of the ECB's policies being undermined by excessive debt increases. It also provides orientation marks for national fiscal policies to be set in accordance with the given monetary policy data. This must not only be achieved by sanctions and threats, but also by better co-ordination between the many national fiscal and the single monetary authorities. It therefore implies a link between art. 103 and 104c of the EU Treaty.

Refining the multilateral surveillance mechanism (art. 103), as suggested by the Commission, could be used to optimize the mix of monetary and fiscal policies, while taking into account national specifics when defining norms for excessive deficits. This could be reached by the following steps:

To assure long-run price stability for the Euro *after* the start of Stage III, but not before, the sustainability of debt levels below 60% should be the primary criterion, and the deficit criteria should be a derived reference value.

Once a country exceeds the limits of the debt to GDP ratio of 60% either when entering the EMU or because of a serious recession afterwards, its government commits itself (under the procedure of Art. 103) to bringing the ratio back to the norm over a period that is agreed. The normative deficit ratio will be modified accordingly.

This concept, designed to prevent excessive fiscal deficits, has the advantage of taking national differences into account. Without threatening the stability of the Euro, national budget policies can be set with reference to national economic performances. Consequently, the upper limit for deficits would no longer have to be rigidly fixed for all member states. Instead, national deficit ratios can be flexibly calculated on the basis of national requirements.

For the calculation of the normative deficit[5], one would use the normative inflation rate set by the ECB for the whole Union as well as the respective national growth rates of productive potentials[6]. These variables will also be used by the ECB when determining its monetary targets. This allows countries with high growth rates to run higher deficits without affecting the debt to GDP ratio. Countries with low growth prospects will not be able to destabilize monetary policy. The formula also indirectly takes into consideration the requests from the European Parliament and countries aiming at catching-up in living, standards according to which deficits for investment purposes are to be treated differently from those for financing current expenditures.

Thus, fiscal policy has to be adjusted to the monetary policy set by the ECB. But it obtains additional room to manoeuvre from the different growth potentials. Based on data from the European Commission, the proposed formula leads to an annual average deficit of 2.7%, for the EU as a whole, but it provides greater margins for states with higher growth rates such as Ireland which is allowed 4%. However, for countries expecting lower growth rates like Greece the allowed normative deficit is correspondingly less (1,8%)[7] which is necessary in order to maintain a sustainable debt to GDP ratio. This fiscal policy rule is compatible with the idea of aiming at a medium term balanced budget in member states, given that the *EU deficit for the community as a whole does not exceed the 3% limit.*

The flexibility in the fiscal policy rule allows enough room for national peculiarities, without undermining the overall stability orientation of the European currency. Therefore, it expresses the principle of subsidiarity in the co-ordination of monetary and fiscal policy.

6. Institutional and Juridical Foundations of the Pact for Stability and Cooperation

Determining and surveying the so-defined maximum deficit limits should be the task of a Stability Council where representatives of the ECB and the European Commission make decisions jointly, based on the shortened procedures regarding article 103 and 104c, as proposed by the Commission. The Stability Council would also have to ensure the coherence between monetary and fiscal policies in EMU.

The Pact for Stability and Cooperation could be joined to the Protocols of the Maastricht Treaty by a unanimous decision in the European Council. This is in accordance with the Treaty[8] and would avoid the difficult procedure of changing the Treaty, which would require new ratification. Provided all countries sign the new protocol, the Pact for Stability and Co-operation is likely to support the convergence of countries with a temporary derogation by fine-tuning the fiscal co-ordination between countries with the stability orientation of the ECB.

In case a unanimous agreement were not forthcoming, the Pact should become a "Gentlemen's agreement". Countries not willing to sign up should not be allowed to make use of the interpretative margins in the Treaty's article 104c. After the start of EMU, they should submit to the valid rules that currently exist to avoid excessive deficits in the most rigid way.

7. Measures when Deficits Exceed the Stipulated Reference Values

When the government deficit of a country exceeds the reference values, the shortened procedures regarding the avoidance of excessive deficits as proposed by the Commission come into play. If a member state fails to comply with the recommendations of the Council, sanctions will be applied. In addition to the administrative fines which were suggested by Germany and have been fine-tuned by the Commission, a market-oriented sanction mechanism could be proposed which would strengthen the disciplining effects by financial markets. The Maastricht Treaty envisaged market sanctions by setting the „No-Bail-Out Rule“. Today, this seems insufficient, given that the solvency risk on European government debt is fortunately very low. However, the market mechanism could be reinforced by adding a liquidity premium to excessive government debt.

At the center of the proposition stands a rule whereby the European System of Central Banks refuses to accept paper issued by governments with excessive deficits as collateral for obtaining central bank liquidity. Such a rule should be clear, obligatory and free of any political bargain, so that it can be anticipated by market participants.

This rule would create a liquidity risk for such paper, requiring a risk premium which is effectively a penalty interest rate. Consequently, governments with excessive deficits have to take measures to regain the trust of investors in order to raise the necessary finances. The rising risk premium increases therefore the pressure on governments with excessive deficits to return to stability. Thus, the disciplining effect exerted by financial markets would be strengthened and national governments would be forced to reconsider their budget policies.

This proposal has greater compatibility with the principle of an open market economy with free competition than with the quasi-tax of automatic sanctions currently being discussed with respect to the stability pact. It is, however, complementary to the proposals made by Germany and the Commission and not an exclusive alternative. Realization could prevent inflexible and high penalties resulting from a stability pact affecting public opinion negatively. The rules which have been proposed here would not require a modification of the Treaty, for they are technical measures taken by the independent ECB in order to maintain price stability.

Figure P.1: Penalties Proposed by Germany

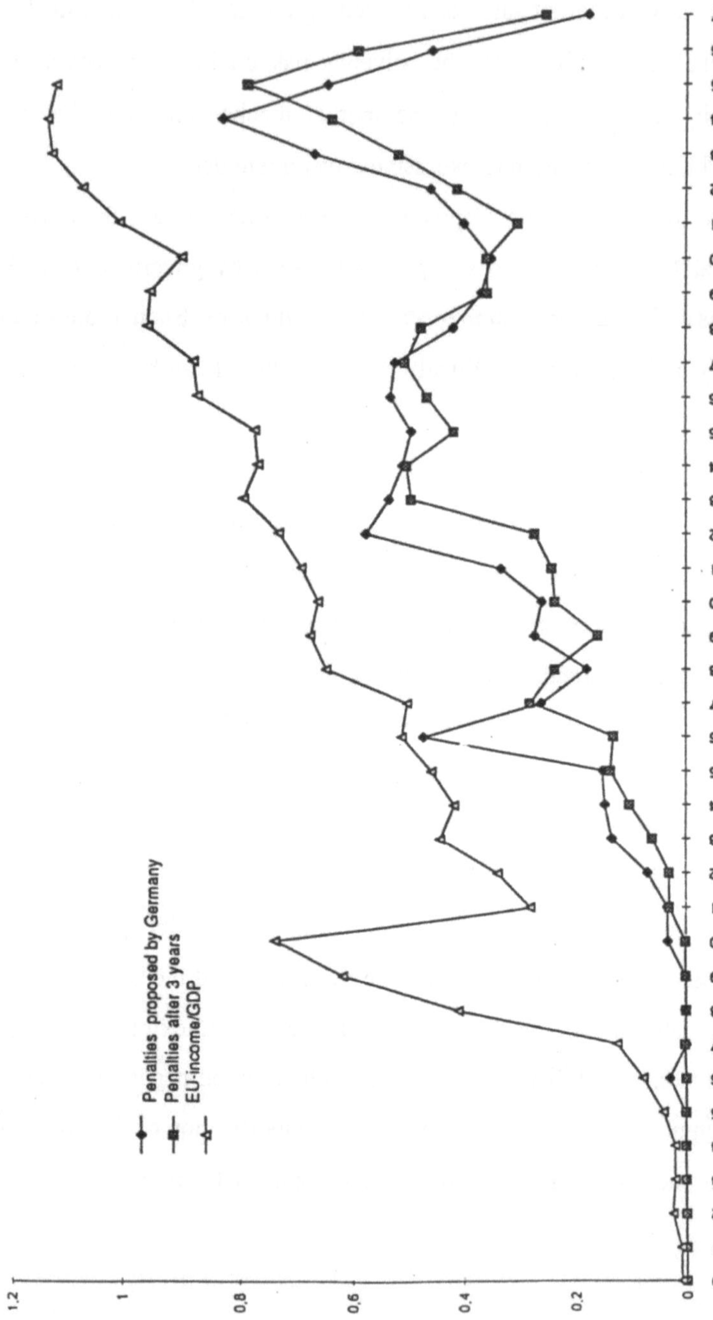

Table P.1: Calculation of the Normative Deficit Ratio

Scenari assuming different growth rates[1]				Growth rate[2] average 1990-97		0.5% higher growth rate[3]		1% higher growth rate[4]	
	Debt/GDP ratio 1995	Growth rate average 1990-97[5]	Normative rate of inflation	Normative deficit[6]	Maximum normative deficit[7]	Normative deficit	Maximum normative deficit	Normative deficit	Maximum normative deficit
B	134.4	2.0	2	2.4	2.1	2.7	2.3	3.0	2.6
DK	73.6	2.2	2	2.5	2.5	2.8	2.8	3.1	3.1
WD	58.8	2.6	2	2.7	2.7	3.0	3.0	3.3	3.3
D	58.8	2.7	2	2.8	2.8	3.1	3.1	3.4	3.4
GR	114.4	1.4	2	1.8	1.8	2.4	2.1	2.7	2.4
E	64.8	2.6	2	2.7	2.7	3.0	3.0	3.3	3.3
F	51.5	2.0	2	2.4	2.4	2.7	2.7	3.0	3.0
IRL	85.9	5.0	2	4.2	4.0	4.5	4.3	4.8	4.6
I	124.9	2.0	2	2.4	2.1	2.7	2.4	3.0	2.6
L	6.3	3.0	2	3.0	3.0	3.3	3.3	3.6	3.6
NL	78.4	2.5	2	2.7	2.6	3.0	2.9	3.3	3.2
A	68.0	2.5	2	2.7	2.7	3.0	3.0	3.3	3.2
P	70.5	2.3	2	2.6	2.5	2.9	2.8	3.2	3.1
SF	63.2	1.6	2	2.1	2.1	2.4	2.4	2.7	2.7
S	81.4	1.4	2	2.1	2.0	2.4	2.3	2.7	2.6
UK	52.5	2.1	2	2.5	2.5	2.8	2.8	3.1	3.1
EUR15-	71.0	2.2	2	2.5	2.5	2.8	2.8	3.1	3.1
EUR15+	71.0	2.3	2	2.6	2.5	2.9	2.8	3.2	3.1

Notes: 1. growth rate of productive potentials; 2. based on values of the second column: growth rate, average 1990-97; 3. assuming second column plus 0.5%; 4. assuming second column plus 1%; 5. data from the European Commission; 6. given by: $x=(\pi+y)\times 60\%$; 7. given by $x^*=(\pi+y)\times d_{t-1}-z^*$; in which d_{t-1} refers to the debt/GDP ratio in 1995 and z^* to the annual reduction of the debt/GDP ratio assuming that the 60% ratio will be achieved after 10 years.

Endnotes

1. This memo is a summary of the forthcoming book by Stefan Collignon (October 1996): Geldwertstabilität für Europa. Die EWU auf dem Prüfstand; Gütersloh, Bertelsmann; as well as the underlying study by Stefan Collignon (April 1996): Defizite, Schulden und die Europäische Währungsunion, Paris, AUME.

2. Compare article 104c of the Maastricht Treaty as well as the Protocol on the Excessive Deficit Procedure.

3. For details see endnote 1.

4. One should also take care that when making some formulations in the Treaty more explicitly defined (e.g. the meaning of words like "exceptional" or "temporary") one does not tie one's hands for the final interpretation.

5. The equation to calculate the normative deficit x (in percentage of GDP) is the following:
a) if the country has a debt/GDP less than 60% it is:

$$x_t = (\pi + y) \times 60\%$$

in which π refers to the inflation rate (e.g. 2%) chosen by the ECB, and y to the growth rate of productive potential (see following note).
b) if it exceeds 60% it is adjusted in the following way:
- first, one will agree over which period the debt/GDP ratio d_{t-1} has to be reduced to 60%
- secondly, the admissible normative deficit is reduced below the amount calculated under a) in accordance to the following formula:

$$x^* = (\pi + y)d_{t-1} - z^*,$$

in which z^* refers to the annual reduction of the debt/GDP ratio.

6. Productive potential reflects national income growth that is compatible with full employment and price stability. It is commonly used for medium term monetary policy targets.

7. See table enclosed.

8. Art. 104c, § 14.

Preparing for EMU

Robert Raymond

1. The project of European Economic and Monetary Union (EMU) gained greater credibility at the Madrid summit in mid-December 1995. The political commitment to adopt the single currency, named the Euro, on 1 January 1999 was confirmed.

This does not mean that all the difficulties have been overcome. One of these is clearly the insufficient preparation of public opinion. This will make it necessary to improve the acceptability of the project.

We know, for instance, that German citizens are proud of the Deutsche Mark and are reluctant to see it replaced by the Euro. They have very good reasons, since the Deutsche Mark has been a stable currency for so long. Stable means that, as an average, the rate of inflation in Germany has been low and has not deviated very significantly from this low average percentage. One has to remember that Germany was seriously marked by the hyper-inflation which prevailed after the First World War and whose resurgence was feared after the Second World War. Added to this distant memory are the more recent experiences of Latin America and even Europe following the oil crises.

However, it should be realized in Germany that the purpose of EMU is not to abandon the Deutsche Mark or to eliminate it, but only to extend its use, under a new name, to a broader geographical area.

Germany succeeded in exporting its culture of stability to the advantage of both its neighbors and itself because it could only benefit from a more sound and stable environment. The lesson has been learnt. At least ten out of fifteen European Union countries fulfill the convergence criterion on inflation. Aversion to inflation is widespread. In most of our countries there are plans to make the central bank more independent. The Maastricht Treaty reinforces the appropriate harmonization efforts. This development promises interest rate cuts and, in particular, a reduction in risk premia vis-à-vis the Deutsche Mark (i.e. lower interest rate differentials vis-à-vis Germany). Moreover, central banks are being made independent from political influence.

This, and the realization of a large and fully integrated market, can only help to improve growth, although it will clearly not per se resolve other structural weaknesses in Europe.

2. We also know that member countries are working very hard to improve convergence in the fiscal field. Progress is being made more or less everywhere. There is a universal awareness that waiting longer would only aggravate the problem and make fiscal consolidation more difficult at a later stage. This, independently from the wording of the Treaty, calls for immediate improvement of the budgetary position and for the reform of social transfer schemes.

In Verona, it was clear that there is full consensus on the principle, of a stability pact among member countries in Stage Three. This will in particular ensure that no free rider will allow its fiscal situation to deteriorate significantly after joining the Euro area.

Finally, appropriate measures are being studied to ensure that no excessive tensions will arise, in particular on the foreign exchange market, between participating and non-participating countries.

3. Third, I should like to emphasize that banks and public administrations have launched projects to review their internal organizations and to see how they could adapt themselves to the new procedures to be applied at the beginning of Stage Three.

A monetary law is under preparation to make the Euro the sole legal currency among the countries which are on the list of initial participants. During a transition period of, at most, three years, existing bank notes will continue to be used. Retail operations such as consumer payments, accounts of households and small or relatively small businesses, relations between the national administrations and the public should continue to be effected in the former national denominations. More generally, the use of the Euro during this transition period will be neither compulsory nor prohibited.

However, various provisions will favor the use of the Euro from the beginning of 1999 in some areas.

It has been decided that, from the first day of Monetary Union in 1999, the accounts of credit institutions held at the central banks will be denominated in Euro. Nevertheless, these central banks will provide their correspondents which are as yet unable to include Euro in their accounting systems with a "courtesy translation" into the customary national currency.

The ESCB will provide the financial community with a real-time funds transfer system for the whole monetary zone, which will be capable of transferring the Euro.

Finally, from January 1999 onwards, government debt instruments will be denominated in Euro, at least those which are actively traded on the markets.

These measures, should induce the capital and exchange markets to use the Euro very quickly, unlike retail operations, which will not do so until later.

This project can only be brought to a successful conclusion if the efforts needed are undertaken in timely fashion. This is why it requires the agreement and participation of all concerned.

Doctrinal Amendments for a Functional EMU ?

A Few Reminiscences of Economic History

Michèle Schmiegelow

Current discussions about the amendments and additions to the EMU part of the Maastricht Treaty focus on the institutional framework. The necessity and timeliness of this focus is suggested by the comparative ease with which agreement on some important issues was reached in late 1995 and early 1996. The large degree of approval won by Finance Minister Theo Waigel for his proposal of a stability pact is one case in point. Another is the swift adoption of the Verona agreement on the relation between the "ins" and the "outs". A third, and perhaps the most important, is the apparent consensus in the currency and bond markets on the scenario of a flexible interpretation of the debt criteria of the Maastricht Treaty in early 1998 combined with a continued firm commitment of EMU members to these criteria after 1999.

Yet though, necessary as the institutional focus evidently is, I am concerned that it may not be sufficient. Sweeping changes under way in the world economy and increasingly acrimonious debates between monetarists, post-Keynesians, post-Schumpeterians, location theorists, managed trade advocates, and new growth theorists suggest that in order to safeguard the EMU project we may have to develop a doctrinal focus as well. In other words, we have to ask ourselves whether the economic model underlying the Maastricht Treaty can continue to serve as a doctrinal underpinning for the implementation phase of the EMU project.

The daily tug-of-war in the currency markets between traders following flow analysis and traders following stock analysis in the theory of exchange rate determination is just one striking example of how directly doctrinal alignments can shape currency (mis-) alignments. As long as dogmatic stalemate prevails, exchange rates are in equilibrium or moved by other factors. But whenever major doctrinal conversions occur, such as the global spread of monetarism in the 1970s or the pragmatic "heresies" of the Federal Reserve and the Treasury in the US since 1985, massive shifts in exchange rate relations follow. The September 1992 ERM crisis may be put in a nutshell as a triumph of the spirit of Anglo-Saxon economic policy pragmatism against a half-hearted British conversion to the Bundesbank model of monetarism.

Some may argue that monetarism, the school of thought which advocates floating exchange rates as the safest way to the recovery of national autonomy in economic policy, was never predestined to serve as a doctrinal "superstructure" for a currency union. But, of course, the currency union may approximate the case of a national economy through convergence and its currency may float against other currencies just as well as that of a national economy. Whisperings about mental reservations of the Bundesbank against EMU can thus safely be ignored, and they indeed seem to be ignored where it matters, i.e. in the currency markets.

After all, the EMU part of the Maastricht Treaty was inspired by the Bundesbank and this is precisely why Anglo-Saxon economists of post-Keynesian persuasion are skeptical about it. They share the monetarist preference for national economic independence, but, of course, they would use economic policy independence for other targets and instruments than monetarists.

Yet, another great doctrinal shift may well be under way. It is suggested by a fundamental change in the world economy. It may weaken both monetarism on the European continent and post-Keynesian opposition to EMU in the UK. Both stock analysts and flow analysts among currency traders have an equally tough problem to solve, if they happen to be short on the Dollar. Among currency and bond market participants focusing on Europe, the changed environment was first perceived in April 1996 as the "German weakness" facilitated European economic convergence. Changing perceptions translated into DM depreciation towards both the Dollar and other European currencies, declining interest rates across Europe and declining risk premia for French Francs, Italian Lira and Spanish Peseta.

The Bundesbank itself helped by a superbly executed package of interest rate reductions on April 18, 1996, reducing the discount rate to a historic low of 2,5 %. It kept expectations of further cuts alive by leaving the money market repurchase rate unchanged. The evident message to the markets was that the Bundesbank cared, after all, about rising unemployment in Germany and the plight of the German export sector under conditions of relentless DM appreciation driven by perceptions in the monetary economy rather than the real economy. Hans Tietmeyer even turned to correcting the Dollar undervaluation of 1995/1996 by applying the same "rhetorical" methods with similar pragmatism as a decade earlier. This was used by James Baker against Dollar overvaluation at the time of the Plaza agreement. Most extraordinarily, all this happened in spite of increased money supply figures. At least to the foreign exchange markets, it looked like an "amendment" to Bundesbank monetarism.

The fundamental change which suddenly seemed to make all this possible without much dogmatic hesitation is, I submit, the global shift from an inflationary to a deflationary environment. Three text book causes of deflation come together in this shift: technological change, wage competition and forced debt reductions. Each of these causes of deflation can be traced back to a period when they attracted the least attention because of overriding concern for inflation, i.e. the 1970s. At that time, post-Schumpeterians could have noticed the take-off of the micro-electronic revolution in the form of Japanese mass production of memory chips and numerical controls in all kinds of products [1]. Part of the structural unemployment that emerged in the 1970s can be analysed as the first, price-cutting and job-killing, phase of technical innovation. While the second, job-creating, phase of the new information technology seems to have long begun since then in the US, technical change is still recognized as the most important cause of mass unemployment in Europe today. One may, or may not, believe in Kondratieff cycles, but Europe's current deflation is strongly reminiscent of historical patterns of the deflationary beginning of a "long wave".

The resulting unemployment is feeding the second type of deflation: wage restraint or decline resulting in price declines from the supply and the demand side alike. The potential of wage competition is amplified by the integration of the former East with its huge labor supply into the world economy. The more sweeping conclusions of the theory of wage equalization are rightly contested (*Bhagwati and Dehejia, 1994*). But that there is no downward pressure on European wages from low cost foreign locations or mobile low cost labor would be difficult to sustain.

Under these conditions, Post-Keynesians may instinctively tend to advocate closing the borders to immigrant labor and "exporting unemployment" through competitive currency devaluation. The problem is that all European countries with post-Keynesian economic cultures are in the same position and the memories of the 1930s are not exactly attractive. Moreover, they may have a hard time competing individually against Dollar depreciations. The Dollar depreciations of the 1990's were certainly not US Treasury policy, although the US Department of Commerce may have welcomed them as a background pressure to its managed trade policies towards Japan. More importantly, though, as Charles Kindleberger has had the merit to make plain (*Kindleberger, 1995*), US banks and US multinationals liked it. US Banks that derived increased portions of their profits from dealing in currencies liked the volatility resulting from philosophical divergences between the monetarism of the Bundesbank and the Bank of Japan (under Mieno) on the one hand and the new pragmatism of the Federal Reserve as well as the Post-Keynesianism of the Bank of England on the other hand. US multinationals welcomed a depreciating Dollar on two accounts: it helped their exports from the US to non-Dollar markets *and* it inflated the income earned from investments abroad in their US balance sheets. Together, the Dollar bears among US banks and US multinationals command for bigger flows of funds than any national government or central bank in Europe or Asia. The only way left for exchange rate policy to succeed against prevailing market perceptions is to co-ordinate action internationally (*Schmiegelow, M., 1995*).

It took German and Japanese industries and central banks quite some time to become aware of the dynamics of this market pattern. When the perception finally came through in 1995, it triggered two remarkable policy changes that, in turn, took the markets by surprise. The first was the co-ordinated intervention of the Federal Reserve, the Bank of Japan and the Bundesbank in the foreign exchange markets in July/August of 1995 that brought the Dollar back from 1,38 DM to 1, 49 DM. The second was the new German consensus that EMU was not only a political target but also an instrument to avoid the economic disruption of the currency volatility inevitable in a multi-currency area in which the currency of one small and open economy, such as the German economy, plays the anchor role.

Monetarists may instinctively think of the opposite exchange rate policy, i.e. "import of wealth" through competitive currency appreciation[2]. In the past, this policy had proven strikingly successful, as initial losses of price competitiveness were subsequently neutralized by higher rates of inflation in countries with depreciating currencies. Of course, this was precisely the policy that the markets perceived, rightly or wrongly, to be the Bundesbank philosophy in the past. The markets gladly obliged by continuously bidding up the DM. The problem for monetarists today is that rates of inflation are down in all industrial countries for very similar reasons. In a way, the proximate cause of monetarist thought in economic history, i.e. the inflation of the 1970s, seems to be gone for much more than the duration of a Keynesian cycle in many more than just one or another national economy. Alexandre Lamfalussy draws a bold conclusion: the good reasons for a regime of floating exchange rates are gone as well[3]. We are back to Friedrich von Hayek's 1935 plea against monetary nationalism. The country trying to go it alone on exchange rates and levels of liquidity will pay for the divergence from the rest of the world by either inflation or deflation depending on the direction of the divergence (*von Hayek, 1964*).

The third type of deflation, which is a particular European problem, supports the case against floating rates, at least within Europe, as it offers an "instrumental" argument for EMU. Indeed, the pressure of public debt is common to most of the prospective EMU members. In the interest of its own national fiscal health, each of the EU members is well advised to do its best to meet the Maastricht criteria on debt and deficit levels. Debt reduction is the target of the policy, convergence a secondary result, a welcome cause for EMU.

Another secondary result is debt-deflation, which is less welcome when it goes beyond the degree of beneficial disinflation. In this context, another historical reminiscence is helpful. In the 1930s, Irving Fisher offered a remedy for the debt-deflation of his time: monetary easing as a way to support growth under conditions of fiscal tightening (*Fisher, 1933*). It is the opposite of the standard monetarist policy-mix, if for a moment we may speak of a policy-"mix" in monetarism. The recent changes of perception and action among market participants and policy-makers suggest that Irving Fisher's lesson is remembered. Targets as well as instruments of economic policy are obviously in the process of changing.

To sum up, the shift from an inflationary to a deflationary environment has perhaps not yet led to a full-fletched doctrinal conversion in all countries concerned. But it has certainly triggered a remobilization of the theory of economic policy. To be sure, by assigning monetary policy to the exclusive target of low inflation, the monetarists did follow Jan Tinbergen's and Robert Mundell's advice not to use one instrument for more than one target (*Tinbergen, 1956,* and *Mundell, 1962*). However, they did so at the cost of leaving the target of full employment unattended. Moreover, after the 1970s, mounting fiscal debts across Europe took away the only instrument left to governments of Keynesian persuasion: to fight unemployment with fiscal means. To recover the potential for fiscal stimulus in the future, debt levels and deficits have first to be reduced as prescribed by the Maastricht criteria. To soften debt deflation, monetarists would have to relinquish the instrument of monetary policy for post-Keynesian uses, as it were. In this way, we would recover a Tinbergian "two-targets-two-instruments" policy-mix with reversed roles. If such a pragmatic opening-up of the two dogmatic mainstreams on the European continent were to occur, it would certainly help to make EMU more functional, exchange-rate relations less volatile and the international monetary system more balanced.

Endnotes

1. See for a discussion of this case in terms of Schumpeterian economics and Tinbergian theory of economic policy *Schmiegelow, M. and Schmiegelow, H. (1989).*

2. For a comparison of the targets and instruments associated with competitive currency undervaluations and overvalutions, see *Schmiegelow, H. (1986).*

3. In an interview with the German weekly magazine Wirtschaftswoche No 9 (February 22, 1996, 14 f).

References

BHAGWATI, J.; DEHEIJA, V. (1994), Trade and Wages, Washington: American Enterprise Institute.

FISHER, I. (1933), The Debt Deflation Theory of Great Depressions, in: Econometrics, Vol. 1, No. 4, (October 1933).

HAYEK, F. v. (1964), Monetary Nationalism and International Stability, New York: Kelley, 51ff.

KINDLEBERGER, C. (1995), Dollar Darkness, in: The International Economy, May/June 1995, 6-9.

MUNDELL, R. (1962), The Appropriate Use of Monetary and Fiscal Policy for Internal and External Stability, IMF Staff Papars IX (March 1962), 70-76.

SCHMIEGELOW, H. (1986), Japan's Exchange Rate Policy: Policy Targets, Non-Policy Variables, and Discretionary Adjustment, in: Schmiegelow, M. (ed.) Japan's Response to Crisis and Change in the World Economy, Armonk: Sharpe, 1986, 29-31.

SCHMIEGELOW, M. (1995), Shiba Shinwa o Kutsugaeshita Nichibeidoku no Kawase Seisaku Kyocho (The shattering of market myth: recent coordination of exchange rate policy between Japan, the US and Germany), Toyo Keizai Shukan (Tokyo), September 9, 1995, 22-25.

SCHMIEGELOW, M.; SCHMIEGELOW, H. (1989), Strategic Pragmatism: Japanese Lessons in the Use of Economic Theory, New York: Praeger.

TINBERGEN, J. (1956), Economic Policy, Principles and Design, Amsterdam: North Holland, 1956, 196-209.

Panel II:

European Monetary Union from a German Perspective

Compromise Should not Undermine the Credibility of the Euro Currency

Hans Jäckel

By now, there is a general perception of an inherent conflict among the three goals for a common European currency. They are as follows: Sticking to the beginning of 1999 as a start date, the strict fulfillment of the convergence criteria and the large number of participants involved. The question of where to compromise will have to be decided on a political level. It is, however, certainly useful to remember that the three goals have different justifications.

1. Three Goals with Different Justifications

The goal to stick to the 1999 start date is based on legal and political criteria. The Treaty is binding in terms of international law. The option to change the Treaty unanimously with regards to the start date has so far been categorically ruled out and would be considered a full change to the official Treaty. It is said that such a move would trigger calls for other major changes and undermine the Treaty as a whole. This would endanger the start of the currency union since such negotiations would require great political energies in order to reach a compromise. Such arguments should be taken seriously. From an economic point of view, it is unclear why an exact start date has such a high priority. It is clear that Europe needs a currency union, as early as possible, but not at any price.

The goal to involve a large group of countries into the initial currency union is natural. A small currency union with six or seven countries would not fully exploit the possible transaction costs savings and other potential benefits would not be utilized. Against this background, a small currency union would only be a temporary solution which could give new momentum to the process of currency integration. This would facilitate and accelerate the integration of non-member countries at a later date.

The choice of the convergence criteria is rather arbitrary in its quantitative requirements. However, one should welcome the initiatives from policy makers to include economic conditions in the Treaty as a basis for a functional currency union without friction, particularly the requirements for a stability oriented fiscal policy. If such requirements are not stated with some degree of arbitrariness, this does not mean that they should be dropped altogether.

2. Can Fiscal Policy Convergence Criteria be Interpreted?

For decades, the scientific evaluation of fiscal policies in the context of macroeconomic effects has been a core field of discussion among economic advisors. Taking into account buzz words in economic literature, such as "cyclical impulse", "structural deficits", "required consolidations" etc., one may view the two fiscal policy criteria (3% for the deficit/GDP ratio and 60% for the debt/deficit ratio) from the Maastricht Treaty as rather simplistic. However, economic science does not offer a consensus analysis to the requirements for a fiscal policy that is compatible with stability. It is quite clear that policy makers prefer some arbitrary limit values, instead of relying on sophisticated concepts which have no broad consensus in economics.

The proposal to interpret the public deficit limit, i.e., 3% of GDP, as the structural or cyclical deficit limit, is reasonable. It would be most regrettable if the immense challenge of forming a currency union failed because of a recession in the EU countries prior to the start date. However, to treat this issue lightly might be interpreted as an excuse for a watering-down of the convergence criteria. It is not yet clear whether the structural deficits in 1997 (regardless of the measurement concepts) will be as far below the actual deficit figures as they were in some countries in 1995 and 1996. While growth may be slow currently in Europe, there is no reason to assume a recession will take place in 1997.

Possibly the strongest argument for the strict criteria is quite different from the previous arguments. Economic policy makers, especially in Germany including the Bundesbank, have stipulated a strict application of the criteria for many years. This has created a strong perception that only through the strict application of the criteria will monetary union create a sense of stability. This perception is held not only by a big part of the German population, but also by the financial markets. The criteria have really been set. A weakening of the criteria requirements would help to undermine the credibility and acceptance of the Euro currency by both the general population and international financial markets. The new currency would get off to a poor start if its credibility and acceptance were not ensured both inside and outside of currency union.

3. Postponement is Ruled out for Political Reasons

If no political and legal obstacles existed, it would be advantageous to postpone the starting date of EMU. The schedule for the monetary union reveals time pressure in a lot of areas. For example the question in which year and on which economic data the convergence criteria will be evaluated could have been discussed in a more relaxed manner, if there had been enough time to examine the fiscal policy of the candidates thoroughly over several years and with a broad variety of indicators. The result of such an review procedure could have created more confidence than the planned examination on a qualifying date.

It is a regrettable but an often observed fact that big and unpopular political plans can be realized more easily in times of crises than in calm periods. The current steps to consolidate the federal budget in Germany confirm this opinion. Under these circumstances, the ideal way into a currency union (as well as ideal consolidation policies) has to be neglected if the begun process is not to lose its momentum.

4. The Remaining Chances for a Credible Constellation

The will to compromise will cease if a timely realization of EMU with the countries recognized as the core members (besides Germany, France and the Benelux-countries Austria and Ireland are possible candidates) is only feasible by giving-up the strict application of the convergence criteria. Especially if a softening of the rules reaches an extent to where it not only jeopardizes the interests of Germany but also the credibility of the currency and the functioning of the currency union as a whole.

Today it is by no means certain that the trilemma will destroy the whole project. If the economy recovers, which current economic figures are revealing, and if governments continue to consolidate their budgets then there is a good chance to realize EMU. This holds true even if some countries slightly exceed the 3%-limit for the budget deficit in 1997, as long as these countries have some economic justifications for it.

EMU: A German Viewpoint

Heinrich Matthes[1]

1. Europe is marked by great tensions between its economic and currency areas (*Predöhl, 1971*). The European economic area, one of the cornerstones of what is fundamentally still a tricentric world economy, is divided into numerous nationally defined currency areas. In Europe this leads to sharp deviations from the optimum spatial situation such as exists, for example, in the United States whose economic area is not subdivided by many national borders with disintegrating effects. Thus there are still fourteen currencies in the European Union alone. In practical terms this means that substitutive core internal trade in Europe, which accounts for some two thirds of cross-frontier European "foreign trade", cannot be organized according to purely economic, spatial laws. For Europe, compared with the United States (and also Japan), this entails the continuation of many barriers to trade and, accordingly, a less than optimum division of labor. The corresponding costs have been estimated by the Commission to be equivalent to 3 to 5% of European national product (Cecchini Report). What is at stake here, given the completion of the internal market, is:

(a) a significant cost reduction because firms can produce for wider sales areas through economies of scale,

(b) increased efficiency in firms, not least because of a rationalization of the industrial structure as a result of more competitive markets,

c) a division of labor between firms that is closer to the optimum situation as a result of a better utilization of comparative cost advantages, and

(d) greater market dynamism and stemming from this, more innovation.

If the internal market has a single currency, additional benefits will accrue: the complete abolition of transaction costs, maximum price transparency, further financial returns to scale and - last but not least - maximum credibility because of the irrevocability of exchange rates. Monetary union therefore comprehensively diminishes the uncertainties associated with investment. This reduces the minimum return on capital and increases the capital stock and output. Finally, a single European currency will have considerable external advantages: it will end the dominant monetary role played by the United States. Underpinned by the spatial potential of Europe, the Euro, which will be the future No. 2 reserve currency alongside the Dollar and the Yen, could withstand turbulence on financial markets much better than any individual European currency.

2. Therefore, the integration task facing Europe is to create the kind of optimum conditions for the basically single European economic area - two thirds of whose foreign trade is accounted for by core internal trade - which the United States, for example, as a single economic area using one currency has never lost. Under the liberal gold standard arrangements, such ideal conditions had more or less already existed. The aim of European integration is therefore to restore those conditions in the European market. Given the globalization of the world economy, in which half of mankind is competing directly with the industrialized world, this is more important than ever.

3. Economically speaking, we are in all probability at the beginning of the fifth Kondratieff cycle. This is the latest in the series of approximately 50-year, long-term, economic cycles which were detected by Schumpeter and which have characterized world economic growth for some 200 years.

In this Kondratieff cycle of world economic globalization, which has probably just begun, technology (once the preserve of the developed industrialized countries) is becoming ubiquitous, i.e. highly specialized manufacturing (e.g. of cars) is now also possible at what was formerly the periphery of the world economy. Furthermore, large sections of the tertiary sector are also being incorporated, through ubiquitous software, into the world division of labor. In this globalized world economic environment, the former dominant powers of the world are suddenly losing income. Wage and welfare levels are all at once becoming directly comparable. It is therefore more than ever necessary for these former dominant powers of the world to exploit every possible cost advantage in competition. This is imperative in large-scale economic contexts.

4. In Europe, therefore, the tensions between the nationally defined currency areas and their corresponding economic area (Europe) have never been greater than they are today. With the globalization of the world economy, the tensions between a nationally defined currency area and an internationally defined economic area are making it increasingly imperative - given the extremely rapid adaptability of the factor capital of both financial *and* physical capital - that those tensions should be reconciled. Such reconciliation entails the integration of currency areas into a single economic area. Otherwise, Europe has no chance of holding its own as the third element in worldwide competition alongside the United States and Asia.

5. In an EMS-type exchange-rate system, however, there is an insurmountable contradiction between the freedom of capital movement, autonomous monetary policy and fixed exchange rates. One of these aims has to be abandoned (incompatibility triad). As long as it was still hoped to reach the Maastricht "haven" quickly, there was no need to face up to the unremitting consequence of this triad. At the same time, it is becoming quite clear that guaranteeing the four basic freedoms (free movement of goods, individuals, services and capital) against the background of the large single market and globalized financial markets is necessitating a *de facto* monetary union. As the Commission has expressed it: one market, one currency! Thus, the alternative to the Maastricht project would not be a fully workable internal market without a single currency but the renationalization of economic policies and thus the dismantlement of

what has been achieved. Free exchange rates breed uncertainty; they are inimical to investment and integration.

This also leads to the following conclusion: only one of two monetary systems can survive in a future Europe, either full monetary union or floating currencies (*Matthes, 1994*). Under flexible exchange-rate arrangements, however, we are deprived of the most important advantage of the large internal market, namely secure planning horizons.

6. With capital movements fully liberalized, all European countries must now submit daily, and indeed hourly, to the markets' verdict even without a single currency. In this context, the large institutional investors forcibly achieve risk minimization for their clients and ensure market reactions that immediately penalize any deviation from the path of economic policy virtue (as systematically set out in the Maastricht entry conditions) with heavy risk premiums[2]. The reference standard in this connection is the currency of the dominant economy, which, in Europe, means the German mark. In the large single market, with its (presupposedly) full liberalization of capital movements, the imbalance in the existing key currency order in Europe has thus still increased considerably: the present European monetary system has in practice developed into a German mark area. With the establishment of the large common market, i.e. with the safeguarding of the four basic freedoms (free movement of goods, individuals, services and capital), the dominant position of German monetary policy has therefore increased still further.

7. The globalization of markets therefore entails also a globalization of financial markets. This normally signifies a monetary reinforcement of the dominant economy. However, from both a political and an economic viewpoint the German mark's level of dominance in Europe is too great:

- viewed politically, it is difficult for Germany to permanently assume a leadership role in the monetary sphere in Europe;

- viewed economically, Germany's potential for the key currency role in Europe is too small. Germany is only one part of the European component in the tricentric world economy. Therefore, it cannot treat its currency's exchange rate with benign neglect, as is the case with the United States (where economic and currency areas are identical). In the long run, therefore, too much is being demanded of Germany by its key currency role, and incidentally it is being forced into periods of suffocating upward revaluation.

8. All European countries except Germany have now recognized that control of their national currencies is illusory in the key currency system dominated by the German mark. Through the setting-up of the European Central Bank and the renunciation of their national currencies under the Maastricht Treaty, these countries are achieving what is for them a fully satisfactory objectification of the European monetary order. Therefore the safeguarding of the four basic freedoms is inevitably leading - in the large single market and with fixed exchange rates - to what is in practice already a monetary union. One market - one currency!

Endnotes

1. The author - Deputy Director-General for Economic and Financial Affairs in the European Commission - is here expressing his own views, which are not necessarily those of the Commission.

2. It should be noted that only some 2% of all transactions on the foreign-exchange market currently relate to trade in goods and services.

References

MATTHES, H. (1994), Damocles-Shadowing - An Innovation in the Second Phase of EMU, in: Intereconomics, Volume 29, No. 2, March/April 1994, 75-77.

PREDÖHL, A. (1971), Außenwirtschaft, 2nd edition, Grundriß der Sozialwissenschaft, Volume 17, Vandenhoeck & Ruprecht, Göttingen.

SCHUMPETER, J. (1953), Theorie der wirtschaftlichen Entwicklung, 5th edition, Munich 1953.

SCHUMPETER, J. (1961), Konjunkturzyklen, Vandenhoeck & Ruprecht, Göttingen.

EMU: A Bank's Perspective

Jürgen Pfister

We still expect the currency union to come on January 1st 1999. It needs to be a success. For one thing, the new currency needs to be as stable as the DM and the conversion must also be organized smoothly. To guarantee this, there are three fields in which political decisions and improvements are necessary.

To begin with fiscal soundness will need to hold after the start of the currency union. According to a famous saying, the most peaceful man can not live in peace if his bad neighbour does not allow him to. To put it differently, a European Central Bank which is oriented to stability cannot function if the fiscal policy rules allow the participating countries to have excessive deficits as it has been the case in most EU countries in the past years. The current rules in the Maastricht Treaty are not sufficient and the "no-bail-out clause" is not credible. Private banks strongly support the proposal of Minister of Finance Waigel to achieve a stability pact for fiscal soundness in Europe that is binding.

If banks are to be successful in their market they will have to rely on the quality of their basic assets and services. Thus a stable money supply is required. Thanks to the Deutsche Bundesbank, Germany has enjoyed a very favorable situation in recent decades. We expect this situation to remain unchanged in the coming Euro era. German banks benefit from the prominent international role of the DM and this would not be possible without the policy successes of the Deutsche Bundesbank.

Our second request in terms of policy is the following: reduce the risk of increasing transfer payments. In a currency union, there could be several economic and reasons why one would expect rising transfers in the EU. This is similar to the interstate financial transfer system within a national state. The first reason is the cancellation of the policy option. This is to influence the national economy with a national monetary policy or to achieve economic policy goals via exchange rate changes. Moreover, there could be growing pressure towards wage equalization across member countries. A third reason is the recently popular call in political circles for equalization between rich and poor regions in Europe.

Beyond political aspects, this is relevant for banks because a massive redistribution will further reinforces the tax burden in Germany. This would undermine locational attractiveness and international competitiveness, respectively. German banks have to rely both nationally and internationally on a sound and dynamic domestic economy.

Finally, I would like to discuss an open core question. To which extent does a successful monetary union require a political union as a complement? This controversial question is often discussed. It becomes increasingly clear that one cannot take only one step and then impose a supranational policy authority with its EU monetary policy. However, other institutional arrangements will have to be modified, too. To create a common fiscal and social policy order or to harmonize other policy aspects will be hardly feasible without strengthening the relevant EU political institutions. The Maastricht II conference which started in March 1996 will focus on these topics. It will discuss issues over at least one year. We expect that by mid-1997 there will be clarity with respect to the paths towards a political union and that the compromise will quickly be ratified in all EU countries. this is also a requirement for a successful EMU.

I hope to have shown with these three examples that our statements in the filed of macroeconomic aspects of monetary union are not in terms of yes or no to EMU. We consider monetary union as a political given. However, taking into account the interest of our clients and of the shareholders, we have to focus on the necessary conditions for success. Here our fundamental interests are expressed. If the political system decides in favour of a currency union, we stipulate that it be organized as a successful change.

There might be other points related to the microeconomic interest of banks and macroeconomic development, but I will skip these here. A particular important one remains, a topic so prominent in the media: Which countries will make the convergence criteria? Semantic sophisms - strict application of criteria versus strict application of the Treaty - are considered with more than skepticism in the financial community where one is used to rely on treaties with an exact wording.

The pragmatic view of a banker is that markets have already made their decisions as to which countries will be participants in EMU. The relevant indicators are interest differentials, swap rates and future market developments. To ignore such signals would imply to incur high cost in terms of risk premisa and volatility, but also not to fulfill the stability promise. I rule out that such experimentation will take place.

Opportunities and Risks Associated with European Monetary Union

Christa Randzio-Plath

The Monetary Union will complete the single market and stimulate European integration. EMU makes sense in both political and economic terms, in particular onemployment policy grounds. It contributes to a European profile and through the introduction of the Euro to a tangible European identity. The denationalization of monetary policy adds to political stability and helps to constrain the rise of nationalism. The DM hegemony, like the hegemony of a member state in any other policy area, contradicts the spirit of equal opportunities and partnership. These are fundamental principles of European integration. Monetary union increases the chance of a better co-ordination of economic, fiscal, employment and social policies and is urgently required in order to improve the EU's international competitiveness. The policy mix where monetary policy stabilizes the economy and secures employment will only be feasible if policies, such as industrial policy, are embedded in a European framework. With the creation of the European Central Bank, the EU will receive its first federal decision-making body.

1. Monetary Union Unifies

European Monetary Union will start with some, but not all the member states. This is due to the provision in the treaty that guarantees European Monetary Union membership only to those countries which satisfy the convergence criteria and have already have achieved convergence and whose economic structures have adjusted so that exchange rate flexibility is no longer required. The majority of member states already satisfies the Maastricht criteria. The German "stability culture" has spread across Europe. Eleven out of 15 countries already meet the important, convergence criterion of a low inflation rate. Problems are apparent with respect to the fiscal criteria set down in the Maastricht Treaty, since only three countries satisfy the deficit criterion.

According to the Maastricht Treaty (Art. 109j II and III) a convergence test will be undertaken for the first time in 1996. The European Parliament's rights of co-determination are quite limited since the Parliament only has the right to publish a statement. The Parliament must be heard. The multi-stage convergence test, which is the basis for the European Council's decision, ensures a very high degree of carefulness, certainty, objectivity and clarity. This is necessary for a credible start of the EMU. There are still debates about the interpretation of the convergence criteria regarding the budget deficit to GDP ratio and the government debt to GDP ratio. Indeed, the Treaty provides some room for interpretation, and this discretion option, should and must be used in accordance with the principles of the Maastricht Treaty. After all, it is the Treaty which should be strictly applied and not the convergence criteria. Some room for interpretation is provided by the Treaty's wording. This is not to argue for the weak application of convergence criteria, but rather that the decision-making opportunities expressly created by the member countries should be used. Nobody wants a lax application of the treaty in order to facilitate a quick entry of all member countries into the monetary union. It is in the interests for everyone that the currency union is a community of stability. This view is supported by the serious efforts of member countries with a convergence program and with rather strict goals for budget consolidation. It is obvious that acceptable degrees of interpretation must be clarified in 1996 - *at the latest in 1997 (editor's note)* so that the public and markets can adjust accordingly. Otherwise, the risk exists that the currency union will lose credibility. Such an approach is not only important for the members of the starting group but also for the countries initially remaining outside, allowing them to pursue their convergence efforts consistently. It is not easy to interpret the meaning of "exceptional" or "temporary" when deviations from deficit reference values are discussed. Certainly, an external shocks such as

German unification justifies an exceptional departure from the reference value. When is a member country moving towards the reference value? Could a temporary fall in economic growth justify a temporary departure from the reference value? Similar questions arise with respect to the debt criterion.

The answer to these questions and clarity about the room for interpretation are important for those participating in the EMU and those member countries with an opt-out clause. Nobody should be discriminated. Thus, no arbitrary decisions should be made which might be regarded as an offense to a member country.

To organize relations among all currencies in the European Union a new system of solidarity and stability, as well as, a new exchange rate mechanism with the Euro as an anchor are required. This mechanism must learn from the experiences of the EMS and should avoid unilateral depreciations and inadequate exchange rate entry levels. Within the context of a new solidarity mechanism, the European Central Bank will have to defend those currencies which are not part of the EMU core against speculative attacks. This approach would underline that the currency union is open for all EU member countries and would avoid a division of the common market.

2. Sticking to the Time Table

The Maastricht Treaty, for good reasons, contains provisions for criteria and a time table. This precision was already added at the Verona and Florence summits. For economic reasons, but also to stimulate employment, EMU should be introduced earlier rather then later. Indeed, a single market with 15 different currencies is a single phenomenon and does not fit into the European and the world economy of today. Reduced growth rates due to exchange rate changes will affect the business community and employment. Due to exchange rate changes, many export-oriented firms face lower profits and reorganize their supplier network. This has negative consequences for Germany. European economies urgently need the Euro area as a zone, in which business calculations and planning associated with investment, production and distribution are made on a secure basis.

A speedy realization of the currency union is of particular interest to Germany since exchange rate changes are very hard to anticipate - between 1989 and 1995 the DM appreciated by 19.7% so that German goods and services became much more expensive abroad. Postponing monetary union would imply further appreciations of the DM with negative consequences for growth and employment.

The postponement of EMU could trigger new turbulences. Disregarding this aspect, it is clear that nobody knows with certainty the ideal starting point. There are always disturbing impulses and potentially erroneous business prognoses as can be seen from the prognoses for 1995/96. A decision in favor of postponement would be interpreted as an indication of political weakness and could face sanctions in the markets. Postponement could also encourage a competition-distorting behavior or new protectionism.

Postponement cannot be justified on the grounds that monetary union should not be restricted to a few countries. Such an approach is indeed explicitly envisaged as a non-discriminatory concept in the treaty. If Germany and France can participate, there will be at least four to six other currencies qualifying as participants. Such a monetary union would represent about 50% of the EU's GDP and a GDP higher than that of Japan and equal to 40% of US GDP. Furthermore, one may assume that other countries, for example Spain, will qualify for membership in EMU before Euro coins and notes are introduced. Thus, a majority of countries will participate before the date of the actual Euro cash conversion.

3. Monetary Union on its Own is not Enough

Mass unemployment is a challenge for the European Union. 18 million unemployed and over 50 million poor people in the European Union are a serious problem. This has to be resolved if the EU is to remain credible. If one is in favor of monetary union, one must fight for more employment. Therefore monetary union should be complemented by an employment chapter during the 1996intergovernmental conference. This chapter should include financing options. There is an urgent need for a European pact on employment. The Social Protocol and the European Social Charta should be embedded in the Treaty. Countries which refuse to ratify these declarations should not be allowed to join EMU.

It is also necessary to reinforce the co-ordination of economic policy, including fiscal and tax policy. Europe must speak with one voice if it is to control its future. This is why the main ideas of the Delors White Paper of 1993 on "Growth, Competitiveness and Employment" were always important as complementary measures to the Maastricht Treaty. The European Council has, however, declined to implement measures proposed by the European Parliament and the European Commission. Moreover, an "Economic and Employment Government" would be a necessary complement to the independent European Central Bank whose monetary policy will be a useful contribution to an adequate and balanced policy mix in the European Union.

LIST OF TABLES

LIST OF FIGURES

LIST OF PARTICIPANTS

Paul Bergin
The Brookings Institution, Washington, D.C., USA

Michael C. Burda
Humboldt University, Berlin, Germany

Emil-Maria Claassen
UN Economic and Social Commission for Asia and the Pacific, Bangkok, Thailand, and University of Paris Dauphine, France

Stefan Collignon
Association for the Monetary Union of Europe (AUME), Paris, France

Max Corden
Paul H. Nitze School of Advanced International Studies, Johns Hopkins University, Washington, D.C., USA

Maria Demertzis
University of Strathclyde, Glasgow, UK

Daniel Gros
Centre for European Policy Studies (CEPS), Brussels, Belgium

Philipp Hartmann
London School of Economics, UK

Heinz Herrmann
Deutsche Bundesbank, Frankfurt/Main, Germany

Karen Horn
Frankfurter Allgemeine Zeitung, Frankfurt/Main, Germany

Andrew Hughes Hallett
University of Strathclyde, Glasgow, UK

Richard Jackman
London School of Economics, UK

Hans Jaeckel
Deutsche Genossenschaftsbank, Frankfurt/Main, Germany

André Jungmittag
University of Münster, Germany

Hans Dietrich von Loeffelholz
Rheinisch-Westfälisches Institut für Wirtschaftsforschung (RWI), Essen, Germany

Heinrich Matthes
European Commission, Brussels, Belgium

Lukas Menkhoff
Rheinisch-Westfälische Technische Hochschule (RWTH), Aachen, Germany

Mathias Moersch
American Institute for Contemporary German Studies (AICGS), Johns Hopkins University, Washington, D.C., USA

Willem Molle
University of Rotterdam, The Netherlands

Hans G. Monissen
University of Würzburg, Germany

Jürgen Pfister
Commerzbank AG, Frankfurt/Main, Germany

Christa Randzio-Plath
European Parliament, Strasbourg, Belgium

Robert Raymond
European Monetary Institute, Frankfurt/Main, Germany

Ole Rummel
European Investment Bank, Luxembourg

Michèle Schmiegelow
Global Economic Strategy Centre, Blanmont-Hévillers, Belgium

Greg Steinmetz
Wall Street Journal, Berlin, Germany

Matti Vanhala
Bank of Finland, Helsinki, Finland

Helmut Wagner
University of Hagen, Germany

Jens Weidmann
University of Bonn, Germany

Paul J.J. Welfens
University of Potsdam and European Institute for International Economic Relations (EIIW), Germany

Jeromin Zettelmeyer
International Monetary Fund (IMF), Washington, D.C., USA

INDEX

Further Publications by *Paul J. J. Welfens*

P. J. J. Welfens, D. Audretsch, J. T. Addison, H. Grupp
Technological Competition, Employment and Innovation
Policies in OECD Countries
1997. VI, 236 pp. Hardcover ISBN 3-540-63439-8

P. J. J. Welfens, H. C. Wolf
Banking, International Capital Flows and Growth in Europe
Financial Markets, Savings and Monetary Integration in
a World with Uncertain Convergence
1997. XIV, 458 pp. 22 figs., 63 tabs. Hardcover
ISBN 3-540-63192-5

P. J. J. Welfens, G. Yarrow
Telecommunications and Energy in Systemic Transformation
International Dynamics, Deregulation and Adjustment in
Network Industries
1997. XII, 501 pp. 39 figs., Hardcover
ISBN 3-540-61586-5

R. Tilly, P. J. J. Welfens
European Economic Integration as a Challenge to
Industry and Government
Contemporary and Historical Perspectives on
International Economic Dynamics
1996. X, 558 pp. 43 figs., Hardcover ISBN 3-540-60431-6

P. J. J. Welfens
Economic Aspects of German Unification
Expectations, Transition Dynamics and International Perspectives
2nd rev. and enlarged ed. 1996. XV, 527 pp. 34 figs., 110 tabs.
Hardcover ISBN 3-540-60261-5

P. J. J. Welfens
Market-oriented Systemic Transformations in Eastern Europe
Problems, Theoretical Issues, and Policy Options
1992. XII, 261 pp. 20 figs., 29 tabs. Hardcover
ISBN 3-540-55793-8

M. W. Klein, P. J. J. Welfens
Multinationals in the New Europe and Global Trade
1992. XV, 281 pp. 24 figs., 75 tabs. Hardcover
ISBN 3-540-54634-0

MIX
Papier aus verantwortungsvollen Quellen
Paper from responsible sources
FSC® C105338

If you have any concerns about our products,
you can contact us on
ProductSafety@springernature.com

In case Publisher is established outside the EU,
the EU authorized representative is:
Springer Nature Customer Service Center GmbH
Europaplatz 3, 69115 Heidelberg, Germany

Printed by Libri Plureos GmbH
in Hamburg, Germany